Communications
in Computer and Information Science 1361

More information about this series at http://www.springer.com/series/7899

Slimane Hammoudi · Luís Ferreira Pires ·
Bran Selić (Eds.)

Model-Driven Engineering and Software Development

8th International Conference, MODELSWARD 2020
Valletta, Malta, February 25–27, 2020
Revised Selected Papers

 Springer

Editors
Slimane Hammoudi
Siège du Groupe ESEO
Angers Cedex 02, France

Luís Ferreira Pires
University of Twente
Enschede, The Netherlands

Bran Selić
Malina Software Corp.
Nepean, ON, Canada

ISSN 1865-0929   ISSN 1865-0937 (electronic)
Communications in Computer and Information Science
ISBN 978-3-030-67444-1   ISBN 978-3-030-67445-8 (eBook)
https://doi.org/10.1007/978-3-030-67445-8

This Springer imprint is published by the registered company Springer Nature Switzerland AG
The registered company address is: Gewerbestrasse 11, 6330 Cham, Switzerland

Preface

The present book includes extended and revised versions of a set of selected papers from the 8th International Conference on Model-Driven Engineering and Software Development (MODELSWARD 2020), held in Valletta, Malta, from 25 to 27 February, 2020.

MODELSWARD 2020 received 66 paper submissions from 26 countries, of which 23% were included in this book. The papers were selected by the event chairs and their selection is based on a number of criteria that include the classifications and comments provided by the program committee members, the session chairs' assessment and also the program chairs' global view of all papers included in the technical program. The authors of selected papers were then invited to submit a revised and extended version of their paper having at least 30% innovative material.

The purpose of the International Conference on Model-Driven Engineering and Software Development, MODELSWARD 2020, was to provide a platform for researchers, engineers, academics and industrial professionals from all over the world to present their research results and development activities in using models and model-driven engineering techniques for Software Development. Model-Driven Development (MDD) is an approach to the development of IT systems in which models take a central role, not only for analysis of these systems but also for their construction. MDD has emerged from modelling initiatives, most prominently the Model-Driven Architecture (MDA) fostered by the Object Management Group (OMG). Within the scope of MDA, technologies have been developed that became the cornerstones of MDD, such as metamodelling and model transformations. MDD relies on languages for defining metamodels, such as the Meta-Object Facility (MOF) and Ecore (developed within the scope of the Eclipse Modelling Framework), and transformation specification languages such as QVT and ATL.

We are confident that the papers included in this book will strongly contribute to the understanding of some of the current research trends in Model-Driven Engineering and Software Development, especially of approaches required to tackle current and future software development challenges. Thus, this book covers diverse but complementary topics such as: reasoning about models, provenance of data models, model quality, generative approaches, model execution and simulation, domain-specific modelling, and model-based testing and validation

We would like to thank all the authors for their contributions and also the reviewers who have helped to ensure the quality of this publication.

February 2020

Slimane Hammoudi
Luis Ferreira Pires
Bran Selić

Organization

Conference Chair

Bran Selić   Malina Software Corp., Canada

Program Co-chairs

Slimane Hammoudi   ESEO, ERIS, France
Luis Ferreira Pires   University of Twente, The Netherlands

Program Committee

Bülent Adak	Aselsan A.S., Turkey
Ludovic Apvrille	Télécom Paris, France
Ethem Arkin	Hacettepe University, Turkey
Marco Autili	University of L'Aquila, Italy
Elarbi Badidi	United Arab Emirates University, UAE
Omar Badreddin	University of Texas at El Paso, USA
Stamatia Bibi	University of Western Macedonia, Greece
Paolo Bocciarelli	University of Rome Tor Vergata, Italy
Marcello Bonsangue	Leiden University, The Netherlands
Juan Boubeta-Puig	University of Cádiz, Spain
Antonio Brogi	Università di Pisa, Italy
Matthias Brun	ESEO Group, France
Christian Bunse	University of Applied Sciences Stralsund, Germany
Renata Carvalho	Eindhoven University of Technology (TU/e), The Netherlands
Olena Chebanyuk	National Aviation University, Ukraine
Yuting Chen	Shanghai Jiao Tong University, China
Dan Chiorean	Babeş-Bolyai University, Romania
Dickson Chiu	The University of Hong Kong, Hong Kong
Antonio Cicchetti	Mälardalen University, Sweden
Andrea D'Ambrogio	Università di Roma "Tor Vergata", Italy
Guglielmo De Angelis	CNR - IASI, Italy
Giovanni Denaro	University of Milano-Bicocca, Italy
Enrico Denti	Alma Mater Studiorum - Università di Bologna, Italy
Dimitris Dranidis	CITY College, Int. Faculty of the University of Sheffield, Greece
Sophie Ebersold	IRIT, France
Holger Eichelberger	Universität Hildesheim, Germany
Achiya Elyasaf	Ben-Gurion University of the Negev, Israel
Andrea Enrici	Nokia Bell Labs, France

Hüseyin Ergin	Ball State University, USA
Rik Eshuis	Eindhoven University of Technology, The Netherlands
Angelina Espinoza	University College Cork (UCC), Ireland
Vladimir Estivill-Castro	Griffith University, Australia
Anne Etien	University of Lille, Inria, CNRS, France
Stephan Flake	S&N CQM Consulting & Services GmbH, Germany
Jicheng Fu	University of Central Oklahoma, USA
Sébastien Gérard	CEA, France
Paola Giannini	University of Piemonte Orientale, Italy
Fabian Gilson	University of Canterbury, New Zealand
Christiane Gresse von Wangenheim	Federal University of Santa Catarina, Brazil
Jean Hauck	Universidade Federal de Santa Catarina, Brazil
Klaus Havelund	NASA Jet Propulsion Laboratory, USA
José R. Hilera	University of Alcalá, Spain
Pavel Hruby	DXC Technology, Denmark
Marianne Huchard	Université de Montpellier, France
Emilio Insfran	Universitat Politècnica de València, Spain
Ludovico Iovino	Gran Sasso Science Institute, Italy
Stefan Jablonski	University of Bayreuth, Germany
Maria José Escalona	University of Seville, Spain
George Kakarontzas	University of Thessaly, Greece
Alexander Kamkin	ISPRAS, Russian Federation
Teemu Kanstren	VTT, Finland
Guy Katz	The Hebrew University of Jerusalem, Israel
Alexey Khoroshilov	ISPRAS, Russian Federation
Jun Kong	North Dakota State University, USA
Uirá Kulesza	Federal University of Rio Grande do Norte (UFRN), Brazil
Rahul Kumar	NASA Jet Propulsion Laboratory, USA
Ralf-Detlef Kutsche	Technische Universität Berlin, Germany
Pierre Laforcade	Le Mans University, France
Youness Laghouaouta	Le Mans University, France
Rafael Lahoz Beltrá	Complutense University of Madrid, Spain
Anna-Lena Lamprecht	Utrecht University, The Netherlands
Ivan Lanese	University of Bologna/INRIA, Italy
Kevin Lano	King's College London, UK
Abderrahmane Leshob	University of Quebec at Montreal, Canada
Timothy Lethbridge	University of Ottawa, Canada
Yannis Lilis	University of Crete, Greece
Lior Limonad	IBM, Israel
Dongxi Liu	CSIRO, Australia
Luis Llana	Universidad Complutense de Madrid, Spain
Francesca Lonetti	National Research Council (CNR) Pisa, Italy
Patricia López Martínez	University of Cantabria, Spain
David Lorenz	Open University, Israel

Der-Chyuan Lou	Chang Gung University, Taiwan, Republic of China
Hong Lu	Software Engineer Institute, China
Juho Mäkiö	Hochschule Emden/Leer, Germany
Frederic Mallet	Université Nice Sophia Antipolis, France
Eda Marchetti	ISTI-CNR, Italy
Beatriz Marín	Universidad Diego Portales, Chile
Johnny Marques	Instituto Tecnológico de Aeronáutica, Brazil
Assaf Marron	The Weizmann Institute of Science, Israel
Steve McKeever	Uppsala University, Sweden
Dragan Milicev	University of Belgrade, Serbia
André Miralles	IRSTEA, France
Anila Mjeda	Lero (The Irish Software Engineering Centre), Ireland
Ambra Molesini	Alma Mater Studiorum - Università di Bologna, Italy
Rodrigo Monteiro	Fluminense Federal University, Brazil
Sébastien Mosser	Université du Québec à Montréal, Canada
Sascha Mueller-Feuerstein	Ansbach University of Applied Sciences, Germany
Hamid Mukhtar	National University of Sciences and Technology, Pakistan
Stefan Naujokat	TU Dortmund, Germany
Clémentine Nebut	LIRMM, Université de Montpellier, France
Andrzej Niesler	Wrocław University of Economics, Poland
Mykola Nikitchenko	Taras Shevchenko National University of Kyiv, Ukraine
Aida Omerovic	SINTEF, Norway
Olaf Owe	University of Oslo, Norway
Gordon Pace	University of Malta, Malta
Ana C. Paiva	University of Porto, Portugal
Dana Petcu	West University of Timisoara, Romania
Rob Pettit	The Aerospace Corp., USA
Elke Pulvermüller	Osnabrück University, Germany
Ansgar Radermacher	CEA, France
Aurora Ramírez	University of Córdoba, Spain
Daniel Ratiu	Siemens AG, Germany
Gil Regev	Ecole Polytechnique Fédérale de Lausanne, Switzerland
Ulrich Reimer	St. Gallen University of Applied Sciences, Switzerland
Iris Reinhartz-Berger	University of Haifa, Israel
Wolfgang Reisig	Humboldt-Universität zu Berlin, Germany
Werner Retschitzegger	Johannes Kepler Universität Linz, Austria
Yassine Rhazali	Moulay Ismail University, Morocco
Laurent Rioux	Thales, France
Colette Rolland	Université Paris 1 Panthèon-Sorbonne, France
José Raúl Romero	University of Córdoba, Spain
Gustavo Rossi	LIFIA, Argentina
Sara Comai	Politecnico di Milano, Italy
Jean-Guy Schneider	Deakin University, Australia

Wieland Schwinger	Johannes Kepler Universität Linz, Austria
Beijun Shen	Shanghai Jiao Tong University, China
Alberto Silva	IST/INESC-ID, Portugal
Pnina Soffer	University of Haifa, Israel
Stéphane Somé	University of Ottawa, Canada
Jean-Sébastien Sottet	Luxembourg Institute of Science and Technology, Luxembourg
Ioanna Stamatopoulou	The University of Sheffield International Faculty, CITY College, Greece
Alin Stefanescu	University of Bucharest, Romania
Jean-Bernard Stefani	INRIA, France
Arnon Sturm	Ben-Gurion University of the Negev, Israel
Hiroki Suguri	Miyagi University, Japan
Hamed Taherdoost	Hamta Group, Canada
Yves Traon	University of Luxembourg, Luxembourg
Naoyasu Ubayashi	Kyushu University, Japan
Christelle Urtado	École des mines d'Alès, France
Sylvain Vauttier	École des mines d'Alès, France
Layne Watson	Virginia Polytechnic Institute & State University, USA
Michael Whalen	University of Minnesota, USA
Hao Wu	National University of Ireland, Maynooth, Ireland
Hüsnü Yenigün	Sabancı University, Turkey
Marc Zeller	Siemens AG, Germany
Chunying Zhao	Western Illinois University, USA
Haiyan Zhao	Peking University, China
Olaf Zimmermann	HSR Hochschule für Technik Rapperswil, Switzerland
Kamil Żyła	Lublin University of Technology, Poland

Additional Reviewers

Vincent Aranega	University of Lille, France
Omar Masmali	University of Texas at El Paso, USA
Khandoker Rahad	University of Texas at El Paso, USA

Invited Speakers

Giancarlo Guizzardi	Free University of Bozen-Bolzano, Italy
Gail Murphy	University of British Columbia, Canada
Sébastien Gérard	CEA, France

Contents

Methodologies, Processes and Platforms

The Smart Grid Simulation Framework: Model-Driven Engineering Applied to Cyber-Physical Systems

David Oudart[1]([✉]), Jérôme Cantenot[2], Frédéric Boulanger[3], and Sophie Chabridon[1]

[1] SAMOVAR, Télécom SudParis, Institut Polytechnique de Paris, Paris, France
david.oudart@gmail.com
[2] EDF R&D, Paris, Palaiseau, France
[3] LRI, CNRS, CentraleSupélec, Université Paris-Saclay, Paris, France

Abstract. Smart grids are complex systems for which simulation offers a practical way to evaluate and compare multiple solutions before deployment. However, the simulation of a Smart Grid requires the development of heterogeneous models corresponding to electrical, information processing, and telecommunication behaviors. These heterogeneous models must be linked and analyzed together in order to detect the influences on one another and identify emerging behaviors. We apply model-driven engineering to such cyber-physical systems combining physical and digital components and propose SGridSF, the Smart Grid Simulation Framework, which automates tasks in order to ensure consistency between different simulation models. This framework consists mainly of a domain specific language for modeling a cosimulation unit, called CosiML for Cosimulation Modeling Language, a domain specific language for modeling the functional architecture of a Smart Grid, called SGridML for Smart Grid Modeling Language, and a tool implementing different transformation rules to generate the files and scripts for executing a cosimulation. Finally, we illustrate the use of SGridSF on the real use case of an islanded grid implementing diesel and renewable sources, battery storage and intelligent control of the production. We show the sequencing of automatic generation tasks that minimizes the effort and the risk of error at each iteration of the process.

Keywords: Cosimulation · FMI · IT · MDE · Smart grid · Cyber-physical system

1 Introduction

Tomorrow's energy systems, or Smart Grids, require the study and development of safer, controlled components, in order to limit the often costly hardware tests and deployments in this sector of activity. Simulation is recognized as a practical way for verifying and validating the systems before deployment. Our work

S. Hammoudi et al. (Eds.): MODELSWARD 2020, CCIS 1361, pp. 3–25, 2021.
https://doi.org/10.1007/978-3-030-67445-8_1

responds to the problem of finding tools and methods to simulate a Smart Grid, and which allow to remain compatible with the constraints, especially economic, of the industry. Smart Grids are complex systems, combining, like all cyber-physical systems, heterogeneous behaviors distributed among several models, themselves developed by persons with different technical profiles and skills. We consider cosimulation with the *Functional Mockup Interface* (FMI)[1] standard as the best way to take into account all these models and assess the behavior of a Smart Grid.

We identified two main challenges to be solved. The first challenge concerns the heterogeneity of the domains involved. Simulating a Smart Grid requires the ability to model and simulate electrical, information processing, and telecommunications behaviors and to integrate them within an FMI cosimulator. These behaviors follow different laws of evolution, continuous for the physical components and discrete for the digital components. One of the current limitations of FMI is its incompatibility with the manipulation of discrete signals, resulting in the absence of compatible Telecom simulators. To overcome this limitation, we have previously proposed in [12] a method to allow the exchange of discrete signals between several FMUs. It consists in an encoding component to transform a discrete signal into two time-continuous signals that can be exchanged over FMI, and a decoding component to perform the reverse operation and obtain the discrete-event signal from the FMI discretization of the time-continuous signals.

The second challenge is to ensure the consistency of models produced by persons specialized in different domains when designing a Smart Grid. We rely on model-driven engineering and more specifically on model transformation to maintain the consistency between the design models of a Smart Grid and simulation models. We propose SGridSF, the Smart Grid Simulation Framework tooled environment, which automates a number of repetitive tasks in order to ensure consistency between different simulation models. This environment consists of a domain specific language for modeling a cosimulation unit, called CosiML for Cosimulation Modeling Language, a tool implementing different transformation rules to generate the files and scripts for executing a cosimulation, a specific language for modeling the functional architecture of a Smart Grid, called SGridML for Smart Grid Modeling Language, two specific modeling languages, called AllocationML for Allocation Modeling Language and CatalogML for Catalog Modeling Language allowing the definition of a transformation from a model written in SGridML to a model written in CosiML, and finally a tool implementing the transformation from three models written in SGridML, AllocationML and CatalogML into a model written in CosiML.

In the next section, we discuss existing solutions to the two challenges we mentioned above. Section 3 presents a global overview of the cosimulation approach and the integration of our Smart Grid Simulation Framework in it. Section 4 and Sect. 5 respectively present how the CosiML and the SGridML languages are build and how to use their associated tools. Section 6 illustrates the approach on a use case. Section 7 presents scenarios to validate our approach.

---

[1] https://fmi-standard.org.

The present article is an extended version of [12], where we already addressed the first challenge and a part of the second challenge. Indeed, we presented the CosiML language and its associated tooling allowing the generation of a cosimulation platform. This new article presents the other tools provided by our automated generation framework, especially the SgridML language, and how they address our second challenge. The use case from [12] is used again and completed to illustrate the whole approach.

2   State of the Art

In the electrical energy community, the challenge of simulating smart grids is not new [9,10,18]. However, it usually consists in the interaction of two domains via two dynamic models. The problem of the synchronization of models and of their consistency is not specifically addressed by these approaches, but is not really challenging when limited to two domains.

For the industrial simulation of complex systems and CPS, it is better to rely on standard technologies, as they address various needs like scalability, modularity or reusability. *The Functional Mockup Interface* (FMI) [2] and *The High Level Architecture* (HLA) [4] are two interoperability approaches allowing the interconnection of several different simulators in an integrated execution.

If both approaches have been declared as standard, FMI benefits from a stronger popularity with more than 80 compatible tools[2]. Its ability to protect industrial property inside FMUs makes it very attractive for industrial projects and makes collaborative design easier [7]. FMI defines a simulation unit format called *Functional Mockup Unit* (FMU), which embeds a model and an execution engine along a standard interface to control the execution of the simulation. FMI cosimulations are driven by a *master algorithm*, which synchronizes the execution of the FMUs and the exchange of data at some communication points.

Because a time-step between two communication points can not be null, FMI is not particularly adapted to reactive systems and discrete-event modeling. Current works already propose FMI extensions, such as zero-size steps [3,8], or absent values [3] to handle discrete-event signals. Optimized master algorithms [15,17] can increase the precision of the simulation while still being compliant with the standard, by trying to locate the occurrence of an event using the optional *rollback* FMI feature (reverting the state of an FMU to a previous communication point), or by optimizing the choice of the time step, which requires FMUs to be exported as white boxes.

The design of complex systems involves several viewpoints from different technical domains, therefore several heterogeneous models developed by different teams are used. In the industry, the interconnection of these models and the consistency links between them are handled using model driven approaches [1, 14,19]. These approaches mainly aim at facilitating the realization of the final system, but only few of them include the simulation in the design process [13].

---

[2] https://fmi-standard/tools/.

The simulation of Smart Grids requires models dedicated to modeling and design, that describe the system and its architecture at a certain level of abstraction. More abstract models can be automatically derived by model transformations into detailed executable models, thus reducing the risk of inconsistency between models at different levels of abstraction. This automation is particularly beneficial in the case of iterative approaches, every change in the design models being quickly and easily reflected in the derived models.

We can distinguish two categories in the existing approaches. The first category relies on system architecture models and derives them into executable models, such as the code of the software parts of the system. This encompasses the model-driven architecture (MDA[3]), PSAL [1] or the SGAM Toolbox [16]. The second category aims at validating the models through simulation. They rely on models of the simulation architecture, which makes it possible to keep the dynamic models of the simulation consistent. Examples in this category are model composition approaches (Ptolemy II[4], ModHel'X[5]) or current cosimulation solutions [7]. Therefore, approaches based on system architecture models do not integrate the models of the dynamics of the system, and approaches focused on simulation do not describe the alignment of the simulation models with the system architecture. In our work, we propose to reconnect the two activities of modeling and simulation, and thus link the design models of a Smart Grid to the simulation models of its behaviour.

3   Overview of the Smart Grid Simulation Framework

3.1   An Approach Based on Model Refinement

One of the main advantages of using a cosimulation environment is to allow the different experts to develop their own model in autonomy, with a minimal interference and in parallel with the others [7]. The choice of the FMI standard ensures the technological compatibility of each simulation unit, or FMU, with the cosimulation environment, without having to develop a specific connector. However it does not ensure structural compatibility. All FMUs produced by the different teams must provide interoperable data structures, namely each input should match an output, in type and meaning.

An example of a cosimulation approach for smart grids [11] identified several steps and actors involved in such a process. The first step is to define all the connections between the simulation models in order to define the interface of the models for each modeling team. But the compliance verification of the models and the creation of the cosimulation artifacts (FMUs, configuration files) are done by hand, which make each iteration time-consuming and error-prone.

The use of a global, architectural model to represent the structural interfaces of the various simulation units and the coupling constraints between them, allows

---

[3] https://www.omg.org/mda/.

[4] https://ptolemy.berkeley.edu/.

[5] https://wdi.supelec.fr/software/ModHelX/.

the use of syntactic tools to automatically check some validation rules. It also creates a unique authoritative artifact to coordinate the work of the various collaborators, and from which more detailed models can be derived.

Following this approach, we developed a toolchain to automate the actions needed to run a cosimulation starting from a global abstract model. This toolchain relies on a domain specific language (DSL), CosiML, to specify the structural interfaces of the simulation units and the configuration of the cosimulation. In our approach, the cosimulation model written with CosiML acts as an intermediate, platform-independent model from which executable simulation artifacts can be generated (see Sect. 4).

SGridML is a DSL developed to identify and connect the functional behaviors of the Smart Grid together. The different domain experts involved in the Smart Grid design are meant to collaborate on the development of a behavior model with SGridML. Then the behavior model is processed to generate the cosimulation model, according to the mapping defined in the allocation model and the catalog model, respectively written with AllocationML and CatalogML (see Sect. 5). Figure 1 illustrates the generation of the cosimulation model and the relations between the four DSL involved in the model transformation.

Our choice to develop our own languages for this purpose, instead of choosing an existing one, such as UML, comes from various reasons:

– in an industrial context, general-purpose languages like UML are not well mastered outside the computer science field,
– such languages contain many concepts, but we only needed a few of them,
– in our approach, adapting UML to model specific concepts would lead to refining generic concepts through profiles.

It appeared more efficient to define only what we needed than to restrict and specialize UML to fit our needs.

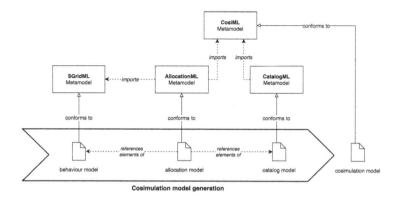

Fig. 1. Cosimulation model generation, with dependency links.

Smart Grid Simulation Framework is the name we give to the tool suite composed by the four languages presented and their associated tools. It is by construction supporting the phases and steps of a cosimulation approach:

1. Phase 1 constitutes the step sequence resulting in the complete model of the Smart Grid. First step consists in the definition of the system to model. Then, the responsability to produce the simulation models is split between the different expert teams involved. The third step specify the interfaces of each model and the interactions between them. Finally, the simulation models can be developed according to these specifications.
2. Phase 2 aims to configure the cosimulation unit to be executable. First the simulation models have to be available in the executable cosimulation format, FMU in our case. Then the simulation parameters and coupling constraints are implemented in the master of cosimulation.
3. Phase 3 consists in the execution and analysis of the cosimulation results. First the results should be assessed to determine if there has been any design mistake compared to the initial expectations (simulation or functional errors). Once the results are validated, further decisions can be make according to the efficiency of the solution. Either the design of the solution is accepted, or it need iterative improvement.

Table 1 presents the correspondence between the phases of the cosimulation approach and the tools of the *Smart Grid Simulation Framework*.

Table 1. Mapping modeling steps with the *Smart Grid Simulation Framework* tools.

Step	Tool to use
Phase 1: Model the solution	
Define a solution	Build an SGridML model
Allocating responsibilities	Build a CatalogML model and an AllocationML model.
Define interfaces and interconnections	Automatically generate the CosiML model
Produce simulation models	Buil simulation models based on already built and generated models
Phase 2: Configuring IMF cosimulation	
Adapting models to FMU	Update the CatalogML model with simulation model information and regenerate the CosiML model Generate the necessary adapters from this CosiML model
Implement the cosimulation scenario in the IMF master text	Generate the DACCOSIM configuration script from the CosiML model
Phase 3: Execute and analyze the results	
Evaluate cosimulation results	The cosimulation execution script is automatically generated from the CosiML model
Make iteration decisions	Facilitated by all our generation and automation tools

This remains a qualitative and human work. Nevertheless, the implementation of iteration decisions is facilitated by all our generation and automation tools.

3.2   Download

Our toolchain is shared on a github repository at: https://github.com/davidouda rt-pro/SGridSF.

The sources of the CosiML language and generation plugins are available, as well as the necessary files to replay the cosimulation of the use case presented in the next section of the article.

4   Modeling and Execution of a Cosimulation Scenario

4.1   CosiML, a DSL for Cosimulation

We implemented CosiML inside the *Eclipse Modeling Framework* (EMF) using the Ecore metamodeling language. Figure 2 shows the metamodel of CosiML. The classical elements of every cosimulation are represented:

CosimulationModel is the root element of the model, it stores the parameters of the cosimulation (start time, stop time, time step, etc.) and contains all the simulation units and their interconnections.

SimulationUnit represents a simulation unit involved in the cosimulation. It contains the Port elements representing the structural interface of the unit.

Input & Output (Port) represents a port of the simulation unit. It has a type, an optional default value and a *variability*, which is the name used by FMI to characterize the discrete or continuous nature of signals.

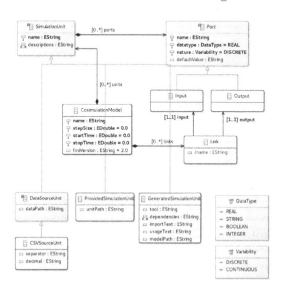

Fig. 2. CosiML metamodel.

Link represents a connection between an output and an input port. A model can be checked to verify that any two connected ports have the same variability, and that they are not contained in the same simulation unit.

Several kinds of SimulationUnits can be instantiated in a cosimulation model, depending on the source format of the simulation unit provided:

ProvidedSimulationUnit is a simulation unit which is completely provided by the user. Such a simulation unit is directly usable in the cosimulation without further action. In our case of FMI cosimulation, a ProvidedSimulationUnit is provided as an FMU resource and we only have to know the path to the artifact.

GeneratedSimulationUnit is a simulation unit which will be generated by the toolchain from a domain model. The attribute `modelPath` stores the path to the domain model. The format of the model and the generator to use for the generation of the simulation unit are specific to the `tool` attribute's value. The `tool` is what is used to build the model, for instance a Java or C++ compiler, or a more complex modeling tool such as OMNeT for communication networks. The generator is part of our toolchain, and will generate the corresponding FMU, which includes the generation of adapters for discrete event signals. The generator relies on naming conventions to access the elements of the model and adapt them to the structure of the FMU. For instance, a Java with a continuous input signal named X should implement a `setX(double value)` method. In order to refer to the model in the generated FMU, the generator uses two generic attributes: `importText` defines how to import the model inside the adapter, and `usageText` tells how to use the model. Finally, the attribute `dependencies` stores the list of all the resource paths required by the model (libraries, data files, binaries) that should be packaged inside the generated simulation unit. Our goal is to stay generic enough to avoid metamodel modifications when we want to support a new tool and add a new generator to the toolchain. For instance, a Java model-based generator would require:

    importText = import package.Classname;

and

    usageText = Classname,

whereas a C++ model-based generator would require:

    importText = #include "filename.h"

and

    usageText = ObjectName.

DataSourceUnit a simulation unit generated by the toolchain from a data file. It only has output ports and will be used as an independent source of timed data. The attribute `dataPath` stores the path to the data file. We are considering that future versions of CosiML and the toolchain may support several format, but for now we only support CSV files to be used as Scenario units.

CSVSourceUnit a particular Scenario element which refers to a CSV data file. Attributes `separator` and `decimal` define the characters used respectively as separator and decimal marker for the CSV content.

4.2   Generation Tools for FMI Cosimulation

We chose the *DACCOSIM NG*[6] software to execute our FMI cosimulation. It implements a master algorithm that is fully compliant with the standard, with advanced discontinuity detection features, and intelligent time step strategies [15]. More importantly, it provides a scripting language allowing the automation of the build and execution of cosimulations. Finally it is designed for distributed executions, which is very useful for industrial use cases potentially involving a large number of FMUs [6].

We developed an Acceleo plugin to generate all the files needed to build the FMI cosimulation from the CosiML model. Figure 3 shows the generation process of these files from a CosiML model. The generators are configured with property files, used to specify platform dependent information, such as library and tool paths.

Whereas CosiML is meant to be fully generated according to the steps defined in Table 1, it is an independent tool which can be adapted to one's own simulation methodology. Because our CosiML metamodel is defined with EMF Ecore, one can use the *Sample Reflective Ecore Model Editor* to instantiate a CosiML model and serialize it in the XMI format, in order to use it with the following associated tools to generate an executable cosimulation unit:

1. **OMNeT Generator:** generates all the files needed to build an FMU from an OMNeT model. It is applied to the GeneratedSimulationUnit instances with the `tool` property set to "java". It generates a JSON configuration file, compatible with our own C++ plugin of the OMNeT simulation core. This plugin allows the FMU export of an OMNeT model. It implements the encoding and decoding components presented in our previous work to allow discrete signal exchanges over FMI. The generator also produces a script to build the corresponding FMU.
2. **Java-tool Generator:** generates all the files needed to build an FMU from a Java model. It is applied to the GeneratedSimulationUnit instances with the `tool` property set to "java". It generates a Java file defining a class adapting the user model to the JavaFMI library[7], along with a MANIFEST.MF file defining the proper classpath. It also generates a script to build the corresponding FMU.
3. **CSV Scenario Generator:** generates the files needed to build an FMU from a CSV file. It is applied to the CSVScenario instances. It generates a Java file defining a class loading the CSV file, and implementing the JavaFMI library, along with the MANIFEST.MF file and the building script, just as with the Java-tool generator.
4. **Cosimulation Scripts Generator:** generates the DACCOSIM cosimulation model in its specific scripting language DNG. It also generates an execution script, which automates the build of all the FMU not yet generated, and the launch of the DACCOSIM simulation.

---

[6] https://bitbucket.org/simulage/daccosim.
[7] bitbucket.org/siani/javafmi/, a set of component to work with FMI. It especially provides a builder component generating an FMU from Java code.

CosiML allows the distinction between discrete and continuous data exchanges, so that the provided generators can automatically implement our discrete-continuous encoding and decoding components [12] in the generated wrappers, and adapt the FMU inputs and outputs accordingly (each CosiML *Port* with a discrete variability causes the creation of two FMI ports). Our CosiML toolchain is meant to be extended with other generators to support more domain specific tools and to be used for cyber-physical systems other than smart grids. The next section presents the SGridML, AllocationML and CatalogML languages, and how they are used to produce the CosiML cosimulation model.

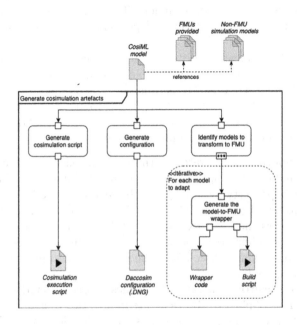

Fig. 3. Generation process of the cosimulation artifacts, from a CosiML model.

5   Functional Architecture for Smart Grid Simulation

5.1   SGridML

As for CosiML, we have a metamodel of SGridML expressed in the Ecore language. This language makes it possible to represent two types of behavior: functional behaviors (for creating and modifying data), and data transmission behaviors. This manipulated data represents information regardless of its form: physical state, digital information, or intangible facts.

Figure 4 shows the complete SGridML metamodel, whose elements are described below:

BehaviorModel: Root element, used for model navigation purposes only. It contains a list of the functional behaviors of the system (`function`), the existing connections between these functions (`connection`), and the possible transmission behaviors of these connections (`transmission`).

SimulationBehavior: Element representing an instance of an elementary simulation behavior, named by its attribute `name`.

Function: Element derived from `SimulationBehavior`, representing a functional behavior of the system simulation. It contains an input interface (list `input`), and an output interface (list `output`). These interfaces are described in a static way, and thus represent all possible data exchanges in and out of this behavior during the system simulation.

Output & Input: These elements represent a data exchange point, part of the interface of a functional behavior. An `Input` is an entry point for a data, allowing us to provide the behavior that contains it with the data necessary to its realization. Similarly, an `Output` is an output point, allowing us to share a data produced by the behavior that contains it, with the other functional behaviors of the model. Each element has a name, the type of data that can be exchanged, and a boolean, `dataType`, indicating whether the data is continuous or discrete in nature.

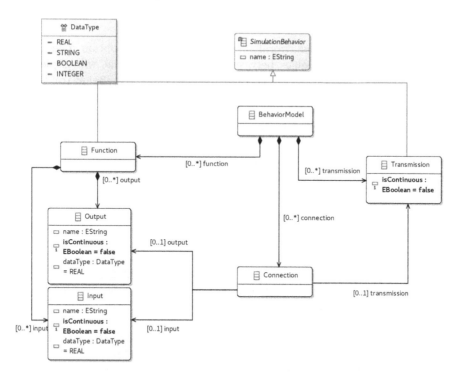

Fig. 4. Ecore metamodel of SGridML.

Connection: Element representing a connection between an output interface point of a functional behavior of the model (attribute `output`), and an input interface point of another (attribute `input`). This indicates that a signal bearing the evolution of a data will be exchanged during the simulation of the system, between the two connected behaviors. The transmission behavior of this connection can be specified by its optional attribute `transmission`. If this attribute is not specified, the transmission is considered instantaneous and perfect (without value modification).

Transmission: Element derived from `SimulationBehavior`, representing a transmission behavior of the system simulation. Transmitted data may be altered, i.e. delayed, deleted or modified by this behavior. However, unlike a functional behavior, a transmission behavior does not have an explicit input or output interface. We explain the nature of this transmission behavior with the `isContinuous` attribute.

DataType: A list representing the different types of data possible. We can have a relative integer (`INTEGER`), a real number (`REAL`), a string (`STRING`) or a boolean value (`BOOLEAN`).

We define an instantiated behavior `SimulationBehavior` as *elementary* by the fact that we do not want to break it down into sub-behaviors, often because they are too strongly coupled and the definition of their interconnections too complex.

By connecting these behavioral instances together, we obtain a model of all the possible data exchanges between the components that will implement these instances. In the way we use this language, a `SimulationBehavior` can be allocated to a simulation unit in an `AllocationML` model. A constraint of this use is that a `SimulationBehavior` must be able to be fully implemented in a single simulation unit, otherwise this element must be re-decomposed.

Eclipse EMF provides an editor for creating or modifying XMI format models that conform to an Ecore metamodel: the *Sample Reflective Ecore Model Editor*. We use it to develop models in CosiML, or to develop our own *concrete syntax*.

5.2 AllocationML and CatalogML: Two DSLs to Define the Transformation

The AllocationML model allows us to map a simulation represented by an SGridML model to the architecture of a cosimulation represented by a CosiML model. Indeed, in order to be able to cosimulate the system modeled with SGridML, the simulation units must respect a minimum interface, and some interconnections must appear in the cosimulation scenario.

These consistency links can be exploited in several ways, for example, by developing a verification and error detection tool between an SGridML model and a CosiML model. A second option, which is the one we choose to develop, is to generate the necessary elements in a CosiML model to be consistent with a given SGridML model.

The generator creates the **Ports** of the **SimulationUnits**, and the **Links** between them in the CosiML model. Rather than providing this generator with an incomplete CosiML model to fill it, we prefer to model the elements that cannot be generated automatically (**CosimulationModel** and the **SimulationUnits**) in reusable component libraries, and to generate the entire cosimulation model.

CatalogML is a DSL developed for this purpose. It is used to define a catalog of simulation units (**SimulationUnit**) with an undefined or incomplete interface (**Port**).

Figures 5 and 6 show the complete AllocationML and CatalogML metamodels, respectively.

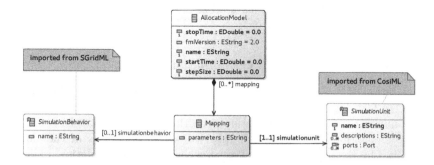

Fig. 5. AllocationML metamodel.

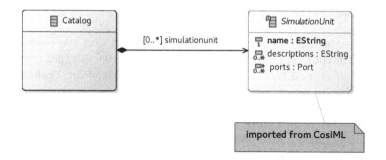

Fig. 6. CatalogML metamodel.

The elements of the AllocationML language are :

AllocationModel: Root element of the allocation model, it contains a list of *mappings* (**mapping**). It also contains the simulation parameters, which are the start date (**starttime**), end date (**stoptime**) and the duration of the time step between the cosimulation communication points (**stepsize**).

Mapping: Element representing an allocation link between a behavior instance (**simulationbehavior**) and a simulation unit (**simulationunit**).

We add a generic attribute called **parameters**, in order to allow the user to parameterize how a behavior instance is linked to a simulation unit (for example to detail how to link the input and output data of the behavior with the model included in the simulation unit). It is up to the user wishing to bring compatibility with a new tool to define how this field should be analyzed (*parsing* operation), if he needs it.

The **SimulationBehavior** and **SimulationUnit** elements are not part of AllocationML. They are imported from the Ecore SGridML and CosiML meta-models.

The CatalogML language contains only one element, which is:

Catalog: Root element of the model, used as a container for a list of simulation units (**simulationunit**).

5.3   Generation of a CosiML Cosimulation Model

The generation of a CosiML cosimulation model requires an SGridML behavior model, a CatalogML catalog model and an AllocationML allocation model. Figure 1 illustrates the dependencies between these different models.

Some transformation rules are simple: the simulation units of the catalog model linked by the allocation model are copied into the cosimulation model, as well as the configuration of the selected cosimulation. But the rules for generating ports and links are more complex because they require many model paths and special generation conditions. The principle is as follows. From a **SGridML::Connection** element of the behavior model:

1. We call In the corresponding **SGridML::Input** and Out the corresponding **SGridML::Output**. We call F_{in} and F_{out} the respective **SGridML::Function** containers of In and Out. If the connection has a **SGridML::Transmission**, we call it T.
2. These grid lines can be allocated to simulation units. Thus, each connection can be between 0 and three simulation units. We call them A, B and C. We're considering a fourth pseudo-simulation unit to mean that a Simulation Behavior hasn't been allocated.
3. Depending on how these three **SimulationBehaviors** can be allocated on these four **SimulationUnits**, between zero and two **Ports** and between zero and two **Links** are generated in the CosiML model.

When T is "allocated" on $\emptyset$, we consider the connection to be an instantaneous transmission. But we decide to prohibit cases where F_{in} or F_{out} are not allocated (the connection is ignored).

For each **SGridML::Connection** element, Table 2 shows the elements to be generated in the CosiML output model depending on the allocation of F_{in}, F_{out} and T to A, B, C and $\emptyset$. We use the following notation for the ports and links to be generated:

- $\in A$ means that the observed grid behavior is allocated to A and $\in \emptyset$ means it is not allocated. We write $\in \emptyset$ for T in cases where T is not allocated, or does not exist (the connection has no `SGridML::Transmission`).
- $\overrightarrow{Out}$ and $\overleftarrow{In}$ represent respectively a `CosiML::Output` and a `CosiML::Input` transformed from In and Out (respectively). $\overrightarrow{Out - In}$ represents a `CosiML::Output` transformed from the (In, Out) pair.
- $A \rightarrow B$ represents a `CosiML::Link` between the generated output ports of A and the generated input ports of B.
- We do not represent the additional synchronization `CosiML:Port` generated in the case of a discrete signal, because it follows the same rules of creation and connection as the information `CosiML::Port`.

Table 2. Transforming a **Connection** element to **Port** and **Link** elements.

Input elements				Generated elements			
Units linked to Connection	SimulationBehavior			Port			Link
	F_{Out}	F_{In}	T	A	B	C	
A	$\in A$	$\in A$	$\in A$	–	–	–	–
$A, \emptyset$	$\in A$	$\in A$	$\in \emptyset$	–	–	–	–
A, B	$\in A$	$\in B$	$\in B$	$\overrightarrow{Out}$	$\overleftarrow{In}$	–	$A \rightarrow B$
	$\in A$	$\in B$	$\in A$	$\overrightarrow{Out}$	$\overleftarrow{In}$	–	$A \rightarrow B$
	$\in A$	$\in A$	$\in B$	$\overrightarrow{OutIn}$	$\overrightarrow{Out - In}$ $\overleftarrow{Out - In}$	–	$A \rightarrow B \rightarrow A$
$A, B, \emptyset$	$\in A$	$\in B$	$\in \emptyset$	$\overrightarrow{Out}$	$\overleftarrow{In}$	–	$A \rightarrow B$
A, B, C	$\in A$	$\in B$	$\in C$	$\overrightarrow{Out}$	$\overleftarrow{In}$	$\overrightarrow{Out - In}$ $\overleftarrow{Out - In}$	$A \rightarrow C \rightarrow B$

6   Use-Case Cosimulation

6.1   The Use-Case of an Islanded Smart Grid

We chose a real use case from the French power utility to illustrate our contribution, and validate our toolchain. The system is an island with a power grid that is independent from the mainland grid, with its own production equipments. A diesel power plant is the main energy producer, and is complemented by a photovoltaic farm. The main issue in the configuration is that the renewable energy supply is intermittent. Indeed, as the photovoltaic source relies on sunlight and needs a clear sky for its production, it makes it as variable and unpredictable as the weather. In order to balance the production with the consumption, it has to be sometimes prevented from producing as much as it could, which causes economic loss and carbon footprint degradation. Therefore, a chosen solution is to add a battery storage to damp the variability of the production, with the purpose of minimizing the limitations of the photovoltaic farm. It could even allow the operator to shut down the diesel plant for some period and rely only on the battery and photovoltaic production.

To maximize the efficiency of the system, we need an Energy Management System (EMS) coupled with a Supervisory Control And Data Acquisition (SCADA) in order to implement an intelligent control of the production. The EMS monitors the state of the power grid (value of the voltage at various control points, state of switches), and drives some of its equipments (giving voltage set-points, limiting the injection of power by a source) through the SCADA. The EMS can collect other information such as weather and consumption forecasts from external information systems, as well as user preferences, in order to optimize the operation of the grid.

Before telling how the EMS controls the equipments on the grid, we have to explain how the power flow is established on a power grid. Knowing the power needed by the consumers, we can set power production set-points to the various sources of the grid in order to balance the consumption. However, losses on transmission lines can never be known, so we need at least one equipment that is not power constrained, and capable of producing the missing power or of absorbing the unpredictable excess. This equipment is generally the one having the biggest generator. In our case it is the diesel plant when it is connected to the grid, and the battery and its converter when it is not.

The EMS sends control signals to the various equipment of the grid:

- *photovoltaic farm*: the EMS decides if the production needs to be limited and how much;
- *battery*: there are two cases for this equipment. When the diesel plant is coupled to the grid and balances the power on the grid, the EMS controls the power absorbed or injected by the battery. When the diesel plant is shut down, the EMS does not control the battery and lets its power converter balance the power on the grid.
- *diesel plant*: the EMS decides if it is coupled to the grid (and produces power) or not. When it is coupled to the grid, it cannot produce less than a minimum power, so it can happen that the photovoltaic farm has its production limited. To avoid it, the diesel is turned off when the battery and the photovoltaic production are able to cover the consumption needs.

Because of all the different modes in which the grid can be, depending on the weather, on the management of the charge of the battery and on the variability of the consumption, simulation is very useful to test and validate a design of the solution, before any deployment on the field and expensive investments.

6.2   Behavior Model with SGridML

The simulation of the islanded smart grid is a good example of a cyber-physical system involving several knowledge fields, and several teams with different modeling tools. The first step to achieve is the development of the behavior model with SGridML. A proposition for the functional behaviors involved in the Smart Grid under design is illustrated in Fig. 7. As shown, all interactions coming to and from the ControlsComputing behavior are discrete, and realised by the TelecomTransmission behavior. All other interactions are continuous and realized by the PhysicalTransmission behavior.

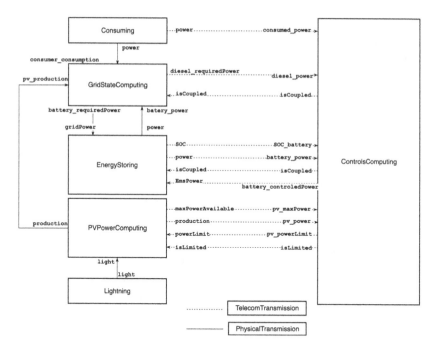

Fig. 7. Behavior model of the islanded power grid to simulate.

6.3 Allocation, Catalog and Simulation Models

Once the functional and transmission behaviors have been identified in the behavior model, they have to be allocated to a specific simulation unit. We decided to use four simulation units, that we describe in the catalog model with CatalogML, as illustrated in Figure 8.

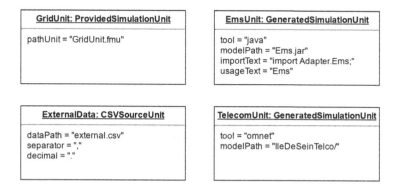

Fig. 8. Simulation units decribed in the catalog model.

The first simulation unit, GridUnit, models the electric behavior. As such, the GridStateComputing, the EnergyStoring, and the PVPowerComputing functional behaviors, as well as the `PhysicalTransmission` behavior, are allocated to this `GridUnit` in the allocation model written with AllocationML. `GridUnit` evaluates the electrical power state of the grid according to production and consumption constraints. We are using Modelica[8] with the Dymola software to model the grid power flow because they are well-known tools among electrical engineers, and they fully support the FMI standard and the export to FMU [5]. `GridUnit` is therefore an instance of `ProvidedSimulationUnit`.

The second simulation unit, `EmsUnit`, models the behavior of the EMS. Only the `ControlsComputing` functional behavior is allocated to it in the allocation model. There is no conventional tool supporting the modeling of reactive systems and also handling FMI. Complex algorithms are usually modeled with textual procedural languages such as C or Java. There are tools supporting the export of such models toward FMU, but they require additional efforts and specific code refactoring and writing. Our Smart Grid Simulation Framework supports the automatic transformation of a Java model into an FMU, with the generation of a wrapper code implementing the JavaFMI Framework library, and the use of the JavaFMI builder tool. `EmsUnit` is therefore an instance of `GeneratedSimulationUnit`. We developed a first, simple Java algorithm of the EMS which takes the current state of the grid as input and does not use forecasts. It computes controls every 15 min, but continuously monitors the current state of the grid equipments in case emergency controls are required. Figure 9 shows an activity diagram, illustrating this process.

The third simulation unit, `ExternalDataUnit` models the independant, external input data used in our use case cosimulation. The `Lightning` and `Consuming` behaviors are allocated to this unit in the allocation model. We chose to provide these timed data in a CSV file, transformed to FMU format thanks to our *CSV source generator*. Therefore, `ExternalDataUnit` is an instance of `CSVSourceUnit` in the catalog model.

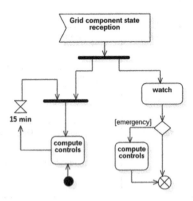

Fig. 9. EMS monitoring process, with periodic and emergency controls.

---

[8] https://www.modelica.org/, component-oriented modeling language based on equations set declaration.

Finally, the fourth simulation unit, `TelecomUnit`, models the telecom transmission behavior. `TelecomTransmission` is allocated to this unit in the allocation model. We are using the OMNeT modeling and simulation software to develop this simulation model. Hence, `TelecomUnit` is an instance of `GeneratedSimulationUnit`, meant to be use with our OMNeT generator to produce the required FMU.

6.4 Simulation Models and Cosimulation Model

The development of a behavior model with SGridML, a catalog model with CatalogML and an allocation model with AllocationML allows us to automatically generate the cosimulation model. This generated model instanciates the same simulation unit as those described in the catalog model, as well as their structural interfaces and coupling constraints.

Through the generation of the cosimulation model, we are now able to generate all the artifacts and scripts to build an executable cosimulation unit. Indeed, all simulation models can be automatically converted to the FMU format, and a configuration file as well as a global execution script are generated by the Smart Grid Simulation Framework.

6.5 Simulation and Decisions

The use case presents two main concerns: *1)* how to optimize the characteristics of the battery in order to implement an efficient management of the production and keep investment as low as possible? And *2)* how to test the efficiency of the chosen EMS algorithm?

From the CosiML model, the toolchain generates the necessary wrapper files to build the EmsFmu and CurvesFmu FMUs, as well as the DACCOSIM model of the cosimulation. In addition, a script is generated to create automatically the missing FMUs, and to launch the DACCOSIM cosimulation.

In our case, the cosimulation evaluates the behavior of the grid on a full day (24 hours), as we did in [12]. Figure 10 shows the average and cumulated per-hour production (over the x-axis) and consumption (below the x-axis) of each equipment on the day, for particular load and photovoltaic maximal production curves (and initial conditions).

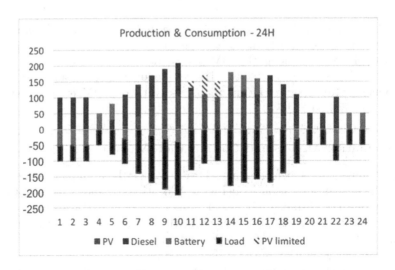

Fig. 10. Consumption and production of electricity over a full day. Source: [12].

The energy balance has been ensured all day (no black-outs) meaning our design solution is effective on this particular scenario. However, between 11am and 2pm, the photovoltaic production has been limited (see hatched bars). Looking at the results (not shown in the figure), we see that the charge of the battery was already maximal and could not absorb the extra production. There is consequently a potential for optimizing our solution. Increasing the capacity of the battery, or improving the algorithm of the EMS are two possible iterations. Once the models are updated, the execution of the toolchain automatically updates the simulation artifacts and executes the cosimulation again.

7   Observations

The key motivation behind our work is to reduce the cost of iterations in the design of systems by automating the cosimulation of the models using a model-driven approach. To be useful in an industrial context, we need to fulfill the following requirements: each iterative step of the process must provide a quick feedback; the upfront modeling cost must be recovered in the following phases of analysis, maintenance, etc.; business experts must concentrate on their core skills.

We presented in this paper a toolchain based on a cosimulation DSL to reference simulation models and characterize some coupling constraints between them. The various generators allow the generation of simulation units and deployment scripts from this cosimulation model. Hence, this automated process provides the possibility to make changes to the cosimulation scenario with minimal efforts. We illustrate this through the following industrial scenarios.

In a first scenario, a functional architect has to compare components from various vendors, for example to find the best EMS solution (EMSGrid in our previous use case). To guarantee the correct integration of the simulation model provided by the vendor, the tender documents include requirements deduced from the CosiML model. The selection of the right component is simplified because:

- Using the tool chain, the architect can quickly build a test environment, by providing input data inside a CSV file, automatically generating a new FMU and a cosimulation model, then testing multiple configurations easily.
- To select the components to be used in the cosimulation, only the *pathFMU* attribute of the *ProvidedSimulationUnit* must be modified and the new cosimulation set up can be generated.

In a second scenario, we want to involve electrotechnical engineers to build a load flow model of the power grid (GridFMI in our previous use case). This is possible without an intensive training because they can use their own specific tools to build the simulation model (Dymola, PowerFactory, etc.), and there are only few basic concepts (input, output, discrete or continuous variability) to be explained in order to build the CosiML model. Once they develop a model conforming to the CosiML metamodel, they can then use an iterative approach to improve the model without involving other collaborators, thanks to our toolchain, which automatically integrates their work to the cosimulation platform.

Finally, in a third scenario, we consider the case of a modification of one simulation model inducing a modification of the CosiML model, and especially among the coupling constraints between models (e.g. adding or renaming several ports). Firstly, the validation rules of our toolchain guarantee the consistency of the CosiML model. Secondly, the automated execution process of the cosimulation will raise errors until each impacted simulation model makes the necessary adjustments. Thirdly and finally, the implementation of the adjustments might be partially done by the generators of the toolchain.

8   Conclusion

By automating some verifications and the generation of cosimulation artifacts, model driven approaches allow shorter, less costly and less error prone iterations on a solution design. Our toolchain relies on an abstract CosiML model of the system to check the consistency of the different simulation units, to generate adapters for discrete event signals that cannot be used as is in an FMI simulation, and to generate FMUs from models developed with different tools. It uses the FMI standard and benefits from its many advantages regarding CPS simulation in the industry. It can also integrate FMUs exported by some modeling tools in the cosimulation, allowing models from different system domains to be developed with the relevant tools, by experimented teams, while protecting industrial property inside FMUs.

We developed the SGridML language to allow several people from various domains to collaborate on an abstract analysis model of the Smart Grid design.

AllocationML and CatalogML allow the distribution of the behavior of the system among different simulation models, whose interfaces and coupling constraints are directly validated by syntaxic rules. In addition, the transformation between SGridML and CosiML ensures the creation of simulation units consistent with the functional design of the system under study.

The Smart Grid Simulation Framework has been used on a real industrial case, which involves both continuous and discrete signal exchanges. The included modeling languages and tools have been designed to be used independently, or to support new modeling tools and generators. The modular nature of the different transformations also helps to adapt the generated artifacts to different versions of FMI. For instance, the support for a more precise detection of discontinuities in FMI v2.1 may lead to a new adapter for discrete event signals, while keeping the current one for cosimulations using older versions of FMI.

References

1. Andrén, F., Strasser, T., Kastner, W.: Engineering smart grids: applying model-driven development from use case design to deployment. Energies **10**(3), 374 (2017). https://doi.org/10.3390/en10030374
2. Blochwitz, T., Otter, M., Arnold, M., Bausch, C., Elmqvist, H., et al.: The functional mockup interface for tool independent exchange of simulation models. In: Proceedings of the 8th International Modelica Conference, pp. 105–114 (2011)
3. Cremona, F., Lohstroh, M., Broman, D., Lee, E.A., Masin, M., Tripakis, S.: Hybrid co-simulation: it's about time. Softw. Syst. Model. **18**(3), 1655–1679 (2019). https://doi.org/10.1007/s10270-017-0633-6
4. Dahmann, J.S., Morse, K.L.: High level architecture for simulation: an update. In: Proceedings. 2nd International Workshop on Distributed Interactive Simulation and Real-Time Applications (Cat. No.98EX191), pp. 32–40, July 1998. https://doi.org/10.1109/DISRTA.1998.694563
5. Elsheikh, A., Awais, M.U., Widl, E., Palensky, P.: Modelica-enabled rapid prototyping of cyber-physical energy systems via the functional mockup interface. In: Workshop on Modeling and Simulation of Cyber-Physical Energy Systems (MSCPES), pp. 1–6. IEEE, May 2013. https://doi.org/10.1109/MSCPES.2013.6623315
6. Évora Gómez, J., et al.: Co-simulation made simpler and faster. In: The 13th International Modelica Conference, pp. 785–794, February 2019. https://doi.org/10.3384/ecp19157785
7. Gomes, C., Thule, C., Larsen, P.G., Vangheluwe, H.: Co-Simulation: a survey. ACM Comput. Surv. **51**(3), 49:1–49:33 (2018)
8. Guermazi, S., Tatibouet, J., Cuccuru, A., Dhouib, S., Gérard, S., Seidewitz, E.: Executable modeling with fUML and ALF in papyrus: tooling and experiments. In: EXE@MoDELS (2015)
9. Li, W., Monti, A., Luo, M., Dougal, R.A.: VPNET: a co-simulation framework for analyzing communication channel effects on power systems. In: 2011 IEEE Electric Ship Technologies Symposium, pp. 143–149 (2011)
10. Nutaro, J.: Designing power system simulators for the smart grid: combining controls, communications, and electro-mechanical dynamics. In: 2011 IEEE Power and Energy Society General Meeting, pp. 1–5, July 2011. https://doi.org/10.1109/PES.2011.6039456

11. Oudart, D., Cantenot, J., Boulanger, F., Chabridon, S.: An approach to design smart grids and their IT system by cosimulation. In: MODELSWARD 19, pp. 370–377. SCITEPRESS - Science and Technology Publications (2019). https://doi.org/10.5220/0007407003700377

12. Oudart, D., Cantenot, J., Boulanger, F., Chabridon, S.: A model based toolchain for the cosimulation of cyber-physical systems with fmi. In: Proceedings of the 8th International Conference on Model-Driven Engineering and Software Development - Volume 1: MODELSWARD, pp. 15–25. INSTICC, SciTePress (2020). https://doi.org/10.5220/0008875400150025, https://www.scitepress.org/PublicationsDetail.aspx?ID=uwfM1k2FY4Y=

13. Paris, T., Ciarletta, L., Chevrier, V.: Designing co-simulation with multi-agent tools: a case study with NetLogo. In: Francesco Belardinelli, E.A. (ed.) 15th European Conference on Multi-Agent Systems (EUMAS 2017). Multi-Agent Systems and Agreement Technologies, vol. 10767, pp. 253–267. Springer, Évry, France (Dec 2017). https://doi.org/10.1007/978-3-030-01713-2_18, https://hal.archives-ouvertes.fr/hal-01687101

14. Suri, K., Cuccuru, A., Cadavid, J., Gerard, S., Gaaloul, W., Tata, S.: Model-based development of modular complex systems for accomplishing system integration for industry 4.0. In: Proceedings of the 5th International Conference on Model-Driven Engineering and Software Development - Volume 1: MODELSWARD, pp. 487–495. ScitePress (2017). https://doi.org/10.5220/0006210504870495

15. Tavella, J.P., Caujolle, M., Vialle, S., al.: Toward an accurate and fast hybrid multi-simulation with the FMI-CS standard. In: Emerging Technologies and Factory Automation (ETFA-2016), Berlin, Germany, September 2016

16. Uslar, M., et al.: Applying the smart grid architecture model for designing and validating system-of-systems in the power and energy domain: a European perspective. Energies **12**(2), 258 (2019). https://doi.org/10.3390/en12020258

17. Van Acker, B., Denil, J., Vangheluwe, H., De Meulenaere, P.: Generation of an optimised master algorithm for FMI co-simulation. In: DEVS Integrative M&S Symposium. DEVS 2015, Society for Computer Simulation International (2015). http://dl.acm.org/citation.cfm?id=2872965.2872993

18. Yang, C.H., Zhabelova, G., Yang, C.W., Vyatkin, V.: Cosimulation environment for event-driven distributed controls of smart grid. IEEE Trans. Ind. Inform. **9**(3), 1423–1435 (2013). https://doi.org/10.1109/TII.2013.2256791

19. Zhao, H., Apvrille, L., Mallet, F.: Multi-View design for cyber-physical systems. In: Ph.D. Symposium at 13th International Conference on ICT in Education, Research, and Industrial Applications, Kiev, Ukraine, pp. 22–28, May 2017. https://hal.inria.fr/hal-01669918

Safety First: About the Detection of Arithmetic Overflows in Hardware Design Specifications

Fritjof Bornebusch[1(✉)], Christoph Lüth[1,3(✉)], Robert Wille[1,2(✉)], and Rolf Drechsler[1,3(✉)]

[1] Cyber-Physical Systems, DFKI GmbH, 28359 Bremen, Germany
{fritjof.bornebusch,christoph.lueth}@dfki.de
[2] Integrated Circuit and System Design, Johannes Kepler University Linz,
4040 Linz, Austria
robert.wille@jku.at
[3] Mathematics and Computer Science, University of Bremen,
28359 Bremen, Germany
drechsler@uni-bremen.de

Abstract. This work proposes an alternative hardware design approach that allows the detection of arithmetic overflows at the specification level. The established hardware design approach describes infinite integer types at that level while the model describes finite types. This opens a semantic gap between both levels, which means that arithmetic overflows cannot be detected at the specification level. To address this problem the CompCert integer library is utilized that describes finite integer types as dependent types using the proof assistant Coq. Properties that argue about these finite types can be specified and verified at the specification level. This closes the semantic gap the established hardware design approach suffers from.

Keywords: Hardware designs · Arithmetic integer overflows · Proof assistants · Functional HDLs · Hardware synthesis

1 Introduction

Circuits are an integral part of our lives. Their area of application extends from airplanes, to medicine, to toothbrushes. These areas of application lead to an increasing number of complexity in circuits. As complexity increases, so does the number of potential errors. For this reason, the increasing complexity needs to be considered in the development phase of hardware designs from the beginning.

To address the increasing complexity, hardware designs are described at different levels. The established hardware design approach starts with a formal specification, e.g. in SysML/OCL [21, 22, 26]. This specification describes the

Research supported by BMBF grant SELFIE, grant no. 01IW16001.

S. Hammoudi et al. (Eds.): MODELSWARD 2020, CCIS 1361, pp. 26–48, 2021.
https://doi.org/10.1007/978-3-030-67445-8_2

functional behavior of the hardware design and allows the verification of properties that argue about that design [8,9]. After specifying and verifying the design it is translated to a SystemC model, which is the de facto standard for high-level synthesis (HLS) [3,24]. This translation step is manually as OCL constraints cannot be translated automatically into executable SystemC code. The final step is the translation of the model to an implementation in a low-level hardware description language (HDL), e.g. Verilog. As SystemC only supports a restricted synthesizeable subset, this translation step is also manually [2].

The established hardware design approach reveals a *semantic gap* between the specification and the model respectively the implementation. The specification describes infinite integer types, while the model and the implementation describe finite integer types. This *semantic gap* lead to properties that hold for the specification, but not for the model, e.g. the absence of arithmetic overflows. Finite integer types describe a wrap-around or overflow behavior, as they implement a quotient ring [11,13–15]. As arithmetic integer operations for finite types are not semantically equivalent to arithmetic integer operations for infinite types, these operations might lead to unintended behavior, which again lead to serious problems in the final hardware design implementation. Through the lack of tool support for automatically detecting arithmetic overflows in the model, the engineer has to detect them manually.

To address the problem of the *semantic gap* of the established hardware design approach an alternative hardware design approach is proposed. This approach describes finite integer types at the specification level using dependent types [7,17]. These types allow the definition of operations, which detect arithmetic integer overflows at the specification level. Properties that argue about these operations can be verified to ensure the reliable detection of these overflows. After the verification process a model in the functional hardware description language (HDL) CλaSH can be extracted automatically [6], which again can be synthesized to an implementation on the Register-Transfer-Level (RTL) [1]. The proposed alternative hardware design approach closes the *semantic gap* the established approach has, by describing finite integer types at the specification level.

To achieve this, we start with a specification for the proof assistant Coq [4,10]. Analog to the established hardware design approach this specification allows the verification of properties. The finite integer types are described by the CompCert integer library [19]. This library implements finite types as *dependent types* [7, 17] and allows the implementation of both signed and unsigned finite types of arbitrary sizes.

Note that this work extends the work [5] already published by the authors. For this reason, some figures and listings are borrowed from that work as can be seen in the captions. The extensions in this work include that, in particular, there may be no overflow in an arithmetic operation implementing the proposed function type, because of specified bounds. It is shown how an operation is specified in this case using the proposed overflow detecting function type. A generic property that has to be proven to show the absence of the overflow is specified. It is also shown why the overflow detecting operation cannot be changed automatically to its corresponding basic arithmetic operation if there is a proof of the absence of the overflow. Furthermore, the closure of functions that implement the function type for the proposed overflow detection pattern is specified and proven. This enables the cascading of overflow detecting operations, analog to their corresponding basic arithmetic integer operations. An evaluation regarding the impact of the speed and space for a synthesized hardware design that implements the overflow detection pattern is provided. This evaluation compares a hardware design using the basic arithmetic integer operations with their corresponding overflow detecting operations and shows the applicability of the proposed overflow detection pattern.

We present our work as follows: First, we explain the established hardware design approach and describe the problem we address in this work. Section 3 discusses the related work and why it is not suitable to address the problem of the established hardware design approach properly. In Sect. 4 and Sect. 5 the proposed hardware design approach is described, how the considered problem is addressed and how the CλaSH model is generated. Section 6 describes the proposed generalizable integer overflow detection pattern. Section 7 evaluates the proposed approach by comparing basic arithmetic integer operations with their corresponding operations, which detect overflows, regarding the speed and consumed space in the final hardware implementations. The Sect. 8 discusses the result of the evaluation and the applicability of the approach proposed in this work, while Sect. 9 concludes this work.

2   Motivation

In this section, we briefly review the established hardware design approach which is the motivation of this work. The established approach relies on a SysML/OCL specification that is later translated to a SystemC model manually. We show why the combination of SysML/OCL and SystemC is a problem for the detection of arithmetic integer overflows.

A traffic light controller serves as a running example to illustrate the established hardware design approach as well as the approach proposed in this work. This controller is inspired by [23].

2.1   The Established Hardware Design Approach

The established hardware design approach starts with a SysML/OCL [21,22,26] specification, which can later be used for the verification of properties [8,9]. The structure of the design is described by SysML class diagrams, while the functional behavior is described by OCL constraints. These constraints are specified as preconditions and postconditions as well as invariants.

Example 1. Figure 1 shows the SysML class diagram for the traffic light controller that serves as a running example in this work. The controller connects three different traffic lights: for the *trams*, *cars* and *pedestrians*. The basis of this controller are two finite state machines (FSMs), implemented by the *switch* and the *tick* function. The OCL constraints for these state machines can be seen in Listing 1.1.

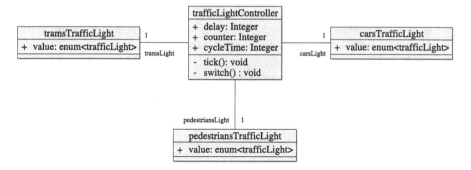

Fig. 1. SysML class diagram of the traffic light controller [5]. This controller serves as a running example in this work.

```
1   context  trafficLightController :: tick ()
2     pre  pre_incr_counter  :  self . counter  < ( self . delay  −1)  ∗  self . cycleTime
3     post  incr_counter  :  self . counter = self . counter@pre +self . cycleTime and
4                              self . delay = self . delay@pre and
5                              self . cycleTime = self . cycleTime@pre
6
7   context  trafficLightController :: tick ()
8     pre  pre_reset_counter  :  self . counter >= ( self . delay  −1)  ∗  self . cycleTime
9     post  reset_counter :  self . counter = 0 and
10                             self . delay = self . delay@pre and
11                             self . cycleTime = self . cycleTime@pre
12
13  context  trafficLightController :: switch ()
14    pre  pre_switch  :  self . counter >= ( self . delay  −1)  ∗  self . cycleTime and
15                          self . tramsLight . value = Red and
16                          self . pedestriansLight . value = Red and
17                          self . carsLight . value = Green
18    post  post_switch  :  self . tramsLight . value = Red and
19                           self . pedestriansLight . value = Red and
20                           self . carsLight . value = Yellow
21
22    inv :  self . counter  > −1
23    inv :  self . delay  > 0
24    inv :  self . cycleTime  > 0
```

Listing 1.1. OCL constraints for the *tick* function and the *switch* function introduced in Fig. 1. Additionally, the range for the variables, *counter*, *delay* and *cylceTime* is restricted by invariants.

The *tick* function represents the clock in the SysML/OCL specification. As seen in Listing 1.1, it increases a *counter* and resets it back to 0 if an upper bound is reached (pre_reset_counter). This *counter* is used to count the amount of nanoseconds until the *switch* function is called. The controller considers traffic situations, such as rush hour. For this reason, the *delay* can be configured at runtime, which allows the configuration of a dynamic transition time. The transition time is the time the *counter* takes to reach its upper bound. Until that bound is not reached, the *counter* is increased by the *cycleTime* as the OCL constraints *pre_incr_counter* and *incr_counter* states. If the upper bound is reached, the *counter* is reset to 0 as state by *reset_counter*. In this case, the

FSM implemented by the *switch* function moves into a new state where the traffic light for the cars is no longer green, but yellow as stated by the constraints *pre_switch* and *post_switch*. The *cycleTime* is constant and indicates the cycle time of the hardware in nanoseconds (nsec). For example, if the transition time is 30 s the *delay* has to be set to 1.500.000.000 with a *cycleTime* of 20 nsec.

The *switch* function implements the state transitions for the traffic lights. This state machine determines whether a traffic light is switched on or off in order to avoid situations such as the lights for cars and pedestrians are both green at the same time. The different states for the lights, are encoded as *Green*, *Yellow* and *RedYellow* and *Red*. An exemplary state transition is stated by the *pre_switch* and the *post_switch* constraints as seen in Listing 1.1. Note that the *delay* might not always be necessary for the state transition, e.g. the pedestrians might have a constant transition time while the transition time for the cars rely on the *delay* (rush hour). Since this work considers arithmetic integer overflows, the state machine is not described in detail, as no arithmetic operations are involved in the state transitions.

After specifying and verifying the behavior of the traffic light controller in SysML/OCL, a model in SystemC is described. This step is manually as indeed the SysML structure can be translated automatically in the form of C++ classes[1]. However, the behavior specified by OCL constraints cannot automatically be translated to executable SystemC code.

Example 2. Listing 1.2 shows the implementation of the *tick* function in the SystemC model.

```
 1  sc_uint <32> counter, delay, cycleTime;
 2  States states;
 3
 4  void tick () {
 5    if ( counter < (delay −1) * cycleTime )
 6      counter = counter + cycleTime;
 7    else
 8      counter = 0;
 9    switch_();
10  }
```

Listing 1.2. Implementation of the *tick* function, introduced in Listing 1.1, of the SystemC model.

As specified by the OCL constraints in Listing 1.1, the SystemC model increases the counter by the *cycleTime* until the upper bound is reached, as seen in Line 5 of Listing 1.2. Otherwise, the counter is reset to 0.

2.2   Considered Problem

To illustrate the problem that motivates this work, we take a look at the safety property that can be derived from the specification, seen in Listing 1.1. This safety property holds for the specification, but not for the model and in this section we show why not.

---

[1] Note that SystemC is a collection of C++ class libraries designed to describe hardware designs.

Example 3. Listing 1.3 shows the safety property that is derived from the SysML/OCL specification. This property is specified as an OCL invariant.

```
1  context  trafficLightController
2    inv:  self.counter < self.delay * self.cycleTime
```

Listing 1.3. Safety property derived from the OCL constraints introduced in Listing 1.1.

This invariant determines that the *counter* is less than the multiplication of the *delay* and the *cycleTime*. As the SysML data type *Integer* is infinite, the property holds for the specification.

To prove that the safety property holds we show that, if the precondition, invariants and safety property hold in the pre state and the postcondition holds in the post state, then the safety property holds in post state as well.

This proof consists of a case analysis of the OCL constraints for the *tick* function, seen in Listing 1.1. The notation x' is used to denote the value of the variable x in the post state. The *self* prefix seen in the OCL constraints is also omitted.

Example 4. In order to show that the safety property, seen in Listing 1.3, holds in the above specification, we take a look at some assumptions that can be derived from the specification, seen in Listing 1.1. We assume that the preconditions and the safety property hold in the pre states and that the postconditions hold in the post states.

Using these assumptions, we want to prove that if we are in a pre state in which both the precondition and the safety property hold, and we move to the post state in which the postcondition holds, then the safety property also holds.

We prove this property by case analysis. The first case is the precondition *pre_reset_counter* and the postcondition *reset_counter*. The second case is the precondition *pre_incr_counter* and the postcondition *incr_counter*. In the first case the *counter* is reset to 0 in the postcondition. The invariants state that the *delay* and the *cycleTime* are both greater than 0, so the safety property holds in the post state. To prove the safety property for the second case, we take a look at the precondition *pre_incr_counter*. Since the monotonicity of the addition holds in $\mathbb{Z}$, we add *cycleTime* to both sides of the precondition. This gives us the postcondition *incr_counter* on the left side. If we dissolve the right side, we see that the safety property holds in the post state.

$$\begin{aligned}
& \text{counter} + \text{cycleTime}' < ((\text{delay}' - 1) * \text{cycleTime}') + \text{cycleTime}' \\
=\ & \text{counter} + \text{cycleTime}' < (\text{delay}' * \text{cycleTime}' - \text{cycleTime}') + \text{cycleTime}' \\
=\ & \text{counter} + \text{cycleTime}' < \text{delay}' * \text{cycleTime}'
\end{aligned}$$

Now that we have proven that the safety property holds in the post states of the SysML/OCL specification, why does it not hold in the SystemC model? If we consider the case analysis of the proof for the SystemC model, we see that for the first case the proof holds. However, for the second case the monotonicity of the addition does not hold. The SystemC model describes the quotient ring $\mathbb{Z}_{>-1}/32\mathbb{Z}_{>-1}$. This ring describes an integer type of limited size and that is precisely the reason why the safety property does not hold in the SystemC model, as the monotonicity of the addition does not hold for quotient rings.

In other words, the multiplication operation in the SysML/OCL specification is not semantic equivalent to the one in the SystemC model, as in SystemC all integer types describe a quotient ring: $\mathbb{Z}/m\mathbb{Z}, m \in \mathbb{N}$ (signed integer) or $\mathbb{Z}_{>-1}/m\mathbb{Z}_{>-1}, m \in \mathbb{N}$ (unsigned integers). The *semantic gap* between SysMLs infinite integer type and SystemCs finite integer types motivates this work and results in the proposal of an alternative hardware design approach that allows the description of finite integer types at the specification level.

Example 5. Let us consider again the translation step of the OCL constraints seen in Listing 1.1 for the SystemC model seen in Listing 1.2. The model assumes that the implementation of the unsigned integer multiplication operation is the same as in the specification. This assumption is understandable at first glance, since the same behavior is apparently described. However, as we have seen above this is not the case, as the integer type in the specification is infinite, while the one in the model is finite. As a result, the SystemC model violates the safety property, shown in Listing 1.3.

This violation bears a direct impact on the change of the configurable delay at runtime and thus on the transition time of the state machine, which considers traffic situations such as rush hour. For instance, a changed delay might lead to unintended behavior as the multiplication operation on the quotient ring $sc\_uint<32>$ implements a wrap-around behavior. In this case, instead of increasing the transition time it is decreased which is a serious problem.

A look in the C++ standard[2] reveals two different behaviors of integer arithmetic regarding overflows.

Unsigned integer arithmetic defines total functions and does not overflow. A result that cannot be interpreted by the resulting data type is reduced by $2^n, n \in \mathbb{N}$, where n is the number of bits in the value representation, e.g. $sc\_uint<32>$. Through the modulo operation, arithmetic operations on these data types implements a wrap-around behavior. So in the case of unsigned arithmetic the operation might lead to unintended behavior.

Signed integer arithmetic does overflow and defines either total functions or partial functions, depending on the underlying hardware platform. The functions are total, if the platform represents the values in the 2's complement. In this case, the same wrap-around behavior is implemented as for the unsigned integer arithmetic. If the platform uses traps[3] to indicate an overflow the arithmetic function becomes partial, as in this case the function does not define a return

---

[2] The current standard for the C++ programming language is specified in ISO/IEC 14882:2017.

[3] A trap is a software interrupt that is triggered due to an instruction execution, e.g. division-by-zero, by the processor.

value for a pair of input values. As the behavior of signed integer arithmetic is platform dependent, it is undefined in general.

The term *arithmetic integer overflow* often refers to both unsigned integer and signed integer arithmetic [13,15]. For this reason, we use that term in the rest of this work to address both behaviors.

The basic problem of the *semantic gap* between SysMLs infinite integer types and SystemCs finite types motivates our work. To address this problem a semantic equivalent finite type is needed at the specification level as hardware descriptions are finite by design and, therefore, rely on these types. Having such types at the specification level enables the clear distinction between the correct result of an arithmetic integer operation and the occurred overflow. We call this distinction the *detection of overflows*. As overflows are inevitable on finite integer types this work proposes an overflow detection pattern by a total function that makes the distinction between the result of an arithmetic integer operation and the overflow explicitly.

In the next section, we evaluate the related work and discuss why it is not suitable to address the problem described above properly. This discussion leads eventually to the alternative hardware design approach.

3   Related Work

In this section we evaluate and discuss the related work to show why a specification in SysML/OCL and a model in SystemC is not suitable to detect integer overflows properly.

To detect integer overflows in the SysML specification the possibility to define finite integer types of arbitrary sizes need to be implemented, but this is not the case in the current standard [22]. Of course, invariants can be used to restrict SysMLs *Integer* type by describing a lower and upper bound. But, these bounds are independent of the integer type used in the SystemC model. For instance, after the automatic generation of the SystemC class structure from SysML: what should the equivalent type to SysMLs *Integer* type be in SystemC? Either a standard type, like *Integer* is always represented as *sc_uint*<32>, but in this case the bounds can never change, or the extracted type of the model is dependent from the bounds chosen in the specification. Such a restriction can be described by OCL invariants, but it is not possible to extract these invariants in executable SystemC code automatically. If these bounds are translated manually to the SystemC model, they might change during the development phase of the model. For example, it was discovered that a different type, e.g. *sc_uint*<31>, is needed which again invalidates the bounds from the specification. The basic problem is that a SysML/OCL specification describes infinite integer types while the SystemC model describes finite ones.

To detect integer overflows directly in the SystemC model, the automatic overflow detection of C++ programs need to be considered. The detection of overflows by a C++ compiler is quite challenging, because of the low level nature of C++. The standard allows bit manipulations, which are very common [15].

This makes it very challenging to detect overflows by the compiler reliably, as it is not always clear whether such a manipulation is intended by the engineer or not. Furthermore, the standard defines undefined behavior semantics that allow optimizations by the compiler [15]. For this reason, C++ compiler can only detect arithmetic overflows in constant-expression evaluation, but not in general. As a result, C++ compilers are not suitable to detect arithmetic integer overflows automatically.

Since there is no support by the compilers static code analysis tools, such as Astrée [13] or Frama-C [14], should to be considered.

Astrée relies on abstract interpretation [12,16] and aims to prove the absence of runtime errors, such as integer overflows, in C programs. Abstract interpretation is used to derive a computational abstract semantic interpretation from a behavior expressed in a programming language. The resulting interpretation does not contain the actual values, but focuses on dedicated parts of the program. The scope of the static analysis is determined by these parts and define what kinds of errors are detected. The limit of abstract interpretation is the analysis of loops, as loops define an infinite number of paths in the interpretation tree. SystemC models are C++ programs, which is not the input language of Astrée. Astrée could, of course, be extended to support C++ programs, but SystemC describes hardware designs. Such designs rely on parallel execution and run in infinite loops. As mentioned above, loops create an infinite number of paths in the interpretation tree. For this reason, Astrée is not suitable to detect integer overflows in hardware designs.

Frama-C is another static code analysis tool which relies on *C Intermediate Language* (CIL) [20] and supports annotations written in *ANSI/ISO C Specification Language* (ACSL) [14]. Frama-C enables the application of different static analysis techniques, such as deductive verification of annotated C programs by automatic provers, e.g. Z3 [14]. The detection of integer overflows is supported by the *Runtime Error Annotation Generation* (RTE) plugin which includes the generation of annotations by syntactic constant folding in the form of assertions. RTE seeds these annotations into other plugins, e.g. for generating weakest-preconditions with proof obligations. Similar to Astrée the input language for Frama-C is a C program, which could , of course, be extended to support C++ programs. But the static analysis of the infinite loops hardware designs rely on is quite challenging. For this reason, Frama-C is not suitable to detect integer overflows in SystemC models.

As discussed in this section a SysML/OCL specification and a SystemC model are not suitable to detect integer overflows. The specification describes infinite types and lacks the definition of finite integer types of arbitrary sizes. The model describes finite integer types and does not get support by compilers or static analysis tools for detecting integer overflows. As a result, the engineer need to detect overflows pro-active and explicitly at the model level.

The problem discussed above in combination with the related work leads to the following question: *Can arithmetic integer overflows in hardware designs be detected at the specification level?*

4   Proposal of the Alternative Design Approach

In this section, we propose an alternative design approach that addresses the problem of the *semantic gap* of the established hardware design approach, described in Sect. 2.

The alternative approach uses the proof assistant Coq [4,10] to specify and verify the functional behavior of hardware designs. Coq describes functional behavior in a specification language, called Gallina, which is based on the *Calculus of Inductive Constructions* (CiC). This calculus combines a higher-order logic with a richly-typed functional programming language. As higher-order logic is too expressive for automatic reasoning, a separate tactic language is used that provides proof methods, but let the user define his own ones as well. Therefore, proof assistants are also known as interactive theorem provers.

As discussed in Sect. 2.2 the problem of the established approach is the *semantic gap* between the infinite integer types in SysML and the finite integer types in SystemC. To address this problem we use *dependent types* [7,17] to implement finite integer types in Coq. These types are used to functionally describe the limited size bit vectors for the inputs and outputs of hardware designs. The idea to describe hardware designs using dependent types is not new and started back in the 1990s. These types allow a type definition that relies on an additional value. For instance, the type A^n defines a vector of the length $n, n \in \mathbb{N}$ with elements of the arbitrary type A. We say that A depends on n that is where the name *dependent type* comes from. Proof Assistants, like Coq, allow the definition of dependent types by the user which gives us the opportunity to describe hardware designs with finite integer types at the specification level. In order to describe such types, we utilized the CompCert integer library to describe both signed and unsigned integer types of arbitrary sizes [19].

In contrast to the established approach, we use the proof assistant Coq at the specification level to specify and verify hardware design. Furthermore, we describe finite integer types using *dependent types*, which enables the detection of integer overflows at the specification level. We describe below how the detection is specified and verified and how a final hardware implementation is generated automatically from a specification written in Gallina.

4.1   Detection of Integer Overflows

As described in Sect. 2.2, we need an explicit distinction between the correct result of an arithmetic integer operation, e.g. multiplication, and the occurred overflow. Therefore, we use a dedicated type which either contains the result of an operation or indicates an occurred overflow. This data type is called *option*, as seen in Listing 1.4, and has two constructors: *None* and *Some* which takes an arbitrary type (A) as parameter.

```
1 Inductive option (A : Type) : Type :=
2 | Some : A -> option A
3 | None : option A.
```

Listing 1.4. Definition of the *option* type in Gallina provided by the Coq standard library (Coq.Init.Datatypes) [5].

The constructor *Some* contains the result, while the constructor *None* indicates the overflow. Consider again the running example introduced in Sect. 2.1. This example uses a multiplication operation of the type:

$$n \in \mathbb{N} \Rightarrow Unsigned^n \rightarrow Unsigned^n \rightarrow Unsigned^n,$$

where an overflow cannot be distinguished from the actual result. We use the term *basic arithmetic operation* for arithmetic integer operations that have the above type. Using the *option* type, we create an alternative multiplication operation, called *safe_mult* seen in Listing 1.5, which has the type:

$$n \in \mathbb{N} \Rightarrow Unsigned^n \rightarrow Unsigned^n \rightarrow option\ Unsigned^n$$

The *safe_mult* operation returns *None* in the case of an integer overflow and *Some(A)* otherwise. Now, the question is: *How are both cases explicitly distinguished?* We take a look at the case where an overflow occurs to answer this question. Note that both a and b are of the type $Unsigned^n$ and $x \mapsto y$ donates: x is transformed to y. The function *max* returns the maximum representable value of a given data type.

$$a * b > max(a) \mapsto b \neq 0 \land a > max(a)/b$$

The condition on the left side (x) indicates the intuitive check of an overflow. If the result of a multiplication is larger than the maximum value of the integer type of the operand (max(a)) than, obviously, an overflow occurred in the multiplication. But, if we implement this using finite integer types this condition always evaluates to true, as by definition there is no larger value of a type than its maximum. For this reason, we need to transform the left side to the right side (y). The condition on the right side evaluates only to true in the case of an integer overflow in the multiplication. If the condition evaluates to false both operands can be multiplied safely. In order to avoid a *division-by-zero* error, we first ensure that b is not equal to zero.

By using the alternative *option* type definition, described above, and the transformed condition, we are able to implement a multiplication operation that detects an occurred overflow, as seen in Listing 1.5.

```
1
2 Definition safe_mult (a b : Unsigned32.int ) : option Unsigned32.int :=
3 if (b >? 0%unsigned32) && (a >? (Unsigned32.max_unsigned / b))
4   then None
5   else Some (a*b)
6 .
```

Listing 1.5. Definition of the *safe_mult* function in Gallina that detects a multiplication overflow for 32-bit unsigned values [5].

Like in the SystemC example, illustrated in Listing 1.2, our multiplication is defined for 32-bit unsigned values (*Unsigned32.int*). This type definition was implemented using the CompCert integer library. As seen in Listing 1.4, our function implementation returns *Some(a*b)* in the case no overflow occurs and *None* otherwise.

After the definition of the *safe_mult* function in Coq, a proof is needed that verifies that the definition satisfies its specification. This specification is formulated as theorems in Coq. Two theorems are formulated in order to proof the *safe_mult* definition: the detection of the occurred overflow and the returning of the result of the unsigned 32-bit multiplication operation if no overflow occurs. To verify this, we show that the multiplication defined for 32-bit unsigned values maps the multiplication for integer values ($\mathbb{Z}$) which is a subset of it, but detects the occurred overflow. Both theorems are shown Listing 1.6.

```
 1  Theorem detect_overflow :
 2    forall a b : Z,
 3    a <= Unsigned32.max_unsigned /\
 4    b <= Unsigned32.max_unsigned /\
 5    a * b > Unsigned32.max_unsigned <->
 6    safe_mult (Unsigned32.repr a) (Unsigned32.repr b) = None.
 7
 8  Theorem no_overflow :
 9    forall a b : Z,
10    a <= Unsigned32.max_unsigned /\
11    b <= Unsigned32.max_unsigned /\
12    a * b <= Unsigned32.max_unsigned <->
13    safe_mult (Unsigned32.repr a) (Unsigned32.repr b) =
14            Some ((Unsigned32.repr a) * (Unsigned32.repr b)).
```

Listing 1.6. Theorems specified Coq to verify that the *safe_mult* function detects the overflow correct and returns the result of the multiplication otherwise [5].

The theorem *detect_overflow* states: if the two values *a* and *b* of type *Z* are less than or equal to the maximum value of the unsigned 32-bit integer type (Unsigned32.max_unsigned) and their multiplication is greater than this value, *None* is returned. The function *Unsigned32.repr* comes from the CompCert Integer library and converts a value of type *Z* into a value of type *Unsigned32.int*. The theorem *no_overflow* states: if two values *a* and *b* of type *Z* are less than or equal to the maximum value and their multiplication is also less than or equal to the maximum value, *Some(A)* is returned. The arbitrary type *A* is in this case the type *Unsigned32.int*.

After specifying and verifying a safe multiplication integer operation, the *tick* function, described in Listing 1.1 has to be specified in Gallina. This specified function has also been changed to use the *safe_mult* function, specified above, as seen in Listing 1.7. Like for the SystemC model, seen in Listing 1.2, we specified an unsigned 32-bit integer value (Unsigned32.int), which was described using the CompCert integer library [19]. The specification of the *tick* function can be seen in Listing 1.7.

```
1  Definition switch (s : State) : State.
2
3  Definition tick (input : Unsigned32.int*Unsigned32.int*Unsigned32.int*States)
4    : option Unsigned32.int*State :=
5  match input with
6    | (counter, delay, cycleTime, state) =>
7      match safe_mult (delay −1%unsigned32) cycleTime with
8        | Some res => if counter <? res
9                      then (Some(counter + cycleTime), state)
10                     else (Some(1%unsigned32), switch state)
11       | _ => (None, state)
12    end
13 end.
```

Listing 1.7. Specification of the *tick* function in Gallina, which used the *safe_mult* function introduced in Listing 1.5.

Note that the *switch* function, seen in Fig. 1, has a different type in the Coq specification, shown below. Pure functional languages, such as Gallina, do not allow internal states, in contrast to a SysML specification. For this reason, the type of the *switch* function had to be changed. As this work considers the detection of arithmetic overflows and there are no arithmetic overflows involved in the state transitions of that function, we omit the function implementation.

Since the unsigned multiplication operation has semantically changed the question is: *How to handle the case where an overflow occurred?* The handling highly depends on the environment the traffic light controller runs in, e.g. return to a safe state or ignore the new configured delay. As this would be out of scope for this work, the *tick* function just returns an instance of the tuple *option Unsigned32.int*State*. The first value of the tuple contains an instance of the type *option Unsigned32.int*, while the second value of the tuple is the new state. This state can either be the same as the old one or be changed by the *switch* function. The overflow is not handled by this function directly, but is propagated to the calling function instead. The state remains unchanged in this case.

After defining the *tick* function in Gallina, the verification of the property is needed that the definition still satisfies the safety property, shown in Listing 1.3. This property had to be translated to Coq first. This transformation results in the definition of two theorems, which is shown in Listing 1.8. Theorem *safety_property_no_overflow* describes the case no overflow occurs and Theorem *safety_property_overflow* describes the case an overflow occurs. The verification of those theorems proves that the *tick* function either changes the *counter* or propagates the detected overflow.

```
1  Theorem safety_property_no_overflow:
2    forall counter counter' delay cycleTime res : Unsigned32.int,
3    forall s s' : State,
4    Some(res) = safe_mult delay cycleTime <->
5    tick (counter, delay, cycleTime, s) = (Some (counter'), s') /\
6    counter' = (delay−1) * cycleTime /\ counter' < res.
7
8  Theorem safety_property_overflow:
9    forall counter delay cycleTime : Unsigned32.int,
10   forall s : State,
11   None = safe_mult (delay −1) cycleTime <->
12   tick (counter, delay, cycleTime, s) = (None, s).
```

Listing 1.8. Theorem in Coq that represents the OCL safety property adapted to finite integer types.

The first theorem states: if no overflow occurred in the multiplication of *delay* and *cycleTime*, the tick function returns the new counter (*counter'*) and the new state (*s'*). Note that the new state might be the old state as it depends on a condition whether the state is changed or not, as seen in Listing 1.7. The new counter (*counter'*) is the result of the multiplication of *delay -1* and *cylceTime* and is less than *res*, which is essentially the safety property, shown in Listing 1.3.

The second theorem states: if the result of the safe multiplication of *delay -1* and *cycleTime* is *None* than the *tick* function returns *None* as well. The state remains unchanged in this case, as described above.

In this section, we illustrated how to specify a safe multiplication operation using *dependent types* in order to detect an overflow for the 32-bit unsigned values. This was the problem, we described in Sect. 2.2. The specification of the *tick* function, shown in Listing 1.1, was transformed into a Coq specification manually and it was verified that the safety property, shown in Listing 1.3 satisfies our specification, as seen in Listing 1.8. This shows that we have successfully addressed the problem of missing finite integer types at the specification level, as described in Sect. 2.

5   Extraction of the CλaSH Model

In this section, we describe how the specification in Gallina, described above, is translated to a CλaSH model and finally to an RTL implementation that can be synthesized on an FPGA.

To illustrate the extraction process from a specification to a model in the functional hardware description language CλaSH [1,18], we take a look at Coq's extended extraction process, proposed in this work [6]. The process allows the extraction of a specification in Gallina into an executable CλaSH model. The extraction is done by syntactical replacement, since Gallina is a functional specification language and follows the same semantic rules as functional programming languages, e.g. Haskell or OCaml. The extraction process has two different modes. The first mode is that it extracts everything that is related to the function that should be extracted, such as other called function or data types. The second mode is the replacement of functions and data types by their semantic equivalent representations in the target language. This mode is used to intrinsic functions or to replace constant functions that have a different syntax. For instance, the constant function *Unsigned32.max_unsigned* used in Listing 1.6 is replaced by $(2^{32}) - 1$ in the CλaSH model, as seen in Listing 1.9. The specification and verification of a behavior by a proof assistant and the extraction of this behavior afterwards to executable code is called *certified programming* [10].

CλaSH borrows its syntax and semantics from the functional programming language Haskell. Combinational circuits are described as recursive functions and synchronous sequential ones as a combination of these functions with a finite state machine, either as a Mealy machine or a Moore machine [1]. After the CλaSH model was extracted the final RTL (Register-Transfer-Level) implementation, e.g. in VHDL or Verilog, it can be synthesized automatically. The unique representation of hardware model and the structured communication between the components, ensured by the type system of CλaSH, allows the automatic analysis of models and the final synthesis into a low-level RTL implementation, e.g. VHDL or Verilog.

```
1  switch  ::  State  -> State
2
3  safe_mult  ::  (Unsigned  32)  -> (Unsigned  32)  -> CLaSH.Prelude.Maybe
4                 (Unsigned  32)
5  safe_mult  a  b  =
6    case  (CLaSH.Prelude.&&)  ((CLaSH.Prelude.>)  (b)  (0))
7                ((CLaSH.Prelude.>)  (a)  (((CLaSH.Prelude.div)  ((2^32)  -1)  b)))  of  {
8     CLaSH.Prelude.True  -> CLaSH.Prelude.Nothing ;
9     CLaSH.Prelude.False  -> CLaSH.Prelude.Just  ((CLaSH.Prelude.*)  a  b)}
10
11  tick  ::  ((,)  ((,)  ((,)  (Unsigned  32)  (Unsigned  32))  (Unsigned  32))  State)  ->
12            (,)  (CLaSH.Prelude.Maybe  (Unsigned  32))  State
13  tick  input  =
14    case  input  of  {
15      (,)  p  states  ->
16      case  p  of  {
17        (,)  p0  cycleTime  ->
18        case  p0  of  {
19          (,)  counter  delay  ->
20          case  safe_mult  ((CLaSH.Prelude.-)  delay  1)  cycleTime  of  {
21          CLaSH.Prelude.Just  res  ->
22            case  (CLaSH.Prelude.<)  counter  res  of  {
23            CLaSH.Prelude.True  -> (,)  (CLaSH.Prelude.Just
24            ((CLaSH.Prelude.+)  counter  1))  states ;
25            CLaSH.Prelude.False  -> (,)(CLaSH.Prelude.Just  1)  (switch  states)};
26          CLaSH.Prelude.Nothing  -> (,)CLaSH.Prelude.Nothing  states}}}}
```

Listing 1.9. Extracted CλaSH model of the *safe_mult* and *tick* function introduced in Sect. 1.5.

6 Overflow Detection Pattern

In this section, we propose a detection pattern that can be used to detect integer overflows in different arithmetic operations. The pattern defines a total function that distinguishes the result of the arithmetic operation from the overflow by the *option* type described in Sect. 4.1. The proposed detection pattern is shown in Listing 1.10.

The pattern requires two definitions. First, a data type that defines two constructors: *None* and *Some A*, where *A* is an arbitrary finite integer type. Second, a function of the type: $A \to A \to option\ A$. This function takes two arguments of the integer type A and returns a value of the previous defined *option* type. Where *None* indicates the overflow and *Some a* indicates the result of the operation that was executed. This case analysis is made by a condition (overflowDetected), e.g. by the one defined in Sect. 4.1 for the multiplication of unsigned 32-bit values.

```
1  data  option  A  =  None  |  Some  A
2
3  f  :  A  →  A  →  option  A
4  f  x  y  =  if  <overflowDetected>  x  y
5             then  None
6             else  Some(x  <operation>  y)
```

Listing 1.10. Proposed overflow detection pattern [5].

The specified function f is used to replace the basic arithmetic operation, e.g. unsigned multiplication, that is not able to distinguish an overflow from the correct result. In order to verify that function f distinguishes the overflow from the correct result, two theorems have to be proven. A proof of the first theorem, as can be seen in Theorem 1, verifies that for all inputs which cause an overflow for the performed arithmetic operation *None* is returned.

Theorem 1 (Detect Overflow in Integer Arithmetic Operation). $\forall x, y$ $\in A$, where A is an arbitrary finite integer type.

$$< overflowDetected> \; x \; y \iff f \; x \; y \; = \; None$$

A proof of the second theorem, as can be seen in Theorem 2, verifies that for all inputs that do not cause an overflow for the performed arithmetic operation the result of this operation is returned.

Theorem 2 (No Overflow in Arithmetic Integer Operation). $\forall x, y \in A$, where A is an arbitrary finite integer type.

$$not \; (< overflowDetected> \; x \; y) \iff f \; x \; y \; = \; Some \; (x \; <operation> \; y)$$

Now, that we have defined the overflow detection pattern, one question remains: *Is this pattern always necessary?*

In the following, we answer this question and explain in which cases it is necessary and in which one it is not. If we look at the general behavior of arithmetic integer operations, an overflow might always occur. The result of an arithmetic operation can potentially be larger than its finite integer type is able to represent. This might lead to an unintended wrap-around behavior, as explained in Sect. 2.2. So in general, the overflow detection pattern, described above, should be applied.

However, there are cases where this pattern can be avoided. First, it has to be verified that the arithmetic operation that is applied on both operands never causes an overflow. The theorem that has to be proven can be seen in Theorem 3.

Theorem 3. $\forall x, y \in A'$, where $A' \subset A$ and A is an arbitrary finite integer type.

$$f \; x \; y \; = \; Some(x \; <operation> \; y)$$

If and only if this theorem holds, then there is no need to replace the basic arithmetic operation with the one defined by f. The general steps for the proposed pattern are the following: first, define the function f for the desired integer type and operation, second, prove the above theorem, to verify that the chosen subset of values is never too large to cause an overflow. As described above, this is not the case in general, but might be in particular.

Now, that we have the proof, that the arithmetic operation defined by function f never returns an overflow, the question is: *Can this proof be used to replace function f in a specification by its corresponding basic arithmetic operation automatically?*

To answer this question, we take a look again at the extraction feature of Coq. As mentioned above, Coq provides the specification language Gallina and a tactic language for property proving. The extraction process only extracts the functional behavior of a specification written in Gallina to an executable target language. Theorems and Lemmas, which state propositions, are ignored during this process, as they do not have a semantic equivalent representation in the target language.

Thus, it is not possible to automatically replace the defined function f by its corresponding basic integer operation using a proof without changing Coq's entire extraction process. Furthermore, as both functions are semantically not equivalent such a replacement would effect the entire specification recursively.

As discussed above, the automation process is quite challenging as the type of function f would change from $A \rightarrow A \rightarrow option\ A$ to $A \rightarrow A \rightarrow A$ what recursively effects the entire specification. A more suitable way is to propagate the value $Some\ A$ of function f through the specification. This avoids the recursive changing of all functions depending on f manually as the type of function f remains the same.

In summary, if and only if Theorem 3 holds, we have a proof that the specification of function f can be changed to just return $Some(x < operation > y)$ as no overflow occurs.

6.1 Closure of Functions

As we propose an overflow detection pattern in this work that has the function type $A \rightarrow A \rightarrow option\ A$, functions that implement this pattern are no longer closed. A set is called closed under an operation if an operation performed on members of a set always produce a member of that set. For this reason, it is not possible to cascade these functions, e.g. *safe_mult (safe_mult 3 4) 5*. In order to address this problem we implement the *option* monad in Coq. Monads come from the mathematical field of category theory and model computations [25]. It is used as a design pattern in functional languages and represents a specific form of computation. Analog to the implementations of monads in other functional languages, e.g. Ocaml, two functions were implemented, seen in Listing 1.11.

Since the cascading of these functions might not always be wanted, we propose this monad instead of changing the proposed pattern, seen in Listing 1.10. This allows a greater flexibility between both use cases.

```
1  Definition ret {A : Type} (x : A) : option A := Some x.
2
3  Definition bind {A : Type} (f : A -> A -> option A) (x y: option A)
4      : option A :=
5    match (x, y) with
6      | (Some x', Some y') => f x' y'
7      | (_,_) => None
8    end.
```

Listing 1.11. Definition of the option monad operations.

The *option* monad contains two functions: *ret* and *bind*. The *ret* function takes an argument of type a and transforms it into a value of the type *option* A. The *bind* function takes a function of the proposed pattern type (f) and two arguments of the type *option* A (x and y). If both arguments contain a value of the type A, the function f is called with these values. Otherwise, *None* is returned.

The *option* monad applies to all functions that require two arguments and return the *option* type. Since it is not restricted to one dedicated type, it can be used for all functions that implement the proposed overflow detection pattern, seen in Listing 1.10. To verify the correct behavior of the *bind* function, two theorems were proved.

```
1  Theorem fIfSome.:
2    forall (A : Type),
3    forall f : (A -> A -> option A),
4    forall x y : option A,
5    forall x' y' : A,
6    x = Some (x') /\ y = Some (y') -> bind f x y = f x' y'.
```

Listing 1.12. Theorem that verifies that the function f is only called by the *bind* function if both arguments are of type A.

The first theorem, seen in Listing 1.12, verifies that if both arguments x and y contain values of type A (x' and y') then the *bind* function calls the function f with these two values, as seen in Listing 1.12. This theorem verifies that only in the case were both arguments for f contain values this function is called.

The second theorem, seen in Listing 1.13, verifies that if either the first argument of the function f (x) or the second (y) is *None* the *bind* function returns *None*, as seen in Listing 1.13. This theorem verifies that the function f is not called with invalid values (*None*).

```
1  Theorem noneIfNone:
2    forall (A : Type),
3    forall f : (A -> A -> option A),
4    forall x y : option A,
5    x = None \/ y = None -> bind f x y = None.
```

Listing 1.13. Theorem that verifies that in the case of invalid arguments for function f *None* is returned by the *bind* function.

The *option* monad closes the operations that implement the proposed overflow detection pattern, which allows the cascading of these functions. e.g. *bind safe_mult (bind safe_mult (ret 3) (ret 4)) (ret 5)*. The cascading of operations enables the formulation of more complex operations based on the application of the basic arithmetic operations. The *bind* function propagates an occurred overflow through the cascaded operations. At the end of the calculation it can be evaluated whether the result is correct or if there was an overflow in one of the operations.

7 Evaluation

In this section, we evaluate the hardware design approach proposed in this work. The foundation of this evaluation is a comparison of basic arithmetic integer operations with their corresponding overflow detecting operations regarding their impact of the speed and consumed space. To determine these values the operations were specified for both signed and unsigned integer operations and used by the traffic light controller, seen in Sect. 4.1. The resulting specification was synthesized on an FPGA using the synthesize process introduced in this work [6].

7.1 Integer Overflow Detection Implementations

This section introduces the different implementations of the overflow detecting arithmetic integer operations used for the evaluation. All implementations follow the pattern introduced in Sect. 6.

```
1  Definition safe_add_unsigned (a b : Unsigned32.int) : option Unsigned32.int :=
2    if a >? (Unsigned32.max_unsigned − b)
3      then None
4      else Some (a+b).
```

Listing 1.14. Definition of the *safe_add_unsigned* function in Gallina that detects an overflow in the addition operation for unsigned 32-bit values.

Listing 1.14 shows the implementation that detects an overflow in the addition operation of two unsigned 32-bit values. The condition that checks whether an overflow occurs or not, follows the transformation pattern, introduced in Sect. 4.1.

Listing 1.15 shows the implementation that detects an overflow for signed 32-bit values. To detect the overflow there are multiple conditions needed, to cover all possible overflow cases. Since signed integer values are negative or positive the *Signed32.min_signed* function determines the minimum representable value of the *Signed32* type and the *Signed32.max_signed* function the maximum representable value.

```
1   Definition safe_mult_signed (a b : Signed32.int) : option Signed32.int :=
2     if (a >? 0%signed32) &&
3        (b >? 0%signed32) &&
4        (a >? (Signed32.max_signed / b))
5       then None
6       else if (a >? 0%signed32) &&
7               (b <? 0) &&
8               (a <? (signed32.min_signed / b))
9         then None
10        else if (a <? 0%signed32) &&
11                (b >? 0%signed32) &&
12                (a <? (Signed32.min_signed / b))
13         then None
14         else if (a <? 0%signed32) &&
15                 (b <? 0%signed32) &&
16                 (a >? Signed32.max_signed / b)
17           then None
18           else Some(a*b).
```

Listing 1.15. Definition of the *safe_mult_signed* function in Coq that detects an overflow in the multiplication operation for signed 32 bit values.

Listing 1.16 shows the implementation that detects an overflow in the addition of two signed 32-bit values. As seen in the previous overflow detection implementations the *Signed32.max_signed* function determines the maximum value and the *Signed32.min_signed* function the minimum value.

```
1  Definition safe_add_signed (a b : Signed32.int ) : option Signed32.int :=
2    if (a >? 0%signed32) &&
3       (b >? 0%signed32) &&
4       (a >? (Signed32.max_signed − b))
5    then None
6    else if (a <? 0%signed32) &&
7            (b <? 0%signed32) &&
8            (a <? (Signed32.min_signed −b))
9    then None
10   else Some (a+b).
```

Listing 1.16. Definition of the *safe_add_signed* function in Gallina that detects an overflow on the multiplication operation for signed 32 bit values.

7.2   Comparison of Integer Arithmetic Operations

In this section, we compare the different arithmetic integer overflow detection implementations proposed in this work regarding their consumed space in LUTs and registers and maximum clock frequency. The foundation for this comparison is the implementation of the traffic light controller, shown in Sect. 4.1, which was specified in Gallina and synthesized on an FPGA. The comparison is between the specified controller with the basic arithmetic operations and their corresponding overflow detecting operations, as seen in Table 1.

Table 1. Evaluation by comparing the consumed space in LUTs and registers and the maximum clock frequency (F_{max}) for signed 32 and unsigned 32 integer operations used by the traffic light controller, described in Sect. 4.1. The *basic operation* column contains the values for the basic arithmetic operations, while the *overflow detection* column contains the values for the arithmetic operations introduced in Sect. 4.1 and Sect. 7.1.

Arithmetic operation	Basic operation		Overflow detection	
	LUTs/Registers	F_{max}	LUTs/Registers	F_{max}
Unsigned multiplication	92/36	72.20 MHz	670/36	65.51 MHz
Unsigned addition	81/36	111.76 MHz	112/36	109.57 MHz
Signed multiplication	112/36	68.19 MHz	122/36	68.84 MHz
Signed addition	81/36	119.82 MHz	148/36	109.24 MHz

Consumed space and maximum clock frequency synthesized for the Cyclone V family using the Quartus Prime tool chain version 18.1.0.

The values in Table 1 cannot necessarily be seen as fixed values, but as a relation between the synthesized traffic light controller specification that uses the basic arithmetic integer operations and the one using the detecting overflow operations. The concrete values highly depend on the FPGA a design is synthesized for. FPGAs are often optimized for a certain purpose, e.g. speed or larger space. As seen in the table above, the consumed space in the form of LUTs and registers differs slightly, except for the unsigned multiplication operation, which we discuss in a moment. The same goes for the maximum clock frequency that has a maximum 10 MHz for the signed addition operation.

The overflow detecting unsigned multiplication operation has a significantly larger amount of LUTs, as during the synthesis process the *lpm divide* megafunction is used. Megafunctions are programmable logic devices (PLD) that describe a certain functionality, e.g. integer multiplication. These functional blocks are ready-made, pre-tested and augment hardware designs so the functionality has not to be implemented again. For unsigned values Quartus Prime includes the *lpm divide* block automatically while for signed integer division it does not. This decision is based on the analysis of the RTL code. For this reason, the amount of LUTs is significantly higher.

8 Discussion

In this section we discuss the proposed overflow detection pattern and the results of the evaluation.

The detection pattern, shown in Sect. 6, leads to arithmetic functions that are no longer closed, since the type of the input values is no longer the type of the output values. This prevents the cascading of these operations, which is possible with their corresponding basic arithmetic operations. We addressed this issue by providing an *option* monad, as seen in Sect. 6.1. This monad closes the operations implementing the proposed arithmetic overflow detection pattern. The closure of functions enables the cascading of those operations which results in the description of more complex calculations similar to the cascading of basic arithmetic operations.

According to the results of the evaluation, the impact on the speed and consumed space by replacing the basic integer arithmetic operations with the corresponding ones that detects the overflow depends on the used operation and the integer type. The difference between the basic arithmetic operations and their corresponding overflow detecting operations for unsigned addition and signed multiplication is even negligible.

In general, this opens a trade-off between safety oriented and performance oriented hardware designs. The additional overflow checks clearly have an impact either on the consumed space or on the maximum clock frequency. But, it depends on the concrete hardware design whether the safety aspect is important enough to except this impact or not. This might not always be the case and the concrete values regarding the speed and consumed space highly depends on the chosen FPGA. Note that in larger hardware designs the arithmetic integer operations represent only a small part of the entire functionality. The impact of the overflow detecting arithmetic operations compared with their corresponding basic arithmetic operations become negligible.

In general, our discussion shows that the overflow detection pattern proposed in this work is applicable. The maximum frequency and the consumed space for the overflow detecting arithmetic operations are slightly slower or even negligible. The only exception is the overflow detecting unsigned multiplication operation, but the Quartus Prime synthesis tool chooses to use the *lpm divide* megafunction automatically during the synthesis process which was omitted for the other operations. But, even in this case, the difference regarding the maximum clock frequency is only slightly slower than in the other implementations used for the evaluation.

9   Conclusion

In this work, the *semantic gap* between the infinite integer types of a SysML/OCL specification and the finite integer types of SystemC was addressed. The issue of this *semantic gap* might lead to arithmetic overflows in the SystemC model which are unknown in the specification, as explained in Sect. 2.2. This gap motivates our work, and we addressed it by the proposal of an alternative approach which extends the work [5] already published by the authors.

We use the proof assistant Coq [4,10] in combination with the CompCert integer library [19] to close this gap. The CompCert Integer library describes both signed and unsigned finite integer types of arbitrary sizes as *dependent types* [7,17]. We utilized this library to describe finite integer types in Coq. This description enables the specification of arithmetic integer operations that verifiable detect overflows, as described in Sect. 4. These descriptions result in a generalizable pattern for detecting overflows in arithmetic integer operations. Furthermore, we provide a method to close the functions that implements the proposed detection pattern, as described in Sect. 6. This allows the cascading of operations implementing the proposed overflow detection pattern, analog to their corresponding basic arithmetic operations to describe more complex calculations.

We evaluated the proposed overflow detection pattern by comparing basic arithmetic operations with their corresponding overflow detecting operations in terms of their maximum clock frequency and consumed space. These values were gathered from an FPGA synthesis process, explained in Sect. 7, which uses the synthesize process introduced in this work [6]. This evaluation opens a trade-off between safety oriented and performance oriented hardware designs, as additional safety checks clearly have an impact on the consumed space and maximum clock frequency, but the impact is sporadically negligible. For this reason, we evaluated the proposed approach to address the *semantic gap* between infinite and finite integer types as promising.

References

1. CλaSH: Structural Descriptions of Synchronous Hardware Using Haskell (2010)
2. Accellera: Accellera Systems Initiative Inc. SystemC Synthesizable Subset (Version 1.5.7) (2016)
3. Arnout, G.: Systemc standard. In: Asia and South Pacific Design Automation Conference (ASP-DAC), pp. 573–578 (2000)
4. Bertot, Y., Castéran, P.: Interactive Theorem Proving and Program Development - Coq'Art: The Calculus of Inductive Constructions. Texts in Theoretical Computer Science. An EATCS Series, Springer (2004). https://doi.org/10.1007/978-3-662-07964-5
5. Bornebusch, F., Lüth, C., Wille, R., Drechsler, R.: Integer overflow detection in hardware designs at the specification level. In: 8th International Conference on Model-Driven Engineering and Software Development (MODELSWARD) (2020)
6. Bornebusch, F., Lüth, C., Wille, R., Drechsler, R.: Towards automatic hardware synthesis from formal specification to implementation. In: Asia and South Pacific Design Automation Conference (ASP-DAC) (2020)

7. Brady, E., McKinna, J., Hammond, K.: Constructing correct circuits: verification of functional aspects of hardware specifications with dependent types. In: Trends in Functional Programming (TFP), pp. 159–176 (2007)
8. Brucker, A.D., Wolff, B.: The HOL-OCL book. Technical Report 525, ETH Zurich (2006)
9. Cabot, J., Clarisó, R., Riera, D.: Verification of UML/OCL class diagrams using constraint programming. In: First International Conference on Software Testing Verification and Validation, ICST, pp. 73–80 (2008)
10. Chlipala, A.: Certified Programming with Dependent Types - A Pragmatic Introduction to the Coq Proof Assistant. MIT Press, Cambridge (2013)
11. Coker, Z., Hafiz, M.: Program transformations to fix C integers. In: 35th International Conference on Software Engineering, ICSE 2013, San Francisco, CA, USA, 18–26 May 2013, pp. 792–801 (2013)
12. Cousot, P.: Formal verification by abstract interpretation. In: NASA Formal Methods - International Symposium, NFM, pp. 3–7 (2012)
13. Cousot, P., et al.: The astreé analyzer. In: European Symposium on Programming, pp. 21–30 (2005)
14. Cuoq, P., Kirchner, F., Kosmatov, N., Prevosto, V., Signoles, J., Yakobowski, B.: Frama-C - a software analysis perspective. In: International Conference on Software Engineering and Formal Methods, pp. 233–247 (2012)
15. Dietz, W., Li, P., Regehr, J., Adve, V.S.: Understanding integer overflow in C/C++. ACM Trans. Softw. Eng. Methodol. **25**(1), 1–29 (2015)
16. Fähndrich, M., Logozzo, F.: Static contract checking with abstract interpretation. In: International Conference on Formal Verification of Object-Oriented Software, pp. 10–30 (2010)
17. Hanna, F.K., Daeche, N.: Dependent types and formal synthesis (1992)
18. Kuper, J., Baaij, C., Kooijman, M.: Exercises in architecture specification using cλash. In: Forum on Specification and Design Languages (FDL) (2010)
19. Leroy, X., Blazy, S., Kästner, D., Schommer, B., Pister, M., Ferdinand, C.: Compcert - a formally verified optimizing compiler. In: Embedded Real Time Software and Systems (ERTS) (2016)
20. Necula, G.C., McPeak, S., Rahul, S.P., Weimer, W.: CIL: intermediate language and tools for analysis and transformation of C programs. In: European Joint Conferences on Theorey and & Practice of Software, pp. 213–228 (2002)
21. OMG: Object Management Group Object Constraint Language (OCL) (Version 2.4) (2014)
22. OMG: Open Management Group System Modeling Language (SysML) (Version 1.6) (2019)
23. Przigoda, N., Wille, R., Drechsler, R.: Analyzing inconsistencies in UML/OCL models. J. Circ. Syst. Comput. **25**(3), 1640021 (2016)
24. Takach, A.: High-level synthesis: status, trends, and future directions. IEEE Des. Test **33**(3), 116–124 (2016)
25. Wadler, P.: Monads for functional programming. In: Jeuring, J., Meijer, E. (eds.) Advanced Functional Programming, First International Spring School on Advanced Functional Programming Techniques, Båstad, Sweden, 24–30 May 1995, Tutorial Text. Lecture Notes in Computer Science, vol. 925, pp. 24–52 (1995)
26. Weilkiens, T.: Systems Engineering with SysML / UML - Modeling, Analysis. Design. Morgan Kaufmann, Burlington (2007)

Systematic Synthesis of Energy-Aware Timing Models in Automotive Software Systems

Padma Iyenghar[(✉)]

Software Engineering Research Group, University of Osnabrueck, Osnabrück, Germany
piyengha@uos.de

Abstract. In automotive embedded software, functions have several performance requirements such as timing, energy, safety and reliability. For such complex software architectures, an early evaluation and decision on the best set of performance configuration (e.g. timing vs energy trade-offs) could save costly corrections of potential errors in the design. For example, appropriate performance analysis workflows and frameworks if employed already during early design stages, allow us to understand the performance aspects and behavior of the system depending on software and hardware characteristics. The main input required for such analysis is the performance-analysis model based on the underlying design model. In this context, this chapter presents a workflow for synthesis of energy-aware timing analysis models for AUTOSAR-based embedded software systems developed using the Unified Modeling Language (UML)/Systems Modeling Language (SysML) domains. A prototype of the model transformations for the synthesis of the energy-aware timing models and its evaluation in an automotive use case is presented.

Keywords: Energy-aware timing model · AUTOSAR · Unified modeling language (UML) · Synthesis · Meta-model · Model transformation

1 Introduction

The Automotive Open System ARchitecture (AUTOSAR) [3] has been created as a worldwide development partnership of vehicle manufacturers, suppliers, service providers and companies from the automotive electronics, semiconductor and software industry. To achieve the technical goals of modularity, scalability, transferability, and function reusability, AUTOSAR provides a common software infrastructure based on standardized interfaces for the different layers [37]. While doing so, AUTOSAR employs component-based software architecture, for the design and implementation of automotive software systems. With the standardized layer between application software and the hardware of an Electronic Control Unit (ECU)[1], the software is largely independent from any chosen micro controller and car manufacturer, making it reusable for several individual ECU systems.

---

[1] An embedded system that controls one or more of the electrical systems or subsystems in a vehicle.

© Springer Nature Switzerland AG 2021
S. Hammoudi et al. (Eds.): MODELSWARD 2020, CCIS 1361, pp. 49–73, 2021.
https://doi.org/10.1007/978-3-030-67445-8_3

At this juncture, the automotive industry not only continues to expand rapidly but also is becoming increasingly complex and heterogeneous with the adoption of multi and many-core processors systems. Further, in automotive embedded architectures, functions have several performance requirements such as timing and energy. For such complex software/system architectures, an early evaluation and decision on the best set of performance configuration (e.g. timing, timing vs energy trade-offs), could save costly corrections of potential errors in the design. For example, appropriate performance analysis workflows and frameworks if employed already during early design stages, allow us to understand the performance aspects and behavior of the system depending on software and hardware characteristics. Further, they help to explore different design architectural choices and quantitatively evaluate their implications on system performance.

On the other hand, the scientific effort provided by academic institutions often does not match the needs of the industry as the proposed solutions fail to consider the state-of-the-practice challenges [36]. Some emerging challenges in the context of performance analysis are, integrating (specification/modeling) performance aspects in the early design stage, an automated synthesis of performance models (e.g. timing, reliability, safety, energy) and early model-based performance analyses in modeling tools or specialized performance analyses tools. In this context, this chapter contributes to the particular aspect of early model-based synthesis of energy-aware timing models in AUTOSAR-based embedded software systems modeled using UML/SysML domain.

1.1 State-of-the Practice by Automotive Organizations

In the race to provide model-based tool support (e.g. architecture design, automatic code generation) for AUTOSAR-based Embedded Software Engineering (ESE) in the Unified Modeling language (UML) [44]/Systems Modeling Language (SysML) [41] domain, UML tools such as Enterprise architect (EA) [8] and IBM Rhapsody Developer [17] emerged as front runners. For instance, AUTOSAR-related UML/SysML profiles for the architectural description of an AUTOSAR model that uses the native AUTOSAR concepts is supported by Rhapsody and EA. At this juncture, a majority of the state-of-the-practice in the automotive industry is that, UML is used at higher abstraction levels, for instance, to create descriptive UML models that describe the overall software and system architecture.

The descriptive models produced in the UML/SysML domain, are then used for various purposes such as (a) to produce more fine grained architecture of the prescriptive models (e.g. using Simulink) and (b) debugging using model execution frameworks[2] in the context of realistic mock-ups of the intended user interface. On the other hand, the automotive software is loaded with numerous non-functional requirements. During the software architecture design of such systems, several non-functional parameters need to be taken into consideration, optimized and fine tuned. Some examples are, studying timing versus energy trade-offs and minimizing CPU load vs meeting safety goals. To achieve this, the non-functional properties such as timing, energy and safety need to be specified in the UML/SysML-based early design model. With this annotated design

---

[2] https://www.nomagic.com/product-addons/magicdraw-addons/cameo-simulation-toolkit.

model as input, a performance analysis model (such as timing/energy/safety model) needs to be synthesized. Such an analysis model can then be used for early performance validation (such as timing analysis in specialized timing analysis tool [11]) and trade-off studies.

1.2 Relation to Author's Previous Work and Novel Contributions

In the above context, a systematic series of steps towards extraction and synthesis of timing analysis models in AUTOSAR-based embedded system design models which are developed in UML tools has been presented in [22]. In this book chapter, the work in [22] is extended and the following novel contributions are presented.

- Extension of the framework introduced in [22] to include energy properties in the AUTOSAR-design model (developed in UML/SysML tools) with the help of stereotypes from the MARTE profile [26].
- Mapping of the energy properties to a generic timing-energy meta model.
- A prototype implementation of the model transformations using Atlas Transformation Language (ATL) [2] in Eclipse Modeling Framework (EMF) [7] for synthesis of energy-aware timing analysis model from AUTOSAR-based design model.
- Evaluation of the above prototype in a practical automotive use case (introduced in [22]).

In the remainder of this paper, background and related work is presented in Sect. 2. The proposed approach for synthesis of energy-aware timing analysis model for AUTOSAR-based design model developed in UML/SysML domain is presented in Sect. 3. An experimental evaluation in an automotive case study is presented in Sect. 4. Section 5 concludes the paper.

2 Background and Related Work

In this section, background and related work pertaining to general modeling options for automotive embedded software systems is presented in Sect. 2.1. In Sect. 2.2, related work on model-based timing and energy specifications and a brief background on AUTOSAR-TE and the MARTE profile are provided. In Sect. 2.3, related work and background on model-based timing and energy analysis is presented.

2.1 Modeling Automotive Embedded Software Systems

Automotive embedded software applications are different than typical embedded software applications that we find on smart devices such as phones, gadgets, etc. In the automotive applications, real-time complex interactions across multiple-systems such as braking, steering, suspension, power-train, body-electronics, etc. are extremely crucial. A single feature might need interactions across 20 or more automotive embedded software applications spread across multiple ECU connected over multiple networking protocols. No single automotive embedded software application performs on its own, it is always part of a much bigger system of systems [27]. To address the increasing complexity in development of such systems, Model Driven Development (MDD) [31], is considered as the next paradigm shift. In MDD, the requirements are specified as models at a higher abstraction level (e.g. using UML diagrams). They are then refined, starting from higher and moving to lower levels of abstraction, via model transformations.

Further, MDD methodology also provides support for analysis of non-functional properties such as timing and reliability parameters. For instance, UML supports generic system and software modeling and also UML profiles for specific aspects such as quality analysis. Some examples of employing UML for MDD and examining quality properties such as timing, energy and reliability are available in [21,23,35].

Matlab/Simulink (M/S) [28] is a popular example for a modeling tool with non-UML modeling language, which is established in the industry, including the automotive domain [10]. It is primarily employed for simulation studies and model-based development of control loops. Further, the Rubus Component Model (RCM) [5] and EAST-ADL are among other established solutions used within the vehicular domain.

AUTOSAR Framework. A promising approach is the standardization of the software architecture used in ECU development [29]. A comprehensive and well- established solution used in the automotive sector is the AUTOSAR standard [3]. It emphasizes to shift the ECU development from an ECU-centric approach to a functionality-based approach. AUTOSAR uses a component-based software architecture, with central modeling elements called *Software Components* (SWCs or SW-Cs). The SWCs describe a completed, self-contained set of functionality. The AUTOSAR methodology describes various steps, namely, *System configuration, ECU configuration and component implementation* involved in the development process. It also describes the artifacts created and interchanged between the steps. In between these steps, the ARXML file format [3] is used for the exchange of development artifacts, which is an XML-based file format. The functionality-based approach aims to specify the functions of the complete vehicle first in the so-called *system configuration*, and afterwards extract specifications for the suppliers to implement an ECU. This way, the automotive software can be interchanged on a function level instead of the ECU level, which increases its reusability.

The various components of the AUTOSAR framework are illustrated together with the mapping of software components to ECUs, in the system configuration step, in Fig. 1. The software components (seen at the top of Fig. 1, e.g., *SW-C1*) are used to structure the AUTOSAR model and group functionality into individual components. These components can be connected together, oblivious of the hardware they will be running on. This is handled by the *Virtual Function Bus* (VFB), which provides an abstraction layer for the SWC to SWC communication. Components distributed over different ECUs however, may use the network bus for communication. This is determined automatically by the *Run-Time Environment* (RTE), which is a communication interface for the software components. The lower part of the Fig. 1 represents the mapping of ECUs to SW-Cs in the system configuration step. Here, the ECUs 1, 2..n are seen communicating over a network bus (e.g. FlexRay, CAN). In each ECU (e.g. ECU 1 in lower part of Fig. 1), the RTE provides interfaces between SW-Cs (e.g. AUTOSAR

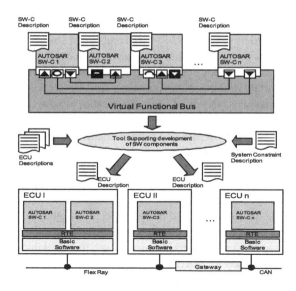

Fig. 1. Mapping of software components to ECUs [3,22].

SW-C 1 and AUTOSAR SW-C 2 in ECU 1) and between SW-C and basic software (BSW). Further it provides the BSW services (as API abstraction) to SW-C.

The underlying software functions which implement the given requirements are contained inside the SW-Cs. These are later on implemented manually by the software developers. The RTE and *Basic Software* (BSW) which are provided by third-party AUTOSAR software vendors are at the disposal of the developer for communication and hardware abstraction. The inner functionality of the application and sensor/actuator SWCs is defined in *Internal Behavior* elements. They encapsulate *Runnable Entities*, which correspond to atomic functions on the code level that are implemented later in the development process. The communication between the SWCs is modeled by using communication ports. In this paper, we deal with the system configuration step and specification of timing and energy properties in the SW-Cs.

2.2 Model-Based Timing Specification

Alternatives for specifying timing behavior in the UML domain have been introduced more than a decade ago [31]. Modeling and Analysis of Real-Time and Embedded Systems (MARTE) [26] is a standardized UML profile, which extends UML and provides support for modeling the platform, software and hardware aspects of an application. There are several approaches in the direction of model-based timing specification in the literature [1,20,33]. But, modeling constraints using AUTOSAR-TE and an automated extraction of timing parameters, synthesis of an analysis model and analysis of the timing analysis model in a state-of-the-art timing analysis tool [11], is missing. In this direction, a workflow for early synthesis of timing models in AUTOSAR-based automotive embedded software systems has been proposed by the author in [22]. In this book chapter, the work in [22] is extended. Thereby, a workflow for synthesis of energy-aware timing models in AUTOSAR-based embedded software developed using UML/SysML domains is presented in this paper along with experimental evaluation.

There are also several modeling alternatives in non-UML domains such as SystemC [4], Event-B[3] and Matlab/Simulink [28] to name a few. Unlike UML-based profiles, support for specification and analysis of timing properties is very limited in SystemC and Event-B. The newly introduced *System Composer* toolbox in M/S [42] provides system engineering capabilities in M/S. It supports creation of custom-defined profiles and custom-defined scripts to analyze the models based on the stereotype values as in the case of UML profile mechanisms and tools. However, there are no studies available yet on the usage of the new features in M/S for energy-aware timing analysis of automotive embedded software models.

Further, several modeling languages, domain-specific languages and a number of generic approaches have emerged that include timing behavior. *PTIDES* [6,45] and *Giotto* [15] provide a good basis for defining an approach to model timing requirements. However, these are often used to analyze system behavior rather than specification of timing properties. In the following a brief background on AUTOSAR-TE and MARTE are provided as they are used in this paper to annotate the AUTOSAR design model with timing and energy properties respectively.

AUTOSAR-Timing Extensions (TE). The AUTOSAR-Timing Extensions (TE) meta-model is separate from the AUTOSAR metamodel, in order to leave the option whether to provide timing specifications or not. They feature an event-based model for the description of the software's temporal behavior and can be defined on top of a system architecture. The AUTOSAR release with timing extensions and own timing model, finds extensive usage in the automotive industry. This is supported by studies including [9,13,34].

The TE metamodel (Fig. 2) provides five different views for timing specification, depending on what kind of timing behavior of the AUTOSAR model is described [3]. The five views are *VfbTiming*, *SwcTiming*, *SystemTiming*, *BswModuleTiming* and *EcuTiming*. In the experimental evaluation, the *SwcTiming* view is employed, as in the system configuration step and timing specification step the SWCs are employed (cf. Sect. 2.1). *SwcTiming* view describes the internal behavior timing of software components. Further explanation of AUTOSAR methodology and AUTOSAR-TE are not provided here because of space limitations (interested readers are referred to [3]).

MARTE Profile. The MARTE profile [26] standardized by the OMG [31] is primarily aimed at modeling and analysis of real time and embedded systems. It is a popular standard which introduces a domain view for time modeling and defines standard UML elements to express timing concepts of real time and embedded systems. MARTE also enhances the UML to support value units with the aid of a Value Specification Language (VSL). Further, the profile extends the UML to be able to model a platform, on which a software application is executed and how the deployment of the software to the platform

---

[3] http://www.event-b.org/index.html.

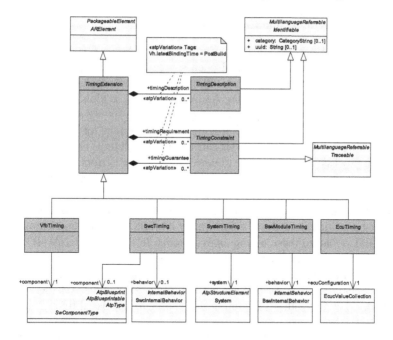

Fig. 2. Overview of AUTOSAR Timing Extensions (TE) metamodel [3].

is made. When modeling a platform, there are (among others) elements for defining processors, schedulers and threads.

In the context of the work presented in this paper, a decision on the usage of standardized profiles such as MARTE for practical scenarios relies on important aspects, among others, such as (1) ease of use of standardized mechanisms (2) support for modeling data, using a specific mechanism, which is required for a basic analysis (e.g. timing, energy) and (3) support for employing a standardized mechanism in a UML modeling tool. But, MARTE is an exhaustive profile with hundreds of stereotypes for annotating aspects pertaining to real-time and embedded software and hardware. Therefore an alternative is to make use of a custom-defined UML with only a handful of elements for defining time and energy properties, which may be required for a first-hand energy-aware scheduling analysis.

Within the scope of this work, on investigating the available alternatives for modeling the energy properties in UML/SysML tools, it was found that this can be achieved with the existing stereotypes of the MARTE profile. Moreover, the MARTE profile is readily available as a profile-plug-in in UML/SysML modeling tools such as Rhapsody [17], EA [8] and Papyrus [32]. Therefore, it is decided to use the existing features in standardized profiles such as MARTE, rather than reinventing the wheel for non-functional properties specification employing UML (e.g. by developing a new custom-defined profile). Further, the new proposals for UML profiles in related work (such as [12]) indicate that, they are neither open source nor available as a model-based plug-in. It is clear that such new proposals have negligible reuse potential.

2.3   Model-Based Timing and Energy Analysis

The specified timing behavior in the design model can be analyzed using dedicated timing analysis tools. There are several open source tools such as Cheddar [40] and MAST [14]. Some popular proprietary timing analysis tools include chronSIM [19], Gliwa T1. timing suite [11] and Timing Architect [43]. These tools are independent of the modeling languages used. Therefore, they require the timing specifications to be in a particular format, although some provide import functions for common modeling languages. However, the timing analysis carried out in such tools are very late it in the development process. It is imperative to note that the design errors realised from such late timing analysis would be costly to fix at a later development stage. Hence, an early model-based timing analysis is necessary to overcome this drawback.

On the other hand, there is no tool support for automated synthesis and export of AUTOSAR-based timing analysis model (from AUTOSAR-based application design model in UML tools) to these timing analysis tools. In the literature, AUTOSAR-TE were used for a model-based timing analysis in works such as [24] and [38]. Further, a review of the literature shows that there is no systematic model-based approach for timing or energy analysis of AUTOSAR-based systems. Except for [22], there exists no related work on early synthesis of timing models for model-based timing analysis of AUTOSAR-based systems.

Further, a related work in [21] deals with a model-driven workflow for energy-aware scheduling analysis of IoT enabled use cases. It carries out energy-aware timing analysis (of UML models) of IoT use cases in state-of-the-art (timing) analysis tools. However, ready made support for energy-aware timing analysis is not available in any of the state-of-the-art timing analysis tools. Hence, in [21], an additional tool-plugin is implemented in a timing analysis tool to include the energy properties and carry out energy-aware timing analysis. Note that the workflow in [21] deals with the synthesis and analysis of energy-aware timing models from hand-written IoT code. Thus, in the literature, there is no published work dealing with the synthesis of energy-aware timing models in AUTOSAR-based embedded software systems developed using UML/SysML domain.

Addressing this gap and in line with the novelties outlined in Sect. 1.2, in the remainder of this paper, the proposed workflow for synthesis of energy-aware timing models in AUTOSAR-based systems and an experimental evaluation are presented in Sect. 3 and 4 respectively.

3   Workflow for Synthesis of Energy-Aware Timing Models

The proposed workflow for a systematic integration of the energy and timing performance requirements in the AUTOSAR-design model and the automated synthesis of an AUTOSAR-based energy-aware timing analysis model is presented in this section. A series of steps involved in this systematic synthesis of energy-aware timing analysis models incorporated in the AUTOSAR development process shown in Fig. 3. The steps involved in the workflow are described in Sect. 3.1. The custom-defined generic timing-energy metamodel used in the workflow is described in Sect. 3.2. The mapping among elements in the AUTOSAR metamodel and the custom metamodel (from Sect. 3.2) w.r.t

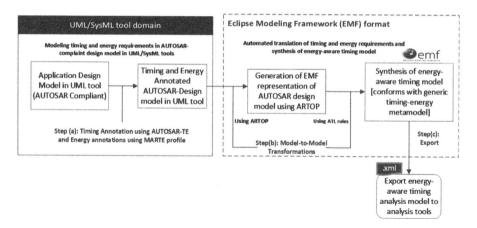

Fig. 3. Steps involved in synthesis of energy-aware timing analysis model incorporated in AUTOSAR development process.

timing properties is described in Sect. 3.3. Similarly, mapping between MARTE stereotypes and custom-defined metamodel (from Sect. 3.2) for energy properties is described in Sect. 3.4. An overview of the M2M transformations used in the workflow is provided in Sect. 3.5.

3.1 Steps Involved in the Synthesis of an Energy-Aware Timing Analysis Model

The proposed workflow for integrating the energy and timing performance requirements in the AUTOSAR-design model and the automated synthesis of an AUTOSAR-based energy-aware timing analysis model is shown in Fig. 3. It comprises of the following steps:

1. In the first step (step (a) in Fig. 3), it is considered that an initial AUTOSAR-based design model of the automotive embedded software application under consideration is already modeled in an UML/SysML tool [8, 17]. Note that step-(a) in Fig. 3 is applied in an early stage of development process. It involves the specification of the timing and energy requirements in the AUTOSAR-based design model using AUTOSAR-TE and MARTE profile respectively. The output of this step is a timing and energy-annotated AUTOSAR-based design model.
2. In line with the main scope of this paper, an AUTOSAR-based energy-aware timing analysis model needs to be synthesised based on the inputs from step-(a) in Fig. 3. For this purpose, given the energy-aware timing annotated design model as input, Model-to-Model (M2M) transformations are implemented for extracting the timing and energy properties. This results in the synthesis of the AUTOSAR-based energy-aware timing analysis model (conforming to a generic metamodel, cf. Sect. 3.2). Thus, the output of step-(b) in Fig. 3 is the synthesized energy-aware timing analysis model.

Note that this resulting model from step (b) can be used for performance validation such as energy-aware timing analysis and trade-off studies. Thus the output (model) from step (b) may be exported (cf. step (c) in Fig. 3), for instance in XML format, to industry standard analysis tools [11,43].

3.2 Generic Timing-Energy Metamodel

A metamodel comprising a set of timing and energy properties is required for the Model-to-Model (M2M) transformations in step-(b) in Fig. 3. A generic, custom-defined metamodel for energy-aware timing analysis introduced in [21], for energy-aware timing analysis of IoT-compliant use cases, is employed in this paper to synthesize an energy-aware timing analysis model for AUTOSAR-based embedded software systems developed using UML/SysML tools. This metamodel bears similarity to the AUTOSAR metamodel with respect to the software and hardware architecture elements. It can be termed as a generic metamodel, as it closely adheres with timing models used in several timing validation tools [11,43]. A simplified view of the custom-defined timing-energy metamodel is shown in Fig. 4.

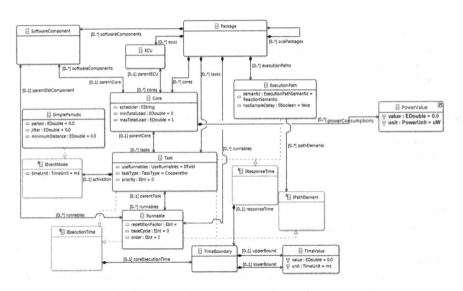

Fig. 4. Excerpt of the timing-energy metamodel [21].

From Fig. 4, it can be seen that the metamodel comprises a package with the elements required for an energy-aware timing evaluation of a software system, in a hierarchy. It consists of elements such as *Packages*, containing the different model elements such as *Runnables* (e.g. an operation), *SoftwareComponents*, *Tasks*, *Cores*, *ECUs* and *ExecutionPaths*. A task may or may not have a *trigger*, depending on its activation. Each task and runnable comprises an attribute to store the execution time. This is used as an input for timing analysis. A result of timing validation, namely the *response time* is an attribute for tasks.

Similarly, the power consumption modes (along with their average power rating) specified in the UML design model can be mapped to the attribute *PowerValue* for a core. Please note that only a simplified (yet sufficient) view of the timing-energy analysis model is presented here, because of space limitations. Interested readers are referred to [22] for a detailed description of the timing elements in the metamodel.

3.3 Mapping Among Metamodels for *Timing* Properties

In this section, the relevant metamodel elements from the custom-defined intermediate timing-energy metamodel (cf. Sect. 3.2, Fig. 4) are mapped to their counterparts in the AUTOSAR-TE metamodel [3]. The AUTOSAR Tool Platform[4] provides an EMF model, which contains the element names as per specification. An evaluation version of this AUTOSAR EMF model is used in this paper for mapping the timing metamodel elements to the AUTOSAR metamodel elements. It is also used as an input metamodel for the automated model transformations (cf. Sect. 3.5). A summary of relevant mappings of elements is shown in Table 1. In the following, these mappings are described in more detail.

Table 1. Mapping of timing-related elements in proposed generic metamodel (in Fig. 4) to AUTOSAR elements.

Nr	Timing element in Fig. 4	AUTOSAR element	Description
1	Model	AUTOSAR	Top-level model element
2	Package	ARPackage	Structuring element
3	SoftwareComponent	AtomicSwComponentType	Encapsulates functionality
4	Runnable	RunnableEntity	Executable operation
	period	Period of TimingEvent	Period of operation
	coreExecutionTime	LatencyTimingConstraint	Execution time of runnable
	order	RtePositionInTask	Execution order of runnable
	baseCycle	RteActivationOffset	First runnable execution
	repetitionFactor	runnable period/task period	How often it is executed
5	ECU	EcuInstance	Electronic control unit
6	Core	HwElement	Processing core
	period	OsSecondsPerTick	Seconds per clock tick
7	System	System	Network of ECUs
8	Task	OsTask	Schedulable unit
	priority	OsTaskPriority	Fixed priority of task
	taskType	OsTaskSchedule	Preemptability of task
	synchronizationMechanism	OsAlarmCounterRef	Reference clock
	synchronizationOffset	OsAlarmAlarmTime	Offset for the reference clock
	activation	OsAlarmCycleTime	Periodic task activation
9	ExecutionPath	TimingDescriptionEventChain	End-to-end path

---

[4] https://www.artop.org/.

1. The top-most element of every AUTOSAR model is the *AUTOSAR* element. It denotes the AUTOSAR revision and links to the corresponding XML schema definition. This element is mapped to the *Model* element, as it represents a dedicated model. Note that this element in Table 1 is not shown in the Fig. 4.

2. The *ARPackage* element gets mapped to the *Package* timing element, as it structures the different AUTOSAR elements in packages and subpackages.

3. The mapping of software components is straightforward, because these elements exist similarly as central modeling elements in the AUTOSAR standard. Every *AtomicSwComponentType* of the AUTOSAR application model is mapped to a *Soft wareComponent* in the timing metamodel. This includes *SensorActuatorSwComponentTypes* and *ApplicationSwComponentTypes*, as they inherit from the atomic software component type.

4. The *Runnable* timing elements exist in AUTOSAR inside the *InternalBehavior* of an *AtomicSwComponentType* as *RunnableEntities*. They represent the executable operations of the software components.

5. The *ECU* elements can be mapped to the AUTOSAR *EcuInstance*. This is used for linking the software components, and therefore runnables, to their dedicated ECUs, on which they are later on implemented and executed.

6. The *Core* elements are mapped to *HwElements* in the AUTOSAR model. They need to be linked to a *HwCategory* of the type *ProcessingCore*. Each core belongs to an ECU and is linked to it in the system mapping.

7. The *System* element in timing metamodel corresponds to a *System* element AUTOSAR model. Overall, they represent a top-level element corresponding to a network of ECUs.

8. *Task* elements are created in the AUTOSAR *Os* configuration as *OsTasks*. A task is defined as a schedulable unit in timing analysis.

9. The end-to-end *ExecutionPaths* in the timing metamodel can be represented in the AUTOSAR model as *TimingDescriptionEventChains*. These event chains group a set of events belonging to the activation and termination of runnable entities.

Note that in place of the custom-defined but generic metamodel used in this paper, an open source metamodel namely, AMALTHEA[5], may be employed for M2M related to timing properties. However, it does not provide ready made support (i.e., elements) for modeling energy characteristics. Hence, in this paper we have employed our custom-defined generic metamodel.

3.4   Mapping Between MARTE Stereotypes and Custom-Defined Timing-Energy Metamodel for *Energy* Properties

For annotating the energy properties, the underlying CPU configuration modes (with power consumption values of the microcontroller) are taken into consideration. This can be obtained from measurements or from data sheets, for instance in the case of Commercial Off-the-shelf (COTS) products. The mapping between the power configuration modes for the CPU core can be added using the *HWComponent* stereotype from MARTE profile (with tagged value *staticConsumption*) [26]. The

---

[5] https://www.eclipse.org/app4mc/.

HWComputingResource stereotype (with tagged value *resMult*) indicating multiplicity of the processing modes, can be additionaly used to link the processing modes to the cores with the tag value *processingUnits* of *SaExecHost* stereotype. Please note that, the aforementioned stereotypes are selected based on an analysis of support for energy modeling in MARTE profile and the requirements for a first hand energy-aware timing analysis of the AUTOSAR-based design models, proposed in this paper.

Table 2. Stereotypes used from MARTE profile for energy/power annotations in the design model and their mapping to elements in Fig. 4.

MARTE Stereotype	Tagged Values	Description	Mapping to element in Fig. 4
SaExecHost	mainScheduler, schedPolicy, utilization, isSched	CPU core and related configuration	Core (also *HWElement* in AUTOSAR), runnable, task
HwComponent	staticConsumption	Average power consumption per processing mode	PowerValue
HwComputingResource	resMult	Linking various core configurations	powerConsumptions in PowerValue

The mapping between the MARTE stereotypes mentioned above and the corresponding elements in the custom-defined timing-energy metamodel in Fig. 4 are shown in Table 2. Each core element in Fig. 4 may comprise of a *PowerValue* denoting the power consumption values of the underlying microcontroller. Thus, the power consumption values specified using the *HWComponent* stereotype from MARTE profile with tagged value *staticConsumption*, are mapped to the *PowerValue* element denoted in Fig. 4. The various core configurations and their power values from *HWComponent* stereotype represented by the *HWComputingResource* stereotype correspond to the multiplicity *powerConsumptions* in *PowerValue* element in the metamodel in Fig. 4. These are required to link the various core configurations (e.g., power configuration modes). Note that, for a first hand energy-aware timing analysis, the power configuration models of the underlying hardware element (one or more cores) are taken into consideration.

3.5 Model-to-Model (M2M) Transformations

As seen in Fig. 3, after step (a), a timing and energy annotated AUTOSAR-based design model is now available in the UML/SysML tool under consideration. It can be exported from the tool as an *ARXML* file [3] as input for step (b) in Fig. 3. Note that while employing Model-to-Model (M2M) transformations, both source and target models must conform with their respective metamodels. Here the *source model* is the *timing and energy annotated AUTOSAR design model* obtained from the system description specification in the UML/SysML tool in ARXML format. This conforms with the AUTOSAR metamodel [3]. The *target metamodel* is the *custom-defined generic timing-energy metamodel* introduced in Sect. 3.2. During the M2M transformations the timing and energy properties are extracted from the annotated AUTOSAR-based design model (source model) and a corresponding instance of the energy-aware timing analysis target metamodel is synthesized. Note that here both the metamodels are available in EMF format.

The synthesized analysis model is also available in EMF and XML formats. This model may now be used for performance validation such as energy-aware scheduling.

In this work, the ATLAS transformation language (ATL) [2] is used for implementing the M2M transformations. ATL is a widely used M2M transformation language and readily available as a plug-in for Eclipse development environment. Thus, using ATL a set of rules can be written to transform the AUTOSAR-based design model to an instance of the intermediate timing-energy meta model, based on the mappings listed in Table 1 and 2. The ATL implementation of the transformations in the prototype implementation of the workflow follows the regular structure of ATL transformations [2]. As stated earlier, the source model, M2M transformation and target models each have their own separate metamodels, which are each based on a common meta-metamodel (ECORE) [7]. The model transformations are implemented as an ATL module, *AUTOSARinUML2TimingEnergy.atl*. These are generic implementations which can be applied across any use case satisfying the source and target models used in the ATL implementations. The implementation specifics of this module are explained in detail in the next section along with examples from the use case.

4   Autonomous Emergency Braking System (AEBS)

This AEBS use case is introduced already in [22]. Since this book chapter is an extension of the work done in [22], only a brief introduction about the AEBS use case is provided here. The main purpose of AEBSs is to warn the driver in case of an imminent frontal collision. This happens through visual and acoustic warning signals as a first step, followed by a tactile warning as the next level. The AEBS in cars use the Time-To-Collision (TTC) value [16, 25] to estimate the danger of the situation. It is defined as the *time left until a collision happens*, if every object continues to move at the same speed. To calculate TTC, AEBS needs data such as the distance to frontal objects (e.g. from rador sensors) and wheel speed sensor input at certain speed ranges.

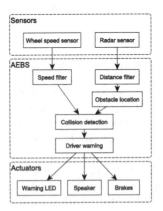

Fig. 5. Control flow and modules of the AEBS.

The control flow and modules of the AEBS are showin in Fig. 5. The AEBS is connected to sensors such as speed and radar sensors and actuators such as the warning LED, speaker and brakes via a software interface. Thus information such as the speed of the car in ms^{-1} (from *wheel speed sensor*), distance in m and relative speed in ms^{-1} (from *radar sensor*) are provided as inputs to the AEBS system. The output from AEBS system can be referenced using port interfaces, which must be processed by the corresponding actuator and issue a corresponding output (e.g. applying brakes, issuing warning signal).

4.1 AUTOSAR Design Model

The AUTOSAR system description of the AEBS is modeled using the IBM Rational Rhapsody Developer modeling tool [18]. Rhapsody is among the most popular UML modeling tool with AUTOSAR support used in the automotive industry. It also supports straight forward usage of the MARTE profile for energy annotations required for the workflow in Fig. 3. The MARTE profile can be added to the model and its stereotypes can be applied to the model elements directly, hence the choice of the tool.

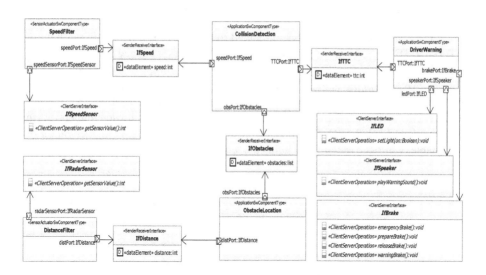

Fig. 6. Software components of AEBS in software component diagram modeled in Rhapsody.

The first step in implementing the AUTOSAR design model is to define the software components, of which the system is composed of as shown in Fig. 6.

– The sensor filter modules on the left-hand side are modeled as *SensorActuator-SwComponentTypes*. They have client ports (*speedSensorPort*, *radarSensorPort*) to be able to connect to the corresponding sensors. These ports are typed by *ClientServerInterfaces* that provide an operation for retrieving the sensor value. This is illustrated by the association between the ports and the interfaces, which is stereo-typed as a *portType*. The rest of the modules are modeled as *ApplicationSwCompo-nentTypes*, as they do not directly represent a sensor or an actuator.

– The communication between the sensor filters and the *CollisionDetection* and *ObstacleLocation* components happens through sender/receiver ports. The filtered *dataElements* get sent to the processing components. Equally, the *ObstacleLocation* sends a list of obstacles (comprising of distance and relative speed) to the *Collision-Detection*. The communication between *CollisionDetection* and *DriverWarning* is also typed as sender/receiver and the corresponding *dataElement* is the TTC value.

– In the end, the *DriverWarning* component is connected by client ports (*ledPort*, *speakerPort* and *brakePort*) to the three actuators. The corresponding interfaces pro-vide the necessary operations for the different levels of driver warning, e.g., setting the warning LED light status (*setLight*), playing a warning sound (*playWarning-Sound*) or performing an emergency brake (*emergencyBrake*).

Thus, the modules for the AEBS use case shown in Fig. 5 are modeled as AUTOSAR software components in the UML tool [17], as seen in Fig. 6.

4.2 Timing Specification

The timing constraints of the AEBS are added to the model in Fig. 6 with the help of AUTOSAR-TE in the UML tool Rhapsody. Figure 7 shows a latency constraint for the *checkTTC* runnable entity of the *DriverWarning* software component (seen at top-right of Fig. 6). An *SwcTiming* is created for each software component in the AEBS, which link to the component's internal behavior with the *l_behavior* association. Inside these elements, two *TDEventSwcInternalBehaviors* are defined for each runnable entity (in this case, *checkTTC* of *IBDriverWarning*). The first event highlights the activation of the runnable, while the second highlights the termination. This is defined by setting the

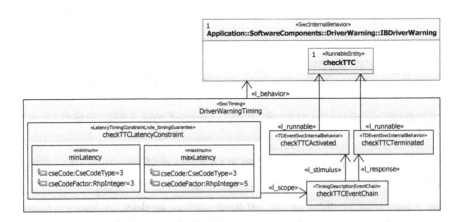

Fig. 7. Timing attributes for the *checkTTC* runnable entity.

tag *tdEventSwcInternalBehaviorType* of the timing event to either *runnableEntityActivated* or *runnableEntityTerminated*. Both these events are now used to form a *TimingDescriptionEventChain*, in which the event chain stimulus is the runnable activation and the event chain response is the runnable termination.

Finally, the core execution time of the runnable *checkTTC* is specified by the *checkTTCLatencyConstraint* that links to its event chain with *l_scope*. The *role_timingGuarantee* stereotype declares that this constraint is the expected execution time instead of a requirement (*role_timingRequirement*). The related timing information can be given as maximum and minimum execution time and is specified by ASAM CSE codes [39]. The *cseCode* specifies the time base (e.g., $2 = 100\,\mu s$, $3 = 1\,ms$ and $4 = 10\,ms$) and the *cseCodeFactor* determines an integer scaling factor. Thus, in this case, the execution time of the *checkTTC* runnable entity lies between 3 ms and 5 ms.

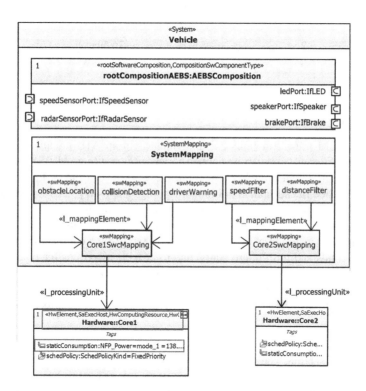

Fig. 8. System diagram containing the system mapping, root software composition and energy annotations for the hardware elements with processing modes for AEBS use case.

4.3   Specification of Energy Properties

In the custom-defined generic metamodel in Fig. 4, each core may comprise of a power value denoting the power consumption values of the underlying microcontroller. Based on the data sheet of the target, the various power ratings for different processor clock rates can be obtained. These power consumption values are specified in the design model using the *staticConsumption* tagged value of *HWComponent*, as per the mapping introduced in Table 2. For the AEBS use case example in this paper, the power consumption modes of an ARM processor [30] is taken into consideration (cf. Table 3). Note that a simple example is used here to demonstrate the direct usage of power consumption values from a COTS product data sheet. For instance, the power consumption during three active power modes shown in Table 3 namely, 23.1 mW, 76.59 mW and 138.6 mW (corresponding to 12 MHz, 48 MHz and 100 MHz clock frequencies) are specified in the design model as shown in Fig. 8.

Table 3. Power consumption modes for an ARM single core processor [30].

Processing Mode	Clock Frequency	Power
1	100 MHz	138.6 mW
2	48 MHz	76.59 mW
3	12 MHz	23.1 mW

4.4 Model Transformations

The generic M2M transformations are implemented in an ATL module, *AUTOSAR-inUML2TimingEnergy.atl*. It can be applied to any use case (e.g. AEBS) which satisfies the source and target model criteria as in the workflow in Fig. 3. In this module, there are 9 matched rules for all conditional mappings and 8 lazy rules for all unconditional mappings. In addition, 15 helpers are implemented which may be invoked by the transformation rules. Th helpers are often used as *getter()* and *setter()* methods. In the prototype, the helpers are implemented, for instance to resolve computation units (e.g. nano/milli seconds and milli/micro watts) and to provide assertions for type of model and timing elements (e.g. a softwareComponent and a runnable). An example for each type of rule (matched and lazy) and helper, from the prototype implementation of the M2M transformations in *AUTOSARinUML2TimingEnergy.atl* is described below.

Matched Rule. The rules consist of a source pattern in the `from` section and a target pattern in the `to` section. The source pattern specifies the type of the source model element to be matched and the target pattern contains the output model element that will be created by the transformation for each source element. In the ATL module *AUTOSAR-inUML2TimingEnergy.atl*, for synthesis of energy-aware timing analysis models, the matched rules are used for source elements such as model, package, classes and for the elements with applied stereotypes from AUTOSAR profile shown in Table 1.

Listing 1.1. An example of an ATL matched rule.

```
1   -- @atlcompiler emftvm
2   -- @path TimingEnergy=/de.uos.te.model/model/timingEnergy.ecore
3   -- @nsURI UML=http://www.eclipse.org/uml2/5.0.0/UML
4   -- @nsURI MARTE=http://www.eclipse.org/papyrus/MARTE/1
5   -- @nsURI AR=http://autosar.org/schema/r4.0/autosar40
6
7   module AUTOSARinUML2TimingEnergy;
8   create OUT: TimingEnergy, from IN : AR
9   rule AtomicSWC2SWComponent extends
10  Identifiable2ICATObject{
11  from
12      input : AR!AtomicSwComponentType
13  to
14      output : TimingEnergy!SoftwareComponent(
15  runnables <- input.internalBehaviors
16      ->collect(ib | ib.runnables)
17      -> flatten())}
```

A simple example of an ATL matched rule is shown in Listing 1.1. Note that in lines 2–5 the various paths of the metamodels invoked in the ATL module are specified (either local or at URI-repository resource). The `AtomicSWC2SWComponent` rule `extends` the parent rule `Identifiable2ICATObject` and thus, its target pattern is inherited. This means that, the target element `SoftwareComponent` automatically receives the name and description attributes from parent rule (i.e., `Identifiable-2ICATObject`-not listed here).

In this matched rule, as seen in lines 11–14, a software component in the source AUTOSAR (meta) model (`AR!AtomicSwComponentType`) is matched to a target software component element (`TimingEnergy!SoftwareComponent`) in the timing-energy (meta) model. Thereby, an instance of the target element (i.e., a software component corresponding to the timing-energy analysis meta-model) is created.

Additionally, it receives the `runnables` (lines 15–17) attribute specified in the new target pattern, to link to the software component's runnables. The `collect` operation iterates through all internal behavior elements (`ib`) and returns the list of runnables for each. As this statement returns a two-dimensional list, the `flatten` operation ensures that a list directly containing the runnables is returned and assigned to the `runnables` attribute. Use an example to describe here all the rules or later on.

Lazy Rule. Lazy rules are used for source elements that satisfy specific conditions and must be called explicitly for creating target elements. Listing 1.2 shows an example of an ATL lazy rule which is used to create a `powerValue` from a `String`. It may be recalled that the power consumption values are specified in the tag values of the respective MARTE stereotype (as a string). The ATL rule in Listing 1.2 converts this specified power value as a string to a corresponding model element `powerValue` in the generic metamodel (cf. Fig. 4, Sect. 3.3, Table 3, Sect. 4.3 & Fig. 8).

Listing 1.2. An example of an ATL Lazy rule.

```
1  lazy rule StringToPowerValue {
2  from
3    string: String
4  using {
5    splitted : Sequence(String) = string.splitPowerConsumption();
6    value: Real = thisModule.valueFromSplitPowerConsumption(splitted);
7    unit: TimingEnergy!PowerUnit =
8    thisModule.unitFromSplitPowerConsumption(splitted);
9  }
10 to
11   timingEneryElement: TimingEnergy!PowerValue (
12     unit <- unit,
13     value <- if value.oclIsUndefined() then
14       OclUndefined
15     else
16       value
17     endif
18   )
19 }
```

Let us consider an example of power value of processing mode 1, namely 138.6mw (cf. Table 3). This is specified in the design model using the tagged value *static-Consumption* of the *HWComponent* MARTE stereotype (cf. Table 2 & Fig. 8). The lazy rule StringToPowerValue in Listing 1.2, splits the above input string *138.6mw* employing the using keyword and expressions in ATL (lines 5–9). The using keyword and expression can be used to define complex target pattern elements, thus employed in this lazy rule. Thus, the resulting variables namely unit and value are assigned to the corresponding target elements in powerValue (cf. powerValue in Fig. 4) in lines 11–17 of Listing 1.2.

Thus in the example in Fig. 8, the lazy rule StringToPowerValue returns the *power value* from a string specified in the tagged value in the stereotypes in model elements. Thus, the power rating for each processing mode such as 138.6mW, 76.59mW and 23.1mW specified in Fig. 8 are returned as output for further calculations.

Helpers. Helpers can be used to define (global) variables and functions. Some examples of include *setter()*, *getter()* methods and functions to resolve attributes involving repetitive pieces of code in one place (e.g. resolving metric units). Helper functions are Object Constraint Language (OCL) [31] expressions. They can call each other by recursion or they can be called from within rules.

Listing 1.3. An example of an ATL Helper.

```
1  helper def: resolveStaticConsumptionFromElement(processingUnit:
2  UML!Element): String = let hwComponent : UML!Stereotype =
3  processingUnit.getHwComponentStereotype() in
4  if not hwComponent.oclIsUndefined() then
5    processingUnit.getValue(hwComponent, 'staticConsumption')
6  else
7    OclUndefined
8  endif;
```

In Listing 1.3, an example of a helper to resolve the tag value `staticConsumption` from the MARTE stereotype element `HWComponent` (cf. Table 2) is presented. In the example in Fig. 8, this helper reads the input value of the tagged value `staticConsumption`, which is highlighted in Fig. 8 in *Hardware::Core1* element and returns the corresponding value of the processing unit.

Similar to the above rules, for the remaining elements in Table 1, a total of 17 ATL rules (9 matched and 8 lazy) and 15 helpers are implemented in the *AUTOSAR-inUML2TimingEnergy.atl* module.

4.5   Synthesis of Energy-Aware Timing Analysis Model of AEBS

In the above steps, the AUTOSAR-based design model and its corresponding timing and energy annotated AUTOSAR-based design model are created in the UML modeling tool Rhapsody (cf. step(a) in Fig. 3). This model is exported from the UML tool in the interchangeable AUTOSAR ARXML format for M2M transformations (cf. step (b) in Fig. 3). The M2M transformations in *AUTOSARinUML2TimingEnergy.atl* module are invoked in the experimental evaluation directly from the Eclipse development environment. The synthesized AUTOSAR-based energy-aware timing analysis model of the AEBS use case is shown in Fig. 9.

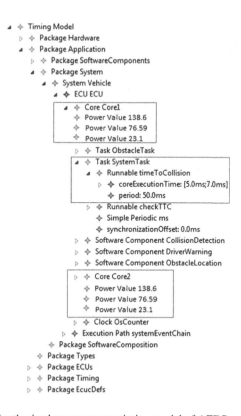

Fig. 9. Synthesized energy-aware timing model of AEBS use case.

The necessary elements for a timing analysis were extracted from the AUTOSAR design model annotated with timing properties (cf. Fig. 6, 7) according to the mapping in Table 1. As seen in Fig. 9, the AEBS model is structured by different *Packages* and the *System* element contains the complete software and hardware elements in a hierarchy. For example, the runnable *timeToCollision* with its corresponding execution time [5 ms, 7 ms] can be seen highlighted in Fig. 9. This runnable is allocated to the *SystemTask*, which is in turn allocated to *Core1* of the ECU. Further, the power consumption modes of the hardware cores are also created corresponding to the annotations in design model. This is highlighted for core1 and core2 in Fig. 9 with the respective power values (138.6, 76.59, 23.1) for each processing mode.

4.6 Performance Analysis

A quantitative performance analysis of the prototype implementation of the workflow in Fig. 3 has been carried out by invoking the transformations for the AEBS use case with varying number of SWCs in the AUTOSAR-based UML design model. This is because, the number of software components (apart from tasks) may be considered as a primary factor for computing complexities involved in schedulability analysis of systems. Further, the number of cores and power consumption modes were also varied to invoke respective M2M transformations for resolving the power consumption modes.

For varying input sizes namely, SWCs and hardware cores in annotated design model), time and memory requirement of the ATL module to synthesize the respective instance of the AUTOSAR-based energy-aware timing analysis model is determined (cf. Table 4). For varying inputs of SWCs, the number of cores were set to two, each having three power consumption modes as described in Sect. 4.3. This is because, the number of SWCs in an AUTOSAR design model can be up to several hundreds. Whereas, the number of cores and their power consumption modes would not scale to such values, hence not provided as a separate set of input in Table 4. The aforesaid experiments were carried out on a standard X-86 based host with Windows-XP OS. The results indicate that the ATL transformations terminate once the generation of the timing analysis model is completed. The generation time and memory requirement is bounded for varying input sizes. This demonstrates the applicability and suitability of the steps involved in the proposed approach for early model-based synthesis of AUTOSAR-based energy-aware timing analysis model from AUTOSAR-based design models developed in UML/SysML tools.

Table 4. Set of inputs, time & memory requirement on a standard X-86 based host for the *AUTOSARinUML2TimingEnergy.atl* ATL module.

SWCs	Time (s)	Memory (MB)
10	26.3	4.1
18	54.2	6.3
23	66.34	8.7
43	136.4	20.7

5   Conclusion

In this book chapter, a systematic workflow for integration of energy and timing requirements in the AUTOSAR-based design model in UML/SysML tools has been presented. Thereby, employing a series of steps, an automated and *early synthesis of energy-aware timing analysis models* is incorporated in the automotive embedded software development process. These performance analysis models may be employed for an early evaluation and decision on the best set of performance configuration and trade-off analysis (e.g. timing vs energy). Thus, employing such performance analysis workflows not only allow us to understand the performance aspects and behavior of the systems during early design stages, but also help to explore different design architectural choices and quantitatively evaluate their implications on system performance. Fine tuning the modeling of energy and timing parameters, such as specification of energy consumption and timing budget per function call is one among the items for future work.

References

1. Anssi, S., Gérard, S., Kuntz, S., Terrier, F.: AUTOSAR vs. MARTE for enabling timing analysis of automotive applications. In: Ober, I., Ober, I. (eds.) SDL 2011. LNCS, vol. 7083, pp. 262–275. Springer, Heidelberg (2011). https://doi.org/10.1007/978-3-642-25264-8_20
2. Atlas Transformation Language (ATL) Technology. https://www.eclipse.org/atl/. Accessed 20 June 2020
3. Automotive Open System Architecture. http://www.autosar.org/. Accessed 20 June 2020
4. Bhasker, J.: A SystemC Primer. Star Galaxy (2010)
5. Bucaioni, A., Cicchetti, A., Ciccozzi, F., Mubeen, S., Sjödin, M.: A metamodel for the Rubus component model: extensions for timing and model transformation from EAST-ADL. IEEE Access **5**, 9005–9020 (2017)
6. Derler, P., Eidson, J., Lee, E.A., Matic, S., Zimmer, M.: Model-based development of deterministic, event-driven, real-time distributed systems. In: Workshop on Model-Based Design with a Focus on Extra-Functional Properties (2011)
7. Eclipse Modeling Framework. https://www.eclipse.org/modeling/emf/. Accessed 20 June 2020
8. Enterprise Architect tool. http://www.sparxsystems.com/. Accessed 25 June 2020
9. Ficek, C., Feiertag, N., Richter, K., Jersak, M.: Applying the AUTOSAR timing protection to build safe and efficient ISO 26262 mixed-criticality systems. In: Proceedings of ERTS (2012)
10. Franco, F.R., et. al: Workflow and toolchain for developing the automotive software according AUTOSAR standard at a Virtual-ECU. In: 2016 IEEE 25th International Symposium on Industrial Electronics (ISIE), pp. 869–875 (2016)
11. GLIWA Embedded Systems-Timing suite T1. https://www.gliwa.com/. Accessed 20 June 2020
12. Hagner, M., Aniculaesei, A., Goltz, U.: UML-based analysis of power consumption for real-time embedded systems. In: IEEE 10th International Conference on Trust, Security and Privacy in Computing and Communications, pp. 1196–1201 (2011)
13. Hans, B., Rolf, J., Henrik, L.: Annotation with timing constraints in the context of EAST-ADL2 and AUTOSAR-the timing augmented description language. In: STANDRTS 2009 (2009)

14. Harbour, M.G., García, J.G., Gutiérrez, J.P., Moyano, J.D.: Mast: Modeling and analysis suite for real time applications. In: 13th Euromicro Conference on Real-Time Systems, pp. 125–134. IEEE (2001)
15. Henzinger, T.A., Horowitz, B., Kirsch, C.M.: Giotto: a time-triggered language for embedded programming. In: Henzinger, T.A., Kirsch, C.M. (eds.) EMSOFT 2001. LNCS, vol. 2211, pp. 166–184. Springer, Heidelberg (2001). https://doi.org/10.1007/3-540-45449-7_12
16. van der Horst, R., Hogema, J.: Time-to-collision and collision avoidance systems. In: Proceedings of the 6th ICTCT Workshop (1993)
17. IBM Software: IBM rational rhapsody developer. https://www.ibm.com/products/systems-design-rhapsody. Accessed 25 June 2020
18. IBM Software: IBM rational rhapsody developer (2019). https://www.ibm.com/software/products/en/ratirhap. Accessed Nov 2019
19. INCHRON: chronSIM (2019). https://www.inchron.com/tool-suite/chronsim.html. Accessed Nov 2019
20. Iqbal, M.Z., Ali, S., Yue, T., Briand, L.: Experiences of applying UML/MARTE on three industrial projects. In: Proceedings of the 15th International Conference MODELS 2012 (2012)
21. Iyenghar, P., Pulvermueller, E.: A model-driven workflow for energy-aware scheduling analysis of IoT-enabled use cases. IEEE Internet Things J. **5**(6), 4914–4925 (2018). https://doi.org/10.1109/JIOT.2018.2879746
22. Iyenghar, P., Huning, L., Pulvermüller, E.: Early synthesis of timing models in AUTOSAR-based automotive embedded software systems. In: Proceedings of the 8th International Conference on Model-Driven Engineering and Software Development, MODELSWARD 2020, pp. 26–38. SCITEPRESS (2020)
23. Iyenghar, P., Noyer, A., Engelhardt, J., Pulvermüller, E., Westerkamp, C.: End-to-end path delay estimation in embedded software involving heterogeneous models. In: 11th IEEE Symposium on Industrial Embedded Systems, SIES, 2016, pp. 183–188 (2016)
24. Kim, J.H., Kang, I., Kang, S., Boudjadar, A.: A process algebraic approach to resource-parameterized timing analysis of automotive software architectures. IEEE Trans. Ind. Inf. **12**(2), 655–671 (2016)
25. Kusano, K.D., Gabler, H.: Method for estimating time to collision at braking in real-world, lead vehicle stopped rear-end crashes for use in pre-crash system design. SAE Int. J. **4**(1), 435–443 (2011)
26. MARTE profile. https://www.omg.org/spec/MARTE/About-MARTE/. Accessed 25 June 2020
27. Martinez, L.R., Prieto, M.D.: New Trends in Electrical Vehicle Powertrains, 1st edn. Intech Open, London (2019)
28. Mathworks Products. https://www.mathworks.com/. Accessed 20 May 2020
29. Navet, N., Simonot-Lion, F. (eds.): Automotive Embedded Systems Handbook. CRC Press, Boco Raton (2009)
30. NXP LPC1768 MCU datasheet. http://www.nxp.com/documents/data_sheet/LPC1769_68_67_66_65_64_63.pdf. Accessed 20 May 2020
31. Object Management Group. http://www.omg.org. Accessed 25 June 2020
32. Papyrus UML Tool. http://www.papyrusuml.org/. Accessed 05 May 2017
33. Peraldi, M., Sorel, Y.: From high-level modelling of time in MARTE to realtime scheduling analysis. In: First International Workshop on Model Based Architecting and Construction of Embedded Systems (2008)
34. Peraldi-Frati, M.A., Blom, H., Karlsson, D., Kuntz, S.: Timing modeling with autosar-current state and future directions. In: Design, Automation Test in Europe Conference, DATE (2012)
35. Petriu, D.C.: Software Model-based Performance Analysis, pp. 139–166. Wiley, Hoboken (2013)

36. Saidi, S., Steinhorst, S., Hamann, A., Ziegenbein, D., Wolf, M.: Special session: future automotive systems design: Research challenges and opportunities. In: 2018 International Conference on Hardware/Software Codesign and System Synthesis (CODES+ISSS), pp. 1–7 (2018)
37. Sangiovanni-Vincentelli, A., Natale, M.D.: Embedded system design for automotive applications. Computer **40**(10), 42–51 (2007)
38. Scheickl, O., Ainhauser, C., Gliwa, P.: Tool support for seamless system development based on AUTOSAR timing extensions. In: Proceedings of Embedded Real-Time Software Congress (ERTS) (2012)
39. Scheid, O.: AUTOSAR Compendium, Part 1: Application & RTE. CreateSpace Independent Publishing Platform (2015)
40. Singhoff, F., Legrand, J., Nana, L., Marcé, L.: Cheddar: a flexible real time scheduling framework. In: ACM SIGAda Ada Letters, vol. 24–4. ACM (2004)
41. SysML specification. http://www.omgsysml.org/. Accessed 20 May 2020
42. System Composer toolbox. https://www.mathworks.com/products/system-composer.html. Accessed 20 May 2020
43. Timing Architects Tool. https://www.timing-architects.com/. Accessed 20 June 2020
44. UML specification. https://www.omg.org/spec/UML/About-UML/. Accessed 20 June 2020
45. Zhao, Y., Liu, J., Lee, E.A.: A programming model for time-synchronized distributed real-time systems. In: Proceedings of 13th IEEE Real Time and Embedded Technology and Applications Symposium, pp. 259–268. RTAS (2007)

Model-Based Virtual Prototyping of CPS: Application to Bio-Medical Devices

Daniela Genius[1(✉)], Ilias Bournias[1], Ludovic Apvrille[2], and Roselyne Chotin[1]

[1] Sorbonne Université, LIP6, CNRS UMR 7606, Paris, France
`daniela.genius@lip6.fr`
[2] LTCI, Télécom Paris, Institut Polytechnique de Paris, Paris, France

Abstract. Virtual prototyping and co-simulation of mixed analog/ digital embedded systems have emerged as a promising research topic, in particular for designing medical appliances. In the paper, we show how the integration of different, analog and digital, Models of Computation (MoC) within an UML/SysML based environment, can offer an efficient assistance for designing a cyber-physical system in a progressive and systematic manner. For this, we rely on formal verification and abstract simulation on a high abstraction level, and on Multi-MoC virtual prototyping on a lower abstraction level. A realistic echo monitoring system illustrates (i) the method, (ii) the modeling languages, and (iii) the different verification techniques.

Keywords: Embedded systems · Analog/mixed signal design · Virtual prototyping

1 Introduction

Embedded systems built upon analog and digital components are also called Cyber-Physical Systems (CPS). These components are commonly built upon Application Specific Integrated Circuits (ASIC), Field Programmable Gate Arrays (FPGA), Digital Signal Processors (DSPs), hardware accelerators, analog/mixed signal (AMS) and radio frequency (RF) circuits on the one hand, and System on chip (SoC) running the software on general purpose processors on the other. The large variety of hardware and software combinations to explore opens up a vast design space which is difficult to handle when designing a CPS.

Often, some parts of the system already exist; for example, some software stemming from previous versions of an embedded system has to be adapted to more recent hardware. Additionally, analog and digital designs are developed in parallel by different teams and have to be integrated.

While in [26], we have already shown how to handle system-level modeling of Cyber Physical Systems, we now propose a complete method for modeling and analyzing such systems, that includes high-level models of all hardware and software components for HW/SW partitioning, and more precise models once partitioning is done. The handling of different MoCs from a high level of

© Springer Nature Switzerland AG 2021
S. Hammoudi et al. (Eds.): MODELSWARD 2020, CCIS 1361, pp. 74–96, 2021.
https://doi.org/10.1007/978-3-030-67445-8_4

abstraction until a low level, main contribution presented in [25], is extended by the handling of software that runs on the digital part, and full-system simulation of the entire system.

The contributions are demonstrated over a realistic case study taken from the early design phase of an ongoing project inside the EchOpen community [17], which is focused on the design of a portable and affordable echo-stethoscope, mostly targeting developing countries. EchOpen is based on the principles of open hardware and open software. While adhering to a top-down approach of successive refinement of the model on the different levels, we also use pre-existing code as an input for our models, both for the application and for the analog part.

The paper first describes the abstractions on our two levels of abstraction and how they can efficiently be used designing CPS. After discussing related work in Sect. 2, we introduce the concepts of both digital and analog modeling in Sect. 3. Our contribution is described in Sects. 4 and 5 and applied to a larger case study in Sect. 6.

2   Related Work

The following tools target analog/mixed signal or multi-domain design and co-simulation.

Ptolemy II [35] is based upon the data-flow model. It addresses digital/analog systems by defining several sub domains. Instantiation of elements controlling time synchronization between domains is left to the designer. Recently, a co-simulation framework for timing verification of cyber-physical systems [28] from Ptolemy models, named *Metronomy*, has been developed.

Metropolis [6] is also based on high level models and facilitates the separation of concerns between computation and communication aspects. While heterogeneous systems are taken into consideration, heterogeneity can only be represented using processes, mediums, quantities and constraints; hierarchical models are not allowed.

Metro II [16] is based on hierarchical high-level models. So-called *Adapters* are used for data synchronization between components belonging to different Models of Computation (MoCs), yet the model designer still has to implement time synchronization. As a common simulation kernel handles the entire process execution (digital and analog), MoCs are not well separated.

Discrete Event System Specification (DEVS, [12]) is a modular and hierarchical formalism for modeling and analyzing general systems. DEVS supports discrete events and continuous systems. Continuous functions can be described by differential equations, or hybrid systems. Although a number of platform implementations based on DEVS exist, ranging from Petri Net over object oriented to Python based approaches, full-system simulation, taking into account hardware, software and an operating system, is not supported.

Modelica [19] is an object-oriented modeling language for component-oriented systems containing e.g. mechanical, electrical, electronic and hydraulic components. Classes contain sets of equations that can be translated into objects running on a simulation engine. Yet, since time synchronization is not predefined, the simulation engine must manipulate objects in a symbolic way in order to determine an execution order between components of different MoCs. Linking simulations with different Models of Computation can be done by using e.g. the Functional Mock-up Interface [9], closely related to the Modelica tools.

From the Micro Electro Mechanical Systems (MEMS) community [10] stems an approach which can transform structural SysML diagrams into VHDL-AMS code. It is thus closely related to our work, but limited to its related domain. Moreover, VHDL specifications are less flexible than most other approaches for expressing different Models of Computation, VHDL being essentially a hardware description language at register transfer level.

SystemC AMS extensions [7,43], is a library of C++ classes based on SystemC [30], extending SystemC with AMS and RF features. In the scope of the BeyondDreams project [8], a mixed analog-digital systems proof-of-concept simulator has been developed, following the SystemC AMS extension standard [18]. Another simulator is proposed in the H-Inception project [29]. All of these approaches rely on SystemC AMS code i.e. they do not provide a high-level interface for specifying the application.

UML/SysML based modeling techniques such as MARTE and Gaspard2 [20, 44] are extremely popular for capturing the behavior of embedded systems, but less widely used for heterogeneous system design [38].

As prototyping on a concrete platform is a slow and costly process, a full-system virtual platform with a real operating system becomes desirable. Moreover, when targeting co-simulation with a significant software proportion running on the digital (i.e. MPSoC) part of the virtual platform, full-system simulation is mandatory : software has to be loaded into different memory sections, parallelism of tasks and processors has to be handled.

With very few exceptions such as [32,41], UML/SysML-based techniques do not support refinement until cycle/bit accurate level virtual prototypes nor provide OS support for full-system simulation. Co-simulation between different MoC is usually out of scope, too.

3 Basic Concepts

Let us briefly introduce the two fundamental concepts and associated tools which are the basis of the present contribution. On the one hand, we follow the multi-level model-based approach of TTool for design (digital) systems [4], as in our previous contributions [22]. On the other hand, we introduce analog concepts in the two modeling levels of TTool. We consider two abstraction levels, hardware/software partitioning, when the decision is taken for tasks to be implemented either in hardware or in software, and software design, considering hardware and software parts separately and deploying the software on the hardware once the partitioning is done. For digital platforms, TTool can generate a SystemC-based virtual prototype from the lowest abstraction level. Thus, the choice of a virtual prototype as a combination of SystemC AMS and System C was natural.

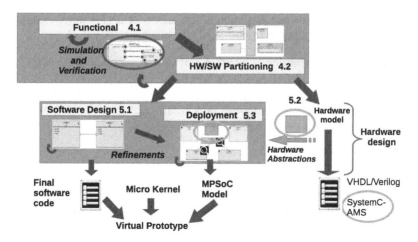

Fig. 1. Methodology: Integration in the TTool partitioning level [25, 26]. Numbers represent section numbers in the paper.

3.1   Multi-level Model-Based Design

Model-based engineering of (digital) embedded systems can be performed at different abstraction levels, grouped into two subsets: *functional* and *partitioning* (high level), *software component design* and *deployment* (low level), as shown in Fig. 1. Specific SysML views and diagrams have already been defined for each abstraction level [22].

The partitioning level features two sub-levels.

1. The purely *functional level* relies on logical time where functional operators describing the behavior of tasks. These operators can describe non deterministic behavior, and model in an abstract way the complexity of computations.
2. The *(system-level) mapping level* gives a physical time to complexity operations, thus giving a physical time to delays. However, the highly abstracted hardware components of our approach make these estimations imprecise: the values obtained—which might be used as a partitioning decision—are expected to be confirmed during the next levels.

At the software design level, tasks are further detailed and then deployed on more concrete hardware components. Thus, software deployment is intended to explore the interaction of software with all other components (digital and analog). The software design level thus includes two sub-levels.

1. At the software component design level, high-level timing constraints of software components can be evaluated by interactive simulation or formal verification, still without hardware.
2. The *deployment level* allows a designer to map software components onto hardware elements (CPU, memory, etc.) and then generating a virtual prototype. A cycle and bit accurate SystemC-based simulation [3] is then used

to obtain cycle-precise measurements. Thanks to this low-level simulation, mapping decisions taken at higher level can be checked again.

To closely analyze the deployment of software components, Analog/Mixed Signal components have to be precisely described. Indeed, since their semantics strongly differ from the one of digital components, the interactions between the two models of computations have to be closely captured. In [25] we further elaborate on semantic aspects, using SysML diagrams.

3.2   SystemC AMS

SystemC AMS makes it possible to model both digital components and analog components. Digital components rely on a a Discrete Event (DE) semantics, while analog components are described with the Timed Data Flow (TDF) Model of Computation, itself based on the timeless Synchronous Data Flow (SDF) semantics [31].

Discrete Event Model of Computation. A Discrete-Event (DE) simulation abstracts a system as a discrete sequence of events in time, where each event signals a change of state, in contrast to continuous simulation in which the system state changes continuously over time. A well-known example of a DE framework is Ptolemy II [35]. DE models in SystemC AMS are essentially SystemC descriptions, using its event-based simulation kernel [30]. DE modules have input and output ports, and contain SystemC code.

Timed Data Flow Model of Computation. In Timed Data Flow (TDF), continuous functions are sampled at discrete intervals. A TDF module is described with an attribute representing the time step and a processing function. A *processing function* is a mathematical function depending on the module inputs and/or internal states. At each time step, a TDF module first reads a fixed number of samples from each of its input ports, then executes its processing function, and finally writes a fixed number of samples to each of its output ports. TDF modules have the following attributes:

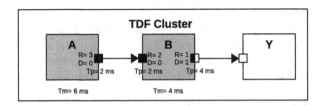

Fig. 2. TDF cluster with two TDF modules and one DE module [25].

- Module timestep (**Tm**) denotes the period during which the module will be activated. One module will only be activated if there are enough samples available at its input ports.
- Rate (**R**). Each module reads or writes a fixed number of data samples each time it is activated. This number is annotated to the ports and it is known as the port rate.
- Port timestep (**Tp**) is the period between module port activation. It also denotes the time interval between two samples that are read or written.
- Delay (**D**) D can be assigned to a port to make it store a given number of samples at each activation, and read or write them in the next activation.

A TDF *cluster* consists of TDF and DE modules connected by signals, which transmit the data samples. Figure 2 shows a TDF cluster with the representation defined in the SystemC AMS standard. [7]. The DE module Y is represented as a white block, the two TDF modules A and B as gray blocks. TDF ports are black squares, TDF converter ports are black and white squares, and DE ports are white squares. TDF signals are arrows. The converter port, shown as black-and white squares, serves as interfaces between the TDF and DE MoC. The module timestep of A is 6 ms, its port timestep 2 ms and its rate 3. B has a port and module timestep of 4 ms and a rate of 1. B has a delay of 1.

The module timestep must be consistent with regards to the rate and time step of all ports of a module. The relation between timesteps and rates is as follows, where T_m is the module timestep, T_{pi} and T_{po} are the input and output port timesteps, R_{pi} and R_{po} the input and output port rates, respectively:

$$T_m = T_{pi} \times R_{pi} = T_{po} \times R_{po}$$

Once this consistency has been validated for a particular cluster by propagating the parameters downstream and upstream [1], the cluster may operate at any frequency. In the example shown in Fig. 2, there are TDF ports between A and B outputs to a converter port. Port rates, delays and timesteps as well as module timesteps are given for the TDF modules. The equation is satisfied for modules A (6 ms = 2 ms × 3) and B (4 ms = 4 ms × 1). A valid *schedule* is the execution order of the TDF modules, in our case A-B-A-B-B.

3.3 Co-Simulation

TDF clusters can contain TDF and DE blocks; in SystemC AMS, they are instantiated together in a common SystemC AMS top cell. Whenever TDF and DE modules coexist in a SystemC AMS specification, they are co-simulated: the SystemC kernel **controls** the AMS kernel which runs continuously until interrupted.

According to [15], when a SystemC AMS simulation is being executed, the execution of the SystemC DE simulation kernel is blocked while the SystemC AMS simulation kernel continues running. As a consequence, the DE simulation time (t_{DE}) does not advance at all, while the TDF simulation time (t_{TDF}) runs according to the time steps of the TDF modules and ports. On access to a TDF converter port, the SystemC AMS simulation kernel is interrupted and yields to the SystemC DE simulation kernel. This way, t_{DE} advances until it is equal to t_{TDF}. In general, t_{TDF} runs ahead of the t_{DE}. Recent contributions have shown how to check these causality aspects before simulation [2] or even before code generation [14,26]; the latter approach has been adopted in TTool.

Obviously, the complexity of this co-simulation also depends on the complexity of software components running in the digital part. It is thus a common situation to run a full-system virtual platform with an operating system and software loaded into a (simulated) memory.

4   Partitioning Level

The paper proposes further extension of the high-level modeling and verification capabilities of an existing framework, named TTool [4], in order to better design such complex applications, where analog parts interact with each other as well as with the digital domain.

In TTool, functionality and hardware are described with SysML-like diagrams, and the behavior of functions is described with activity diagrams [5]. Just like for digital functions, the behavior of each SystemC AMS module is captured with an extended SysML activity diagrams. Once functions have been associated with hardware components, C++ simulation code can be generated automatically from these. In Fig. 1, the red circle points out the analog extensions at partitioning level, and the orange circles highlight the extensions at software design level. A separate SystemC AMS prototype is generated for co-simulation (lower right).

4.1   Functional Modeling and Verification

The following paragraph extends the formalization of the two levels of modeling and their interaction [23,25].

Structural Modeling. A partitioning $\mathcal{P}$ is defined as a set of models $\mathcal{P} = (F, A, M)$, with F a Functional Model, A an Architecture Model, and M a Mapping Model. The functional model is defined as $F = (T, C)$ where T is a set of tasks, and C is a set of communications between tasks. A Task t is defined as $t = (Attr, B)$ with $Attr$ a set of attributes, and B a behavior. From a SysML point of view, block definition and internal block diagrams are used to capture functions and architectural components. Mapping is performed with allocations.

Behavioral Modeling. We model all tasks $t \in T$, be they later implemented in hardware (analog or digital) or software. Essentially, we use an extended form of *activity diagrams* as e.g. in [5]. Behavioral diagrams capture control flow in the form of e.g. non-deterministic and guarded choices, and general control operators. Specific operators can be used for read and write operations on channels, and sending and receiving of events. Data abstraction is a key point: channels do not convey values, but only a number of samples, while events are used as control signals. Events can only occur in the digital part or at the interface between the analog and digital part, the notion of channel in TDF clusters being flow-based.

More formally, a behavior $B = (Ctrl, CommOp, CompOp, Con())$ consists of interconnected control operators $Ctrl$, communication operators $CommOp$ and complexity operators $CompOp$ modeling the complexity of algorithms through the description of a min/max interval of integer/float/custom operations. $Con : op \mapsto op$ connects operators together. The left hand side of Fig. 3 shows typical operators of activity diagrams. Their basic translation into SystemC AMS is given on the right.

Modeling DE Modules. Discrete Event (DE) modules can easily be captured as functions. A customized activity diagram is associated to each of them, as for other functions [25].

- To capture the semantics of transfer of data between DE modules, channel and event communications between functions can be used.
- Choices are obviously modeled with the choice operator. Non deterministic choices are not allowed. Choices can thus be translated with "if"/"else" statements in SystemC.
- To capture the estimated execution time of the module, we have added a *complexity* operator abstracting an algorithm. In lower levels (e.g, software component design), these operators are expected to be replaced by their related algorithm.

Modeling Analog Modules. Capturing analog modules at a high abstraction level is much less obvious, since activity diagrams have a discrete-based semantics. All communication between primitive modules is done by exchange of data samples via channels, activation is based on data reception; events are not permitted. Between analog modules and the MPSoC, events can be used: thus we model the fact that the MPSoC regularly requests data from the cluster.

From a behavioral point of view, extended activity diagrams are used as follows:

- Branches stemming from choices (simulation code relies on "if" statements in the TDF *processing* function) can be directly translated into guarded branch control structures in the activity diagram.
- A TDF *Module Timestep* is abstracted with a *physical delay* operator of our activity diagrams. The schedule, i.e. the execution order of TDF modules in its cluster, is either estimated or derived from the SystemC AMS model, if the latter already exists.

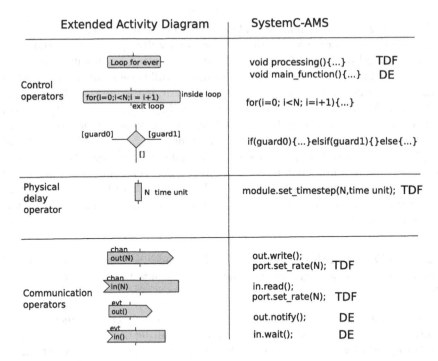

Fig. 3. Relation between operators in extended activity diagrams of the TTool functional level (on the left) and their counterparts in SystemC AMS [25] (on the right).

- Activity diagrams support read and write operations on channels. They allow to specify a *number of data samples* written to/read from a channel, which can be interpreted as the port rate at which samples are written to/read from a port in TDF.
- Infinite repetition of the cluster schedule (in a data flow-like fashion) is captured by an infinite loop in the activity diagram.
- To represent transition between TDF and DE, we use composite components (i.e. composite SysML blocks). A composite component may contain either TDF or DE modules but not both; converter ports are modeled by composite ports. TDF converter ports are represented by composite ports.

Port timesteps are not represented in the functional view, neither are delays (in the sense of SystemC AMS: they are not related to delays in activity diagrams): they can be used at software/hardware design level only, in the SystemC AMS representation. The specification of delays makes it possible to calculate the schedule and enforce causality (see Sect. 3.2).

Figure 3 shows the relation between TDF/DE cluster and activity diagrams.

For the example in Fig. 2, Fig. 4(a) shows the functional view and related activity diagrams. Block A writes a signal which is read by block B, which in turn communicates with block Y; the conversion port is represented by a composite port.

4.2 Hardware Components

At partitioning level, hardware components are very abstract: communication, execution and storage nodes are defined separately. A CPU and its operating systems are defined as a set of parameters such as an average cache-miss ratio, go-to-idle time, context switch penalty, etc. We take into consideration the following execution nodes:

– Central Processing Unit (CPU)
– Hardware Accelerator (HWA)
– Field Programmable Gate Array (FPGA)

We relate tasks (i.e. blocks of the Functional View) to architectural blocks using allocations. A task mapped to a processor will be implemented in software, while a task mapped to a hardware accelerator or FPGA will be implemented in hardware. In the case of CPUs or FPGAs, several tasks can be mapped to the same node. However, only one task can be allocated to a hardware accelerator. Simulation of mapping models helps understanding the performance of the mapped system.

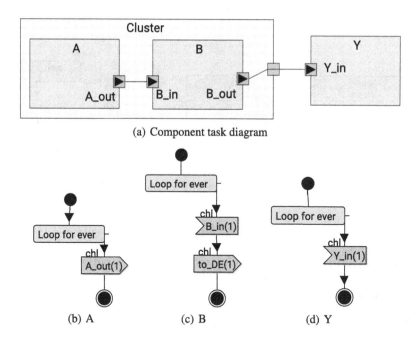

Fig. 4. Functional view: (a) Component task diagram (b, c, d) Activity diagrams.

5 Software Design Level

Once a satisfactory partitioning has been found, the software design level is intended to refine software functions and to validate them with more concrete hardware components. This latter validation is performed thanks to a model-to-virtual-prototype transformation described in [22].

5.1   Software Components

In order to switch from the partitioning to the software design level, we generalize the technique of model refinement described in [23]. We use AVATAR [34], a SysML-like representation, to represent software. Our implementation does not entirely comply with the OMG-based SysML, in so far as our block instance diagrams merge block and internal block diagrams, modify SysML parametric diagrams to express properties and do not support continuous flows. The software model $S = (T, I)$ can thus be defined as a set of tasks t and interactions i between tasks. While a partitioning model expresses algorithms as abstract complexity operations and communications in terms of their size, a software design model models the controllers of software tasks in a more precise way.

In the example of Fig. 2, let us suppose that software running on the MP-Soc consists in one task that sends an integer value to another task. On this level, block diagram and state machine show the software only, which would yield the block diagram (left) and state machines (right) in Fig. 5.

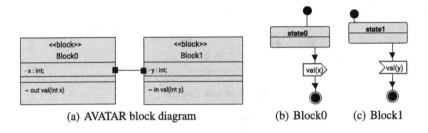

(a) AVATAR block diagram   (b) Block0   (c) Block1

Fig. 5. Software design view of the example in Fig. 2.

Algorithms and communications are described in more detail too. Complexity operators refer to the number of times a computation unit (e.g. the integer computation unit) must be used. Depending on the related execution node capacity, this results in a number of clock cycles of the related component. These operators are translated into either a time function $TF()$ or a sub-behavior $subB$. More formally, the transformation relation of partitioning behavior to software design behavior can be expressed as [23]: $B_P = (Ctrl, Comm, Comp) \rightarrow B_S = (Ctrl', Comm', TF, subB)$

When tasks of the functional view are split into several software components, the set of control/communication operators the initial functions used may change. If a Partitioning task t1 is split into multiple Software Design tasks t'_{11}, t'_{12}, then t_1's communications with other tasks may be to only t'_{11} or t'_{12}, or both, and new communications between t'_{11} and t'_{12} may be added. In a simple case, the complexity $Comp$ can be translated exclusively into *after* operations.

On the other hand, when the Software Design models add more detail on the implementation of algorithms, complexities are translated into a 'sub-behaviors', with a mix of control operators, communications, and time functions TF.

5.2   Analog and Digital Hardware Components

A specific SysML block diagram, named "SystemC AMS Panel" in TTool, is used to capture TDF clusters, including modules and port rates, delays, modules and port timesteps. It also contains those DE modules intended to be implemented on FPGA or ASIC, and TDF components. The TTool SystemC AMS panel [27] was designed to mimic as much as possible the graphical SystemC AMS notation from [1] as shown in Fig. 2.

Representing Hardware Clocks. As sampling plays a crucial role in the signal processing part of the EchOpen application, TTool SystemC AMS panel has been enriched with clocks. From a hardware point of view, a *clock* is a boolean signal that changes from 0 to 1 and vice versa at regular intervals. Most DE modules are thus sensitive to a clock signal, i.e. they read a Boolean value from a clock port. On the rising edge of the clock, the data arriving on the input port is transferred to the output port.

The same clock can be shared between several DE modules. It is also very frequent that the entire system has the same master clock, but there may be multiple clocks (e.g. for subsampling purpose). In order not to overload diagrams, we do not draw the interconnection of clock signals to the modules, but indicate the clock's name as a parameter in the DE module. A clock can be parameterized with frequency, units, start time, and other information (left side of Fig. 6).

Signal Processing Data Types. Signal processing applications in general, and medical imaging electronics in particular, require various data types, which were not implemented in the initial version of TTool's AMS extension, more targeted to control-bound applications like robotics and automotive. An enriched menu and code generation now covers a wide range of data types, like floating point or, particularly important for hardware design, bit vectors (right side of Fig. 6).

Lines of code for clock instantiation in the SystemC AMS topcell (the equivalent of a main program which among others instantiates hardware components and connects them by signals) can be automatically generated from the above information, thus saving a lot of time compared to a manual implementation.

5.3   Deployment Diagram

The software model can at first be functionally simulated, using the AVATAR interactive simulator, taking into account temporal operators but ignoring hardware, operating system and middleware.

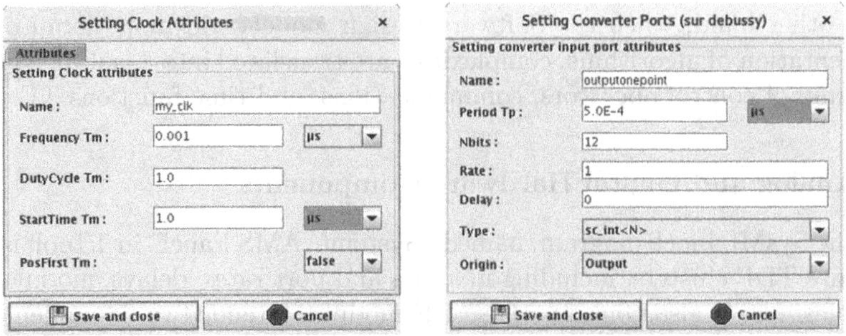

Fig. 6. Clock dialog window for DE components (left) Data type menu (right).

In order to get an overview of the entire platform consisting of software (running on digital components of the MPSoC part), digital and analog components in the TDF clusters, SystemC AMS clusters are displayed in the AVATAR deployment panel. The two simulators, one for the digital part in SystemC [40] and another for the analog part in SystemC AMS [18], are interconnected by an interface, guaranteeing correct timing by detecting causality problems early in the design process [14]. This simulation helps to identify logical modeling bugs, while the concrete performance can be obtained by generating a C code of the software tasks and executing it.

Taking up the small introductory example from Sect. 4.1, as shown in (Fig. 7), we present on the left the AMS representation; the DE block Y is clocked. The right hand side shows the deployment for two software tasks *Block0* and *Block1* mapped to the CPU and one integer channel *val* mapped to memory. We also have to add the interface to the MPSoC (not shown here).

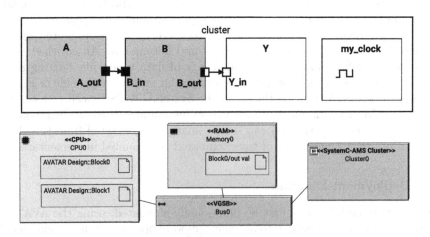

Fig. 7. Introductory example AMS (top) and deployment (bottom) representation.

Now, on the one hand, from the SysML-like representation of SystemCAMS clusters in TTool, SystemC AMS code is generated. On the other hand, from the software, C-POSIX threads running on a MPSoC under an lightweight operating system are generated [3, 21].

6   Case Study

The aim of the following section is to illustrate the use of our new extensions as well as the interactions between the two abstraction levels. By choosing a complex and realistic system with multiple facets, we show the whole range of capabilities of our extensions.

The case study stems from the early design phase of a low-cost echo-stethoscope developed in the EchOpen project [17], where system-level designers cooperate closely with hardware designers, with the aim of designing low-cost and portable echography device for pre-echography medical exploration, primarily for emerging countries but also in case of difficult circumstances [33, 42]. An echo-stethoscope is an equivalent of the doctor's stethoscope that is used to auscultate the body and reveal diseases, but with ultra-sound signals.

Fig. 8. EchOpen system.

The objective of the system described by Fig. 8 is to acquire ultrasound signals with a probe (transducer), then to extract the useful signals and to store them to a memory before sending them by wifi to a smartphone for image processing.

Signal Acquisition. The signal acquisition is represented by a TDF module featuring a sine wave generator (*SineGenerator*) and an Analog to Digital Converter (*ADC*), which takes the samples from the probe and converts them into digital values.

Envelope Detection. The envelope of the ultra-sound power gives the echographic image. So, the role of envelope detection [36] is to extract the useful signal: a number of samples are compared to those produced by a sample generator (sampling rate defined by the designer) and the highest value is extracted among them. Envelope detection is modeled as digital (DE) blocks.

Finally, the values are transferred by hardware allowing Direct Memory Access (*DMA*) in order to be sent to the processor for image processing. The SPI module, which is in charge of this, waits until the envelope detection for the whole image is completed and then sends it to the SoC interface.

Scan Conversion. The scan conversion [39] is used to build the image from ultrasound signals envelope and is usually done by software, which the echOpen design team intends to run on a smartphone. That consists of translating a point from polar coordinates to Cartesian ones in order to display it on a screen. In fact, it can be viewed as a chain of operations. First, image data is read from the Envelope Detection hardware. In our setting of early design space exploration, a data file serves for test purposes. From data read from the file, a data structure is built, containing the image and several parameters. Two operations are applied one after another, scan conversion itself and modification of the image background. Finally, the resulting image, which should be of sufficient quality, can either be displayed on the smartphone or used for other purpose.

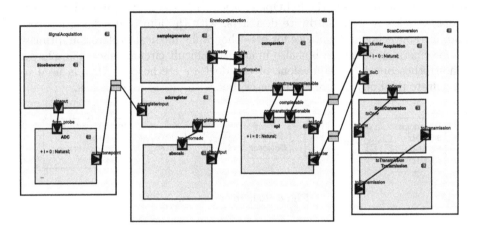

Fig. 9. EchOpen application functional view [25] (left, center) software part (right).

6.1   Partitioning Level

Functional View. Figure 9 shows the functional view. Green blocks represent functional components connected through ports to data channels (in blue) and event channels (in mauve). Yellow blocks represent composite components. On the left of the figure, the analog modules *SineGenerator* and *ADC* are shown as distinct sub components within the *SignalAcquisition* composite components. Figure 10 shows selected *activity diagrams* capturing behavior. The first one, represents the analog-to-digital converter module ADC, the second is what will later become a software task reading the image line by line. Computation times are taken, where possible, from the original SystemC AMS model as explained in Sect. 4; this is the case for ADC but not for SoC Interface and Acquisition, which we newly developed.

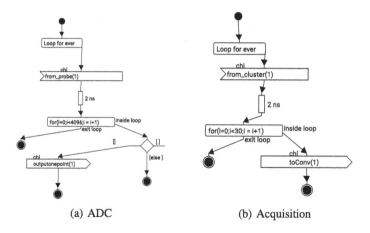

(a) ADC   (b) Acquisition

Fig. 10. Activity diagrams of selected functional blocks.

Mapping View. While all other functionalities are to be implemented in hardware, scan conversion must be implemented in software running a general purpose CPU. The mapping view thus contains an FPGA, which is at this level of abstraction simply simulated as a n-core processor, with n being the number of tasks mapped. An alternative mapping, where all DE tasks are implemented in software and thus mapped to a second CPU, can easily be evaluated as well. This modification of the diagrams takes only a few seconds, unlike for a real ASIC of FPGA implementation.

All diagrams are converted into C++ before being simulated or formally verified (the simulator can among others generate a reachability graph, which in our case has around 900 states). The simulation engine is predictive: each processing element advances at its own pace until a system event (data transfer, a synchronization event, etc.) invalidates current transactions. Then, the latter are cut back as much as necessary in the past, and the simulation continues from the cut transactions.

6.2   Component Design Level

Once the hardware/software partitioning has been decided—in the following we take as a starting point a possible partitioning shown in Fig. 11—hardware and software are modeled apart. On the one hand, from the SysML-like representation of SystemC AMS clusters in TTool, after checking schedulability and causality [13, 26], SystemC AMS code is generated. On the other hand, from the software, which can be of significant size and require full-system simulation, Posix threads running on a MPSoC under an lightweight operating system are generated [3, 21].

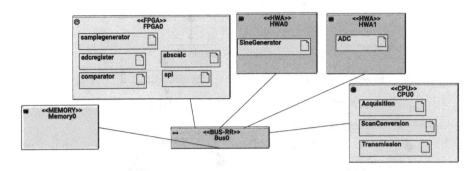

Fig. 11. Initial partitioning level architecture and mapping diagram [25].

SystemC AMS Representation. Figure 12 shows TTool's representation for our System C AMS model. The block on the lower right represents a General Purpose Input/Output (GPIO) interface that is responsible for the synchronization with the MPSoC [13]. The blocks from partitioning level can easily be recognized: these are the blocks of the left and central part of Fig. 9 (sample generator, comparator, ...). Analog blocks are, like in the SystemC AMS standard graphical representation, colored in grey.

In Fig. 12, two clocks (see Sect. 5.2) are captured with two specific blocks on the lower left of the cluster. In order to improve readability, our design choice was to not show the signals between clocks and the clock input ports of the DE modules. As shown in Fig. 6, every DE model contains the name of the clock that commands it. All modules except *adcre* use *my_clock*, which is the working frequency (i.e. the global clock) of the digital circuit(a FPGA in our case), while the latter uses *my_clock1* for rate conversion (super-sampling of the ADC signal), which runs at a slower frequency.

Software Component Design. The fact that EchOpen in an open hardware and software project allowed us to access realistic image processing code. An experimental implementation of the scan conversion software in C already existed and served as basis for the modeling of the software components in AVATAR. Fig. 13 shows the AVATAR block-based representation of the scan conversion software. The first block, *Acquisition*, reads a fixed number of lines from the file emitted by the EnvelopeDetection, then builds a structure with some additional parameters. Sticking to the method described in Sect. 5.1, we refine the scan conversion part so that the two distinct tasks of image processing, ScanConversion and ChangeBackground, become explicit (sub-tasks in our terminology). Also, the transmission of the resulting image is now split into two tasks, *SaveOrTransmit*, which extracts the image from the data structure and either stores it or sends it to the mobile network and *Disallocation*, which frees the memory of the data structures.

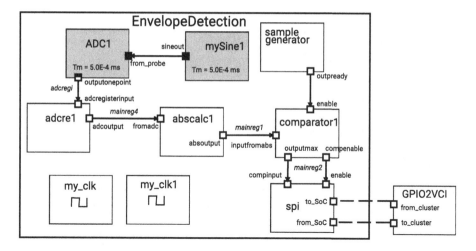

Fig. 12. SystemC AMS representation in TTool.

Note that this data structure model is strongly simplified, since the actual structure contains sub-structures for tensors, as well as floating point parameters. Missing in the block diagrams, they are still present in the actual C code that is inserted in the prototyping part of the block.

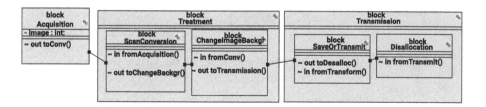

Fig. 13. Scan conversion modeled in AVATAR.

Figure 14 shows the acquisition state which makes the connection to the SystemC AMS cluster. Using an *entry code* mechanism available for AVATAR state machine diagram states—inserting C code that is taken over in the generated POSIX tasks—we represent the reading from the EnvelopeDetection cluster (Fig. 14) by a read primitive from the GPIO interface. A counter keeps track of the number of lines that are transmitted from the file and written into the Image part of the data structure.

Fig. 14. Acquisition block modeled in AVATAR (left) and entry code (right).

Deployment. On this level, we determine the mapping of blocks to processors, the mapping of channels to memory banks, the choice of interconnect (bus, mesh network, ...). Time- and resource- consuming tasks such as the scan conversion algorithm itself, may be deployed on a dedicated CPU in an exploration process. Figure 15 shows a deployment on a three-processor platform, where the software blocks *Acquisition*, *ScanConversion* and *Transmission* are mapped to one CPU each. In the prototype generated from the deployment diagram, software appli-

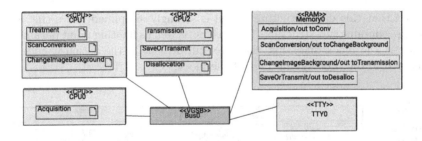

Fig. 15. Possible mapping of software tasks on the virtual prototype.

cations (in the case of EchOpen, the scan conversion) run on the CPU(s) of the digital platform and write or read values from the TDF clusters. Thus, for a precise simulation of **all** parts of the system, whether mapped to analog hardware, FPGA or general purpose processors, have to appear in the deployment diagram. A specific SysML block diagram (grey in the upper right of the figure) is used to capture the interface to the SystemC AMS cluster.

Validation of the AMS Schedule. From a TDF block diagram, a coherent schedule can be computed, and causality issues between DE and TDF modules automatically detected.

Figure 16 shows TTool with SystemC AMS/SystemC co-simulation for the case study application as featured by the virtual machine available under [24]. On the upper left, the invocation of the two simulators is shown. The lower right shows the TTY (the console log) of the SystemC simulation, tracing the progress of the software part. In the background, the TTool AMS panel is shown, with the validation and code generation window.

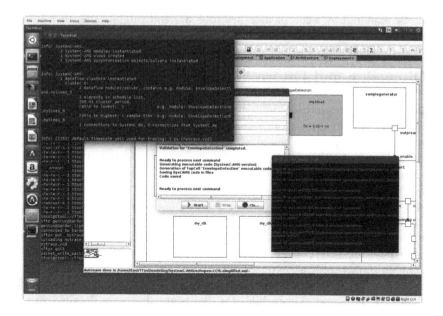

Fig. 16. Tool overview: screen shot of the virtual machine.

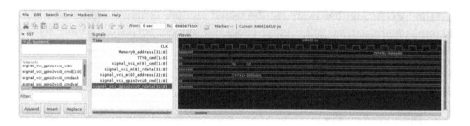

Fig. 17. Trace generated from the SystemC simulation.

Validation of the Generated Code. In the work described in [25], the digital platform running the scan conversion software had not yet been modeled; only the SystemC AMS part was simulated in a stand-alone manner.

Now, we can validate the full system on both partitioning and software design level. The integration of SystemC AMS made it necessary to add facilities for tracing analog, thus continuous, signals, in the virtual prototype. We thus obtain one trace for the SoCLib part and one for the SystemC AMS part. Figure 17 shows part of the trace for a mono-processor platform, using the gtkwave tool [11]: a snapshot of the clock signal, the processor command (m_0 is processor 0), the TTY, address and data transmitted from the processor and the signal transiting via *gpio2vci*, the GPIO interface between the SystemC and SystemC AMS parts of the platforms. There is also an analog counterpart of this trace tan can be explored by a complementary tool [37] and validated against a hand-written SystemC AMS model.

7   Discussion and Future Work

We show how to take into account digital and analog aspects of an embedded system from the very first modeling phases onwards, until a low-level virtual prototype. For that purpose, we extend TTool with new SysML models able to capture SystemC AMS components in an abstract way and reuse the existing simulation and validation methods.

We can now take into account software running on the digital part of the platform for full-system simulation. Simulation parameters at partitioning level are initially based on first assumptions; once software design and deployment levels have been designed, more accurate estimations of the execution time and valid schedules for TDF clusters can be fed back to the partitioning levels.

What we show here is an extensive case study stemming from the early very design process of an echo-stethoscope. SystemC AMS itself is an abstraction of the analog hardware. Meanwhile, the hardware design is detailed further; a first validation on a FPGA prototype is still under way. Moreover, the real system uses a WIFI interface. While developing the SystemC AMS models of the wireless connections, we use read/write on files instead. Most importantly, once the FPGAs and hardware can be tested and performance evaluated with a real implementation, we will counter-check our models, then start a more refined design space exploration of the software.

References

1. Accellera Systems Initiative: SystemC AMS extensions Users Guide, Version 1.0 (2010)
2. Andrade, L., Maehne, T., Vachoux, A., Ben Aoun, C., Pêcheux, F., Louërat, M.M.: Pre-simulation formal analysis of synchronization issues between discrete event and timed data flow models of computation. In: Design, Automation and Test in Europe, DATE Conference (2015)
3. Apvrille, L., Becoulet, A.: Prototyping an embedded automotive system from its UML/SysML models. In: ERTSS 2012, Toulouse (2012)
4. Apvrille, L.: Webpage of TTool (2003). https://ttool.telecom-paris.fr/
5. Apvrille, L., Muhammad, W., Ameur-Boulifa, R., Coudert, S., Pacalet, R.: A UML-based environment for system design space exploration. In: 2006 13th IEEE International Conference on Electronics, Circuits and Systems, pp. 1272–1275. IEEE (2006)
6. Balarin, F., Watanabe, Y., Hsieh, H., Lavagno, L., Passerone, C., Sangiovanni-Vincentelli, A.L.: Metropolis: an integrated electronic system design environment. IEEE Comput. **36**(4), 45–52 (2003)
7. Barnasconi, M., Einwich, K., Grimm, C., Maehne, T., Vachoux, A.: SystemC AMS Extensions 2.0 Language Reference Manual. Accellera systems initiative (2016)

8. Beyond Dreams Consortium: Beyond Dreams (Design Refinement of Embedded Analogue and Mixed-Signal Systems) (2008–2011). projects.eas.iis.fraunhofer.de/beyonddreams
9. Blochwitz, T., et al.: The functional mockup interface for tool independent exchange of simulation models. In: 8th International Modelica Conference, Dresden, Germany, pp. 105–114 (2011)
10. Bouquet, F., Gauthier, J.M., Hammad, A., Peureux, F.: Transformation of SysML structure diagrams to VHDL-AMS. In: 2012 Second Workshop on Design, Control and Software Implementation for Distributed MEMS, pp. 74–81. IEEE (2012)
11. Bybell, T.: GtkWave electronic waveform viewer (2010). gtkwave.sourceforge.net
12. Concepcion, A.I., Zeigler, B.P.: DEVS formalism: a framework for hierarchical model development. IEEE Trans. Softw. Eng. 14(2), 228–241 (1988)
13. Cortés Porto, R.: Integration of SystemC-AMS Simulation Platforms into TTool. Master's thesis, Technische Universität Kaiserslautern (2018)
14. Cortés Porto, R., Genius, D., Apvrille, L.: Modeling and virtual prototyping for embedded systems on mixed-signal multicores. In: RAPIDO (2019)
15. Damm, M., Grimm, C., Haas, J., Herrholz, A., Nebel, W.: Connecting SystemC-AMS models with OSCI TLM 2.0 models using temporal decoupling. In: FDL, pp. 25–30 (2008)
16. Davare, A., et al.: A next-generation design framework for platform-based design. In: DVCon, vol. 152 (2007)
17. EchOpen community: designing an open-source and low-cost echo-stethoscope (2017). http://www.echopen.org/
18. Einwich, K.: SystemC AMS PoC2.1 Library, COSEDA, Dresden (2016)
19. Fritzson, P., Engelson, V.: Modelica—a unified object-oriented language for system modeling and simulation. In: Jul, E. (ed.) ECOOP 1998. LNCS, vol. 1445, pp. 67–90. Springer, Heidelberg (1998). https://doi.org/10.1007/BFb0054087
20. Gamatié, A., et al.: A model-driven design framework for massively parallel embedded systems. ACM Trans. Embed. Comput. Syst. 10(4), 39 (2011)
21. Genius, D., Apvrille, L.: Virtual yet precise prototyping: an automotive case study. In: ERTSS 2016, Toulouse (2016)
22. Genius, D., Li, L.W., Apvrille, L.: Model-driven performance evaluation and formal verification for multi-level embedded system design. In: MODELSWARD (2017)
23. Genius, D., Li, L.W., Apvrille, L.: Multi-level Latency Evaluation with an MDE Approach. In: MODELSWARD (2018)
24. Genius, D.: Webpage of TTool AMS extensions (2020). https://www-soc.lip6.fr/trac/ttool-ams
25. Genius, D., Bournias, I., Apvrille, L., Chotin, R.: High-level partitioning and design space exploration for cyber physical systems. In: MODELSWARD (2020)
26. Genius, D., Cortés Porto, R., Apvrille, L., Pêcheux, F.: A tool for high-level modeling of analog/mixed signal embedded systems. In: MODELSWARD (2019)
27. Genius, D., Cortés Porto, R., Apvrille, L., Pêcheux, F.: A framework for multi-level modeling of analog/mixed signal embedded systems. In: Hammoudi, S., Pires, L.F., Selić, B. (eds.) MODELSWARD 2019. CCIS, vol. 1161, pp. 201–224. Springer, Cham (2020). https://doi.org/10.1007/978-3-030-37873-8_9
28. Guo, L., Zhu, Q., Nuzzo, P., Passerone, R., Sangiovanni-Vincentelli, A., Lee, E.A.: Metronomy: a function-architecture co-simulation framework for timing verification of cyber-physical systems. In: Proceedings of the 2014 International Conference on Hardware/Software Codesign and System Synthesis, p. 24. ACM (2014)
29. H-Inception Consortium: Heterogeneous Inception Project (2012–2015). https://www-soc.lip6.fr/trac/hinception

30. IEEE: SystemC. IEEE Standard 1666–2011 (2011)
31. Lee, E.A., Messerschmitt, D.G.: Synchronous data flow. Proc. IEEE **75**(9), 1235–1245 (1987)
32. Li, L.W., Genius, D., Apvrille, L.: Formal and virtual multi-level design space exploration. In: Pires, L.F., Hammoudi, S., Selic, B. (eds.) MODELSWARD 2017. CCIS, vol. 880, pp. 47–71. Springer, Cham (2018). https://doi.org/10.1007/978-3-319-94764-8_3
33. Mancuso, F.J.N., et al.: Focused cardiac ultrasound using a pocket-size device in the emergency room. Arquivos brasileiros de cardiologia **103**(6), 530–537 (2014)
34. Pedroza, G., Knorreck, D., Apvrille, L.: AVATAR: a SysML environment for the formal verification of safety and security properties. In: The 11th IEEE Conference on Distributed Systems and New Technologies (NOTERE), Paris, France (2011)
35. Ptolemy.org (ed.): System Design, Modeling, and Simulation using Ptolemy II. Univ. Berkeley (2014)
36. Qiu, W., Yu, Y., Tsang, F.K., Sun, L.: An FPGA-based open platform for ultrasound biomicroscopy. IEEE Trans. Ultrason. Ferroelectr. Freq. Control **59**(7), 1432–1442 (2012)
37. Quillevere, H.: Gtk Analog Wave viewer (2019). http://www.rvq.fr/linux/gaw.php
38. Selic, B., Gérard, S.: Modeling and Analysis of Real-Time and Embedded Systems with UML and MARTE: Developing Cyber-Physical Systems. Elsevier, Amsterdam (2013)
39. Sikdar, S., Managuli, R., Mitake, T., Hayashi, T., Kim, Y.: Programmable ultrasound scan conversion on a media-processor-based system. In: Medical Imaging: Visualization, Display, and Image-Guided Procedures, vol. 4319, pp. 699–711. Int. Society for Optics and Photonics (2001)
40. SocLib consortium: The SoCLib project: An Integrated System-on-Chip Modelling and Simulation Platform (2003). www.soclib.fr
41. Taha, S., Radermacher, A., Gérard, S.: An entirely model-based framework for hardware design and simulation. In: Hinchey, M., et al. (eds.) BICC/DIPES -2010. IAICT, vol. 329, pp. 31–42. Springer, Heidelberg (2010). https://doi.org/10.1007/978-3-642-15234-4_5
42. Tse, K.H., Luk, W.H., Lam, M.C.: Pocket-sized versus standard ultrasound machines in abdominal imaging. Singapore Med. J. **55**(6), 325 (2014)
43. Vachoux, A., Grimm, C., Einwich, K.: Analog and mixed signal modelling with SystemC-AMS. In: ISCAS (3), pp. 914–917. IEEE (2003)
44. Vidal, J., de Lamotte, F., Gogniat, G., Soulard, P., Diguet, J.P.: A co-design approach for embedded system modeling and code generation with UML and MARTE. In: DATE, pp. 226–231. IEEE (2009)

Applications and Software Development

ProvAnalyser: A Framework for Scientific Workflows Provenance

Anila Sahar Butt$^{(\boxtimes)}$ and Peter Fitch

CSIRO Land and Water, Canberra, Australia
{anila.butt,peter.fitch}@csiro.au

Abstract. The increasing ability of data-driven science is resulting in a growing need for applications that are under the control of data-centric workflows, also known as scientific workflows. The focus of this work is on provenance collection for these workflows, necessary to validate the workflow and to determine the quality of generated data products. However, the act of instrumenting a workflow engine for provenance collection is burdensome. This complex task requires adding hooks to the workflow engine to capture provenance, which can cause perturbation in execution. We address the challenge of extracting provenance data in the form of a knowledge graph from the event logs of the workflows to record critical information about the applications and the workflows. We present an ontology-based framework for provenance collection using the event logs of workflow engine. Further, we reduce provenance use cases to SPARQL queries over captured provenance knowledge graph. Performance evaluation demonstrates that the framework is capable of reconstructing complete data and invocation dependency graphs from one or various execution traces.

Keywords: Provenance model · Workflow provenance · Provenance use cases

1 Introduction

The advent of inexpensive specialised devices and sensor networks is promoting data-driven science by feeding data into scientific applications [29]. Data-driven scientific workflows are a tool to model such data-driven scientific investigations where data passes from process to process as it is transformed and used in complex models [4]. Scientific workflows are tools for specifying and automating scientific investigations as repetitive experiments [10]. Once specified and shared, a workflow becomes a useful building block that can subsequently be combined or modified to develop new experiments [4].

Workflows are implemented in many ways such as bash or Python scripts [25] and using frameworks such as Apache Spark and its variations [16]. However,

This paper is an extended version of [5].

© Springer Nature Switzerland AG 2021
S. Hammoudi et al. (Eds.): MODELSWARD 2020, CCIS 1361, pp. 99–120, 2021.
https://doi.org/10.1007/978-3-030-67445-8_5

they are commonly modelled and executed using engines named Scientific Workflow Management Systems (SWfMSs) [9]. SWfMSs have become a necessary tool for many applications, enabling the composition and execution of complex analysis on distributed resources [7]. Various SWfMSs have been proposed and developed for specifying and enacting workflows (e.g., Taverna [19], Kepler [2], Triana [30], and YAWL [31]). These systems leverage distributed and high-performance computing technologies to provide cutting edge data analytic services to the data scientists for implementing data-intensive pipelines [22]. The underline technologies have evolved a line of research i.e., provenance collection and representation alongside the research into the workflow systems.

Provenance is defined in Oxford English Dictionary as *"the source or origin of an object; its history and pedigree; a record of the ultimate derivation and passage of an item through its various owners."* In the context of scientific workflows, provenance concerns the reliability and integrity of workflows and their potentially complex data processes. Understanding provenance of a workflow is crucial to its users to identify bottlenecks, inefficiencies, learn how to improve them, and establish trust in data produced by these workflows. Moreover, to understand a workflow and how it may be used and(or) reproduced for their needs, scientists require access to some additional resources, such as annotations describing the workflow, datasets used and produced by the workflow, and provenance traces recording workflow executions.

Scientific workflow engines can integrate provenance component, which is an elegant solution but requires a significant effort to implement. It requires modifying the engine architecture to collect provenance data by adding hooks, which can lead to perturbation in execution. Another method is to collect provenance directly from the event logs of workflow engines. This method allows a thorough understanding of the provenance collection, storage and access requirements before integrating provenance component to these engines and avoid any performance issues. Furthermore, this approach provides a mean of collecting provenance of already executed workflows using their event logs. Since workflow provenance is event-based, i.e., capturing the significant events within a system, the event log is an essential source of provenance data. Logs are traditionally beneficial for auditing and identifying the root causes of failures in large systems. In addition, logs contain essential information about the events occur within a system, which result in generation of the data objects. It is established that intelligent logging and careful analysis of logs support extraction of the critical information about the system [27]. The provenance queries can be answered through manual analysis of workflows and their execution traces using their event logs. However, the rapid growth in size of the event logs and the cloud-based multi-tenant nature of these engines make such solutions increasingly inefficient.

In this paper, we show our work on workflow provenance collection from their event logs. We present **ProvAnalyser**[1], an ontology-based solution to collect and query provenance of the scientific workflows. The proposed solution transforms event logs into knowledge graphs using an ontology that supports a set of

---

[1] https://github.com/CSIRO-enviro-informatics/ProvAnalyser.

provenance queries. The initial version of this work is presented in [5]. In this paper, we extend our work in many ways: we present (1) **SWfPROV** ontology, a workflow engine independent model to collect and query the provenance of scientific workflows. Previously, we used an existing provenance model that has a few limitations as discussed later in this paper, (2) a generic architecture of a provenance collection and querying framework and a prototype for SenapsLAND workflow engine, (3) a revised architecture of ProvAnalyser by using WePROV provenance API for storage and analysis of provenance data instead of storing provenance knowledge graph in a local RDF store, (4) improved evaluation by collecting event logs of six months instead of three months event logs. Furthermore, we included one provenance use case and two provenance queries to analyse the impact of provenance on a workflow engine and its client applications.

The rest of the paper is organised as follows. In Sect. 2, we discuss the detail design of ProvAnalyser. In Sect. 3, we present a prototype of ProvAnalyser for SenapsLAND workflow engine. In Sect. 4, we present provenance use cases and queries. In Sect. 5, we discuss the steps required for large-scale deployment of the technology within the organisation. In Sect. 6, we review state-of-the-art and in Sect. 7, we conclude outlining future directions of research and development.

2 Scientific Workflow Provenance

In this section, we present ProvAnalyser that collects provenance data from event logs and stores it in an Quad store through WePROV provenance API. The users can perform analysis and exploration on provenance data through predefined or customised provenance queries.

2.1 Scientific Workflows

A workflow $\mathcal{W}$ is a directed graph, i.e., $\mathcal{W} = (\mathcal{M}, \mathcal{C})$ where $\mathcal{M}$ is a set of nodes representing workflow modules while the edges $\mathcal{C}$ describe dependencies between the modules. The modules $\mathcal{M}$ of the workflow $\mathcal{W}$ process data as input and generates output data. The data $\mathcal{D} = (\mathcal{I} \cup \mathcal{O})$ refer to inputs $\mathcal{I}$ and outputs $\mathcal{O}$ of the modules $\mathcal{M}$. The data could be structured, semi-structured or even unstructured data. In order to process $\mathcal{D}$, modules of the workflow $\mathcal{W}$ may require execution parameters $\mathcal{P}$. The general graph model for a workflow introduced above covers different, more constrained graph models, which coincide with workflow types used in various domains. For instance, depending on a domain, edges in $\mathcal{C}$ may represent data or control dependencies.

Based on the general workflow model described above, we further define a generic workflow execution model. In general, we assume that a workflow module $m \in \mathcal{M}$ is a black box where we have no knowledge about its semantics or performed computation. Then, m requires input data $\mathcal{I}_m$ and parameters $\mathcal{P}_m$ to produce output $\mathcal{O}_m$. The execution of a workflow yields an execution trace $\mathcal{T}$.

Here $\mathcal{T}$ is a directed acyclic graph $\mathcal{T} = (\mathcal{E}, \mathcal{UG})$ where $\mathcal{E}$ represents executions of modules during workflow execution (i.e., activation of modules in the workflow) and $\mathcal{UG}$ represents causal dependencies between these events (i.e., generation and usage of data of the modules in $\mathcal{W}$).

2.2   Scientific Workflow Provenance Model

To capture the provenance of workflows, we require a data model capable of capturing provenance metadata. Some generic and extendable provenance models do exist in the literature. PROV-DM is the World Wide Web Consortium (W3C)-recommended data model to record inter-operable provenance in heterogeneous environments, such as the Web [23]. PROV-DM is generic and domain-independent and does not cater to the specific requirements of particular systems or domain applications; rather, it provides extension points through which systems and applications can extend PROV-DM for their intended domains.

However, Scientific workflows are concerned with capturing provenance from complex computational pipelines commonly referred to as scientific workflows. Several recent community efforts have culminated with the development of generic models to represent the provenance of scientific workflows. To capture the provenance of scientific workflows, OPMW, Wf4Ever and ProvONE are considered as the most expressive workflow provenance models [28]. *OPMW* [13] is a conceptual model for the representation of prospective and retrospective provenance collected from the execution of scientific workflows. It is a specialisation of PROV and the OPM provenance models. *Wf4Ever* [4] extends PROV to present wfdesc and wfprov ontologies to describe prospective and retrospective provenance respectively. ProvONE [8] is a data model, built on PROV-DM, for scientific workflow provenance representation. It provides constructs to model workflow specification provenance (i.e., a set of instructions specifying how to run a workflow) and workflow execution provenance (i.e., the record of how the workflow is executed). ProvONE is a widely accepted workflow provenance model and is capable of capturing most of the provenance metadata discussed in Sect. 2.1. However, there are a few limitations that our proposed model aims to overcome:

- ProvONE models the relationship between processes through **Controller** class; However, the model does not specify the ports through which two processes connect to each other.
- ProvONE includes some classes that increase the size of the provenance knowledge graph, generated according to the model, without adding any value to the model. For instance, **Association** class in ProvONE connects processes to its execution and agent. This relationship is modelled as a binary relationship between process-to-execution and execution-to-agent. Such modelling reduces the size of knowledge graph, hence improving its query processing time.

We present SWfPROV - **S**cientific **W**ork**f**low **PROV**enance model shown in Fig. 1. The generalised workflow model, presented in Sect. 2.1, provides a basis for the provenance model. This model is designed by following a modular approach to enable its reusability, and has two main components.

The first component of the model defines **Workflow** as a set of {Process, DataLink, Port, Parameter}. These concepts correspond to {Module, Edge, Data, Parameter} as presented in Sect. 2.1. The various tasks which consti-tutes a workflow are represented by the **Process** class. The process can either be atomic or composite, the later case is specified through the *hasSubProcess* self-association. A workflow itself is a process. Each process may have a series of **Ports** that function as input ($\mathcal{I}$) or output ($\mathcal{O}$) ports. Processes are connected through a **DataLink**. A DataLink connects two processes through two Ports. The default parameters are represented by a **Parameter**.

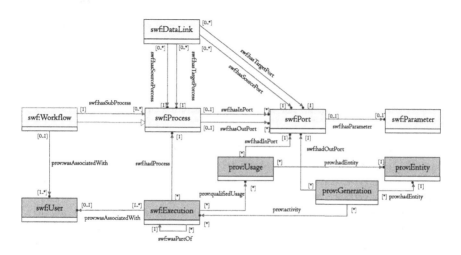

Fig. 1. Core structure of SENProv.

The second component of the model defines **Traces** as a set of {Execution, Usage, Generation, Entity, Agent}. An **Execution** represents the execution of a Process. If the process is a workflow, the execution represents a trace of workflow execution. The **Usage** class belongs to PROV Ontology and is the utilisation of an entity by execution at an inport. The **Generation** class also belongs to PROV Ontology and represents a generation of an entity by execution at an outport. An **Agent** is a person responsible for the execution. Its specification serves attribution and accountability purposes.

2.3   Architecture

Figure 2 shows the architecture of our proposed solution. It works as follows:

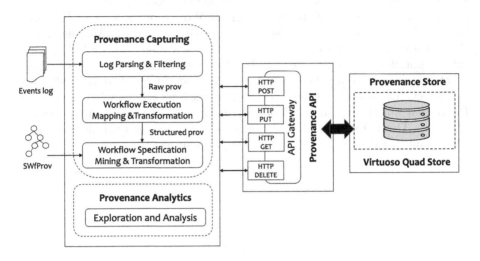

Fig. 2. The ProvAnalyser architecture.

1. For each workflow execution request, all traces related to the very request are parsed and provenance information (e.g., execution time, workflowId, processId, ports, and data ids) is filtered. **Log parser and filter** component transforms a verbose event log into concise raw provenance data.
2. **Execution mapping and transformation** component maps the raw provenance data to SWfPROV and generates structured provenance for that particular execution trace. This structured provenance is the RDF[2] description of retrospective provenance [18] (i.e., workflow execution).
3. **Specification mining and transformation** component infers prospective provenance [18] (i.e., workflow structure) from the retrospective provenance using SWfPROV. Further, it also links the retrospective provenance associated with the prospective provenance.
4. The extracted provenance data is stored or updated in a QuadStore[3] using the **WePROV provenance API**[4], which is a CSIRO's open-source RESTful provenance API.
5. **Provenance analysis component** allows users to explore and analyse provenance by designing provenance use cases, executing them as SPARQL queries over RDF store, and showcasing the results to their clients.

---

[2] https://www.w3.org/RDF/.

[3] http://docs.openlinksw.com/virtuoso/.

[4] RESTful API code is available at https://github.com/anilabutt/weprov.

ProvAnalyser supports a range of provenance use cases, such as explaining and reproducing the outcome of a workflow, tracing the effect of a change, and provenance analytics. It gives a structure to provenance information, which makes provenance data machine-readable and inter-operable. Moreover, it reduces the time needed for analysing workflow execution traces and allows semantic web experts to perform the task, thus distributing the load.

3 SenpsLAND Provenance: A ProvAnalyser Case Study

SenapsLAND[5] is a custom build workflow engine designed through the need of hosting applications from multiple domains (e.g., marine sensing, water management, and agriculture). The focus of SenapsLAND is on hosting, adapting, and sharing existing scientific models or analysis code across organisations and groups who use the sensor, climate, and other time-series data. In lieu of the dynamic nature of the platform, SenapsLAND considers its workflow provenance, which concerns the reliability and integrity of workflows and their potentially complex data processes. ProvAnalyser is implemented as a provenance web service to collect and query over data and workflow provenance within Senaps-LAND.

3.1 Workflows in SenapsLAND

The UML diagram in Fig. 3 represents the conceptual model for a workflow specification and execution in SenapsLAND.

A **workflow** is a multi-directed acyclic graph[6] made up of vertices and edges, which are referred as nodes and connections in SenapsLAND. A node can either be a **data node** or an **operator node**. An operator node hosts a model (executable code and its supporting files). The operator node has multiple **ports**, whereas a data node can only connect to an operator node through a port. Currently, a data node offers support for multi-stream, document, and grid data formats. A user **group** or an **organisation** puts a workflow execution request. With a **workflow execution** request, a **user** needs to specify a workflow to execute, a data node (i.e., input data), and a port on which a data node is connecting to an operator node. A workflow execution id is assigned to the run when it executes. Each operator node of a workflow is executed and has its operator node execution id, and corresponding input and output data nodes. Therefore, one complete workflow execution is composed of all of its operator nodes executions.

---

[5] https://research.csiro.au/dss/research/senaps/.
[6] https://en.wikipedia.org/wiki/Directed_acyclic_graph.

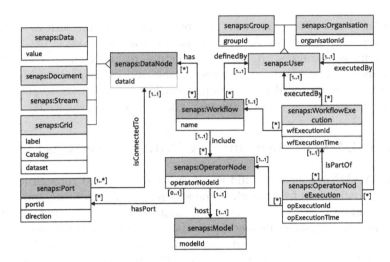

Fig. 3. SenapsLAND workflow specification (constructs in blue) and execution (constructs in grey) conceptual model UML diagram [5]. (Color figure online)

3.2 SENProv: Provenance Ontology for SenapsLAND

We use SWfPROV model to represent provenance data of SenapsLAND. We specialise SWfPROV in SENProv to capture the provenance of SenapsLAND workflows. In this regard, we need to model the relationship of SenapsLAND constructs with PROM-DM and SWfPROV constructs. Table 1 shows the mapping between SenapsLAND and PROV-DM or SWfPROV. In SENProv, each SenapsLAND class shown in *'SenapsLAND Concept'* column extends from its corresponding class presented in *'SWfPROV/PROV-DM'* column of the table, and SWfPROV or PROV-DM associations are used to model the corresponding SenapsLAND associations.

Based on the SenapsLAND conceptual model and its mapping to SWfPROV and PROV-DM, we present SENProv– an ontology to capture and represent SenapsLAND workflow provenance. Figure 4 highlights the most important classes and relationships that make up the SENProv ontology. The green ovals (i.e., PROV Entities), rectangles (i.e., PROV Activities), and pentagons (i.e., PROV Agents) represent the concepts in SenapsLAND whereas yellow and blue presents PROV-DM and SWfPROV concepts, respectively.

Table 1. SenapsLAND constructs mapping to SWfPROV and PROV-DM constructs.

SenapsLAND aspect	Construct type	SenapsLAND concept	SWfProv/ PROV-DM
Workflow	Class	Workflow	swf:Workflow
		OperatorNode	swf:Process
		DataNode	prov:Entity
		Port	swf:Port
		Model	prov:Plan
	Property	include	swf:hasSubProcess
		hasPort	swf:hasInPort
			swf:hasOutPort
Workflow execution	Class	WorkflowExecution	swf:Execution
		OperatorNodeExecution	swf:Execution
		Organisation	swf:Agent
		Group	swf:Agent
		Document	prov:Entity
		Stream	prov:Entity
		Grid	prov:Entity
	Property	initiatedBy	prov:agent
			prov:wasAssociatedWith
		isPartOf	swf:wasPartOf
		isConnectedTo	prov:hadEntity
		wfExecutionTime	prov:atTime
		opExecutionTime	prov:atTime
		value	prov:value

3.3 SenapsLAND Provenance Knowledge Graph

The provenance is captured from the event logs of SenapsLAND, which are configured for INFO level logging. At INFO level, informational messages that are most useful are logged for the monitoring and managing an application during execution. For example, an INFO level message describes an event type, timestamp, data used, and data generated by a workflow. Moreover, it considers an operator node and the model as a black box. Hence, INFO level logging enables the collection of coarse-grained provenance [18].

An entry in a SenapsLAND event log comprises of three main components: **DateTime** – Date and time of an event, **EventType** – the type of an event (e.g., EmptyWorkflowCreatedEvent, OperatorNodeAddedEvent, and DataUpdateEvent), and **Payload** – contains the information of an event including workflow and operator node execution ids, operator node, data nodes, ports, and data type (depending upon the event type). When a workflow executes in SenapsLAND, the event log records twelve to fourteen different events for each operator node of a workflow. However, all the information required to capture provenance of an operator node execution is available from the payload of 'ExecutionRequestedEvent' entry of an execution. Other event type

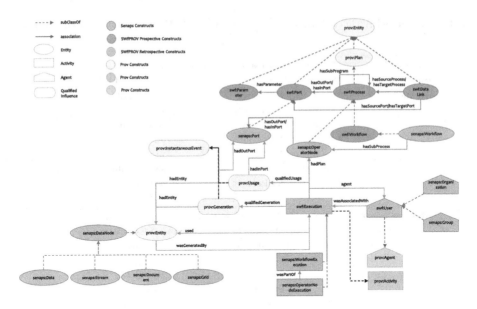

Fig. 4. Core Structure of SENProv, showing relationship to PROV-DM and SWfPROV - The constructs are represented in this diagram using PROV-like elements. (Color figure online)

entries of an operator node execution record incomplete and(or) duplicate information. Therefore, ProvAnalyser extracts the provenance from the payload of 'ExecutionRequestedEvent' and ignores other entries of the same operator node execution id while capturing provenance. The current implementation of Prov-Analyser records the provenance of only successfully executed workflows; however, we plan to capture unsuccessful workflow provenance to understand the root causes of workflow execution failure. This information is obtained from 'ExecutionSuccessfulEvent' entry for an operator node execution of a workflow.

Provenance extraction from the log files is done by the **Log Parser and Filter** component of ProvAnalyser. The entries with event type 'ExecutionSuccessfulEvent' are filtered from a log file, the workflow execution Id for each such event is extracted from the payload and recorded into a 'Successful workflows list'. Next, the entries with an event type 'ExecutionRequestedEvent' are selected to retrieve the provenance of successfully executed workflows. The information about operator node, connected data nodes, model and ports are retrieved from the payload as raw provenance data, as shown in Listing 1.1. Using the SENProv, raw provenance data is transformed into a structured provenance (i.e., an RDF document). ProvAnalyser retrieves prospective and retrospective provenance according to the SENProv model, as shown in Listing 1.2 and 1.3, respectively. The structured provenance is subsequently stored using WePROV provenance API.

Listing 1.1. Raw Provenance [5].

```
{"workflowExecId" : "c49ff96d-cc5771b5d689",
"opNodeExecId" : "c49ff96d-forecast.template",
"opExecutionTime" : "2018-07-17T03:43:11.474Z",
"operatorNodeId" : "forecast.template-selector",
"modelId" : "apsim-template-selector",
"Ports" : [
    {
        "portId" : "location",
        "portDirection" : "Input",
            "connectedData" : {
                "dataNodeId" : "02b5ffde3e18",
                "dataNodeType" : "Document" }
    }
    {
        "portId" : "parameters",
        "portDirection" : "Input",
        "connectedData" : {
                "dataNodeId" : "7096195c361f",
                "dataNodeType" : "Document" }
    }
    {
        "portId" : "apsim_template",
        "portDirection" : "Output",
        "connectedData" : {
                "dataNodeId" : "673aeb335602",
                "dataNodeType" : "Document"}
    } ]
}
```

Listing 1.2. Prospective Provenance.

```
<c49ff96d-cc5771b5d689> a senaps:Workflow;

<forecast.template-selector> a senaps:OperatorNode;
    senaps:host <apsim-template-selector>;
    swf:hasInPort <location>;
    swf:hasInPort <parameters>;
    swf:hasOutPort <apsim_template>.

<apsim-template-selector> a senaps:Model.

<location> a senaps:Port.

<parameters> a senaps:Port.

<apsim_template> a senaps:Port.
```

Listing 1.3. Retrospective Provenance.

```
<c49ff96d-cc5771b5d689> a senaps:WorkflowExecution;

<c49ff96d-forecast.template> a senaps:OperatorNodeExec;
    senaps:partOf <c49ff96d-cc5771b5d689>
    prov:atTime 2018-07-17T03:43:11;
    prov:hadPlan <forecast.template-selector>;
    prov:agent <Graincast>.
    prov:qualifiedUsage <c49ff96d-02b5ffde3e18-forecast>;
    prov:qualifiedUsage <c49ff96d-096195c361f-forecast>;
    prov:qualifiedGen <c49ff96d-673aeb335602-forecast>;
    prov:used <02b5ffde3e18>;
    prov:used <7096195c361f>.

<c49ff96d-02b5ffde3e18-forecast> a prov:Usage;
    swf:hadInPort <location>;
    prov:hadEntity <02b5ffde3e18>.

<c49ff96d-096195c361f-forecast> a prov:Usage;
    swf:hadInPort <parameters>;
    prov:hadEntity <096195c361f>.

<c49ff96d-673aeb335602-forecast> a prov:Generation;
    swf:hadOutPort <apsim_template>;
    prov:hadEntity <673aeb335602>.

<673aeb335602> a senaps:Document;
    prov:wasGeneratedBy <c49ff96d-forecast.template> .

<02b5ffde3e18> a senaps:Document;

<7096195c361f> a senaps:Document;

<Graincast> a senaps:Group;
    prov:wasAssociatedWith <c49ff96d-forecast.template>.
```

3.4   Implementation and Performance

In the current implementation of ProvAnalyser, we have automatise the process of importing and processing the most recent event logs. Previously, we were updating our provenance data weekly by importing new log files and extracting structured provenance from them. The previous version had two limitations: it required human intervention and the system was updated once every week. We have now fully automated the process to import daily event logs and extract provenance knowledge graph from them. Secondly, we have updated the backend storage structure of ProvAnalyser. Instead of maintaining a local RDF repository for the storage of provenance knowledge graph, we are using WePROV provenance API, which provides built-in features for provenance data validation and privacy. It allows detailed, system-specific, and less detailed system-independent provenance to validate through rulesets. The detailed discussion of this API is out of scope of this paper.

The Provenance Capturing module, implemented in Java (jdk-1.8.0), processes the log files and uses Apache's Jena RDF API (apache-jena-3.7.0) to extract the provenance and WePROV provenance API to store the structured provenance. For the evaluation and testing purposes, we extracted the provenance from SenapsLAND event logs of 180 days. All the processing was performed on a 64-bit Windows 10 Enterprise computer using an Intel Core i7 6600U CPU with 2 cores and 8 GB memory. We processed log files of variable sizes (i.e., from 3 to 590 MBs), and the execution takes between 2 to 41 s in parsing and extracting provenance from a log file and storing the provenance data in the Quad store.

However, the time ProvAnalyser takes to process a log file depends on the number of successfully executed workflows in the log file and not on its size. Moreover, we collected provenance for 10951 workflow runs and 564,154 operator node executions in the Quad store of 4.89 GB from log files of 14.68 GB by using ProvAnalyser. This result of the provenance-enhanced RDF data being smaller in size than the raw logs echos other log-to-PROV experiences [6].

4   Querying Workflow Provenance

ProvAnalyser is capable of understanding and validating workflows, and determines the quality of its data products. Therefore, we present the evaluation use cases in Sect. 4.1 followed by some sample queries in Sect. 4.2.

4.1   Evaluation Use Cases

Understanding a scientific workflow and reproducing its results are essential requirements to trust workflows and their results. These two requirements lead to the reuse of workflows and data generated by them across or within organisations. Therefore, our focus in this work is to explore use cases addressing these two essential requirements. For instance, ProvAnalyser should be able to answer queries like 'track the lineage of the final output of a workflow'. The lineage of output should explain which workflow(s) generated it, when the output was generated, who was responsible for it, what dataset(s) and models were used while generating this output. How did the process use the input data, and how were the steps configured? The result of this query will enable a user to repeat a series of steps on original data to reproduce the outcomes. This ability of a workflow engine is useful for both the clients and developers of a workflow. A scientist needs a provenance knowledge to assess the reliability of the outcomes or reuse a model in another workflow. Likewise, a workflow developer could be interested in investigating whether the workflow execution traces conform to the workflow structure by executing specific models in a particular order. In this paper, we also discuss additional use cases related to traceability, attribution, and provenance analytics. This brings us to discuss the primary use cases for ProvAnalyser and provide their sample queries.

Use Case 1: Understandability – Explain a Workflow. This use case helps in understanding the workflow by producing the leading intermediate operators or models used in the execution of a particular workflow. A scientist could demand to examine workflow processes in detail to assess the reliability of results or to reuse operators in another workflow.

Use Case 2: Reproducibility – Find Information to Reproduce. Organisations may want to reproduce their own or others' work. A scientist should be able to begin with the same inputs and methods (models) used previously and observe if a prior result can be confirmed. This is a particular case of repeatability where a complete set of information is obtained to verify a final or intermediate result. In the process of repeating a workflow and especially in reproducing an output the scientist needs to know which models were used to derive an output and how a model used the input data.

Use Case 3: Traceability – Trace the Effect of a Change. This use case traces the effect of a change. It identifies the scope of a change by determining workflows and their executions that are (or have been) affected. Moreover, tracing the effect can be used to minimise the re-computations to only those parts of a workflow that are involved in the processing of the changed data or a model.

Use Case 4: Provenance Analytics. Provenance-based analytics help scientists to discover new research opportunities, identify new problems, and challenges hidden in the traces of workflow executions. Most importantly, it helps scientists to discover and address anomalies. ProvAnalyser's current implementation can partially answer many such provenance analytics related queries.

Use Case 5: Attribution - Assign Responsibility. Attribution is to determine the responsibility by identifying who authored or executed a workflow. This information is useful to establish copyright and ownership of data, enable its citation, or determine liability for erroneous data. This use case is important for communication between users since it clarifies actions performed by each collaborator.

4.2   Provenance Queries

In order to demonstrate the effectiveness of the ProvAnalyser, we evaluated the system against a set of basic provenance related queries that are designed based on the use case requirements mentioned in the Sect. 4.1. Some of the provenance queries are:

Query1: What Structure Was Followed by a Given Workflow Execution Trace? A typical understandability question to be addressed to understand the outcome of a complex scientific process. Listing 1.4 shows a SPARQL query to retrieve the structure of a workflow execution trace.

Listing 1.4. SPARQL to get workflow specification.

```
PREFIX senaps:<http://www.csiro.au/ontologies/senaps#>
PREFIX rdf:<http://www.w3.org/1999/02/22-rdf-syntax-ns#>
PREFIX swf:<http://swfprov.csiro.au/>
PREFIX prov:<http://www.w3.org/ns/prov#>

CONSTRUCT {
?sourceOpNode swf:hasOutPort ?outport.
?desOpNode swf:hasInport ?inport.
?dataLink swf:hasSourceProcess ?sourceOpNode.
?dataLink swf:hasTargetProcess ?desOpNode.
?dataLink rdf:type swf:DataLink.}
WHERE {
<wfExecId> senaps:hasSubProcess ?sourceOpNode.
?sourceOpNode senaps:operatorNodeId ?sourceOpNodeId;
        swf:hasOutPort ?outport.
?outport senaps:portId ?outportId.
?entityGen swf:hadOutPort ?outport;
        swf:hadEntity ?entity.
?entityUsed swf:hadEntity ?entity;
        swf:hadInPort ?inport.
?inport senaps:portId ?inportId.
<workflowExecId> swf:hasSubProcess ?desOpNode.
?desOpNode swf:hasInPort ?inport;
        senaps:operatorNodeId ?desOpNodeId.
BIND (URI(CONCAT(STR( ?sourceOpNode), \".\",
    STR(?outportId), \"_to_\", STR( ?desOpNodeId),
        \".\",STR(?inportId))) AS ?dataLink)}
```

For a workflow execution, the query constructs the detail of a workflow structure. Consider an example of an execution of **Forecast Grains workflow**. For this execution, the result of the query identifies all intermediate operator nodes, their ports, and how the data were routed among the operator nodes as shown in Fig. 5.

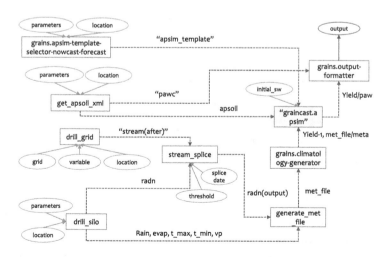

Fig. 5. A graphical view of a SPARQL query result; the query is given in Listing 1.4.

Query2: Find What and How to Use Input Data to Result in a Specific Yield Prediction. Listing 1.5 presents a SPARQL query to answer this question.

Listing 1.5. SPARQL to find input information.

```
PREFIX senaps:<http://www.csiro.au/ontologies/senaps#>
PREFIX swf:<http://swfprov.csiro.au/>
PREFIX prov:<http://www.w3.org/ns/prov#>

SELECT DISTINCT ?model (?portId AS ?variableName) ?data
WHERE {
    <output> (prov:wasGeneratedBy/prov:used)* ?data.
    OPTIONAL {?data prov:wasGeneratedBy ?exec.}
    OPTIONAL {?usage swf:hadEntity ?data.
        ?usage swf:hadInPort ?port.
        ?port senaps:portId ?portId.
        ?opNode swf:hasInPort ?port.
        ?opNode senaps:host ?model. }
FILTER (!bound(?exec)) }
```

The query returns the details of inputs to a workflow to generate a specific output, including input ids, ports the inputs were connecting to an operator node, and the model hosted by an operator node. For instance, for an output (outputId: <42b838a7-786c-42a0-a4b9-f7dbed9df292>) generated by an execution of **Forecast Grains workflow** the query returns all input ports in Fig. 5, input data provided to these input ports, and models that used these input data.

Query3: Identify all Workflow Executions that Used (a Specific Version of) the APSIM Model and Group them by their Organisations. The result of this query helps to communicate all the organisations which are likely to be affected by a change in the APSIM model. Listing 1.6 shows the SPARQL syntax of this query.

Listing 1.6. SPARQL to trace the affect of change.

```
PREFIX senaps:<http://www.csiro.au/ontologies/senaps#>
PREFIX rdf:<http://www.w3.org/1999/02/22-rdf-syntax-ns#>
PREFIX swf:<http://swfprov.csiro.au/>
PREFIX prov:<http://www.w3.org/ns/prov#>

SELECT DISTINCT ?orgs ?workflowExec
WHERE {
    ?opNodes senaps:host senaps:graincast.apsim.
    ?assoc prov:hadPlan ?opNodes;
        prov:agent ?orgs.
    ?orgs rdf:type senaps:Organisation.
    ?opExecution prov:qualifiedAssociation ?assoc;
            senaps:partOf ?workflowExec.
    } Group By ?orgs ?workflowExec
```

Query4: Is the Behavior in a Second Workflow Execution Conformant with the Workflow's Behavior in the First? This query helps to find the impact (due to intentional changes in workflows) and(or) cause (due to accidental changes in workflows) analysis in case of any change in the behavior of workflow on two separate days. To date, ProvAnalyser can partially answer the query by providing the implicit workflow structure of two workflow executions using query presented in Listing 1.4.

Query5: What Users (Agent or Organisation) are Involved in Designing a Workflow? This query is useful to identify copyright and ownership of a workflow. Listing 1.7 shows the SPARQL syntax of this query. This query returns agents and organisations of a workflow and its sub-workflows.

Listing 1.7. SPARQL to identify workflow ownership.

```
PREFIX senaps:<http://www.csiro.au/ontologies/senaps#>
PREFIX rdf:<http://www.w3.org/1999/02/22-rdf-syntax-ns#>
PREFIX swf:<http://swfprov.csiro.au/>
PREFIX prov:<http://www.w3.org/ns/prov#>

SELECT DISTINCT ?workflowId ?user
WHERE {
    ?workflowId a swf:Workflow;
    prov:wasAssociatedWith ?user.
    FILTER (?workflowId = ?workflow)
    {
      SELECT ?workflow
      WHERE {
          <workflowId> (swf:hasSubProcess/swf:hasSubProcess)+ ?
              ↪ workflow.}
    }
}
```

Query6: Find the Collaborative Researchers Who Collaborated in Designing Workflows Together? This query retrieves researchers (i.e., agents) who collaborate in designing workflows. Listing 1.8 shows the SPARQL syntax of this query.

Listing 1.8. SPARQL to identify collaborations.

```
PREFIX senaps:<http://www.csiro.au/ontologies/senaps#>
PREFIX rdf:<http://www.w3.org/1999/02/22-rdf-syntax-ns#>
PREFIX swf:<http://swfprov.csiro.au/>
PREFIX prov:<http://www.w3.org/ns/prov#>

SELECT DISTINCT ?workflowId ?agent1 ?agent2
WHERE {
    ?workflowId a swf:Workflow;
    ?workflowId prov:wasAssociatedWith ?agent1; ?agent1 a prov:
        ↪ Agent.
    ?workflowId prov:wasAssociatedWith ?agent2; ?agent2 a prov:
        ↪ Agent.
    FILTER (?agent1 != ?agent2)
}
```

5   Discussion

Provenance knowledge graph extracted from the event logs can be used to answer a range of relevant provenance queries and exhibit high usability compared to the event logs. Nevertheless, some issues are planned to be addressed in the future.

A significant concern is that provenance collected from then event logs captures retrospective provenance only i.e., execution traces. A partial prospective provenance can be extracted using metadata like SWfPROV; however, a complete prospective provenance and workflow evolution provenance cannot be inferred from workflow execution traces only. Workflow specification and evolution provenance are required to address many provenance analytic queries. For instance, a scientist faces divergent outcomes during reproducibility analysis, i.e., two executions of the same workflow produce different results. The scientist is interested to know **what is (are) the reason(s) of divergent results of two executions of a workflow?** One such reason could be the data or workflow evolution, or it could be some unintentional changes in the workflow. For any provenance solution to identify the cause, it should capture the workflow evolution and prospective provenance. Our solution ProvAnalyser produces implicit prospective provenance through reverse engineering, as shown in Listing 1.4. However, for conformance checking [24], a user is required to compare the implicit workflow specifications with explicit workflow specifications manually. The ProvAnalyser needs to capture workflow retrospective provenance explicitly to automate the conformance checking.

Another limitation is the unavailability of a user-friendly provenance exploration and analysis mechanism. ProvAnalyser uses SPARQL as the only mechanism to query stored provenance. Although query-based access mechanisms (e.g., SPARQL, SQL, XPath or XQuery) are amongst the most popular provenance access methods [28], it is usable for expert users (people with query language expertise) or, for naïve users, to answer pre-formulated queries. An appropriate method of provenance data visualisation or exploration can improve the data interpretation, facilitate decision making, and lead scientists to unexpected science discovery from the provenance traces.

Based on the discussion above, we plan to extend ProvAnalyser to address the limitations including capturing and storing workflow prospective and evolution provenance; and a visualisation tool for interactively exploring provenance in future.

6   Related Work

The provenance of workflows has been investigated in a number of areas, including experimental research, business and data analytics [18]. Workflow provenance ability to replicate findings from previous runs, explain surprising results, and organize results for sharing and interpretation is the biggest motivation for employing it in science. State-of-the-art scientific workflow engines (e.g.,

Kepler [1], Taverna [26], WINGS/Pegasus [21], Galaxy [15] and VisTrails [3]) automatically record the provenance of their workflows in the form of execution traces. Moreover, there are several stand-alone provenance capture and analytics methods [28]. However, most solutions rely on proprietary formats that make it difficult to interchange and interoperate provenance information. In addition, these approaches harvest provenance directly from the system at runtime work-flow execution traces rather than log archives, requiring instrumentation of the source code of the systems.

LogMaster [11] uses system logs to extract event correlations to build failure correlation graphs by using log files to understand the root causes of failures, SherLog [33] leverages large system logs to analyse source code of the system. Through integrating fault signals with event messages, Jiaang et al. [20] suggests a mechanism for root cause analysis of fault in large systems. Xu et al. [32] detect problems in large scale systems by mining logs along with the source code that generated the logs. Gaaloul et al. [12] analyses process logs to classify transaction behaviours in the process and to then optimise and correct the corresponding recovery function. Similarly, NetLogger [17] captures and analyses event logs for distributed applications' performance, but it requires instrumentation of the source code. All these methods, however, do not gather provenance information directly from log files.

While logs provide relevant information for the analysis of failures, they can also be used to collect relevant information about workflows execution and data objects. To create a web service request citation, Car et al. [6] extracted PROV-O compliant provenance from the Web service log. Ghoshal and Plale [14] presented the most relevant approach to ProvAnalyser by exploring the options of deriving workflow provenance from existing log files. Their emphasis, though, is on gathering provenance from various forms of distributed applications logs. Our approach leverages SenapsLAND event logs to capture interoperable provenance and analyse it to understand and reproduce workflow outputs.

7   Conclusion

In this work, we captured the provenance of scientific workflows from their event logs to verify the quality of their data products. The event logs are filtered and transformed into a provenance knowledge graph using a specialised provenance model. This transformation makes it possible to record the useful information into a structured, interoperable and workflow system-independent format. The captured provenance enabled the analysis of workflows' execution traces to make them understandable and reusable. Moreover, the provenance recorded to perform data and workflow quality assessments and analysis are smaller in volume than the event log. This reduction in volume indicates the practical scalability of this provenance extraction process. While workflow execution provenance recorded from the event logs can answer most of the user queries, it is not always enough and, where it is not, workflow prospective provenance can be inferred and used. The systems can, however, consider collecting prospective and evolution provenance information in their logs to enable detailed provenance analytics.

References

1. Altintas, I., Barney, O., Jaeger-Frank, E.: Provenance collection support in the Kepler scientific workflow system. In: Moreau, L., Foster, I. (eds.) Provenance and Annotation of Data. IPAW 2006. Lecture Notes in Computer Science, vol. 4145. Springer, Heidelberg (2006). https://doi.org/10.1007/11890850_1406
2. Altintas, I., Berkley, C., Jaeger, E., Jones, M., Ludascher, B., Mock, S.: Kepler: an extensible system for design and execution of scientific workflows. In: Proceedings. 16th International Conference on Scientific and Statistical Database Management, 2004, pp. 423–424. IEEE (2004)
3. Bavoil, L., et al.: VisTrails: enabling interactive multiple-view visualizations. In: VIS 05 IEEE Visualization, pp. 135–142 (October 2005). https://doi.org/10.1109/VISUAL.2005.1532788
4. Belhajjame, K., et al.: Using a suite of ontologies for preserving workflow-centric research objects. J. Web Semant. **32**, 16–42 (2015)
5. Butt, A.S., Car, N., Fitch, P.: Towards ontology driven provenance in scientific workflow engine. In: Proceedings of the 8th International Conference on Model-Driven Engineering and Software Development, MODELSWARD 2020, Valletta, Malta, February 25–27, 2020, pp. 105–115 (2020)
6. Car, N.J., Stanford, L.S., Sedgmen, A.: Enabling web service request citation by provenance information. In: Provenance and Annotation of Data and Processes - 6th International Provenance and Annotation Workshop, McLean, VA, USA, June 7–8, 2016, Proceedings, pp. 122–133 (2016). https://doi.org/10.1007/978-3-319-40593-3_10
7. Cohen-Boulakia, S., et al.: Scientific workflows for computational reproducibility in the life sciences: status, challenges and opportunities. Future Gener. Comput. Syst. **75**, 284–298 (2017)
8. Cuevas-Vicenttín, V., et al.: Provone: a prov extension data model for scientific workflow provenance (2015). https://purl.dataone.org/provone-v1-dev. Accessed 12 Dec 2019
9. Deelman, E., Gannon, D., Shields, M., Taylor, I.: Workflows and e-science: an overview of workflow system features and capabilities. Future Gener. Comput. Syst. **25**(5), 528–540 (2009)
10. Deelman, E., et al.: The future of scientific workflows. Int. J. High Perform. Comput. Appl. **32**(1), 159–175 (2018)
11. Fu, X., Ren, R., Zhan, J., Zhou, W., Jia, Z., Lu, G.: LogMaster: mining event correlations in logs of large-scale cluster systems. In: 2012 IEEE 31st Symposium on Reliable Distributed Systems, pp. 71–80 (October 2012). https://doi.org/10.1109/SRDS.2012.40
12. Gaaloul, W., Gaaloul, K., Bhiri, S., Haller, A., Hauswirth, M.: Log-based transactional workflow mining. Distrib. Parallel Databases **25**(3), 193–240 (2009)
13. Garijo, D., Gil, Y.: A new approach for publishing workflows: abstractions, standards, and linked data. In: Proceedings of the 6th Workshop on Workflows in Support of Large-scale Science, WORKS 2011, pp. 47–56. ACM, New York (2011). https://doi.org/10.1145/2110497.2110504
14. Ghoshal, D., Plale, B.: Provenance from log files: a bigdata problem. In: Proceedings of the Joint EDBT/ICDT 2013 Workshops, EDBT 2013, pp. 290–297. ACM, New York (2013). https://doi.org/10.1145/2457317.2457366
15. Goecks, J., Nekrutenko, A., Taylor, J.: Galaxy: a comprehensive approach for supporting accessible, reproducible, and transparent computational research in the life sciences. Genome Biol. **11**(8), R86 (2010)

16. Guedes, T., Silva, V., Mattoso, M., Bedo, M.V., de Oliveira, D.: A practical roadmap for provenance capture and data analysis in spark-based scientific workflows. In: 2018 IEEE/ACM Workflows in Support of Large-Scale Science (WORKS), pp. 31–41. IEEE (2018)
17. Gunter, D., Tierney, B., Crowley, B., Holding, M., Lee, J.: NetLogger: a toolkit for distributed system performance analysis. In: Proceedings 8th International Symposium on Modeling, Analysis and Simulation of Computer and Telecommunication Systems (Cat. No. PR00728), pp. 267–273. IEEE (2000)
18. Herschel, M., Diestelkàmper, R., Ben Lahmar, H.: A survey on provenance: what for? what form? what from? VLDB J.-Int. J. Very Large Data Bases **26**(6), 881–906 (2017)
19. Hull, D., et al.: Taverna: a tool for building and running workflows of services. Nucleic Acids Res. **34**(suppl-2), W729–W732 (2006)
20. Jiang, W., Hu, C., Pasupathy, S., Kanevsky, A., Li, Z., Zhou, Y.: Understanding customer problem troubleshooting from storage system logs. In: Proceedings of the 7th Conference on File and Storage Technologies, FAST 2009, pp. 43–56. USENIX Association, Berkeley (2009). http://dl.acm.org/citation.cfm?id=1525908.1525912
21. Kim, J., Deelman, E., Gil, Y., Mehta, G., Ratnakar, V.: Provenance trails in the WINGS/Pegasus system. Concurr. Comput.: Pract. Exp. **20**(5), 587–597 (2008)
22. Liu, J., Pacitti, E., Valduriez, P., Mattoso, M.: A survey of data-intensive scientific workflow management. J. Grid Comput. **13**(4), 457–493 (2015)
23. Moreau, L., Missier, P.: World Wide Web Consortium "PROV-DM: The PROV Data Model" W3C Recommendation (2013). https://www.w3.org/TR/prov-dm/. Accessed 12 Dec 2019
24. Moreau, L.: Aggregation by provenance types: a technique for summarising provenance graphs. arXiv preprint arXiv:1504.02616 (2015)
25. Murta, L., Braganholo, V., Chirigati, F., Koop, D., Freire, J.: noWorkflow: capturing and analyzing provenance of scripts. In: Ludäscher, B., Plale, B. (eds.) Provenance and Annotation of Data and Processes. IPAW 2014. Lecture Notes in Computer Science, vol. 8628. Springer, Cham (2015). https://doi.org/10.1007/978-3-319-16462-5_6
26. Oinn, T., et al.: Taverna: a tool for the composition and enactment of bioinformatics workflows. Bioinformatics **20**(17), 3045–3054 (2004). https://doi.org/10.1093/bioinformatics/bth361
27. Oliner, A., Stearley, J.: What supercomputers say: a study of five system logs. In: 37th Annual IEEE/IFIP International Conference on Dependable Systems and Networks, pp. 575–584. IEEE (2007)
28. Oliveira, W., Oliveira, D.D., Braganholo, V.: Provenance analytics for workflow-based computational experiments: a survey. ACM Comput. Surv. (CSUR) **51**(3), 53 (2018). https://doi.org/10.1145/3184900
29. Simmhan, Y.L., Plale, B., Gannon, D.: A framework for collecting provenance in data-centric scientific workflows. In: 2006 IEEE International Conference on Web Services (ICWS 2006), pp. 427–436. IEEE (2006)
30. Taylor, I., Shields, M., Wang, I., Harrison, A.: The Triana workflow environment: architecture and applications. In: Taylor, I.J., Deelman, E., Gannon, D.B., Shields, M. (eds.) Workflows for e-Science. Springer, London (2007). https://doi.org/10.1007/978-1-84628-757-2_20
31. Van Der Aalst, W.M., Ter Hofstede, A.H.: YAWL: yet another workflow language. Inf. Syst. **30**(4), 245–275 (2005)

32. Xu, W., Huang, L., Fox, A., Patterson, D., Jordan, M.I.: Detecting large-scale system problems by mining console logs. In: Proceedings of the ACM SIGOPS 22nd Symposium on Operating Systems Principles, SOSP 2009, pp. 117–132. ACM, New York (2009). https://doi.org/10.1145/1629575.1629587

33. Yuan, D., Mai, H., Xiong, W., Tan, L., Zhou, Y., Pasupathy, S.: SherLog: error diagnosis by connecting clues from run-time logs. SIGPLAN Not. **45**(3), 143–154 (2010). https://doi.org/10.1145/1735971.1736038

A Multi-Model Reviewing Approach for Production Systems Engineering Models

Felix Rinker[1,2(✉)] ⬤, Laura Waltersdorfer[1,2] ⬤, Manuel Schüller[2],
Stefan Biffl[2] ⬤, and Dietmar Winkler[1,2] ⬤

[1] Christian Doppler Laboratory for Security and Quality Improvement
in the Production System Lifecycle (CDL-SQI),
Technische Universität Wien, Vienna, Austria
{felix.rinker,laura.waltersdorfer,dietmar.winkler}@tuwien.ac.at
[2] Institute of Information Systems Engineering,
Technische Universität Wien, Vienna, Austria
{manuel.schueller,stefan.biffl}@tuwien.ac.at

Abstract. *Background.* In *Production Systems Engineering* (PSE) models, which describe plants, represent different views on several engineering disciplines (such as mechanical, electrical and software engineering) and may contain up to 10,000s of instance elements, such as concepts, attributes and relationships. Validating these models requires an integrated multi-model view and the domain expertise of human experts related to individual views. Unfortunately, the heterogeneity of disciplines, tools, and data formats makes it hard to provide a technology-independent multi-model view. *Aim.* In this paper, we aim at improving Multi-Model Reviewing (MMR) capabilities of domain experts based on selected model visualisation methods and mechanisms. *Method.* We (a) derive requirements for graph-based visualisation to facilitate reviewing multi-disciplinary models; (b) introduce the MMR approach to visualise engineering models for review as hierarchical and linked structures; (c) design an MMR software prototype; and (d) evaluate the prototype based on tasks derived from real-world PSE use cases. For evaluation purposes we compare capabilities of the MMR prototype and a text-based model editor. *Results.* The MMR prototype enabled performing the evaluation tasks in most cases considerable faster than the standard text-based model editor. *Conclusion.* The promising results of the MMR approach in the evaluation context warrant empirical studies with a wider range of domain experts and use cases on the usability and usefulness of the MMR approach in practice.

Keywords: Multi-disciplinary engineering visualisation · Production systems engineering · Model-driven engineering · Domain-specific modeling · Model review · Model quality assurance

© Springer Nature Switzerland AG 2021
S. Hammoudi et al. (Eds.): MODELSWARD 2020, CCIS 1361, pp. 121–146, 2021.
https://doi.org/10.1007/978-3-030-67445-8_6

1   Introduction

Engineering models for the design and construction of industrial production plants or work cells typically follow a hierarchical structure and represent dependencies and connections to related model views and elements, e.g., conveyors connected to robotic arms [3]. Engineers, e.g., mechanical or electrical engineers, model their discipline-specific views, which need to be integrated into a common and comprehensive view on the system later in the process. The size of such models can reach up to tenthousands of model elements that take up several GBs of computer memory, making the processing and editing increasingly difficult. However, assuring the quality of underlying models is a challenging and critical task for evaluating the correctness of system designs. Model reviews, comparable to code reviews [1, 26] are established software engineering practices, used increasingly to check for design evolution, logical correctness and completeness of models [38]. However, compared to code reviews that focus on software code, in model engineering heterogeneous data artefacts have to be analysed (e.g. spreadsheets, technical documentation in PDFs, or data in standardized languages, such as *AutomationML* (AML)).

In *Production Systems Engineering* (PSE), a simulation engineer builds up a holistic model, which combines discipline-specific views and parameterises the model according to provided data. Changes in one discipline can trigger effects in other disciplines (e.g., using a motor of a different size may require changes to the mechanical design), so the models are highly dependent on the input. Therefore, engineers need to propagate system changes in a *Round-Trip Engineering* (RTE) process [37]. Instead of waiting for the completion of design steps by colleagues, engineers iteratively push their updates and incorporate changes of others including the risk of inconsistencies [13] or information losses [27]. Proprietary file formats and description languages make data integration and the common view on the system model more complex. Simultaneous contributions to and adaptations of the common view and data model result in big and complex model files, around 30 MBs to several GBs composed of up to potentially tenthousands of elements, making them hard to process and manage. Moreover, model inspection and manipulation tools in industry traditionally focus on text-based representation and are not optimised for human experts or automation supported operations, such as automated reasoning [33].

Until now, only a few useful alternative approaches for integrated modeling of PSE structures have been developed: *Systems Modeling Language* (SysML)[1], based on the Unified Modeling Language (UML) and the AML[2] standard, based on *Extensible Markup Language* (XML) provide common data formats, used in the engineering of production systems. As the main concern of our work is the process of engineering data exchange, we focus on the application of AML, which is tailored to the exchange of engineering data and implements the industry standard IEC62714 [16]. Although, AML is already a popular industry format, the

---

[1] SysML: sysml.org.

[2] AutomationML: www.automationml.org.

modeling editing support is limited to text-based and tree-focused capabilities. In the context of code review this approach seems suitable since traditional editing tools of software architects rely on textual representations to visualise changes. However, textual representations are not sufficient for model review because additional information such as semantic dependencies are required for model understanding. Our assumption is that making element and attribute changes and their effects on their related dependencies visible to involved stakeholders could have the potential to increase data exchange efficiency. The visualisation of production system models can support the model review process to (a) support achieving and keeping data consistency, (b) track changes across engineering disciplines, and (c) facilitate defect detection in multi-disciplinary engineering models.

Information Visualisation (InfoVis) is a sub research field of computer science, human-computer interaction, and computer graphics focusing on the human perception of data and process improvement by implementing best practices and lessons learned [25]. One main concern of InfoVis is that unstructured and large data sets are challenging to be analysed by humans experts, if these data are not represented and optimized for human processing. Graph-based data visualisations can support effective and efficient model processing [7] and reduce the cognitive load as well as search time for users. The goal is to support human experts by providing patterns and highlight data changes.

Therefore, our goal is to apply selected information visualisation methods in the PSE context to improve the review process of engineering models in the PSE domain. This work builds on previous work on model inspection, published at the *Modelsward 2020* conference [31]. Based on the *Design Design Science Cycle* [36], we analyse requirements of the application use case, develop a software prototype (i.e., the Multi-Model Reviewing (MMR) prototype) to support *multi-model reviewing* capabilities and evaluate it against a standard PSE tool, i.e., the *AutomantionML Editor* (AMLEditor). Therefore, we derived the following research issues (RIs):

RQ1. Model Visualisation Requirements. *What requirements are critical to facilitate visualising and reviewing multi-disciplinary models in the PSE domain?*
PSE models are complex, including a variety of elements, nested structures, and dependencies requiring the integration of various tools and data formats [34]. The high complexity makes it hard for human experts to efficiently manage and review such files. Hence, we propose the application of selected *information visualisation* concepts [25], specifically graph-based techniques, to improve the processing of large-scale models and to improve the collaboration of domain experts for better understanding system models and for decision-making in case of quality issues (such as defects). We discuss fundamental findings of the information visualisation community for application in model engineering in PSE (see Sect. 2). However, these general guidelines are not tailored to the specific application domain. Therefore, we additionally

investigate the needs for modeling domain-specific PSE models and common user actions in the form of use cases as requirements in Sect. 3.

RQ2. Multi-Model Reviewer System Design. *What system design facilitates the information visualisation of PSE models?*

Based on identified requirements and use cases derived from RQ1, we developed a MMR approach, including a system design and architecture to visualise AML model hierarchies in a space-efficient way. The visualisation is based on an AML-specific instance model hierarchy. We implemented a customized force-directed graph algorithm for efficient space allocation. We applied modern development principles, such as *service-oriented architecture* and the Model View Controller (MVC) pattern. In Sect. 3, we discuss and introduce functionalities and capabilities of theMMR-prototype.

RQ3. Multi-Model Reviewer Performance Analysis. *How does the information visualisation prototype approach perform when compared to a PSE modeling tool?*

We compared the MMR software prototype to the AMLEditor, as one example of a standard tool for a text-based model editing and a standard tool for AML data management and editing. We applied the Keystroke-Level Method (KLM) [7] for evaluating the static performance of both approaches. KLM is a static measure to analyse data management and editing performance regarding the graphical user interface and modeling capabilities by measuring the time required to correctly conduct selected tasks that reflect the requirements. An initial analysis shows the advantages of the MMR approach, however extensive additional analysis is further required to strengthen external validity.

From this work, we expect the following contributions to the model-driven engineering community: i) requirements for the PSE domain as application area, ii) insights on the MMR approach as foundation for application in other domains that include models with hierarchical structures, and iii) a system design architecture for AML graph visualisation.

The remainder of this work is structured as follows: Sect. 2 provides background information on common visualisation techniques, the data exchange format AML, and an AML approach for domain-specific data modeling. Section 3 presents identified requirements and common use cases for model editing and review. We describe the MMR approach based on information visualisation in the context of PSE in Sect. 4. Section 5 introduces the MMR software prototype for the graphical model review. Section 6 discusses our research findings and limitations. Section 7 presents related work on domain-specific modeling approaches and visualisation techniques for the PSE domain. Finally, Sect. 8 concludes and identifies future work.

2   Background

This section summarizes background on data and graph structures and visualization in *Production Systems Engineering* (PSE) and *AutomationML* (AML).

2.1   Visualisation Techniques for Structural Data

There are multiple well-established visualisation techniques for structural data [15], also used in PSE artefacts. They include *Rooted Trees*, *Tree Maps*, *Radial Trees* and *Force-directed Tree*.

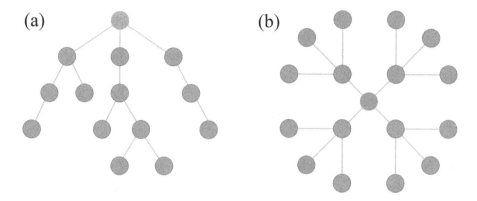

Fig. 1. Example of (a) *Rooted Trees* and (b) *Radial Trees*.

Rooted Trees are tailored for the visualization of hierarchical relations (cf. Fig. 1a). They typically have a single root node in the top level position. Based on this top level position, child nodes move downwards. Nodes on the same hierarchical level share the same vertical depth. However, for large data structures this representation requires additional functionality for searching vertically in the tree. Hence, it is challenging to keep the overview on the overall tree structure.

Radial Trees. Compared to the rooted tree, this representation starts from a central node (Fig. 1b). Based on this root node, all other nodes are grouped in circles, leading to a more efficient utilization of the available space.

Tree Maps presents data in rectangular formation related to the data size (Fig. 2a). Although Tree Maps support the presentation of larger data structures this approach is not well-suited for representing cross-references.

Force-Directed Graphs. (Figure 2b) are devised by algorithms calculating the position of nodes based on force simulation (the force between nodes, attracting or repelling each other). The algorithms are optimized for space usage. However, this method often does not represent graphs that are visually attractive for human experts.

(a)

(b)

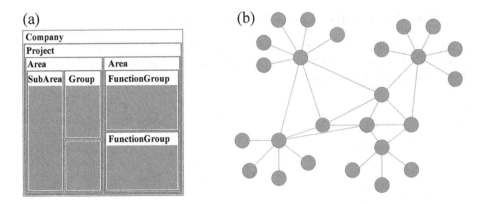

Fig. 2. Example of (a) a *Tree-Map* and (b) a *Force-directed Tree*.

2.2 AutomationML – The Open PSE Data Exchange Standard

AutomationML (AML) is a standardised data exchange format for the storage
and exchange of modeling hierarchical structures common to plant structures.
The data format is taking advantage of different industry standards, like IEC
62424, COLLADA and PLCOpenXML to represent the different views needed
for the interdisciplinary design of production systems [9]. *Computer-Aided Engineering eXchange* (CAEX) supports object orientation [11], with different elements providing specific functions: System unit classes describe system objects
and can be organised in system unit libraries. RoleClasses define the semantics
of an object. Interface classes describe abstract relations of an object or relevant information that is not covered by the other language concepts. AML files
are described in a hierarchical structure, also called Instance Hierarchy, defined
by a set of Internal Elements (IE). Since AML files are based on *Extensible
Markup Language* (XML), they can be manipulated in text editors. However,
especially in the context of *Production Systems Engineering* (PSE), engineering
data artefacts with thousands of components, knowledge extraction and review
tasks can become cumbersome and entail errors through manual manipulation.

An established tool is the *AutomantionML Editor* (AMLEditor)[3]. Note that
the editor has been designed to support engineers in managing AML files and
represents the recommended tool in the PSE context. Figure 3 shows the representation of tree structure of the AMLEditor (1). On the right (2), shows
the SystemUnitClass libraries, bottom left RoleClass libraries (3) and bottom
right InterfaceClass libraries (4). Individual nodes can be inspected to view
sub-nodes and the side panel helps to understand the project instance hierarchy
(5). The top panel is compromised of edit options, saving, importing etc. (6).
The overall design focuses on text-based representation and structure. However,
a major disadvantage of the editor is the poor utilisation of the given screen
space and limited visualisation of the system model. The tree representation

---

[3] AutomationML Editor: www.automationml.org.

mostly expands downwards (1), requiring users to scroll and search extensively for components especially in larger structures. Also, the search function is currently limited, attribute search is not enabled and complete spelling of names is required to find elements. Further, the search functionality is quite limited, e.g., searching for attribute values of a certain device is not supported yet.

Because AML represents the foundation for modern (a) engineering data representations and model exchange in PSE and (b) enables a common view on the system model there is the need to support engineers by improving AML data management and editing.

2.3 Domain-Specific Data Modeling with AutomationML

In industrial use cases the planning and design of Production Systems (PSs) is a complex process, involving the collaborative work of several heterogeneous engineering disciplines. During the work process the engineers exchange data across the involved disciplines constitute an engineering network.

A common method to manage the collaborative work is the *Round-Trip Engineering* (RTE) [37] process that proposes a centralised data management system where domain experts can commit their work progress to a unified data model and pull updates coming from other disciplines.

Implementing a centralised data management system in the PSE context is a main challenge because of the discipline-specific tool data and formats that support only their discipline-specific concepts and model hierarchies. Additionally, these tools are not necessarily compatible with each other, which can lead to data inconsistencies, information loss, or duplication of data during the data integration. This makes it difficult to extract and integrate engineering tool data into a unified model that is also reasonable for other domains. Often, it is also not possible to reconstruct the original model information without supporting meta data which provides information about the mapping between the origin model and the unified model. This leads, to the loss of the previous structure and semantic meaning.

Lüder et al. [23] propose a data exchange architecture to integrate domain-specific tools in an engineering network utilising a central data management system as described in the RTE process. The unified model in the data management system follows the IEC 62714 standard [24]. Compared to existing approaches in asset management such as Siemens COMOS[4] the information about local data models a is persevered and can be partially reconstructed on export to a domain-specific tool. To enable the reconstruction of local data hierarchies and structures Lüder et al. [21, 22] introduces the modeling concept of defining local and global views in two separate concept models based on AML:

The local model view is called **AML-2** and describes the local discipline-specific concepts and model hierarchies and defines links and mappings to the original data sources, e.g., tool data. The common model view is called **AML-1** and constitutes the unified model of all described AML-2 models.

---

[4] Siemens COMOS: https://www.siemens.com/comos.

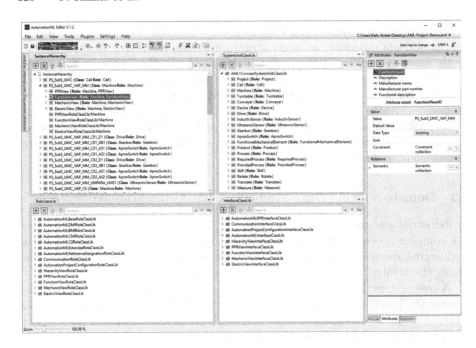

Fig. 3. AMLEditor components and a sample instance hierarchy in PSE.

AML-2 Local View Modeling. A key success factor in a PSE project is the strong inter-connection and integration of the different discipline-specific data. Indeed, each discipline uses their own concept space and definition for data modelling. Also, the engineering tools provide their own data models and data formats, which makes it hard to integrate the data into other model spaces without a mapping language. AML-2 supports the modelling of local concept and data hierarchies to ensure the availability of these information for the integration into the unified model and the export back into local data models.

To describe the local data model with AML-2, we use AML features such as Role Class (RC) and Role Class Library (RCLib) to describe the semantics of local concepts. A domain-specific local concept is described as a RC that defines the concept-related attributes and the mapping to the corresponding source data. AML Interface Class Libraries (ICLibs) are used to link external artefacts like technical data-sheets or drawings on instance level. System Unit Classes (SUCs) are used to define local modeling elements, e.g., a *motor* or a *gear* that can be used to define a specific device. When a local data model is imported the defined AML-2 model elements are instantiated in a local instance model hierarchy.

AML-1 Hierarchy Modeling. AML-1 contains all RC and Interface Classes (ICs) defined in the single local AML-2 models. The discipline-specific SUCs, are grouped together in a common SUC consisting of sub-groups for each local model view containing the discipline-specific attributes and semantic links. Sub-groups specify the sameRCs as the corresponding SUC in the AML-2 concept view.

When a local AML-2 is integrated into an AMl-1 model the existing hierarchy is flattened into a list of Internal Elements (IEs). The discipline-specific *mother-child* relations are defined with Internal Link (ILnk) connected to *toMother* and *toChild* Interfaces.

The flattened list of elements and links between elements allows that all local hierarchies can be displayed and preserved in the unified model (AML-1). On top, attributes in sub-groups can be mapped to other attributes in the same subgroup by a specified mapping language that enables attribute mappings that enables the data propagation to other discipline-specific model views.

3   Requirements for the Visualisation of Multi-disciplinary Engineering Data

This section summarises identified requirements for the visualisation and common use cases for modeling of PSE data.

3.1   Requirements for Engineering Data Visualisation

Information Visualisation aims at increasing human processing and cognition abilities through different principles and techniques [7]. One mechanism is to reduce cognitive load for users through displaying less information. Furthermore, search efforts are reduced and the displayed results illustrated in a way meaningful for the user to minimize required scanning time. Another characteristic for information visualisation is the recognition of patterns and relationships in the data. The human perception of patterns in numerical data is limited, so visual hints have to be provided for better recognition.

Based on the insights of information visualisation research and input from our company partners, we focused on identifying capabilities for system model editors in the PSE domain.

R1. Project Hierarchy. AML and PSE-related models use a hierarchical structure for representing the topology of the plant. Connections are not easily recognizable, due to the structural organisation and size of files. Thus, a visualisation approach needs to support a hierarchical project structure by showing the connections between different nodes to understand the organisation of components.

R2. Cross-references. This requirement describes relationships and dependencies between different concepts and attributes apart from topology. In order to avoid consistency errors, cross-references between different disciplines need to be visible. These references are required to be able to visualise dependencies and triggered changes in next steps.

R3. Representation of Large Data Structures. Typical AML files can become quite large (up to GBs of structured information in XML format and several thousands of elements). Therefore, engineers need to have a concise and efficient overview over this structure to assess individual elements. Possibility to filter irrelevant, but also displaying detailed data for specific tasks while utilizing the available screen space is required.

R4. Discipline-neutral View. In the context of PSE different disciplines, such as electrical, mechanical, and software disciplines, have to exchange and edit data. However, stakeholders might want to focus on local or in other words discipline-specific views without getting bothered by information that are not relevant for them. Therefore, discipline-neutral views are needed.

3.2 Context and Use Cases

Traditionally model engineering in PSE has mainly focused on paper plans and slowly has transformed to the digital era over the last decades. However, discipline-specific views have prevailed and the integration of engineering data is still an open challenge in every complex PSE project. Figure 4 displays an approach for a multi-model unification into a common view and thus, identifying common concepts for holistic system understanding and modeling [29].

On the left and right side we have the local glossaries that represent the local vocabularies and views of discipline-specific engineers in their specific domain. In the middle we can see the unified view over all concepts. If concepts can be semantically linked in a moderated negotiation process, they build up a glossary of common concept models. These concepts are domain-crossing and are constructed from parameters and values from different views and domains. However, local characteristics such as names or units might differ between each other and the identification of mapping relationships is a non-trivial task. The entire system is constructed from these boundary-crossing concepts that combine the different discipline-specific concepts relevant to the project.

To achieve this vision, we aim to visualise AML-structures supporting the Multi-Model Reviewing (MMR) capabilities for improved PSE model engineering.

To show the feasibility of our approach, we have derived the four basic use cases from common AMLEditor functionalities for AML data handling. These basic data management functions consist of importing and exporting AML files, add, modify and remove functionalities for AML data elements and search for AML data. Furthermore, we include desired functions not available in the current version of AMLEditor, such as search via attribute values. To enable model capabilities, we extend the requirements with the following set of use cases:

UC-1: Import & Export of an AML file. In PSE a *round-trip engineering* process as described in [37] with frequent update cycles of preliminary discipline-specific designs is required for the engineering of complex PSE systems. Therefore, the *import* (UC-1.1) and *export* (UC-1.2) of AML files is essential for data management. Users frequently start with the import of an AML file in

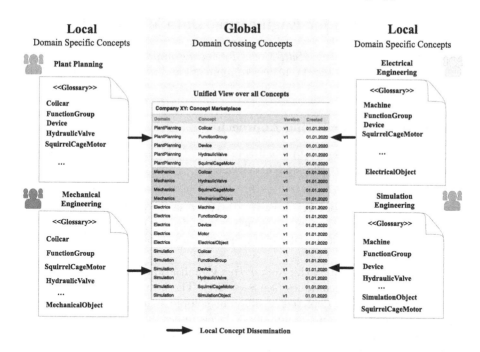

Fig. 4. Multi-disciplinary use case: the common concepts glossary process.

order to view or modify data in the received artefact. The export function is required for distributing changes to other engineers or stakeholders or to import data into other software tools for further manipulation.

UC-2: Navigation in Project Data. Engineers have to edit data based on the designs of other disciplines. In order to be able to view the designs, users require navigation capabilities to process the data: *(UC-2.1)* Selection of specific disciplines or *(UC-2.2)* the routing of dependencies to other disciplines are needed for holistic, targeted understanding.

UC-3: Search in Project Data. Since project structures can become large and complex, a search functionality is relevant for efficient data management: *(UC-3.1)* Users can search for a specific name of a component or *(UC-3.2)* users can search for a specific attribute value of a component.

UC-4: Modify Project Data. This use case concerns the data modification capabilities and is similar to the Create, Read, Update and Delete (CRUD) functions for persistent storage: *(UC-4.1)* to add a component, *(UC-4.2)* to edit a component, *(UC-4.3)* to move component within the hierarchical structure, or *(UC-4.4)* to delete a component.

To support elicited requirements and identified use cases, we developed a prototypical solution based on a graph-based visualisation to support model review of AML files.

4 System Design for Engineering Data Visualisation

This section introduces the *Multi-Model Reviewing* approach and *Multi-Model Reviewer* system design based on the requirements and modeling capabilities as described in Sect. 3.1.

4.1 Multi-model Reviewing Approach

The *Multi-Model Reviewing* approach considers four engineering model visualisation aspects to support the model reviewer.

Visualisation of Project Hierarchy. To visualise the project hierarchy (e.g. the plant structure) the applied approach is a *Node-link graph*. Users can intuitively view the hierarchical structure of the system without the need to train in this specific method.

Due to space constraints the *Radial Tree* visualisation was selected from the different visualisation techniques (see Sect. 2.1). The branches, which represent different disciplines, are depicted in different colors as shown in Fig. 5. In the current implementation a maximum of two levels under the root level is shown to the user to avoid cognitive overload. Additional information such as node names are available when hovering over the particular node.

Visualisation of Cross-References. The *Radial Tree* technique is not entirely suited for visualising cross-references. Our solution is to show cross-references in a different color than the discipline-specific views.

A cross-reference between mechanical and electrical engineering could concern, e.g., an electrical motor. The electrical view details power supply and cabling of the motor, while mechanical engineers specify other parameters e.g. the size dimensions of the motor.

We draw information for cross-references from the InstanceHierarchy and show connections relative to the selected node. Aside from the selected node, other nodes are greyed out to focus on the current selection as seen in Fig. 6.

Space-Efficient Visualisation. To declutter the visual space and provide space-efficient means of visualisation for the PSE context the decisions taken are explained in the following:

Force-directed graph algorithm combined with *radial tree* was implemented to arrange the nodes in an optimal way. For an optimal distribution of nodes, additional refinements in the force directed graph algorithm were made to keep child and parent nodes close while ensuring sufficient space between unrelated nodes without overlapping.

Labels are available but only partially visible: the label for the root node, for nodes representing views (e.g. *Mechanical view*), currently selected nodes and connected nodes to the current selection.

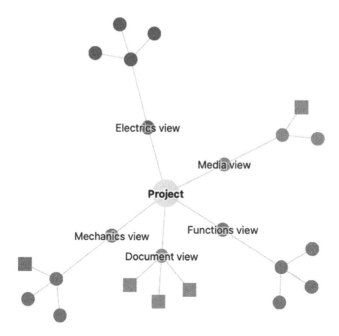

Fig. 5. Overview on discipline-specific views in a *radial tree* representation of a multi-disciplinary AML structure.

Color is used to emphasize the different disciplines. In the figures, the *Electrics view* is colored in pink, orphaned nodes (without a parent), are colored in red to draw the attention to them. The color schema can be adapted for instance to grayscale in case of addational needs. This would limit the number of possible discipline branches to six.

Shapes provide additional information concerning node hierarchy in the implementation:

> *Circles* illustrate components that have one or more sub-components and belong to the regular project hierarchy.
>
> *Squares* show components without sub-components.
>
> *Triangles* represent orphaned nodes.

Size was only used for the root node, being bigger than the others. However for future work, the number of children nodes or other features could be also illustrated in the size of nodes to provide quicker visual analysis capabilities.

Discipline-Neutral View. User can switch in the main view between the general view, showing all disciplines and the entire project hierarchy, and the selection of single disciplines. Single branches can be clicked to center them and view connections between all nodes, irrelevant data are getting filtered out. Parts of the tree that do not belong to the selected discipline are hidden.

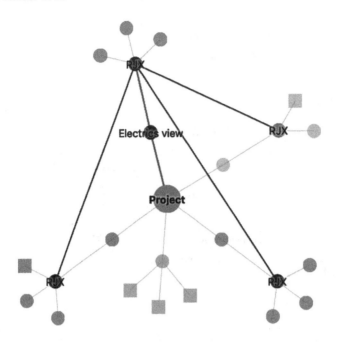

Fig. 6. Visualisation of cross-references between discipline-specific views.

4.2 Multi-Model Reviewer System Design

To support the *Multi-Model Reviewing* approach the decision was made to build a modular, light-weight web application to support the modeling capabilities and apply information visualisation methods to the underlying model. The system design of the *Multi-Model Reviewer* is divided into two main parts: the user interface in a web application and the service backend with a REST-interface. An overview of the system components is shown in Fig. 7.

User Interface. To support the multi-model reviewer on working with the engineering model, the *Multi-Model Reviewer* frontend consists of two modules: (a) *aml-graph* (b) *aml-graph-visualization.* The *aml-graph-visualization* module provides components and modules for a general graph visualisation. This module is utilised by the *aml-graph* module to provide the model, functionalities and services to draw and interacting with the AML graph. For the communication with the service backend a dedicated service is provided.

Service Backend. In the *Multi-Model Reviewer* service backend an overlying *Backend REST API* is responsible for the communication with the frontend and provides services for the import and export of an AML graph. Like the frontend, the backend consists of an model and services. An AML graph instance is persisted by the *graph-persistence* service to a database.

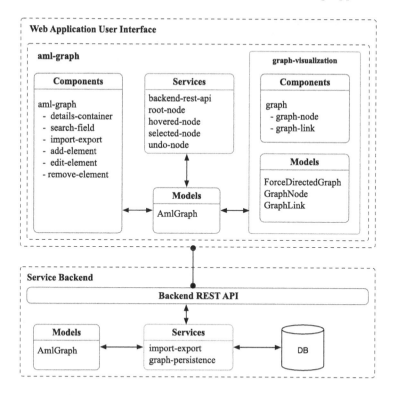

Fig. 7. Architectural system design of the *Multi-Model Reviewer*.

5   Prototype and Evaluation

This section demonstrates the *Multi-Model Reviewer* prototype and reports on the evaluation results of the applied graph-based techniques in the PSE domain.

5.1   Multi-Model Reviewer Prototype Implementation

The *Multi-Model Reviewer* prototype, provides a frontend web application connected to a backend service for data model management and proved the feasibility of the chose visualisation approach for PSE structures. The frontend is built using *Angular 8*[5]. Additionally used libraries are *Reactive Programming library RXJS*[6] and *JavaScript (JS) library Data-Driven Documents (D3)*[7]. The backend is built using *Spring Boot*[8]. Figure 8 shows the graphical interface, which is created of a main view, displaying the project hierarchy (1) as well as import and export functionality (2). Nodes can be double-clicked to re-arrange the view

---

[5] Angular: angular.io.
[6] RXJS: reactivex.io.
[7] Java Script Library D3: d3js.org.
[8] Spring Boot: spring.io/projects/spring-boot.

around them. On the top right of the window, detailed information is shown, such as the name, id or parent node (3). The different discipline-specific views are shown in (4). Add, remove and edit functions are also supported (5).

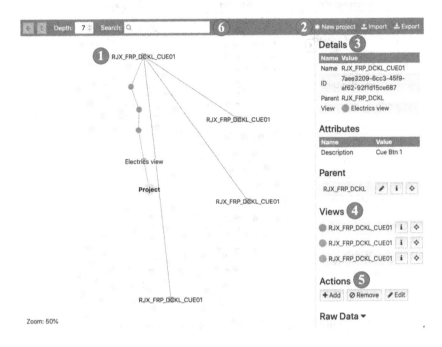

Fig. 8. User interface of the *Multi-Model Reviewer* prototype.

The search function (6) currently supports full text search and search via element or attribute name and is shown in Fig. 9 (a). Results are listed as real-time suggestions in a drop-down window under the search bar.

A more detailed demonstration of the different capabilities is shown in the provided screencasts.[9]

To investigate the feasibility of our approach initially, a small and simple AML-data set was created to test the capabilities. The data set consists of 98 components modelled in different views (disciplines).

In comparison to the standard *AutomationML Editor*, the presented prototype has as a main advantage the graphical visualisation of cross-references and the entire project structure. Users can easily filter for discipline-specific branches visually and inspect relationships in the context menu. Furthermore, orphaned nodes can easily be detected. Another feature is the search function that enables users to search by name or attribute, which is currently not possible in the *AutomationML Editor*.

---

[9] Prototype Screencasts: https://qse.ifs.tuwien.ac.at/2019-graph-visualization/.

In Fig. 9 (b), one main modeling capability is shown, the add function. The connected views and parameters can be added, as well as parent element, id and name. Similar dialogues are available for edit and remove actions.

Fig. 9. The *Search* (a) and *Add New Element* (b) feature in the *Multi-Model Reviewer* prototype.

However, there are further features that are not implemented in the current version: Not all AML language concepts are yet built into the presented prototype, for example `RoleClasses`.

5.2   Multi-Model Review Performance – Evaluation Design

This section described the design of the performance evaluation. We selected a common human interaction measure, the Keystroke-Level Method (KLM) [8], for the performance measurement. The aim is to evaluate the time an expert user needs in a computer system to correctly conduct a routine task (described in Sect. 3.2). For that a routine task is split into atomic keystroke-level actions. In Table 1 standardized *Operators* are shown that reflecting common user interactions in computer systems (such as keystroke or mouse pointing, etc) with average empirical data. Additionally, *Mental Operators*, which considers time frames in which the users stops an action for different reasons (e.g. thinking) are used. The time efficiency between different systems is measured by adding up all execution times at the end of an action process recording.

To measure the performance between the *AutomationML Editor* and the *Multi-Model Reviewer Prototype* we created a small but illustrative data set with 98 components. To imitate the multi-disciplinary engineering environment, we modeled discipline-specific views such as *Functions view*, *Mechanics view*, *Electrics view*, *Media view* and *Document view*. According to the derived

Table 1. List of standard KLM *operators*, associated *symbols* and estimated *execution time* (in seconds) [19].

Symbol	Operator	Execution time (sec)
K	Keystroke	0.12–1.2 (typically 0.28)
T(n)	Type sequence of n characters	$n * K$
P	Point with mouse to target on display	1.1
B	Press or release mouse button	0.1
BB	Click mouse button	0.2
H	Move hand to keyboard or mouse	0.4
M	Mental act of routine thinking	0.6–1.4
W(t)	Waiting for the system to respond	t

needs following tasks were measured and grouped by the scenarios introduced in Sect. 3:

UC-1 Import and export of an AML file
  Task-1a Import an AML file.
  Task-1b Export an AML file.
UC-2 Navigate in project data
  Task-2a Show only components relevant to a specific engineering discipline.
  Task-2b Show a component with related views.
UC-3 Search in project data
  Task-3a Search for a component by name.
  Task-3b Search for a component by attribute value.
UC-4 Modify the project data
  Task-4a Add a new component.
  Task-4b Edit the details of a component.
  Task-4c Change the hierarchy of a component.
  Task-4d Remove a component.

5.3   Performance Evaluation Results

This section illustrates a calculation for a representative task in model reviewing and also the results of all other tasks. The task *UC 3.3a: Search for a component by name* is executed in both the AMLEditor and the *MMR Prototype* and the corresponding calculations are shown below:

UC 3.3a: Search for a Component by Name

AutomationML Editor. (1) Initiate the search (decide to carry out the task) **M** (2) Find, point to and double click (expand) the "Project" component **M, P, 2BB** (3) Find, point to and click (select) the "Mechanics view" component **M, P, BB** (4) Hit the Ctrl + F keys (actives the search function) **T(2)** (5) Find, point to and click the revealed search bar **M, P, BB** (6) Move hand from mouse to keyboard **H** (7) Enter the name of the searched component ("RJX_FRP_DCKL_JOG01_DIAL") **T(23)** (8) Hit the Enter key **K** (9) Find the highlighted component **M** (10) Validate that the component name is the one that was searched for **M**

Total time = 6**M** + 3**P** + **H** + **K** + 4**BB** + **T**(25) = $6*1.2 + 3*1.1 + 0.4 + 0.28 + 4*0.2 + 25*0.28 = 18.98$ s

Multi-Model Reviewer Prototype. (1) Initiate the search (decide to carry out the task) **M** (2) Find, point to and click the search bar **M, P, BB** (3) Move hand from mouse to keyboard **H** (4) Enter a part of the searched component's name ("01_dial") **T(7)** (5) Go through the two results of the revealed search result list **M** (7) Recall that the color green is assigned to components of the "Mechanics view" **M** (8) Find the result with the green color coding **M** (9) Find, point to and click the "Select" button of that search result **M, P, BB**

Total time = 6**M** + 2**P** + **H** + 2**BB** + **T**(7) = $6*1.2 + 2*1.1 + 0.4 + 2*0.2 + 7*0.28 = 12.16$ s

Table 2 presents the summarized results of all use cases (for details refer to [30]). These results, measured with the KLM method, show that, except from two scenarios *Import an AML file* and *Edit the details of a component*, the proposed prototype fares better. These results are promising that the designed solution could help PSE engineers to manage engineering models more efficiently. However, this hypothesis must be tested in more detail in future work.

Table 2. Average execution times based on KLM [8] for the tasks (in seconds), performed with *AMLEditor* and the *MMR Prototype* solution based on [31].

Tasks	AML editor	MMR prototype
Task-1a	8.1	9.6
Task-1b	12.4	9.4
Task-2a	-	4.4
Task-2b	36.3	13.9
Task-3a	19.0	12.2
Task-3b	-	12.4
Task-4a	35.3	22.4
Task-4b	13.2	13.7
Task-4c	9.0	8.7
Task-4d	35.6	10.4

6   Discussion

This section discusses results of the research questions introduced in Sect. 1. The goal of this work was to initially study the requirements and needs for AML modeling in the PSE domain. The heterogeneous data flow and divergent tool landscape in the PSE domain hinder a seamless data and model integration. Text-based manipulation is a standard for engineering models, but have their disadvantages regarding understandability and transparency of interdependencies between domains and boundary-crossing objects. Visualisation can help to infer knowledge that could not be extracted from a pure text-based representation and support experts in their modeling tasks. This way, common concepts and integration of discipline-specific views as described in Sect. 3 can be discovered in a more illustrative and intuitive way to pave the way towards a discipline-crossing overview and negotiation method. The prototype and developed concepts build a basis for more advanced use cases and modeling capabilities.

RQ1. Model Visualisation Requirements. *What requirements are critical to facilitate visualising and reviewing multi-disciplinary models in the PSE domain?*
We derived requirements and actions that are usually performed by engineers in multi-disciplinary environments in Sect. 3. The following requirements were identified: (a) *The ability to represent project hierarchy*, (b) *The capability to represent cross-references between components*, (c) *An efficient way to represent large data structures* and (d) *A discipline-neutral view*. Furthermore, we derived the following four basic use cases described in Sect. 3.2, which are representative for the daily work of an engineer in PSE: *UC-1 Import & Export of an AML file, UC-2 Navigate in Project Data, UC-3 Search in Project Data, UC-4 Modify the Project data.*

RQ2. Multi-Model Reviewer System Design. *What system design facilitates the information visualisation of PSE models?*
To answer this research question, we designed and developed the *Multi-Model Reviewer* prototype, applying graph-based visualisation to AML-hierarchies, which is described in Sect. 4. The requirements derived from addressing RQ1 were transformed to prototype functionality for AML data handling and management. Different information visualisation techniques were applied, such as use of appropriate color, size or form and restriction of displayed data to reduce cognitive load.

RQ3. Multi-Model Reviewer Performance Analysis. *How does the information visualisation prototype approach perform when compared to a standard text-based PSE modeling tool?*
We used a comparative analysis for evaluation. The four main use cases described in RQ1 were measured in both modeling tools, the *Multi-Model Reviewer* and AMLEditor. Through the static KLM, we estimated time required for these tasks of domain experts. Except for import functionality and editing the details of a component, all other tasks are performed in a quicker way in the *Multi-Model Reviewer*, the search function is more extensive.

Limitations. Threats to validity to this work include that the prototype in its current form is at an initial stage. The tool only covers the presented use cases and functionalities. However, for a operational engineering tool advanced features have to be introduced to cover and integrate the frequent update cycle required for complex PSE modeling and move towards an agile working process in the industrial domain. Such features are consistency and semantics checks, change tracking or version management. The generated test data was relatively simple and small in comparison to real-world production system data sets. Furthermore, it does not cover the whole functionality of the AML standard, such as `SystemUnitClasses`, `RoleClasses`, and references to external resources. Additionally, the visual aspects for graph-based model reviews need to be validated regarding efficiency and quality assurance factors.

At this stage, the prototype is of academic nature and has not been yet tested with a significant number of domain experts.

7 Related Work

In this section we discuss related work on domain modeling in PSE and domain-specific model visualisations.

7.1 Domain Modeling in Production Systems Engineering

Local data models are oftentimes only known to the engineers who model them in the discipline-specific tools, however for improved standardisation and reuse of data models, visibility of local data models is necessary [10]. Change and consistency management are essential topics in production systems modeling, but are challenging due to the multitude and heterogeneity of data sources common to the PSE domain [12].

Proprietary formats and languages create an additional lock-in effect due to the incompatibility with tools and artefacts from other domains [2]. The externalisation of element or attribute changes and effects on interconnected dependencies (between these elements) to involved stakeholders can increase system model exchange efficiency and can improve the quality of the overall engineering model [4]. In multi-disciplinary PSE, system designs and plans are typically modeled based on hierarchical structures including a set of different views.

Although, tools help to increase productivity and product quality, there are still several shortcomings to be addressed: Lack of usability and interoperability and high complexity require high training effort and lots of domain expertise [6].

However, consistency and changes tracking is a crucial property to guarantee high quality of outputs, such as control code or simulation models for parameter estimation [13]. Mustafa and Labiche also present various requirements for a generic traceabilty model, which specific different manipulation tasks such as modeling traceability between model at elements in different degrees of detail [28]. Traceability modeling in heterogeneous systems is also more tailored to specific formats, such as Ecore [28].

Domain experts can benefit from the combination of textual analysis paired with visualisation and graph analytics of their domain-specific concepts, [18] performing better than purely text-based approaches concerning knowledge extraction. Therefore, we aim to visualise the growing hierarchical structure of plant topologies, as an important step towards increasing the efficiency in domain-specific modeling in terms of providing a better overview about data model structures. Vathoopan et al. describe how mechatronic AML models can be visualised to enable model-based automation engineering [35] and report positive initial experiences from prototype development.

CAEX [9], a XML-based format for modeling engineering data, is a representative example for data modeling formats in PSE which needs to be considered for domain modeling.

7.2 Domain-Specific Model Visualisation

Visualisations have multiple benefits for model management and curation in domain-specific contexts: Use cases include data analysis, improved querying capabilities and exploration [14].

Jäger et al. [17] visualised technical dependencies in PSE using cause-effect-diagrams as a visualisation means. The authors conclude, that not all information is always needed for specific tasks, and therefore the facilitation to curate and select is important. Knowledge graphs are one established form of visualisation of data sets to gain and reason on existing data, that are generated by different algorithms in semantic web technologies. In [32], the authors presented a knowledge graph, to semantically analyse Industry 4.0 related standards.

Zoubek et al. [38] discuss the difficulty of developers switching back and forth between the textual and graphical representation for review tasks. To improve this, they propose coordinated visualisations to better perceive changes to graphical models and a prototypical implementation in *Eclipse Papyrus*.

Biffl et al. [5] discuss a model-driven engineering approach for AML and the subsequent benefits such as versioning and view-linking support. However, they also point out that additional work has to be done regarding quality assurance and fault management.

Kovalenko et al. [20] provide an overview on advantages of model-based and semantic web technologies methods applied to AML. One limitation is that, there is still a high entry level for engineers who need a sufficient understanding of these techniques to gain their functionalities. However they also mention that it could be beneficial to bridge both worlds to benefit from both approaches.

8   Conclusion and Future Work

Visual and graph-based model review and inspection methods and tools in *Production Systems Engineering* have not yet been researched extensively. However, the growing complexity of system models speaks in favour of such information extraction approaches.

Graphical tools for model management can support the engineering process and guide the knowledge discovery process and improve quality assurance in identifying faulty designs. Data integration can be improved by gaining an understanding of dependencies between disciplines. For improved tool and concept development, domain experts and model engineers' collaboration is of high importance. Information visualisation is a growing discipline from which both communities, the model engineering and PSE industry, can benefit.

The *Multi-Model Reviewer* tool is the first step towards visual inspection and multi-model review of AML files. The requirements and findings of applying information visualisation techniques focused on graph-based approaches in an industrial context can further increase the model quality in PSE.

The *Multi-Model Reviewing* approach provides a guideline to visualise multi-disciplinary engineering models. Discipline-specific model views are linked into a unified graph and shown in a space-efficient way. Besides a discipline-neutral view that shows all information, cross-references are highlighted when a node is selected, and unnecessary parts of the graph are faded. This helps a multi-model reviewer to focus on the relevant task and displays only needed information.

Future Work. Empirical data on the management and review activities of large system models in PSE are needed to base future research on a quantitative foundation. The combination of model-based and semantic approaches (e.g. knowledge graphs) seem to be promising to support domain experts with challenging tasks in the future.

Acknowledgment. The financial support by the Christian Doppler Research Association, the Austrian Federal Ministry for Digital & Economic Affairs and the National Foundation for Research, Technology and Development is gratefully acknowledged.

This work has been funded by the project OBARIS, which has received funding from the Austrian Research Promotion Agency (FFG) under grant 877389.

References

1. Ackerman, A.F., Buchwald, L.S., Lewski, F.H.: Software inspections: an effective verification process. IEEE Softw. **6**(3), 31–36 (1989)
2. Biffl, S., et al.: Technical debt analysis in parallel multi-disciplinary systems engineering. In: 2019 45th Euromicro Conference on Software Engineering and Advanced Applications (SEAA), pp. 342–346. IEEE (2019)
3. Biffl, S., Lüder, A., Gerhard, D.: Multi-Disciplinary Engineering for Cyber-Physical Production Systems. Springer, Heidelberg (2017). https://doi.org/10.1007/978-3-319-56345-9
4. Biffl, S., Lüder, A., Rinker, F., Waltersdorfer, L.: Efficient engineering data exchange in multi-disciplinary systems engineering. In: Giorgini, P., Weber, B. (eds.) Advanced Information Systems Engineering. CAiSE 2019. Lecture Notes in Computer Science, vol. 11483. Springer, Cham (2019). https://doi.org/10.1007/978-3-030-21290-2_2

5. Biffl, S., Mätzler, E., Wimmer, M., Lüder, A., Schmidt, N.: Linking and versioning support for AutomationML: a model-driven engineering perspective. In: 2015 IEEE 13th International Conference on Industrial Informatics, pp. 499–506. IEEE (2015)

6. Bordeleau, F., Liebel, G., Raschke, A., Stieglbauer, G., Tichy, M.: Challenges and research directions for successfully applying MBE tools in practice. In: MODELS (Satellite Events), pp. 338–343 (2017)

7. Card, S.K., Mackinlay, J.D., Shneiderman, B. (eds.): Readings in Information Visualization: Using Vision to Think. Morgan Kaufmann Publishers Inc., San Francisco (1999)

8. Card, S.K., Moran, T.P., Newell, A.: The Psychology of Human-Computer Interaction, vol. 15. CRC Press, Boca Raton (1983)

9. Drath, R.: Datenaustausch in der Anlagenplanung mit AutomationML: Integration von CAEX. Springer-Verlag, PLCopen XML und COLLADA (2009)

10. Drath, R., Barth, M.: Concept for managing multiple semantics with AutomationML–maturity level concept of semantic standardization. In: Proceedings of 2012 IEEE 17th International Conference on Emerging Technologies & Factory Automation (ETFA 2012), pp. 1–8. IEEE (2012)

11. Drath, R., Lüder, A., Peschke, J., Hundt, L.: AutomationML-the glue for seamless automation engineering. In: 2008 IEEE International Conference on Emerging Technologies and Factory Automation, pp. 616–623. IEEE (2008)

12. Egyed, A., Zeman, K., Hehenberger, P., Demuth, A.: Maintaining consistency across engineering artifacts. Computer $51(2)$, 28–35 (2018)

13. Feldmann, S., Wimmer, M., Kernschmidt, K., Vogel-Heuser, B.: A comprehensive approach for managing inter-model inconsistencies in automated production systems engineering. In: 2016 IEEE International Conference on Automation Science and Engineering (CASE), pp. 1120–1127. IEEE (2016)

14. Fluit, C., Sabou, M., van Harmelen, F.: Ontology-based information visualization: toward semantic web applications. In: Geroimenko, V., Chen, C. (eds.) Visualizing the Semantic Web. Springer, London (2006). https://doi.org/10.1007/1-84628-290-X_3

15. Holten, D.: Hierarchical edge bundles: visualization of adjacency relations in hierarchical data. IEEE Trans. Vis. Comput. Graph. $12(5)$, 741–748 (2006)

16. International Electrotechnical Commission: IEC 62714 - engineering data exchange format for use in industrial automation systems engineering - Automation markup language

17. Jäger, T., Fay, A., Wagner, T., Löwen, U.: Mining technical dependencies throughout engineering process knowledge. In: 2011 IEEE International Conference on Emerging Technologies and Factory Automation, pp. 1–7. IEEE (2011)

18. Kejriwal, M., Peng, J., Zhang, H., Szekely, P.: Structured event entity resolution in humanitarian domains. In: Vrandečić, D., et al. (eds.) The Semantic Web – ISWC 2018. ISWC 2018. Lecture Notes in Computer Science, vol. 11136. Springer, Cham (2018). https://doi.org/10.1007/978-3-030-00671-6_14

19. Kieras, D.: Using the keystroke-level model to estimate execution times. Tech. rep., University of Michigan (2001). http://www-personal.umich.edu/~itm/688/KierasKLMTutorial2001.pdf

20. Kovalenko, O., Wimmer, M., Sabou, M., Lüder, A., Ekaputra, F.J., Biffl, S.: Modeling AutomationML: semantic web technologies vs. model-driven engineering. In: 2015 IEEE 20th Conference on Emerging Technologies & Factory Automation (ETFA), pp. 1–4. IEEE (2015)

21. Lüder, A., Kirchheim, K., Pauly, J.L., Biffl, S., Rinker, F., Waltersdorfer, L.: Supporting the data model integrator in an engineering network by automating data integration. In: IEEE 17th International Conference on Industrial Informatics (2019)
22. Lüder, A., Pauly, J.L., Kirchheim, K., Rinker, F., Biffl, S.: Migration to AutomationML based tool chains - incrementally overcoming engineering network challenges. In: 5th AutomationML User Conference (2018). https://www.automationml.org/o.red/uploads/dateien/1548668540-17_Lueder_Migration-ToolChains_Paper.pdf
23. Lüder, A., Pauly, J.L., Rosendahl, R., Rinker, F., Biffl, S.: Support for engineering chain migration towards integrated multi-disciplinary engineering chains. In: 14th IEEE International Conference on Automation Science and Engineering (2018)
24. Lüder, A., Schmidt, N.: AutomationML in a Nutshell. In: Vogel-Heuser, B., Bauernhansl, T., ten Hompel, M. (eds.) Handbuch Industrie 4.0 Bd.2. Springer Reference Technik. Springer, Heidelberg (2017). https://doi.org/10.1007/978-3-662-53248-5_61
25. Mazza, R.: Introduction to Information Visualization. Springer, Heidelberg (2009). https://doi.org/10.1007/978-1-84800-219-7
26. McIntosh, S., Kamei, Y., Adams, B., Hassan, A.E.: The impact of code review coverage and code review participation on software quality: a case study of the QT, VTK, and ITK projects. In: Proceedings of the 11th Working Conference on Mining Software Repositories, pp. 192–201 (2014)
27. Mordinyi, R., Biffl, S.: Versioning in cyber-physical production system engineering: best-practice and research agenda. In: Proceedings of the First International Workshop on Software Engineering for Smart Cyber-Physical Systems, pp. 44–47. IEEE Press (2015)
28. Mustafa, N., Labiche, Y.: Towards traceability modeling for the engineering of heterogeneous systems. In: 3rd International Conference on Model-Driven Engineering and Software Development, pp. 321–328. IEEE (2015)
29. Rinker, F., Waltersdorfer, L., Meixner, K., Biffl, S.: Towards support of global views on common concepts employing local views. In: 2019 24th IEEE International Conference on Emerging Technologies and Factory Automation (ETFA), pp. 1686–1689. IEEE (2019)
30. Rinker, F., Waltersdorfer, L., Schüller, M., Winkler, D.: Information visualization in production systems engineering. Tech. rep. CDL-SQI 2019–15, TU Wien (June 2019). http://qse.ifs.tuwien.ac.at/wp-content/uploads/CDL-SQI-2019-15.pdf
31. Rinker, F., Waltersdorfer, L., Schüller, M., Winkler, D.: Graph-based model inspection tool for multi-disciplinary production systems engineering. In: Proceedings of the 8th International Conference on Model-Driven Engineering and Software Development, MODELSWARD, pp. 116–125 (2020). https://doi.org/10.5220/0008990001160125
32. Rivas, A., Grangel-González, I., Collarana, D., Lehmann, J., Vidal, M.E.: Unveiling relations in the Industry 4.0 standards landscape based on knowledge graph embeddings. arXiv preprint arXiv:2006.04556 (2020)
33. Schiffelers, R.R., Luo, Y., Mengerink, J., van den Brand, M.: Towards automated analysis of model-driven artifacts in industry. In: 6th International Conference on Model-Driven Engineering and Software Development, pp. 743–751 (2018)
34. Trunzer, E., Kirchen, I., Folmer, J., Koltun, G., Vogel-Heuser, B.: A flexible architecture for data mining from heterogeneous data sources in automated production systems. In: 2017 IEEE International Conference on Industrial Technology (ICIT), pp. 1106–1111. IEEE (2017)

35. Vathoopan, M., Walzel, H., Eisenmenger, W., Zoitl, A., Brandenbourger, B.: AutomationML mechatronic models as enabler of automation systems engineering: use-case and evaluation. In: 2018 IEEE 23rd International Conference on Emerging Technologies and Factory Automation (ETFA), vol. 1, pp. 51–58. IEEE (2018)
36. Wieringa, R.J.: Design Science Methodology for Information Systems and Software Engineering. Springer, Heidelberg (2014). https://doi.org/10.1007/978-3-662-43839-8
37. Winkler, D., Rinker, F., Kieseberg, P.: Towards a flexible and secure round-trip-engineering process for production systems engineering with agile practices. In: Winkler, D., Biffl, S., Bergsmann, J. (eds.) Software Quality: The Complexity and Challenges of Software Engineering and Software Quality in the Cloud. SWQD 2019. Lecture Notes in Business Information Processing, vol. 338. Springer, Cham (2019). https://doi.org/10.1007/978-3-030-05767-1_2
38. Zoubek, F., Langer, P., Mayerhofer, T.: Visualizations of evolving graphical models in the context of model review. In: Proceedings of the 21th ACM/IEEE International Conference on Model Driven Engineering Languages and Systems, pp. 381–391 (2018)

Augmenting Deep Neural Networks with Scenario-Based Guard Rules

Guy Katz[⊠]

The Hebrew University of Jerusalem, Jerusalem, Israel
guykatz@cs.huji.ac.il

Abstract. Deep neural networks (DNNs) are becoming widespread, and can often outperform manually-created systems. However, these networks are typically opaque to humans, and may demonstrate undesirable behavior in corner cases that were not encountered previously. In order to mitigate this risk, one approach calls for augmenting DNNs with hand-crafted *override rules*. These override rules serve to prevent the DNN from making certain decisions, when certain criteria are met. Here, we build on this approach and propose to bring together DNNs and the well-studied *scenario-based modeling* paradigm, by encoding override rules as simple and intuitive scenarios. We demonstrate that the scenario-based paradigm can render override rules more comprehensible to humans, while keeping them sufficiently powerful and expressive to increase the overall safety of the model. We propose a method for applying scenario-based modeling to this new setting, and apply it to multiple DNN models. (This paper substantially extends the paper titled "Guarded Deep Learning using Scenario-Based Modeling", published in Modelsward 2020 [47]. Most notably, it includes an additional case study, extends the approach to recurrent neural networks, and discusses various aspects of the proposed paradigm more thoroughly).

Keywords: Scenario-based modeling · Behavioral programming · Machine learning · Deep neural networks

1 Introduction

Deep learning technology [20] is bringing about dramatic changes in the world, by allowing engineers to use automated learning algorithms to create complex models [21]. Deep learning algorithms can generalize examples of how a desired system should behave into an artifact called a *deep neural network* (*DNN*). The DNN is then capable of correctly handling new inputs—including inputs that it had not encountered previously. In many cases, DNNs have been shown to *significantly outperform* manually-crafted software. Notable examples include the AlphaGO Go player [64], which defeated some of the world's strongest human Go players; systems for image recognition with DNN components that achieve superhuman precision [65]; and systems in various other domains, including recommender systems [16], natural language processing [12], and bioinformatics [10].

© Springer Nature Switzerland AG 2021
S. Hammoudi et al. (Eds.): MODELSWARD 2020, CCIS 1361, pp. 147–172, 2021.
https://doi.org/10.1007/978-3-030-67445-8_7

As DNNs are becoming more accurate and easier to create than manually-crafted systems, their use is expected to grow and intensify in the coming decades. Recently it has even been proposed to incorporate DNNs in *highly critical systems*, such as autonomous cars and unmanned aircraft [7,45].

Although DNNs have been demonstrating extraordinary performance, their use poses new challenges [1]. A notable difficulty is the extreme *opacity* of DNNs: because DNNs are generated by computers and not by humans, we can empirically determine that they perform well, but fully understanding their internal decision making is highly difficult. As a result, it is nearly impossible for humans to manually reason about the correctness of DNNs. For example, in many state-of-the-art systems for image recognition, which appeared highly accurate, it has been observed that slight input perturbations could cause DNN to make problematic misclassifications [69]. This phenomenon raises serious concerns about these networks' reliability and safety. In recent years initial attempts have been made to automatically reason about DNNs using formal methods (e.g., [19,41,48,50,54,71]), but these approaches currently afford only limited scalability. Moreover, DNN verification approaches typically focus on detecting erroneous DNN behaviors, but do not specify how to correct such behaviors after their discovery—which is also a difficult task.

As an illustrative example, consider the DeepRM system [57]. The goal of DeepRM is to perform resource allocation: the system has certain available resources (e.g., memory and CPUs), and also a queue of pending jobs. In each time step, the system needs to either schedule a pending job and allocate some of the available resources to this job; or perform a "pass" action, which means that no new jobs are assigned resources while the system waits for executing jobs to terminate and free up resources. DeepRM's goal is to perform scheduling in a way that maximizes job throughput. In order to achieve this goal, the system maintains a model that contains information about resource allocation and pending jobs, and uses a pre-trained DNN to choose which action to perform in each step. When compared to manually created state-of-the-art solutions that tackle the same problem, DeepRM has been shown to perform very well [57].

In spite of its overall satisfactory performance, it has been observed that the DeepRM system may sometimes behave in undesirable ways. For example, DeepRM's creators reported that its DNN controller might sometimes request that a job x be allocated resources, even though no job x exists in the job queue. In order to address this issue, *override rule* were added to DeepRM's implementation [58]. An override rule is a small piece of code that can examine the current state of the system, and then overrides the decision of the DNN controller when certain conditions are detected. In the case described above, the override rule will change the controller's selection to "pass" whenever the DNN requests to allocate resources to a job that is non-existent. There are additional override rules included within the DeepRM implementation [58], and also in implementations of other systems that use DNN controllers (e.g., the Pensieve system [59]). Further, additional undesirable behaviors have been discovered in DeepRM since its release [52]; and removing these behaviors might require augmenting the system with yet additional override rules.

These cases, and others like them, demonstrate the integral role that override rules are beginning to play in DNN-based models. Because erroneous behaviors may be discovered after such models are deployed, override rules may need to be added, extended, refactored and enhanced at many points throughout the system's lifetime. In this paper, we argue that this situation calls for leveraging suitable modeling techniques, in order to facilitate the creation and maintenance of override rules—in a way that would increase the system's overall reliability.

As part of this work we advocate using the *scenario-based modeling* (*SBM*) framework [13,40] in creating override rules. In SBM, the individual behaviors of a system are modeled as independent scenarios, which are then automatically interwoven when the model is executed—in a way that produces cohesive system behavior. SBM has been shown to afford multiple benefits in the design and automated maintenance of systems. In addition, it is particularly suited for *incremental development*, which is a desirable trait when dealing with override rules. We propose here an approach and a method for applying SBM to systems with DNN components, in a way that allows engineers to specify override rules as SBM scenarios. We discuss the benefits that this approach affords (for example, through the amenability of SBM to automated analysis [38]), and demonstrate its applicability on three recently proposed systems. Although we focus here on systems with DNN components, our proposed approach could be adjusted to also accommodate systems with additional kinds of opaque components.

The rest of this paper is organized as follows. In Sect. 2 we provide the necessary background on SBM, DNNs and override rules. Next, in Sect. 3 we present our method for applying SBM to systems with DNN components. In Sect. 4 we describe how the proposed approach is applied to three case-studies. Next, in Sect. 5 we extend the proposed technique to recurrent neural networks. A discussion of related work appears in Sect. 6, and we conclude in Sect. 7.

2   Background

2.1   Scenario-Based Modeling

Scenario-based modeling [40] is a modeling approach for creating complex reactive systems. The basic notion at the core of this approach is that of a *scenario object*: an object that describes a single behavior, either desirable or undesirable, of the system being modeled. Each scenario object is created separately and independently of other scenarios, and does not directly interact with them; instead, it only interacts with a global execution mechanism. This global execution mechanism is the component in charge of managing the execution of a set of scenario objects, in a way that produces cohesive system behavior.

Several flavors of scenario-based modeling have been proposed, which differ from each other primarily in the idioms that a scenario object uses to interact with the execution mechanism, and thus to affect the overall system execution.

Our work here focuses on the most commonly used idioms, namely the *requesting*, *waiting-for* and *blocking* of events [40]. When the system is executed, each scenario object may declare that it has reached a *synchronization point*, in which the global execution mechanism must trigger an event. The object then specifies three sets of events: events that it *requests* be triggered; events that it *blocks* from being triggered; and events that it does not actively request, but should be notified in case they are triggered by the global execution mechanism (*waited-for events*). The execution mechanism waits for all the individual scenario objects to synchronize (or, alternatively, just for a subset thereof—depending on the semantics in use [27]). Then, it selects an event e that is requested and not blocked for triggering, and informs any relevant scenario object that e has been triggered.

An example of a small, scenario-based model appears in Fig. 1. This model belongs to a system that controls the water level in a tank that has hot and cold water taps. Each of the model's scenario objects is depicted as a transition system, whose nodes represent the (predetermined) synchronization points. The ADDHOTWATER scenario object repeatedly waits for WATERLOW events, and requests three times the event ADDHOT; and the ADDCOLDWATER scenario object performs a symmetrical operation with cold water. When a model that includes only the ADDHOTWATER and ADDCOLDWATER objects is executed, three ADDHOT events and three ADDCOLD events may be triggered in any order. If an additional requirement is added that the water temperature in the tank be kept stable, the scenario object STABILITY may be used to enforce the interleaving of ADDHOT and ADDCOLD events through the use of event blocking. The execution trace that is generated by the resulting model appears in the event log.

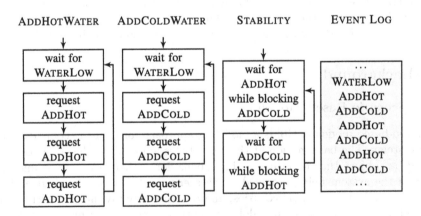

Fig. 1. (From [37]) A scenario-based model of a system that controls the water level in a tank with hot and cold water taps.

Scenario-based modeling has been implemented on top of a variety of programming languages, such as JavsScript [4], Java [39], ScenarioTools [22] and

C++ [30]. The SBM methodology has been successfully applied to model complex systems, such as robotic controllers [25], cache coherence protocols [32] and web-servers [30]. For simplicity, in the rest of this paper, we often describe scenario objects in terms of transitions systems.

We take after the definitions given in [46], and formalize the SBM framework as follows. A scenario object O over event set E is defined as tuple $O = \langle Q, \delta, q_0, R, B \rangle$, which is comprised of the following components:

- Q is a set of states, each representing one of the predetermined synchronization points;
- q_0 is the initial state;
- $R : Q \to 2^E$ and $B : Q \to 2^E$ map states to the sets of events requested and blocked at these states (respectively); and
- $\delta : Q \times E \to 2^Q$ is a transition function, indicating how the object reacts when an event is triggered.

Two scenario objects can be composed into a single, combined scenario object, as follows. For objects $O^1 = \langle Q^1, \delta^1, q_0^1, R^1, B^1 \rangle$ and $O^2 = \langle Q^2, \delta^2, q_0^2, R^2, B^2 \rangle$ over a common event set E, we define the composite scenario object $O^1 \parallel O^2$ as $O^1 \parallel O^2 = \langle Q^1 \times Q^2, \delta, \langle q_0^1, q_0^2 \rangle, R^1 \cup R^2, B^1 \cup B^2 \rangle$, where:

- $\langle \tilde{q}^1, \tilde{q}^2 \rangle \in \delta(\langle q^1, q^2 \rangle, e)$ if and only if $\tilde{q}^1 \in \delta^1(q^1, e)$ and $\tilde{q}^2 \in \delta^2(q^2, e)$; and
- The union of the labeling functions is defined in the natural way; e.g. $e \in (R^1 \cup R^2)(\langle q^1, q^2 \rangle)$ if and only if $e \in R^1(q^1) \cup R^2(q^2)$, and $e \in (B^1 \cup B^2)(\langle q^1, q^2 \rangle)$ if and only if $e \in B^1(q^1) \cup B^2(q^2)$.

The composition operator can be applied repeatedly to compose any number of scenario objects into a single scenario object.

We define a *behavioral model* M to be a collection of scenario objects, $O^1, O^2, \ldots, O^n$. The executions of M are defined to be the executions of the composite scenario object, $O = O^1 \parallel O^2 \parallel \ldots \parallel O^n$. Each execution of M starts from the initial state of O; and in each state q visited throughout the execution an enabled event e is chosen for triggering, if such an event exists (i.e., $e \in R(q) - B(q)$). Then, the execution proceeds to a state $\tilde{q} \in \delta(q, e)$, and so on.

Several extensions have been proposed for the basic variant of SBM described above. In one such extension, which will be particularly useful in our context, events are treated as *typed variables* [51]. For example, an event e can be declared to be of type integer, allowing a scenario object to *request* $e \geq 5$. Another scenario object might block $e \geq 7$. In this setting, the execution framework employs a *constraint solver*, such as an SMT solver [5], in order to resolve the various constraints and find a value assignment for e. In this case, the event $e = 6$ might be triggered. We omit here the formal definition of this extension, which is straightforward; the interested reader is referred to [51].

2.2   Deep Neural Networks and Override Rules

Deep, feed-forward neural networks (DNNs) are directed, weighted graphs, in which the nodes (also known as *neurons*) are organized into layers. The first and last layers are the input and output layers, respectively, and the multiple remaining layers are referred to as hidden layers. Each neuron in the network (except for input neurons) is connected to neurons from the preceding layer, and each edge is assigned a predetermined weight value (an illustration appears in Fig. 2). The selection of appropriate weight values is key; this is performed when the DNN is created during the *training* phase, which goes beyond the scope of this paper (for additional details, see [20]). In order to evaluate the DNN, values are first assigned to its input neurons, and then propagated forward through the network in an iterative process. In each iteration, values for another layer are computed using the values assigned to neurons in its predecessor. Eventually, the values of the output neurons are computed, and these values constitute the outputs of the DNN which are returned to the user. It is typical for DNNs to be used as controllers or classifiers, in which case the user usually cares about which output neuron received the highest value—as this neuron represents the action, or classification, that the DNN has selected among the possible options.

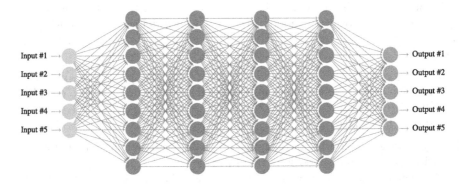

Fig. 2. (From [47]) A fully connected DNN with 5 input nodes (in green), 5 output nodes (in red), and 4 hidden layers containing a total of 36 hidden nodes (in blue). (Color figure online)

For our purpose here, it is usually sufficient to treat DNNs as black boxes, that transform an input into an output in some unknown way. However, for completeness, we briefly describe the evaluation procedure of a DNN. After the input neurons are assigned values, the value of each hidden node is computed in two steps: first, we compute a weighted sum of the node values from the previous layer, according to the predetermined edge weights. Then, we apply a non-linear *activation function* to this weighted sum [20], and the output of this activation function becomes the value of the node being computed. One common activation function is the Rectified Linear Unit (ReLU) [61], computed by $\text{ReLU}(x) = \max(0, x)$. Thus, when a neuron's value is computed using the ReLU activation function, it is taken to be the maximum between the linear combination of node values from the previous layer and 0.

Figure 3 depicts a small DNN (with 7 neurons in total), which will serve as a running example. This DNN acts as a controller: it takes two inputs, x_1 and x_2, computes values for its three hidden neurons v_1, v_2 and v_3, and then computes its output values y_1 and y_2, which represent scores for two possible actions. The hidden nodes v_1, v_2 and v_3 all use the ReLU activation function. We slightly abuse notation here, and use y_1 and y_2 to denote both the neurons and the actions/classes represented by these neurons. The action that is assigned the higher score is the one selected by the DNN. For example, the input assignment $x_1 = 1, x_2 = 0$ results in output values $y_1 = 1, y_2 = 0$, which mean that action y_1 is selected. In contrast, the input assignment $x_1 = 0, x_2 = 1$ leads to $y_1 = 0, y_2 = 3$, and so action y_2 is selected.

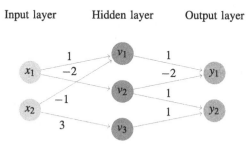

Fig. 3. (From [47]) A small neural network with a single hidden layer.

We formalize the notion of an *override rule* as a triple $\langle P, Q, \alpha \rangle$, where: (i) P is a predicate over the inputs of the network; (ii) Q is a predicate over the outputs of the network; and (iii) α is an override action. The semantics of an override rule $\langle P, Q, \alpha \rangle$ is that whenever P and Q hold for a network's evaluation, then output action α should be the one selected, regardless of the actual output of the DNN. For example, consider the following override rule

$$\langle x_1 > 0 \wedge x_2 < x_1, true, y_2 \rangle.$$

As we saw previously, for input values $x_1 = 1, x_2 = 0$ the DNN normally selects y_1; but, with this override rule, the selection would be changed instead to y_2. Note that this is so because this particular input satisfies the input condition, i.e. it holds that $x_1 > 0$ and $x_2 < x_1$. Our choice of setting Q to true means that this override rule only examines the DNN's inputs, and does not depend on its outputs. If we were to set Q, e.g., to $y_2 > 10$, then the override rule would not be triggered for $x_1 = 1, x_2 = 0$. By adjusting P and Q as needed, this definition is sufficient for expressing many common override rules, such as those in the DeepRM example described in Sect. 1.

3   Modeling Override Scenarios

In the case of DeepRM, engineers have added override rules as unrestricted Python code that resides within the code module that invokes the DNN controller, and then processes its result [58]. Thus, while the DNN component itself is clearly structured and well defined, the more recently added override rules are expressed as arbitrary pieces of code. This coding convention could lead to several undesirable issues: (i) if the number of override rules was to increase significantly, they could become convoluted and difficult to comprehend, maintain and extend; (ii) the semantics of existing override rules might, in time, become unclear. For example, does a more recent override rule supersede a previous rule if both can be applied? Is there a particular order in which override rules should be checked? Can multiple rules interact with one another? etc; and (iii) the conditions encoded within override rules might, in time, become more complex than originally intended, thus hiding away some of the model's logic where engineers might not know to look for it.

Here, we advocate the modeling of override rules using SBM, in a way that is designed to mitigate the aforementioned difficulties. SBM is particularly geared towards incremental modeling, which is a likely scenario when DNNs are involved: because DNNs are opaque, some of their undesirable behaviors are likely to be detected only post-deployment, thus requiring that new override rules be added. Moreover, SBM's simple semantics serve to guarantee that all interactions between the override rules are well defined. Finally, a substantial amount of work has been carried out on automatically analyzing, verifying and optimizing SBM models; and building on top of this work could prove useful in simplifying override rules and in detecting conflicts between them, as their numbers increase.

3.1   Modeling DNNs and Override Rules in SBM

We now propose a method for creating SBM models, in a way that combines scenario objects with a DNN controller. The core idea is to use a dedicated scenario object, O_{DNN}, to abstractly represent the DNN within the scenario-based model. This O_{DNN} is a non-deterministic scenario that models the DNN controller, and allows it to interact with other scenario objects which are present in the system. For the sake of simplicity, for now we assume that the set of possible inputs to the DNN, denoted $\mathbb{I}$, is finite (we relax this limitation later). Let $\mathbb{O}$ denote the set of possible actions from which the DNN chooses. We add the following new events to our event set E: an *input event* e_i for every $i \in \mathbb{I}$, and an *output event* e_o for every $o \in \mathbb{O}$. We introduce the convention that our new scenario object O_{DNN} repeatedly waits for all input events e_i, and then request all output events e_o. This behavior represents the black-box nature of the neural network component, at least as far as the rest of the model is concerned: engineers only know that after an input event is triggered, one of the output events will be selected, without knowing which. However, when the model is deployed, the execution infrastructure resolves the non-determinism of O_{DNN} by invoking the actual DNN and triggering precisely the output event that corresponds to the DNN's selection. For example, assuming there are only precisely two possible inputs, e.g. $i_1 = \langle 1, 0 \rangle$ and $i_2 = \langle 0, 1 \rangle$, the DNN depicted in Fig. 3 would be represented by the O_{DNN} scenario object that appears in Fig. 4.

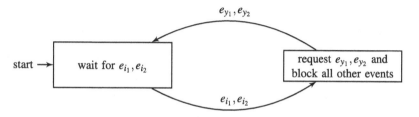

Fig. 4. (From [47]) A scenario O_{DNN} for the neural network in Fig. 3. Events e_{i_1} and e_{i_2} represent the inputs to the neural network, and events e_{y_1} and e_{y_2} represent its outputs.

In order to render the resulting model compatible with the actual DNN, we introduce a convention that states that other scenario objects in the system may not block any input event e_i. These scenario objects may, however, wait-for these events. A single dedicated scenario object, called a *sensor*, is responsible for requesting an input event when it is time for the DNN needs to be evaluated (e.g., following some user action). By another convention that we introduce, no scenario object besides O_{DNN} may request any output event e_o; however, other scenario objects in the system may wait-for, or block, these events. During system execution, it is possible for the neural network to assign the highest output score to an event that is currently blocked by another scenario object. When this happens, we resolve the non-determinism of O_{DNN} by selecting another output event, which represents the output with the next-to-highest score, etc. If no output events are left unblocked, then the system is deadlocked—and the execution terminates.

The motivation that underlies our definitions is to allow various scenario objects to monitor the inputs and outputs of the neural network controller, by waiting for the input and output events associated with them; and then to interfere with the DNN's recommendation by blocking certain output events. This is precisely the use-case of a typical override rule. We note that a scenario object may force the neural network to produce some specific output, by blocking all other possible outputs; alternatively, it may interfere more subtly, by blocking some events while allowing the DNN to choose among the remaining, unblocked events.

Recall our earlier assumption that the sets $\mathbb{I}$ and $\mathbb{O}$ of possible DNN inputs and outputs, respectively, are finite. In practice, this assumption might become a limiting factor: for example, considering the override rule described in Sect. 2.2, the triggering of the override rule was affected by the values assigned to x_1 and x_2, and so it is desirable to express these exact values in our model. Of course, in this case the number of possible value assignments is infinite. To overcome this limitation we again turn to an extension of the SBM semantics [51], which allows engineers to treat events as typed variables. We adjust our formulation slightly: we allow scenario objects in the system to wait-for a single, composite event, whose triggering indicates that values have been assigned to (all of) the neural network's inputs or outputs. Scenario objects may then access the fields of this composite event, which indicate the individual values assigned to each input or output neuron, and act according to these values.

With this extension in place, the override rule from Sect. 2.2 can be expressed as the scenario object in Fig. 5. This scenario enforces the following override rule: whenever $x_1 > 0$ and $x_2 < x_1$, output event y_2 (and not y_1) should be triggered. Here, the tuple $\langle e_{x_1}, e_{x_2} \rangle$ represents a single event, whose triggering indicates that values have been assigned to the neural network's inputs. This is a composite event that contains two real values, x_1 and x_2, that the override scenario can access and use in order to determine its next state. Output event e_{y_1} indicates, as before, that the override scenario forbids the neural network from selecting y_1 as its output action.

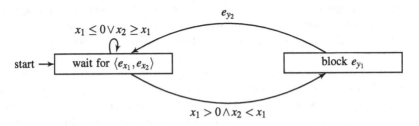

Fig. 5. (From [47]) A scenario object enforcing the override rule that whenever $x_1 > 0$ and $x_2 < x_1$, output event y_2 should be triggered.

3.2 Liveness Properties

Override rules are most often used to enforce *safety properties*. These properties state that "bad things never happen". However, sometimes there is a need to enforce also *liveness* properties, which state that "good things eventually happen". Specifically, this need can arise in the context of online reinforcement learning [68], in which the DNN controller changes over time. In this context we may wish to ensure, for example, that the DNN controller eventually tries out new output actions. If these output actions prove beneficial, the online RL mechanism will ensure that the neural network controller repeats them in the future. Liveness properties are relevant also when there are *fairness constraints*; for example, we may wish to ensure that in a resource management system, every pending job is eventually scheduled.

An example in which we wish to enforce liveness properties appears in [52], where the authors describe the *Custard* system: a congestion control system, which uses a neural network controller. Custard monitors the conditions of a computer network, and then select a bitrate for sending information across this network—with the goal of minimizing congestion while maintaining high throughput [43]. In [52], the authors examine Custard in order to determine whether there exist cases in which the DNN controller chooses a *sub-optimal* sending rate, i.e. a sending rate that does not utilize all available bandwidth, and never attempts to increase this bitrate. Clearly, such behavior constitutes a liveness violation, which can be corrected using an override rule.

Using SBM, we can encode the fact that one (or multiple) DNN output actions should eventually be blocked. Because blocking some actions forces the DNN controller to pick a different action, it can be used to enforce a liveness property. In practice, this blocking can be performed by having a scenario object wait for a sequence of n consecutive rounds in which a particular output event is triggered, and then block it in round $n + 1$. An example for $n = 3$ appears in Fig. 6: the scenario therein looks for 3 consecutive DNN evaluations where event y_2 is triggered, after which it blocks y_2 once, forcing the neural network to select another output action. An alternative approach is to have the override scenario block a particular output event with a very low probability [37], thus eventually blocking that event with probability 1.

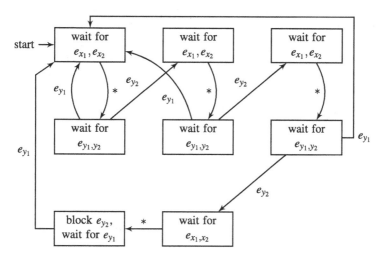

Fig. 6. (From [47]) A scenario object that enforces a liveness property for the network from Fig. 4.

3.3 Automated Analysis

Various studies indicate that using scenario-based modeling may serve to facilitate automated formal analysis (e.g., [38]). More specifically, the simple synchronization constructs employed by SBM scenario objects to communicate with each other render tasks such as automated repair [46], compositional verification [28] and model checking [49] simpler than they would be for less restricted models. We argue that the amenability of SBM to formal analysis adds to its attractiveness as a formalism for expressing override rules.

We illustrate this claim through one particular use case that involves deadlock freedom. As a DNN-based system is deployed and additional override rules are slowly added to it, potentially by different engineers, we run the risk that a certain sequence of inputs to the DNN controller could cause a deadlock. A simple illustrative example appears in Fig. 5: this figure depicts an override rule that enforces that whenever $x_1 > 0$ and $x_2 < x_1$, output y_2 should be selected. Suppose now that at some later point in time, a different engineer is concerned about the possibility that the DNN might always advise y_2. This engineer then creates a new override rule, depicted in Fig. 6, to the effect that after 3 consecutive y_2 events, a different event must be triggered. When run simultaneously, these two override rules could produce a deadlock: for example, if the neural network is given the inputs $x_1 = 2, x_2 = 1$ three consecutive times, both override rules would be triggered, causing output events e_{y_1} and e_{y_2} to be simultaneously blocked.

The absence of such deadlocks can be guaranteed through the use of formal verification. The verification process can be carried out, e.g., after the addition of each new override rule, or on a periodic basis. Whenever a deadlock is detected, the counter-example provided by the verification tool could help the modeler in identifying and altering the conflicting override rules—after which verification can be run again, in order to ensure that the system is now indeed deadlock free. Clearly, additional system-specific properties, beyond deadlock freedom, could also be formally verified.

4   Three Case-Studies

In order to evaluate our approach, we implemented it on top of the BPC framework for scenario-based modeling in C++ [30] (other SBM frameworks could, of course, be used instead). The BPC package allows engineers to leverage many of the useful and expressive constructs of C++, while enforcing that they adhere to the SBM principles: i.e., each scenario is modeled using a separate object, and inter-scenario interactions are performed strictly through the global execution mechanism provided by BPC. Here, we used BPC to model override rules for the DeepRM system for resource management [57], the Pensieve system for adaptive bitrate selection [59], and the Custard system for congestion control [43].

4.1   Override Rules for DeepRM

The DeepRM system [57] (mentioned in Sect. 1) is a resource allocation system: it assigns available resources to pending jobs, in order to maximize job throughput. In order to evaluate our approach we implemented an override rule that prevents DeepRM's DNN controller from attempting to assign resources to non-existent jobs, which is undesirable system behavior that occurs in practice [58].

The BPC code for an override rule that addresses this situation, implemented as a scenario object, appears in Fig. 7. We assume here that the queue of pending jobs is of length 5, and we use $y_0, y_1, \ldots, y_5$ to denote the DNN's output actions. Output actions $y_1, \ldots, y_5$ indicate that the job in slot i of the queue should be selected for resource allocation, whereas the special action y_0 is the "pass" action—which indicates that no job should be allocated resources at this time. We denote by x an event that indicates that the neural network needs to be evaluated on certain input values, which are available as parameters of x. The job queue's state is included in the input to the DNN controller. Specifically, we use $x[1], \ldots, x[5]$ to denote Boolean values that indicate whether or not there is currently a pending job in the corresponding slot of the queue.

Our override scenario object is implemented as a single class, which inherits from BPC's special BThread class. The override scenario object uses the special bSync() method in order to indicate that it has reached a synchronization point, and wishes to synchronize with the other scenarios in the model (including O_{DNN}, the special scenario object that models the DNN controller). The bSync() method takes as input three Event vectors—the first with the set of requested events, the second with the set of waited-for events, and the third with the set of blocked events. The bSync() call then suspends the object's execution, until the BPC execution mechanism has selected and triggered an event. Then, if the event that was triggered was requested or waited-for by a scenario object, that scenario is woken up and resumes its execution. In that case, the scenario object can also retrieve the triggered event using the lastEvent() method.

Our override scenario object runs in an infinite loop. In each iteration it synchronizes and waits for the input event x to be triggered; and once that triggering has occurred, the scenario examines x to determine which slots of the job queue are occupied. Finally, it synchronizes once again, in order to block event y_i for any unoccupied slots. Note that this scenario object can never cause a deadlock, because it never blocks the special "pass" event, y_0.

4.2   Override Rules for Pensieve

In online video streaming, a client wishes to download a video from a server and play it. The video is typically available in multiple levels of quality, known as *definitions*, that the client can choose from. The typical client will attempt to choose the highest definition that is reasonable for the current bandwidth conditions—i.e., the highest definition for which the video can be viewed without pauses for *rebuffering*, which are known to be detrimental to the viewer's experience. Further, bandwidth conditions might change while the video is being downloaded and played (e.g., if additional users start using the same physical link), in which case the choice of definition might need to be adjusted. An algorithm for selecting the definition rates in which a video is to be downloaded is called an *adaptive bitrate (ABR)* algorithm. Recently, DNN-based ABR algorithms have been shown to perform exceedingly well when compared to manually designed solutions [59].

The Pensieve system [59] is one such DNN-based ABR system. The system's goal is straightforward: given previous bitrate choices and statistics about how successful they were (i.e., how quickly parts of the video, called *chunks*, have previously been downloaded), the system selects the bitrate in which the next chunk is to be downloaded. Internally, Pensieve employs a DNN controller that takes as input: (i) a list of past bitrate selections; (ii) a list of past throughput

```
class EnsureJobExists : public BThread {
  void entryPoint() {
    Vector<Event> emptySet = {};
    Vector<Event> allInputs = { x };
    Vector<Event> allOutputs = { y_0,...,y_5 };

    while ( true ) {
      bSync( emptySet, allInputs, emptySet );
      lastInput = lastEvent();
      Vector<Event> blocked = {};

      for ( int i = 1; i <= 5; ++i ) {
        if ( !lastInput[i] )
          blocked.append( y_i )
      }

      bSync( emptySet, allOutputs, blocked )
    }
  }
}
```

Fig. 7. (From [47]) A scenario object for preventing the DeepRM DNN controller from assigning resources to non-existing jobs.

rates (indicating how quickly past chunks were downloaded); (iii) the number of remaining video chunks to be downloaded; and (iv) the current *buffer size*, which indicates how many seconds of already-downloaded content are available for playing, before rebuffering occurs. The DNN controller has a fixed number of outputs (6, in our case study), each corresponding to a possible definition in which the next chunk can be downloaded; and the definition associated with the output to which the DNN assigns the highest score is the one selected for the next video chunk.

Despite Pensieve's overall excellent performance [59], formal verification of this system has recently revealed many corner cases in which it makes undesirable bitrate selections [52]. For example, consider the following properties:

- When there is a single video chunk left to download, the client's buffer is quite full, and all recently downloaded video chunks were downloaded in the highest definition available (HD), the last chunk should be downloaded in HD.
- When there is a single video chunk left to download, the client's buffer is nearly empty, and all recently downloaded video chunks were downloaded in the lowest definition available (SD), the last chunk should be downloaded in SD.

Both properties describe extreme cases, in which the correct choice of bitrate is clear: either conditions are excellent and so the best definition should be used, or conditions are so poor that the worst definition should be used. However, even for these simple properties, dozens of violations (i.e., cases where the DNN selects some other definition) have been discovered [52].

As part of our evaluation, we use scenario-based override rules to enforce correct system behavior in both of these cases. To this end, we introduce scenario objects that wait until there are n chunks left in the video; and then monitor whether they are all downloaded in a fixed definition d. Then, if all chunks except for the very last one have been downloaded in definition d, the blocking idiom is applied to enforce that definition d is selected also for the last chunk. See Fig. 8 for an illustration. Of course, this override rule may be enhanced to include additional criteria (e.g., constraints on the client's buffer size) before the blocking is applied.

4.3   Override Rules for Custard

As we briefly mentioned in Sect. 3.2, Custard is a DNN-based system for congestion control. Custard's DNN controller receives as input various readings about the current, and previous, state of the computer network (e.g., loss rates, throughputs and latency readings). Then, it selects the next sending bit rate. Custard is a reactive system, in the sense that it was designed to run continuously and use the results of its past decisions (as they are reflected in past network readings) in order to make its next choice of bitrate.

Due to the opacity of Custard's DNN controller, one concern is that it might make selections that are overly *conservative*. Specifically, we typically wish to avoid a situation in which the state of the computer network is completely steady, and yet Custard's DNN controller never tries to increase the sending bitrate— and consequently never finds out whether some of the available bandwidth is currently unused.

Figure 9 depicts a scenario object that prevents the situation described above. This scenario attempts to identify situations in which the DNN's inputs and outputs have been completely steady for the last $n = 10$ rounds. Once this situation is detected, the scenario object blocks the previous output action from being triggered again, forcing the DNN to try an alternative. Note that event x represents here an input assignment (which is comprised of multiple input values) on which the neural network has been evaluated; whereas event y represents the DNN's output selection. For simplicity, we do not examine here the actual values of x, and instead only look for steady, repeating assignments (however, in practice we may wish to apply this override rule only if the computer network's conditions are both *steady* and *good*, which serves to indicate that there may be additional, unused bandwidth).

5   Recurrent Neural Networks

5.1   Memory Units

So far, we have focused on models that incorporate *feed-forward* neural networks. These networks, described in Sect. 2.2, are designed so that each of their

```
const int n = 10;

class EnsureLastChunkDefinition : public BThread {
  void entryPoint() {
    Vector<Event> empty;
    Vector<Event> allInputs = { x };
    Vector<Event> allOutputs = { y };

    Event lastInput;
    Event lastOutput;

    bool steadyState = false;

    int d;

    while ( true ) {
      bSync( empty, allInputs, empty );
      lastInput = lastEvent();

      if ( lastInput.remainingChunks > n )
        continue;

      else if ( lastInput.remainingChunks == n ) {
        steadyState = true;
        bSync( empty, allOutputs, empty );
        lastOutput = lastOutput();
        d = lastOutput.definition;
        continue;
      }

      else if ( lastInput.remainingChunks == 1 ) {
        if ( steadyState ) {
          bSync( empty, empty, allOutputs.erase( d ) );
          steadyState = false;
        }
        continue;
      }

      else {
        bSync( empty, allOutputs, empty );
        lastOutput = lastOutput();
        if ( steadyState && lastOutput.definition != d )
          steadyState = false;
      }
    }
  }
}
```

Fig. 8. A scenario object for forcing the Pensieve DNN to maintain the same definition for the last chunk.

```
const int n = 10;

class PreventSteadyState : public BThread {
  void entryPoint() {
    Vector<Event> empty;
    Vector<Event> allInputs = { x };
    Vector<Event> allOutputs = { y };

    Event lastInput;
    Event lastOutput;

    while ( true ) {
      bSync( empty, allInputs, empty );
      lastInput = lastEvent();

      bSync( empty, allOutputs, empty );
      lastOutput = lastOutput();

      bool steadyState = true;
      int i = 1;
      while ( i < n && steadyState ) {
        bSync( empty, allInputs, empty );
        if ( lastInput != lastEvent() )
          steadyState = false;

        bSync( empty, allOutputs, empty );
        if ( lastOutput != lastEvent() )
          steadyState = false;

        ++i;
      }

      if ( steadyState ) {
        bSync( empty, allInputs, empty );
        bSync( empty, allOutputs, lastOuptut );
      }
    }
  }
}
```

Fig. 9. (From [47]) A scenario object for enforcing the Custard DNN to choose a different action if the state has been steady for $n = 10$ iterations.

evaluations is independent of previous evaluations. This is suitable, for example, in image recognition: each image is classified independently, regardless of how images encountered previously were classified. However, this kind of neural network might be ill-suited for certain tasks that require *context*. Consider, for example, a DNN designed to interpret words that form a sentence, which are passed to the DNN one word at a time. As the DNN reads a word, it must consider the previous words in the sentence in order to properly interpret its meaning.

To address this need, the machine learning community has designed a variant of deep neural networks called *recurrent neural networks* (*RNNs*) [20]. Much like its feed-forward counterpart, an RNN is evaluated each time on a set of input values and produces a set of output values. However, it also maintains, using internal *memory units*, some aggregated information from the previous evaluations. This stored information affects the future evaluations of the RNN. RNNs have proven remarkably useful for a variety of tasks that involve context, such as machine translation [15], health applications [56], and speaker recognition [70].

We demonstrate the concept of an RNN through a simple example, depicted in Fig. 10. This network has two input nodes, x_1 and x_2, two output nodes, y_1 and y_2, and a single hidden node v. The new construct is the memory unit, $\tilde{v}$, which is connected to v. When the network is evaluated on input $\langle x_1, x_2 \rangle$, it computes the output $\langle y_1, y_2 \rangle$ using weighted sums and activation functions, same as before. However, the value stored in the memory unit also participates in this computation; and once the evaluation is performed, the value computed for node v is stored in $\tilde{v}$, to be used in the next evaluation. By convention, we assume that the memory unit is first initialized to 0. Suppose the network is initially evaluated on input $\langle x_1, x_2 \rangle = \langle 1, 0 \rangle$; for this input, $v = 1$ and $\langle y_1, y_2 \rangle = \langle 1, 2 \rangle$. The value $v = 1$ will now be stored in $\tilde{v}$ for the next evaluation. Next, if the network is again evaluated on $\langle 1, 0 \rangle$, the new value computed for v will be 2, and now this value will be stored in $\tilde{v}$; and the network's outputs will be $\langle 2, 4 \rangle$. It is straightforward to show that the memory unit in this particular RNNs computes the sum of the ReLUs of all previously received x_1 values.

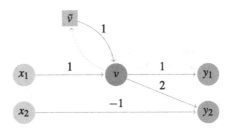

Fig. 10. A recurrent neural network.

5.2 Undesirable Behaviors in RNNs

Much like with feed-forward neural networks, various models that incorporate RNN components have been shown to demonstrate undesirable behavior. One common example is that of *adversarial inputs*—inputs that the network classifies correctly, but which, when they are slightly perturbed in subtle ways, cause the network to make severe misclassification errors [69]. Adversarial inputs are mostly known to plague feed-forward neural networks that perform image recognition tasks [55,69], but recently they have also been shown to exist in RNNs; for example, slight perturbations to audio files, which are inaudible to the human ear, were shown to cause RNN misclassification [11].

These errors, and others, indicate that RNN-based models suffer from the same intrinsic drawbacks of feed-forward networks: although they perform well in general, they may behave in undesirable ways in some cases; and because they are completely opaque to the human eye, manually maintaining, extending and correcting them is impractical. The verification community has also observed this and has begun devising techniques for RNN verification [42,74]. However, just like in the feed-forward case, these techniques can detect a bug but do not provide a framework for removing bugs after they are detected. It is thus highly likely that as RNN-based models continue to be deployed in various systems, override rules will need to be added to these models.

5.3 Override Rules for RNNs

We extend our previous notion of an override rule to the RNN setting, as follows. We define an *RNN override rule* as the quadruple $\langle P, M, Q, \alpha \rangle$, where: (i) P is a predicate over the inputs of the network; (ii) M is a predicate over the memory units of the network; (iii) Q is a predicate over the outputs of the network; and (iv) α is an override action. The definitions of P, Q and α are as before, but we now include a fourth element, the predicate M, which can render the activation of the override rule conditional on the state of the RNN's memory units. The semantics of an override rule $\langle P, M, Q, \alpha \rangle$ is that whenever P, M and Q hold for a network's evaluation, then output action α should be the one selected, regardless of the actual output of the RNN.

We demonstrate with an example, Consider again the RNN depicted in Fig. 10, and the following override rule:

$$\langle x_1 > 0, \tilde{v} > 0, true, y_1 \rangle.$$

As we saw previously, for input values $x_1 = 1, x_2 = 0$ the RNN outputs $y_1 = 1, y_2 = 2$, and so y_2 is selected. At this point, the override rule is not triggered: although $x_1 > 0$, the predicate $M = (\tilde{v} > 0)$ does not initially hold, because $\tilde{v} = 0$. If the network is again evaluated on $x_1 = 1, x_2 = 0$, it would normally compute $y_1 = 2, y_2 = 4$ and select y_2; however, now $\tilde{v} = 1$, the predicate M is satisfied, and so the override rule is triggered and the network is forced to select y_1 instead.

5.4 Modeling RNN Override Rules in SBM

Similarly to the feed-forward case, we propose SBM as an attractive paradigm for modeling RNN override rules. We achieve this by again representing the RNN using a dedicated, non-deterministic scenario, O_{RNN}. This scenario repeatedly waits for a composite event that represents an assignment to the RNN's *inputs* and also to its *memory units*; and then it requests all possible composite events, each of which represents a possible evaluation of the RNN's outputs. The intention is, once more, to simulate the black-box nature of the RNN: we do not allow the rest of the model to affect (i.e., block) the values of the RNN's inputs or memory units, but we allow it to observe (wait for) these values and affect the RNN's output values. When the system is deployed, the non-determinism of O_{RNN} is resolved using the actual input values that the RNN is given, and the actual values stored in its memory units at that time.

Using this formulation, override rules for the RNN case can again be expressed as scenario objects. We demonstrate this for the override rule discussed before, namely

$$\langle x_1 > 0, \tilde{v} > 0, true, y_1 \rangle,$$

whose corresponding override scenario is depicted in Fig. 11. The tuple $\langle e_{x_1}, e_{x_2}, e_{\tilde{v}} \rangle$ represents a single composite event, whose triggering indicates that values have been assigned to the neural network's inputs and memory unit. This composite event contains three real values, x_1, x_2 and $\tilde{v}$, that the override scenario can access and use in order to determine its next state. As before, the blocking of output event e_{y_2} indicates that the override scenario forbids the selection of y_2 as the RNN's output action.

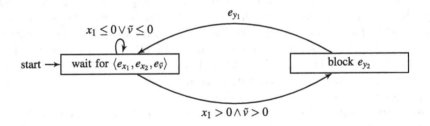

Fig. 11. An override rule for an RNN.

The same desirable properties that we discussed for the feed-forward case carry over to RNNs; i.e., (i) RNN override scenario can be used to encode both safety and liveness override rules; and (ii) automated SBM analysis can be used to ensure the consistency of override rules.

6   Related Work

Override rules, which are sometimes also referred to as *shields*, have been applied ad-hoc in various DNN-enabled systems. Some examples, which we have already mentioned, include DeepRM [57] and Pensieve [59]. Override rules, and related forms of runtime monitors, are found also in drones [14], control systems for robots [62], and in various other formalisms which are not directed particularly at deep learning [18,26,44,63,73]. In recent years, the formal methods community has started studying override rules for systems with DNNs: for example, recent papers have proposed techniques for synthesizing override rules that affect the controller in minimal ways [3,72].

SBM and its various aspects, especially those pertaining to the formal analysis of scenario-based models, have been thoroughly studied over the last decade. These aspects include the automatic verification [31], repair [36], optimization [24,29,35,66,67] and synthesis [23] of scenario-based models. SBM has also played a key role in the Wise Computing initiative [33,34,60], which seeks to make the computer a proactive team member, capable of developing complex models hand-in-hand with human engineers.

In this work we focused on SBM as a possible formalism for expressing override rules. There exists other, related modeling schemes, which could also be used for similar purposes. For example, the publish-subscribe framework for parallel composition shares many traits with SBM [17], and could be applied in a similar way. Aspect oriented programming [53] is another formalism, which allows developers to specify and execute cross-cutting program instructions on top of a base application. Both publish-subscribe and aspect oriented programming, however, do not directly support the blocking idiom, which appears quite useful for specifying override rules. Other behavior- and scenario-based models, such as LEGO Mindstorms leJOS [2], Branicky's behavioral programming [8], and Brooks's subsumption architecture [9], all suggest constructing systems from individual behaviors. One advantage that the scenario-based approach affords compared to these formalisms is that it is language-independent, and has been implemented on top of multiple platforms. It can thus extend, in a variety of ways, the arbitration and coordination mechanisms in use by these architectures.

Another related formalism is the BIP formalism (behavior, interaction, priority) [6]. BIP uses the notion of *glue* for assembling components into cohesive systems. The goals that BIP pursues are similar to those of SBM, although BIP focuses mostly on correct-by-construction systems. SBM, in contrast, is more geared towards executing intuitively-specified scenarios, and resolving the constraints that they pose at run-time.

7   Discussion and Next Steps

As the use of DNNs is becoming widespread in multiple and varied systems, ensuring the safety of these systems is quickly turning into an urgent need— specifically by using override rules. We argue here that by using modeling schemes that model together the DNN and its override rules, progress can be made towards this important goal. We propose to use a scenario-based modeling approach for this purpose, explain how a basic scenario-based scheme can be adjusted to incorporate DNNs, and demonstrate the approach on multiple, recently-proposed DNNs.

Moving forward, we believe that applying a more structured methodology for modeling override rules raises the following key question: as the number of override rules increases and as they become more complex, could they fully capture the DNN's logic and eventually replace it? We believe that the answer is negative, because override rules typically forbid some specified behavior, but rely on the DNN controller to prioritize among the remaining possible options. We thus believe that a more realistic approach is to combine a DNN controller together with appropriately crafted override rules, in a way that allows engineers to maintain, enhance and extend both components throughout the system's lifetime.

We consider our work to date a first step, which we intend to extend. Specifically, we plan to work on (i) leveraging the other advantages of scenario-based modeling, specifically its amenability to automated analysis and verification, in proving the overall correctness of DNN-based models; and (ii) customizing the idioms of scenario-based modeling, or similar techniques, to better suit integration with deep neural networks, and guard them in more subtle ways. In the longer run, we envision that work in this direction will eventually lead to the creation of DNN-enabled systems that are more robust, reliable, and easier to maintain and extend.

Acknowledgements. We thank Yafim (Fima) Kazak for his contributions to this project. This work was partially supported by grants from the Binational Science Foundation (2017662) and the Israel Science Foundation (683/18).

References

1. Amodei, D., Olah, C., Steinhardt, J., Christiano, P., Schulman, J., Mané, D.: Concrete Problems in AI Safety (2016). Technical report. https://arxiv.org/abs/1606.06565
2. Arkin, R.C.: Behavior-Based Robotics. MIT Press, Cambridge (1998)
3. Avni, G., Bloem, R., Chatterjee, K., Henzinger, T.A., Könighofer, B., Pranger, S.: Run-time optimization for learned controllers through quantitative games. In: Dillig, I., Tasiran, S. (eds.) CAV 2019. LNCS, vol. 11561, pp. 630–649. Springer, Cham (2019). https://doi.org/10.1007/978-3-030-25540-4_36
4. Bar-Sinai, M., Weiss, G., Shmuel, R.: BPjs: an extensible, open infrastructure for behavioral programming research. In: Proceedings 21st ACM/IEEE International Conference on Model Driven Engineering Languages and Systems (MODELS), pp. 59–60 (2018)
5. Barrett, C., Tinelli, C.: Satisfiability modulo theories. In: Clarke, E., Henzinger, T., Veith, H., Bloem, R. (eds.) Handbook of Model Checking, pp. 305–343. Springer, Cham (2018). https://doi.org/10.1007/978-3-319-10575-8_11
6. Bliudze, S., Sifakis, J.: A notion of glue expressiveness for component-based systems. In: van Breugel, F., Chechik, M. (eds.) CONCUR 2008. LNCS, vol. 5201, pp. 508–522. Springer, Heidelberg (2008). https://doi.org/10.1007/978-3-540-85361-9_39
7. Bojarski, M., et al.: End to End Learning for Self-Driving Cars (2016). Technical report. http://arxiv.org/abs/1604.07316
8. Branicky, M.: Behavioral programming. In: Working Notes AAAI Spring Symposium on Hybrid Systems and AI (1999)
9. Brooks, R.: A robust layered control system for a mobile robot. Robot. Autom. **2**(1), 14–23 (1986)

10. Chicco, D., Sadowski, P., Baldi, P.: Deep autoencoder neural networks for gene ontology annotation predictions. In: Proceedings 5th ACM Conference on Bioinformatics, Computational Biology, and Health Informatics (BCB), pp. 533–540 (2014)
11. Cisse, M., Adi, Y., Neverova, N., Keshet, J.: Houdini: fooling deep structured prediction models. In: Proceedings of the 31st Conference on Neural Information Processing Systems (NeurIPS) (2017)
12. Collobert, R., Weston, J., Bottou, L., Karlen, M., Kavukcuoglu, K., Kuksa, P.: Natural language processing (almost) from scratch. J. Mach. Learn. Res. (JMLR) **12**, 2493–2537 (2011)
13. Damm, W., Harel, D.: LSCs: breathing life into message sequence charts. J. Formal Methods Syst. Des. (FMSD) **19**(1), 45–80 (2001)
14. Desai, A., Ghosh, S., Seshia, S., Shankar, N., Tiwari, A.: SOTER: Programming Safe Robotics System using Runtime Assurance (2018). Technical report. https://arxiv.org/abs/1808.07921
15. Devlin, J., Chang, M.W., Lee, K., Toutanova, K.: BERT: Pre-training of Deep Bidirectional Transformers for Language Understanding (2018). Technical Report. http://arxiv.org/abs/1810.04805
16. Elkahky, A., Song, Y., He, X.: A multi-view deep learning approach for cross domain user modeling in recommendation systems. In: Proceedings of the 24th International Conference on World Wide Web (WWW), pp. 278–288 (2015)
17. Eugster, P., Felber, P., Guerraoui, R., Kermarrec, A.: The many faces of publish/-subscribe. ACM Comput. Surv. (CSUR) **35**(2), 114–131 (2003)
18. Falcone, Y., Mounier, L., Fernandez, J., Richier, J.: Runtime enforcement monitors: composition, synthesis, and enforcement abilities. J. Formal Methods Syst. Des. (FMSD) **38**(3), 223–262 (2011)
19. Gehr, T., Mirman, M., Drachsler-Cohen, D., Tsankov, E., Chaudhuri, S., Vechev, M.: AI2: safety and robustness certification of neural networks with abstract interpretation. In: Proceedings of the 39th IEEE Symposium on Security and Privacy (S&P) (2018)
20. Goodfellow, I., Bengio, Y., Courville, A.: Deep Learning. MIT Press, Cambridge (2016)
21. Gottschlich, J., et al.: The three pillars of machine programming. In: Proceedings of the 2nd ACM SIGPLAN International Workshop on Machine Learning and Programming Languages (MAPL), pp. 69–80 (2018)
22. Greenyer, J., et al.: ScenarioTools – a tool suite for the scenario-based modeling and analysis of reactive systems. J. Sci. Comput. Program. (J. SCP) **149**, 15–27 (2017)
23. Greenyer, J., Gritzner, D., Katz, G., Marron, A.: Scenario-based modeling and synthesis for reactive systems with dynamic system structure in ScenarioTools. In: Proceedings of the 19th ACM/IEEE International Conference on Model Driven Engineering Languages and Systems (MODELS), pp. 16–23 (2016)
24. Greenyer, J., et al.: Distributed execution of scenario-based specifications of structurally dynamic cyber-physical systems. In: Proceedings of the 3rd International Conference on System-Integrated Intelligence: New Challenges for Product and Production Engineering (SYSINT), pp. 552–559 (2016)
25. Gritzner, D., Greenyer, J.: Synthesizing executable PLC code for robots from scenario-based GR(1) specifications. In: Seidl, M., Zschaler, S. (eds.) STAF 2017. LNCS, vol. 10748, pp. 247–262. Springer, Cham (2018). https://doi.org/10.1007/978-3-319-74730-9_23

26. Hamlen, K., Morrisett, G., Schneider, F.: Computability classes for enforcement mechanisms. ACM Trans. Program. Lang. Syst. (TOPLAS) **28**(1), 175–205 (2006)
27. Harel, D., Kantor, A., Katz, G.: Relaxing synchronization constraints in behavioral programs. In: McMillan, K., Middeldorp, A., Voronkov, A. (eds.) LPAR 2013. LNCS, vol. 8312, pp. 355–372. Springer, Heidelberg (2013). https://doi.org/10.1007/978-3-642-45221-5_25
28. Harel, D., Kantor, A., Katz, G., Marron, A., Mizrahi, L., Weiss, G.: On composing and proving the correctness of reactive behavior. In: Proceedings of the 13th International Conference on Embedded Software (EMSOFT), pp. 1–10 (2013)
29. Harel, D., Kantor, A., Katz, G., Marron, A., Weiss, G., Wiener, G.: Towards behavioral programming in distributed architectures. J. Sci. Comput. Program. (J. SCP) **98**, 233–267 (2015)
30. Harel, D., Katz, G.: Scaling-up behavioral programming: steps from basic principles to application architectures. In: Proceedings of the 4th SPLASH Workshop on Programming based on Actors, Agents and Decentralized Control (AGERE!), pp. 95–108 (2014)
31. Harel, D., Katz, G., Lampert, R., Marron, A., Weiss, G.: On the succinctness of idioms for concurrent programming. In: Proceedings of the 26th International Conference on Concurrency Theory (CONCUR), pp. 85–99 (2015)
32. Harel, D., Katz, G., Marelly, R., Marron, A.: An initial wise development environment for behavioral models. In: Proceedings of the 4th International Conference on Model-Driven Engineering and Software Development (MODELSWARD), pp. 600–612 (2016)
33. Harel, D., Katz, G., Marelly, R., Marron, A.: First steps towards a wise development environment for behavioral models. Int. J. Inf. Syst. Model. Des. (IJISMD) **7**(3), 1–22 (2016)
34. Harel, D., Katz, G., Marelly, R., Marron, A.: Wise computing: toward endowing system development with proactive wisdom. IEEE Comput. **51**(2), 14–26 (2018)
35. Harel, D., Katz, G., Marron, A., Sadon, A., Weiss, G.: Executing scenario-based specification with dynamic generation of rich events. In: Hammoudi, S., Pires, L.F., Selić, B. (eds.) MODELSWARD 2019. CCIS, vol. 1161, pp. 246–274. Springer, Cham (2020). https://doi.org/10.1007/978-3-030-37873-8_11
36. Harel, D., Katz, G., Marron, A., Weiss, G.: Non-intrusive repair of reactive programs. In: Proceedings of the 17th IEEE International Conference on Engineering of Complex Computer Systems (ICECCS), pp. 3–12 (2012)
37. Harel, D., Katz, G., Marron, A., Weiss, G.: Non-intrusive repair of safety and liveness violations in reactive programs. Trans. Comput. Collect. Intell. (TCCI) **16**, 1–33 (2014)
38. Harel, D., Katz, G., Marron, A., Weiss, G.: The effect of concurrent programming idioms on verification. In: Proceedings of the 3rd International Conference on Model-Driven Engineering and Software Development (MODELSWARD), pp. 363–369 (2015)
39. Harel, D., Marron, A., Weiss, G.: Programming coordinated behavior in Java. In: D'Hondt, T. (ed.) ECOOP 2010. LNCS, vol. 6183, pp. 250–274. Springer, Heidelberg (2010). https://doi.org/10.1007/978-3-642-14107-2_12
40. Harel, D., Marron, A., Weiss, G.: Behavioral programming. Commun. ACM (CACM) **55**(7), 90–100 (2012)
41. Huang, X., Kwiatkowska, M., Wang, S., Wu, M.: Safety verification of deep neural networks. In: Majumdar, R., Kunčak, V. (eds.) CAV 2017. LNCS, vol. 10426, pp. 3–29. Springer, Cham (2017). https://doi.org/10.1007/978-3-319-63387-9_1

42. Jacoby, Y., Barrett, C., Katz, G.: Verifying recurrent neural networks using invariant inference. In: Proceedings of the 18th International Symposium on Automated Technology for Verification and Analysis (ATVA) (2020)
43. Jay, N., Rotman, N., Brighten Godfrey, P., Schapira, M., Tamar, A.: Internet congestion control via deep reinforcement learning. In: Proceedings of the 32nd Conference on Neural Information Processing Systems (NeurIPS) (2018)
44. Ji, Y., Lafortune, S.: Enforcing opacity by publicly known edit functions. In: Proceedings of the 56th IEEE Annual Conference on Decision and Control (CDC), pp. 12–15 (2017)
45. Julian, K., Lopez, J., Brush, J., Owen, M., Kochenderfer, M.: Policy compression for aircraft collision avoidance systems. In: Proceedings of the 35th Digital Avionics Systems Conference (DASC), pp. 1–10 (2016)
46. Katz, G.: On module-based abstraction and repair of behavioral programs. In: McMillan, K., Middeldorp, A., Voronkov, A. (eds.) LPAR 2013. LNCS, vol. 8312, pp. 518–535. Springer, Heidelberg (2013). https://doi.org/10.1007/978-3-642-45221-5_35
47. Katz, G.: Guarded deep learning using scenario-based modeling. In: Proceedings of the 8th International Conference on Model-Driven Engineering and Software Development (MODELSWARD), pp. 126–136 (2020)
48. Katz, G., Barrett, C., Dill, D.L., Julian, K., Kochenderfer, M.J.: Reluplex: an efficient SMT solver for verifying deep neural networks. In: Majumdar, R., Kunčak, V. (eds.) CAV 2017. LNCS, vol. 10426, pp. 97–117. Springer, Cham (2017). https://doi.org/10.1007/978-3-319-63387-9_5
49. Katz, G., Barrett, C., Harel, D.: Theory-aided model checking of concurrent transition systems. In: Proceedings of the 15th International Conference on Formal Methods in Computer-Aided Design (FMCAD), pp. 81–88 (2015)
50. Katz, G., et al.: The marabou framework for verification and analysis of deep neural networks. In: Dillig, I., Tasiran, S. (eds.) CAV 2019. LNCS, vol. 11561, pp. 443–452. Springer, Cham (2019). https://doi.org/10.1007/978-3-030-25540-4_26
51. Katz, G., Marron, A., Sadon, A., Weiss, G.: On-the-fly construction of composite events in scenario-based modeling using constraint solvers. In: Proceedings of the 7th International Conference on Model-Driven Engineering and Software Development (MODELSWARD), pp. 143–156 (2019)
52. Kazak, Y., Barrett, C., Katz, G., Schapira, M.: Verifying deep-RL-driven systems. In: Proceedings of the 1st ACM SIGCOMM Workshop on Network Meets AI & ML (NetAI) (2019)
53. Kiczales, G., et al.: Aspect-oriented programming. In: Akşit, M., Matsuoka, S. (eds.) ECOOP 1997. LNCS, vol. 1241, pp. 220–242. Springer, Heidelberg (1997). https://doi.org/10.1007/BFb0053381
54. Kuper, L., Katz, G., Gottschlich, J., Julian, K., Barrett, C., Kochenderfer, M.: Toward Scalable Verification for Safety-Critical Deep Networks (2018). Technical report. http://arxiv.org/abs/1801.05950
55. Kurakin, A., Goodfellow, I., Bengio, S.: Adversarial Examples in the Physical World (2016). Technical report. http://arxiv.org/abs/1607.02533
56. Lipton, Z., Kale, D., Elkan, C., Wetzel, R.: Learning to diagnose with LSTM recurrent neural networks. In: Proceedings of the 4th International Conference on Learning Representations (ICLR) (2016)
57. Mao, H., Alizadeh, M., Menache, I., Kandula, S.: Resource management with deep reinforcement learning. In: Proceedings of the 15th ACM Workshop on Hot Topics in Networks (HotNets), pp. 50–56 (2016)

58. Mao, H., Alizadeh, M., Menache, I., Kandula, S.: Resource Management with Deep Reinforcement Learning: Implementation (2016). https://github.com/hongzimao/deeprm
59. Mao, H., Netravali, R., Alizadeh, M.: Neural adaptive video streaming with pensieve. In: Proceedings of the Conference of the ACM Special Interest Group on Data Communication (SIGCOMM), pp. 197–210 (2017)
60. Marron, A., et al.: Six (im)possible things before breakfast: building-blocks and design-principles for wise computing. In: Proceedings of the 19th ACM/IEEE International Conference on Model Driven Engineering Languages and Systems (MODELS), pp. 94–100 (2016)
61. Nair, V., Hinton, G.: Rectified linear units improve restricted Boltzmann machines. In: Proceedings of the 27th International Conference on Machine Learning (ICML), pp. 807–814 (2010)
62. Phan, D., Yang, J., Grosu, R., Smolka, S., Stoller, S.: Collision avoidance for mobile robots with limited sensing and limited information about moving obstacles. J. Formal Methods Syst. Des. (FMSD) 51(1), 62–68 (2017)
63. Schierman, J., et al.: Runtime Assurance Framework Development for Highly Adaptive Flight Control Systems (2015). Technical report. https://apps.dtic.mil/docs/citations/AD1010277
64. Silver, D., et al.: Mastering the game of go with deep neural networks and tree search. Nature 529(7587), 484–489 (2016)
65. Simonyan, K., Zisserman, A.: Very Deep Convolutional Networks for Large-Scale Image Recognition (2014). Technical report. http://arxiv.org/abs/1409.1556
66. Steinberg, S., Greenyer, J., Gritzner, D., Harel, D., Katz, G., Marron, A.: Distributing scenario-based models: a replicate-and-project approach. In: Proceedings of the 5th International Conference on Model-Driven Engineering and Software Development (MODELSWARD), pp. 182–195 (2017)
67. Steinberg, S., Greenyer, J., Gritzner, D., Harel, D., Katz, G., Marron, A.: Efficient distributed execution of multi-component scenario-based models. Commun. Comput. Inf. Sci. (CCIS) 880, 449–483 (2018)
68. Sutton, R., Barto, A.: Introduction to Reinforcement Learning. MIT Press, Cambridge (1998)
69. Szegedy, C., et al.: Intriguing Properties of Neural Networks (2013). Technical report. http://arxiv.org/abs/1312.6199
70. Wan, L., Wang, Q., Papir, A., Lopez-Moreno, I.: Generalized End-to-End Loss for Speaker Verification (2017). Technical Report. http://arxiv.org/abs/1710.10467
71. Wang, S., Pei, K., Whitehouse, J., Yang, J., Jana, S.: Formal security analysis of neural networks using symbolic intervals. In: Proceedings of the 27th USENIX Security Symposium (2018)
72. Wu, M., Wang, J., Deshmukh, J., Wang, C.: Shield Synthesis for Real: Enforcing Safety in Cyber-Physical Systems (2019). Technical report. https://arxiv.org/abs/1908.05402
73. Wu, Y., Raman, V., Rawlings, B., Lafortune, S., Seshia, S.: Synthesis of obfuscation policies to ensure privacy and utility. J. Autom. Reason. 60(1), 107–131 (2018)
74. Zhang, H., Shinn, M., Gupta, A., Gurfinkel, A., Le, N., Narodytska, N.: Verification of recurrent neural networks for cognitive tasks via reachability analysis. In: Proceedings of the 24th Conference on European Conference on Artificial Intelligence (ECAI) (2020)

Modeling Languages, Tools and Architectures

Resilient Business Process Modeling and Execution Using BPMN and Microservices

Frank Nordemann[1]([✉]), Ralf Tönjes[1], Elke Pulvermüller[2], and Heiko Tapken[1]

[1] Faculty of Engineering and Computer Science,
Osnabrück University of Applied Sciences,
Albrechtstr. 30, 49076 Osnabrück, Germany
{f.nordemann,r.toenjes,h.tapken}@hs-osnabrueck.de
[2] Institute of Computer Science, University of Osnabrück,
Wachsbleiche 27, 49090 Osnabrück, Germany
elke.pulvermueller@informatik.uni-osnabrueck.de

Abstract. Process Modeling Languages (PMLs) help to define, structure and organize operational workflows. The Business Process Model and Notation 2.0 (BPMN), one of the most prominent PMLs, allows the definition and execution of process models including distributed participants and systems. An increasing number of BPMN use cases take place in unreliable communication environments, where connectivity may be intermittent or broken. Resilient processes need to avoid failures that may result in process interruptions or complete breakdowns.

Considering the particular requirements of unreliable communication environments, this paper addresses shortcomings when modeling and executing business processes. With *resilient BPMN* (*rBPMN*), the BPMN meta model is extended to allow resilient process designs by domain experts. Exemplary realizations of the introduced resilience strategies use state of the art technologies such as microservices and container virtualization. A proof-of-concept implementation illustrates the resilient design and execution of process models, serving as a guide for other use cases exposed to unreliable communication.

Keywords: Business processes · Meta modeling · Unreliable communication environments · Microservices · Container virtualization · BPMN

1 Introduction

The Business Model and Notation 2.0 (BPMN) represents a universal Process Modeling Language (PML), capable of being customized for the requirements of different application domains [30]. Besides traditional process modeling for banks, logistics, and sales, it is being applied to use cases taking place in unreliable communication environments. Examples include scenarios in rural areas

© Springer Nature Switzerland AG 2021
S. Hammoudi et al. (Eds.): MODELSWARD 2020, CCIS 1361, pp. 175–199, 2021.
https://doi.org/10.1007/978-3-030-67445-8_8

like agriculture, forestry and wildlife monitoring as well as scenarios including limited devices such as Internet of Things (IoT) and Cyber-Physical Systems (CPS). Since handling limited, intermittent or failing connectivity is not in the focus of BPMN, modeling of resilient processes is challenging for domain experts of many application domains.

When modeling a process taking place in unreliable environments using BPMN, a significant part of the process model is dedicated to handling communication failures. Alternatives for possibly unavailable message flows have to be added. Changes to the workflow and its activities may be required. Domain experts are forced to address communication aspects and loose focus on the technical objectives of the designated task. Eventually, domain experts may get stuck at a point where BPMN fails to provide the tools to fix a communication-related issue. Alternatively, experts modeled a process but are unable to verify resilient process operation. This may result in process failures or breakdowns at process runtime.

This paper introduces *resilient BPMN (rBPMN)*, an extension of the BPMN meta model to enable the design and verification of resilient processes even in the case of failing connectivity. New modeling elements allow to address the specific challenges of unreliable communication environments. This includes elements to move functionality across participants, to add alternatives for failing message flows and to dynamically adapt process operation according to connectivity at runtime.

State of the art paradigms and technologies may be used to implement the resilience strategies introduced by *rBPMN*. For instance, movable functionality between participants may be realized by microservices. Being autonomously operable by self-containing all required dependencies and data artifacts, microservices represent a convenient way of moving service functionality. Encapsulation of microservices into virtualized containers facilitates service exchange by including required software platforms and components. Service discovery mechanisms allow to find, load-balance and replace services dynamically.

However, most microservice ecosystems are designed for cloud environments [24]. While they may replace failing service instances rapidly, they do not have to cope with intermittent, delayed or broken connectivity on a large scale. microservice ecosystems are typically owned by one organization, having full control regarding services, data, infrastructure, software, and communication. In contrast, many use cases in unreliable communication environments include participants of different organizations. Every participant may employ a custom set of software and communication techniques.

rBPMN has been originally introduced in [26]. This paper covers a revised version of the *rBPMN* meta model including optional message flows, mechanisms to describe movable functionality and elaborated concepts for the decision making on alternatives. Major parts of the paper are dedicated to illustrate realization and evaluation of the resilience strategies of *rBPMN*. The main research contributions include:

1. A revised version of *rBPMN* including optional message flows, functionality descriptions and elaborated decision making concepts.
2. Strategies to realize resilient process models (e.g. movement of functionality, discovery/usage of neighbors/services, decision making on alternatives).
3. Elimination of shortcomings in the resilient execution of business processes using state of the art paradigms and technologies (e.g. microservices).
4. An agricultural real-world example, illustrating resilient process modeling and execution in unreliable communication environments.
5. An open source proof-of-concept implementation [25] ready for extension and adaptation, serving as a guide for other application domains.

The paper is organized as follows: a case study motivates the need for a BPMN meta model extension in Sect. 2. Concepts and strategies for resilient process modeling and execution are described in Sects. 3 and 4. An evaluation is presented in Sect. 5, followed by an overview of related work in Sect. 6. Finally, a conclusion is presented in Sect. 7.

2   Case Study: An Environmental-Friendly Slurry Application

An agricultural case study of an environmental-friendly slurry application illustrates the shortcomings of BPMN when modeling and executing processes taking place in unreliable communication environments. Based on regulations of the European Union, legal guidelines have to be addressed when applying slurry to fields in Europe. The objective is to prevent over-fertilization and its negative impact on the environment.

2.1   BPMN Process Model

The slurry application is depicted by the BPMN process model in Fig. 1. It includes a central process management entity *MGMT*, a slurry spreader *SP* and supporting services.

MGMT creates and deploys the slurry task to *SP*. During the slurry application, *MGMT* verifies and adapts process operation. Based on the status of *SP*, *MGMT* coordinates supporting vehicles bringing the slurry form the storage area to the field. Since the case study focuses on operation of *SP*, the supporting vehicles are not part of the BPMN model. When receiving the task log, the process documentation is created and may be submitted to an authority.

After being initialized by the task deployment of *MGMT*, *SP* is driving to the field. The slurry ingredients (e.g. nitrogen, phosphor, potassium) are identified using an Online Slurry Analysis Service (*OSAS*). Application accuracy is increased by an Online GPS Correction Service (*OGCS*). At the same time, the process status is transferred from *SP* to *MGMT*, which may adapt operation by sending instructions back to *SP*.

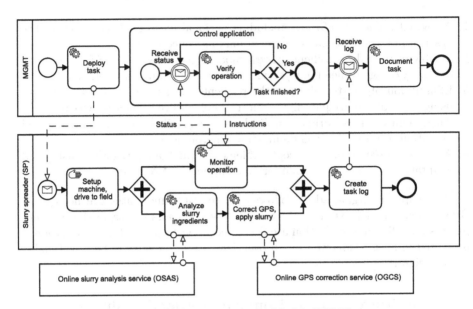

Fig. 1. A slurry process modeled in BPMN.

2.2 BPMN Model Weaknesses

The BPMN process model of the slurry application has the potential to work well in environments featuring reliable connectivity between *MGMT, SP, OSAS* and *OGCS*. However, a typical surrounding of an agricultural slurry process is a rural area that is lacking cellular communication coverage. Even when combining infrastructure-based (e.g. cellular networks, WiFi in access-point mode) with infrastructure-free (e.g. WiFi in ad-hoc mode) communication technologies, there is no continuous communication path between all process participants at all times.

In case of intermittent or broken connectivity, message flows between *SP* and the other process participants may be significantly delayed or non-existing. This will result in various critical issues for the process and in particular for participant *SP*:

Regarding Message Flows between *SP* and *MGMT*. *MGMT* might not be able to verify and adjust operation of *SP*. Coordination of supporting vehicles may be limited, resulting in process interruptions at *SP*.

Regarding Message Flows between *SP* and *OSAS*. *SP* might not be able to request and receive a slurry ingredients analysis, unable to calculate the slurry output amount. As a result, the process would break down.

Regarding Message Flows between *SP* and *OGCS*. *SP* might not be able to determine its position with the required accuracy. The slurry application might fail to comply with legal requirements (e.g. distance to water bodys during slurry application).

Sending the initial slurry task from *MGMT* to *SP* and sending back the task log at the process' end are not considered to fail. *SP* is located at a farm with reliable connectivity at the beginning. Transfer of the slurry log can be done when coming back to the farm at the end of the day.

Concluding observations: The BPMN process model is vulnerable to process interruptions and breakdowns based on connectivity issues. Domain experts are not able to verify operation of the model, preventing optimizations for a resilient execution.

3   Resilient Process Modeling

This section introduces *resilient BPMN (rBPMN)*, a valid BPMN meta model extension for modeling resilient processes in unreliable communication environments. After identification of modeling requirements, extension concepts and the meta model are presented in detail.

3.1   Process Modeling Requirements

Preventing process interruptions and complete breakdowns based on insufficient connectivity is a main objective of resilient processes. Derived requirement:

Req. M1: Ensure resilient process operation even if connectivity is intermittent or broken.

Domain experts are most familiar with their processes and are best-suited to model alternatives for failing message flows. Since they are rarely IT-experts, integration of and decision making on alternatives should be straightforward without overloading the model. Derived requirements:

Req. M2: Ability to model alternatives for failing message flows.
Req. M3: Ability to define decision making on available alternatives.

Especially in unreliable communication environments, process conditions may change unexpectedly and interfere with the process model. Derived requirement:

Req. M4: Ability to dynamically identify optimal process operation at runtime.

Resilient modeling requires domain experts to evaluate and optimize process models at design time. Derived requirement:

Req. M5: Ability to verify resilient process operation at design time.

Communication characteristics are not a key attribute of BPMN - the main gap when considering process execution in unreliable communication environments. While message transfers between different participants/systems may be modeled, no option exists to specify the required Quality of Service (QoS) of a data transmission. Alternatives for failing message flows may be integrated by

XOR-Gateways or *Business-Rule* tasks. However, resulting process models are prone to lose focus on the problem domain, are often complex and inflexible [26]. In case of insufficient connectivity, BPMN provides no tools to prevent process breakdowns based on failing message flows. There is no mechanism to verify resilient operation of a process model. This illustrates the need for a BPMN meta model extension supporting the challenges of unreliable communication environments.

3.2   Extension Concepts

rBPMN introduces new modeling concepts to the BPMN meta model. The concepts address the determined requirements for processes in unreliable communication environments. Extensions allow to describe communication requirements for message flows, to define alternatives in case of connectivity failures and to dynamically decide on the optimal alternative available at process runtime.

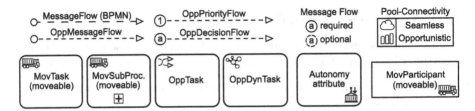

Fig. 2. *rBPMN* message flows, tasks and attributes.

Figure 2 depicts the graphical representations of the extension concepts. *rBPMN* adds new message flow types to model unreliable communication. *Opportunistic Message Flows* (abbreviated: *OppMessageFlows*) describe possibly intermittent or broken communication segments and may be used in conjunction with existing BPMN activities and participants. *OppMessageFlows* may be annotated with communication requirements and scenario-based connectivity descriptions to enable evaluation of message flow resilience prior to process runtime. *OppPriorityFlows* and *OppDecisionFlows* represent specializations of *OppMessageFlows* to define alternatives in case of broken connectivity. With *OppPriorityFlows*, each message flow within an alternatives group is labeled with a priority for decision making. During process execution, the highest-prioritized *OppPriorityFlow* that is available and fulfills the connectivity requirements is chosen. In contrast, *OppDecisionFlows* identify the best-suited alternative by comparing criteria of the available alternatives at process runtime. A criterion is a characteristic of the corresponding BPMN element (e.g. accuracy, cost or time of a task).

With *required* and *optional*, two variants of the opportunistic message flow types (*OppMessageFlows, OppPriorityFlows, OppDecisionFlows*) exist. Using the required variant, one of the opportunistic message flows part of an alternatives group needs to be available for resilient operation. This is graphically indicated by a solid circle containing the alternatives group label (cf. Fig. 2). As a second variant, message flows may be optional in terms of resilient operation. This is illustrated by opportunistic message flows containing a dashed circle for the alternatives group label.

rBPMN adds new task types to the BPMN tool pallet:*MovTasks*, *MovSubProcesses*, and *MovParticipants* (in short: movables) offer movable functionality to other participants / systems. Functionality is often represented by services, offering interfaces to perform operations. In case of connectivity issues, the functionality acts as a local backup, allowing process operation to continue. *OppTasks* can execute offered functionality locally. *OppDynTasks* extend flexibility by the dynamic identification of suitable alternatives at process runtime.

Graphical attributes for seamless (cloud sign) and opportunistic connectivity (signal bar) of participants with the cloud are defined. The autonomy attribute of tasks allows to graphically indicate locally moved functionality as a backup for failing communication. All attributes do not affect process operation. Their purpose is to graphically point out characteristics of the modeling element.

3.3   Meta Model Extension

The BPMN meta model has been extended to include the new modeling concepts of Sect. 3.2. Following the guidelines for developing valid BPMN meta model extensions [41], a Context Domain Model of the Extension (CDME) has been created. It is split into Fig. 3 and Fig. 4 for better readability.

Figure 3 illustrates the connectivity-related concepts of *rBPMN*. Opportunistic message flows are based on traditional BPMN message flows. A number of extension concepts allow to verify resilient process operation at design time: Every opportunistic message flow is able to describe its message properties (e.g. message size and interval) and its QoS requirements (e.g. max delivery delay). In addition, a scenario-based connectivity can be modeled for opportunistic message flows. This includes expected minimum and average bandwidth, failure probability and a failure recovery time. The actual resilience verification is described in the following Subsect. 3.4.

OppMessageGroups define sets of message flow alternatives and configure them as required or optional. Concepts for a decision engine and decision criteria allow to examine the best-suited alternative based on connectivity, priorities and features (e.g. accuracy, cost, time). The extension concepts for communication and decision making aspects are listed in Table 1.

The CDME of movability-related concepts is depicted in Fig. 4. Movement of functionality is supported by extending BPMN activities and participants. *MovTasks, MovSubProcesses* and *MovParticipants* may offer functionality to be used by *OppTasks*. Alternatively, *OppDynTaks* may be used to integrate dynamically appearing participants that have not explicitly been modeled at design time.

Consistency of functionality descriptions is realized by additional concepts. Either functionality and its interfaces is described directly in process models

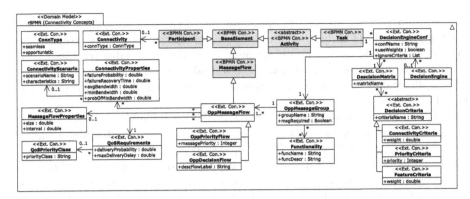

Fig. 3. CDME (part 1) of *rBPMN* including connectivity-related concepts.

or a reference to an interface description is provided. Extension concepts for collaboration are elaborated in Table 2.

In accordance to the work of [41] and [4], the CDME may be used as a foundation to derive the BPMN+X model and the BPMN-XML-schemas. The publications provide model translation rules and an example to automate the translation.

Table 1. Extension concepts addressing communication modeling.

Concept	Semantics of communication modeling
OppMessageFlow	Possibly intermittent or broken communication with other participants. May be used with existing BPMN concepts
OppPriorityFlow	Opportunistic message flow with explicitly defined priority. A number within the message flow circle states the priority
OppDecisionFlow	Opportunistic message flow with implicit, criteria-based decision making for alternatives. An alphabetic character within the message flow circle states the decision group
MessageFlowProp.	Describes message properties (e.g. frequency, size, relevance)
QoSRequirements	Defines QoS requirements for a message flow
QoSPriorityClass	Defines a QoS hierarchy, to be used by QoSRequirements
Connectivity	Defines a type of connectivity (seamless, opportunistic) for a participant
ConnectivityProp.	Describes connectivity at the time of a message flow
ConnectivityScen.	Allows to group ConnectivityProperties to different scenarios
OppMessageGroup	Group of OppMessageFlows that defines a set of alternatives
DecisionEngine	Chooses OppMessageFlows based on engine configuration
DecisionEngineConf	Configures decision engine, assigns DecisionMatrix
DecisionMatrix	Foundation of decisions on alternatives, uses DecisionCritera
DecisionCriteria	Decision criteria used by decision matrix. Available criteria: ConnectivityDecision, PiorityDecision, FeatureDecision

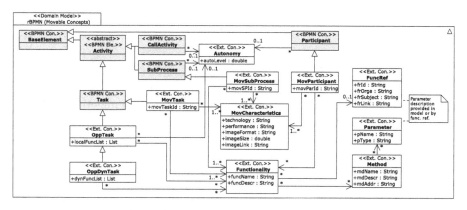

Fig. 4. CDME (part 2) of *rBPMN* including movable-related concepts.

3.4   Model Resilience Verification

Verifying the resilience of a process model at design time allows domain experts to identify and optimize imperfections of the model avoiding process failures at runtime. *rBPMN* is able to evaluate the resilience *i)* based on connectivity estimations or *ii)* based on connectivity statistics gathered in previous process executions.

The first step in the resilience verification of a message flow is to calculate the required number of data frames N_f: the message size M_s is divided by the frame payload size F_{pl} in Eq. 1.

Table 2. Extension concepts addressing collaboration modeling.

Concept	Semantics of collaboration modeling
MovPraticipant	Participant offering movable functionality
MovTask	Task offering movable functionality
MovSubProcess	Sub-process offering movable functionality
MovCharacteris	Technical information regarding functionality movement
OppTask	Task capable of executing locally moved functionality
OppDynTask	An OppTask that dynamically identifies alternatives (using functionality descriptions) not explicitly modeled at design time
Autonomy	Defines autonomy level for tasks (e.g. 4 OppMessageFlows, 3 with local functionality ⇒ autonomy level of 75%)
Functionality	Defines and ensures consistency of functionality
Method	Describes method of functionality in process model
Parameter	Describes parameter of method directly in model
Method	Describes method of functionality directly in model
FuncRef	Alternatively describes functionality using external link

$$N_f = \left\lceil \frac{M_s}{F_{pl}} \right\rceil \tag{1}$$

With the number of frames on hand, the time it takes to transfer the required data frames can be calculated. Equation 2 provides a formula to calculate a basic time T_b by including the minimum bandwidth BW_{min} in conjunction with the message size and the frame header size F_h.

$$T_b = \frac{M_s + N_f * F_h}{BW_{min}} \tag{2}$$

Alternatively, an advanced time T_{adv} may be calculated by combining minimum bandwidth BW_{min}, average bandwidth BW_{avg} and their probabilities to a common bandwidth BW in Eq. 3. Following, BW is combined with a data transfer failure probability P_f and a failure recovery time T_f (Eq. 4).

$$BW = BW_{min} * P_{BWmin} + BW_{avg} * (1 - P_{BWmin}) \tag{3}$$

$$T_{adv} = \frac{M_s + N_f * F_h}{BW} + P_f * T_f \tag{4}$$

Comparing the maximum delivery delay for a message flow T_d with the actual time required for the transmission $T_{b/adv}$ reveals whether or not a message flow i) is resilient ($T_d \geq T_{b/adv}$) or ii) is not resilient ($T_d < T_{b/adv}$).

For repeating message flows, the message flow interval T_i can be divided by $T_{b/adv}$ to get the number of messages N_m able to be transferred within the interval (Eq. 5). Resilience of repeating message flows depends on the required delivery probability P_d. Operation is resilient for $N_m \geq P_d$ and not resilient for $N_m < P_d$.

$$N_m = \frac{T_d}{T_{b/adv}} \tag{5}$$

rBPMN has been originally introduced in [26], where a more detailed description of the concepts and calculations can be found. Since first publication, rBPMN has been revised for required/optional message flows, decision making and functionality descriptions.

4   Resilient Process Execution

This section identifies requirements for the resilient execution of process models. Following, solution strategies addressing determined requirements are presented. The elaborations' focus is on illustrating how state of the art paradigms, technologies, and frameworks help to meet the requirements, what shortcomings exist and how they can be solved.

4.1   Process Execution Requirements

The requirements for the execution of a resilient process modeled in *rBPMN* are identified subsequently.

The start of a process requires an initial set-up configuration to specify process variables and communication parameters. In unreliable communication environments, infrastructure-based (e.g. cellular networks, WiFi in access point mode) and infrastructure-free (e.g. WiFi in ad-hoc mode) technologies are frequently combined to hybrid networks. Configuration settings are required to operate and access the networks. Derived requirement:

Req. E1: Ability to set-up the initial process and communication configuration prior to runtime.

rBPMN introduces movable process elements offering functionality to be executed locally at other participants. Hence, a mechanism for moving functionality to interested participants is needed. It should not matter whether the participants belong to a common or to different organizations. Derived requirement:

Req. E2: Ability to move functionality between participants of different organizations.

A running process needs to recognize neighbor participants dynamically, since they may be part of the same process model. Also, a process may identify and use offered functionality of neighbors to adapt its operation to the best-suited alternatives available. Derived requirements:

Req. E3: Ability to discover participants dynamically at runtime.
Req. E4: Ability to identify and use functionality offered by other participants at runtime.

Finally, decisions about the best-suited alternatives need to be made at runtime. Derived requirement:

Req. E5: Ability to decide on the best-suited alternatives for optimal process execution at runtime (decision making).

The following subsection presents detailed solution strategies to address the requirements for executing processes.

4.2   Initial Participant Configuration

The strategy for the initial configuration (*Req. E1*) includes a management entity linebreak (*MGMT*) located in the cloud, providing configurations to all participants. *MGMT* is contacted by every participant to retrieve their configuration, including process variables and communication settings. Since network addressing may change rapidly and a participant may be part of multiple networks at the same time, a *participant ID* is used for identification. Participants transfer

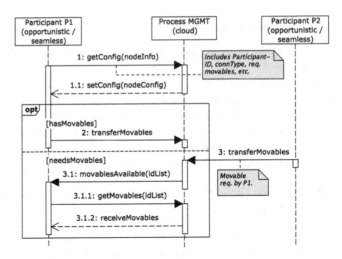

Fig. 5. Participant configuration and transfer of movable functionality for local execution during the initial set-up sequence of a process.

their offered, movable functionality to *MGMT* for distribution to other participants. Figure 5 summarizes the initial configuration sequence, supposed to take place before process execution when reliable connectivity is available.

The configuration messages contain relevant data to prepare the participants for the process execution. Most use cases will find three configuration categories useful:

i) Process-related instructions such as process variables/parameters, offered and consumed functionality, IDs of all process participants.

ii) Network-related configuration settings such as addressing, naming, user credentials, routing settings.

iii) Service-related information such as service and functionality IDs, service addressing of seamlessly connected participants.

A JSON-formatted example is included in the source code of the proof-of-concept implementation (Sect. 5.2).

4.3 Movement of Functionality

A local backup of (limited) functionality ensures process operation for participants even if no connectivity is available (*Req. E2*). Functionality needs to be movable in the sense of mobile code/code on demand [15]. Depending on the software platform and BPMN runtime engine used in a scenario, several approaches are applicable to design movable process parts:

Engine-bound Process Modules. If all participants agree on the same BPMN runtime engine, process parts may be exchanged directly as engine modules.

A common format for process modules are Java-archives (.jar) since many runtime engines are based on Java. It is important to add all required libraries to the archive, as they need to be present at other participants.

Microservices. Realizing functionality as a microservice allows convenient functionality movement across participants. All dependencies and data artifacts required for execution are part of the microservice. BPMN runtime engines can be integrated into a microservice, eliminating the need for a local runtime instance at other participants. However, required software platforms such as Java still need to be present on the remote participants.

Container Virtualization. Mobile code may be realized by container virtualization techniques like *docker* [9] and *rkt* [35], especially if different software platforms and BPMN runtime engines are applied by the participants. The provided functionality is encapsulated within a container with all its dependencies and can be run locally by other participants. All participants need to run the required container technology.

For seamless integration into the process, the participants' service registry may be used to register and dynamically access the functionality within the running process. Service registries are part of the service discovery, outlined in Sect. 4.5. To ensure availability of local components, the initial configuration sequence moves required functionality to the corresponding participants prior to process runtime (Fig. 5).

4.4   Discovery of Neighboring Participants

An essential part of process operation is to recognize neighboring participants (*Req. E3*). Cloud-connectivity of these participants may be opportunistic or non-existing, often supplemented by high mobility. Neighboring participants may be part of the process model serving as functionality providers to run/optimize a process.

The proposed strategy realizes neighbor detection using routing algorithms for Mobile Ad-hoc Networks (MANETs). Proactive routing algorithms such as Destination-Sequenced Distance-Vector (DSDV [33]) and Optimized Link State Routing (OLSR [8]) detect neighbor nodes by picking up periodic *hello* broadcast messages emitted by every node of the network. The frequency of the *hello* broadcast determines the speed of neighbor detection and should ensure detection in a reasonable amount of time, depending on the applied use case. The frequency can be aligned for every participant separately and is part of the initial configuration sequence (Sect. 4.2).

Figure 6 illustrates the neighbor discovery mechanism. When a neighbor is detected by a proactive routing algorithm, its IP-Address is entered into a custom neighbor participant table. After detection, the participant is identified by requesting node information on a fixed port (e.g. port 9876). Node information includes a *participant ID* and may state the port number of the local service registry if the participant offers functionality. A custom table is required to group participants by their IDs, since participants part of multiple networks may have diverse IP addressing information. Also, a custom table helps to maintain functionality information offered by neighbors. The offering of functionality will be discussed in the following subsection.

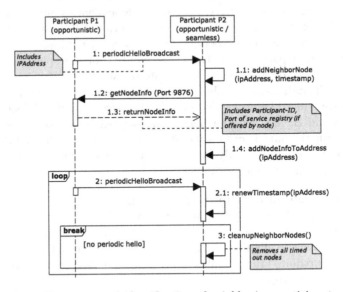

Fig. 6. Discovery and identification of neighboring participants.

When a participant exits the communication range of the MANET, *hello* broadcasts are no longer received by the applied routing algorithm. The participant is removed after a timeout period from the neighbor table. Since the seamlessly connected service providers keep their cloud address settings during process runtime, their addressing is part of the initial configuration sequence.

4.5   On-Demand Usage of Functionality

After discovering neighboring participants, mechanisms for identification and usage of offered functionality are required (*Req. E4*).

Identification of Functionality. Offering functionality to other participants requires having a common understanding of what kind of functionality is provided and how it is used. The ontology in Fig. 7 is guiding functionality development, offering, and usage: Functionality is provided by services, is described semantically by metadata, includes input/output parameters and has a Path-URL based on the service's Base-URL. For identification, every service and functionality is labeled with a unique ID as part of its metadata. Finding suitable functionality is guided by a taxonomy, grouping services into categories.

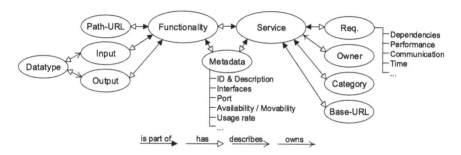

Fig. 7. Ontology describing provisioning of functionality for participants.

Usage of Functionality. Using functionality requires a description of interfaces with input and output parameters. While in the days of web services *WSDL* [7] and *WADL* [42] have been used for interface descriptions, application of technologies like *OpenAPI* [31] and *RAML* [34] is common for microservices. Organizations may standardize interfaces to support interoperability of implementations. For certain use cases, guidance provided by the HATEOAS principle of REST may be appropriate. With HATEOAS, the service is offering links for functionality currently available based on service state information [13].

Due to the opportunistic nature of unreliable communication environments, the following guidelines have to be followed:

1) Services describe their functionality using metadata.
2) Services are registered in a service registry.
3) Participants with opportunistic connectivity run their own service registry.
4) Every participant runs an information service following a well-defined interface for identification needs/as entry point for usage of service functionality.

The solution strategy to dynamically identify and use functionality is illustrated by Fig. 8. A neighboring participant with opportunistic connectivity is asked for a service list on its service registry port. The returning services are queried for service metadata to identify the service categories, IDs and interfaces. In the case of HATEOAS, functionality links are provided based on the current state. The functionality may be used by calling the appropriate service interfaces.

4.6 Dynamic Decision Making on Alternatives

Connectivity of participants is a key factor for deciding on alternatives in a process. This is solved by a neighbor table based on proactive routing protocols. The neighbor table lists participants that have been reachable in the recent past. More precise connectivity information may be obtained by periodic measurements of available bandwidth, latency, connection failures, and packet loss. With this data on-hand, predictions for the future connectivity of individual participants may help to decide on alternatives.

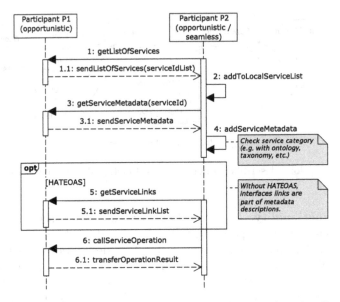

Fig. 8. Dynamic identification and usage of service functionality.

Decision making on available alternatives is based on *OppPriorityFlows* or *OppDecisionFlows* in *rBPMN*. Hence, different strategies for the realization of decision making are introduced (*Req. E5*).

OppPriorityFlows. The optimal process execution is defined by priorities for alternatives at design time. When reaching a point of choosing an alternative at runtime, the alternative with the highest priority that is available in terms of connectivity is chosen.

OppDecisionFlows. For *OppDecisionFlows*, the problem of choosing an alternative can be described as a multi-criteria decision analyses problem (MCDA). The solution strategy proposes to use a weighted decision matrix to decide on alternatives. The matrix contains a set of criteria relevant for the decision, in which every criterion may be weighted regarding its impact factor. The highest-rated alternative that is available is chosen for process operation. In the case of *OppDynTasks*, matching functionality offered by other participants not part of the original process model is also considered as an alternative. This results in a loosely coupled service decision making mechanism since no adaptation of the actual service implementations is required to change process operation. Decision making based on *OppDecisionFlows* is summarized in Fig. 9.

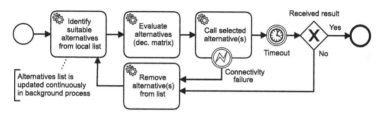

Fig. 9. Process of decision making based on *OppDecisionFlows*.

5   Evaluation

This section evaluates the concepts and strategies for the modeling and execution of resilient processes. The evaluation is based on the agricultural case study presented in Sect. 2.

5.1   Adding Resilience to the Slurry Process Model

The BPMN model of the slurry application of Sect. 2.1 can be extended using *rBPMN* modeling elements. A domain expert may add opportunistic message flows wherever there is a chance for connectivity issues. Adding message flow properties, QoS requirements and connectivity descriptions to opportunistic message flows allows to verify resilience of the process model. This has been done in Fig. 10, showing the result of a resilience analysis on an adapted slurry process model. The red/grey parts of the model indicate process failures due to insufficient connectivity. The slurry application is in danger of failing at the monitoring, the ingredients analysis and the GPS correction tasks.

A domain expert optimized the process model in Fig. 11. With a Near-Infrared Spectroscopy Sensor (*NIRS*) and a Local GPS Correction Station (*LGCS*), additional alternatives for the slurry ingredients analysis and the GPS correction have been added. While *NIRS* is part of the slurry spreader, *LGCS* is a station located in the fields proximity. Unreliable connectivity of *SP*, *NIRS*, and *LGCS* with the cloud is easily identified by the connectivity attributes of the participants (signal bars in Fig. 11).

The sub-process *Control application* of *MGMT* has been designed as movable functionality, which may be moved to *SP* and executed there. The same applies to the slurry ingredients analysis of *OSAS*. The choices for an analysis service (*alternatives group a*) and for a GPS correction service (*alternatives group b*) are designed as *OppDecisionFlows*. The decision for one or another service is made at runtime, comparing characteristics of the alternatives in a weighted decision matrix. The available option with the highest accuracy is chosen in this evaluation. A final analysis confirms resilient operation of the modified process model (cf. red/grey parts in Fig. 11).

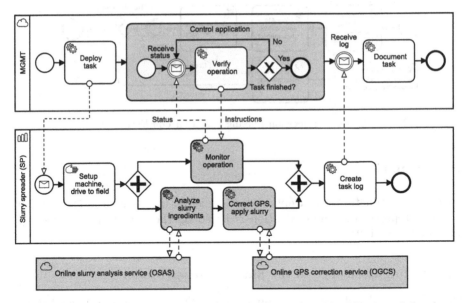

Fig. 10. A slurry process modeled in *rBPMN*. The resilience verification of the slurry model failed due to unavailable message flows. (Color figure online)

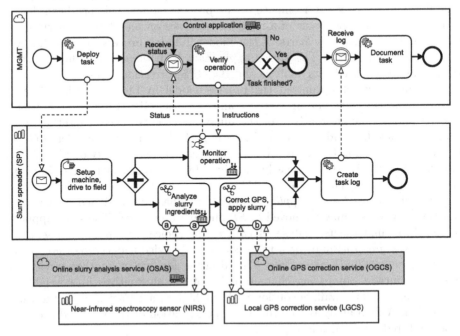

Fig. 11. A resilient slurry process model, including message flow alternatives, locally moved functionality and dynamic decision making. (Color figure online)

5.2   Realizing a Resilient Slurry Process Execution

The slurry application has been evaluated by a proof-of-concept implementation, following the architectural overview depicted in Fig. 12. *MGMT* and the online services for analysis (*OSAS*) and GPS correction (*OGCS*) are located in the cloud. Execution of the *MGMT* process model is realized by the open source version of *Camunda BPM* [6], a BPMN runtime engine. *OSAS* and *OGCS* are implemented as microservices using *Spring Boot* [40]. A common service registry implemented in *Spring Eureka* [40] acts as a broker for all cloud services.

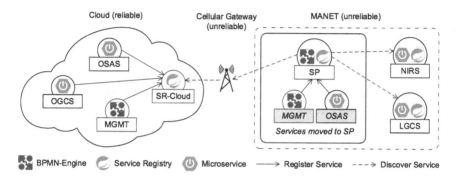

Fig. 12. Architectural overview of the slurry process and its participants. Services are registered, discovered and used in an unreliable communication environment.

The BPMN runtime module for the sub-process *Control application* of *MGMT* is integrated into a microservice to realize functionality movement to *SP*. In contrast, movable functionality of *OSAS* is designed as a microservice excluding any BPMN components. The locally moved service instances act as a backup in case of connectivity issues with the cloud. During local execution, these services register at the Eureka server instance of *SP* to be part of the alternatives decision making. While *NIRS* and *LGCS* are also realized as microservices, they include their own service registries. Since they represent dynamically appearing participants, they may offer their services to participants (such as *SP*) using the participant information service with its well-defined interface (Sects. 4.4/4.5).

Communication between *SP*, *NIRS*, and *LGCS* takes place in a MANET. OLSR is used as a proactive routing protocol for the identification of neighboring participants and routing of data. A cellular gateway on *SP* allows communicating unreliably with services placed in the cloud. Information exchange between all participants is based on REST. All participants agreed on standardized interfaces during the process design phase.

With *Spring Boot*, *Spring Eureka* and *Camunda BPM*, the proof-of-concept implementation uses widely spread technologies to realize microservices, service discovery and BPMN process model execution. While usage of these technologies is a good starting point, extensions have been made to address the solution strategies presented in Sect. 4.

Examples for the initial set-up sequence configuration file and the design of service functionality interfaces with JSON-based data transfer objects are provided as part of the proof-of-concept. Considerable effort was invested to discover and identify service alternatives across multiple distributed Eureka servers in an unreliable network. By querying metadata of reachable service instances, a network-wide set of alternatives including locally moved functionality is created as an input for decision making. Decision making is realized as a decision matrix, containing weighted characteristics (e.g. operational accuracy) gathered from metadata of the alternatives. In case of broken connectivity, a new alternative is provided instantly by the decision making process.

Figure 13 summarizes the novelties in the proof-of-concept implementation, serving as a template for other application domains. The code is available on Github [25].

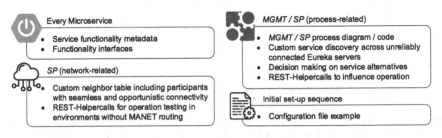

Fig. 13. Implementation novelties part of the scenario evaluation.

5.3   Discussion of Evaluation Results

The evaluation using an agricultural slurry process has been able to confirm resilient business process execution in an unreliable communication environment.

The extension concepts of *rBPMN* allow domain experts to adapt existing BPMN processes for unreliable communication environments. By using opportunistic message flows, imperfections of the model may be identified in a resilience analysis. The addition of alternatives for possibly failing message flows and the integration of dynamic decision making on available alternatives lower the risk of process interruptions and breakdowns. Finally, the movement of functionality across participants allows to continue process operation even if no connectivity is available.

Integration of state of the art technologies like microservices and container virtualization helps to implement the resilience strategies in real-world environments. An on-demand identification and usage of service offering participants guarantees to include all available alternatives at process runtime. Concepts and implementation are open for extension and adaptation [25]. All technologies used in the proof-of-concept are open source.

Deciding on alternatives is realized in a highly dynamic manner by identifying, comparing, rating and selecting alternatives at runtime. A lesson learned at this point of implementation is the need to check service availability information gathered from Eureka service registries. Depending on the Eureka configuration, services may be shown as available while they already disappeared. Connectivity checks prior to service usage have been used to rapidly exclude unavailable services and to decide on a new alternative (cf. Fig. 9).

Instead of querying and combining service information of different Eureka servers, a single query to the local Eureka server may identify all available services by using Eurekas replication mechanism. Services of other Eureka servers become part of the local server instance. While this principle facilitates service discovery, replication configuration of servers in highly dynamic scenarios may be challenging.

Caution is advised when using the Circuit-Breaker-Pattern [14], which is part of frameworks like Spring. While the pattern helps to avoid overload situations in cloud environments, it may falsely prevent access to services in dynamic, intermittent scenarios.

Movement of functionality is illustrated by moving process modules of the BPMN engine (.jar-files) and Spring-Boot-Microservices. Container virtualization may be used alternatively.

Attention is required when configuring network settings. For instance, frequent *hello* broadcast messages (e.g. every five seconds) may be required to recognize rapidly moving participants in a scenario.

Adaptation effort for existing microservices or container-based implementations is reasonable. The implemented methods for participant and service discovery as well as decision making need to be integrated. While *Spring Boot, Spring Eureka* and *Camunda BPM* have been used in the evaluation, other technologies such as *Signavio, jBPM, docker, rkt, Zookeeper*, and *Consul* may be used as BPM runtime engines, to implement and move microservices and to discover services. Alternatively, an integration of tools like the Spring Framework with BPMN runtime engines like Camunda and the *rBPMN* meta model may simplify the effort for resilient process execution.

A combination of configuration and deployment aspects into existing deployment tools such as Kubernets is reasonable. In addition, scientific research on cross-layer information exchange between application and communication layer is a promising approach to optimize communication and decision making aspects. Another interesting topic is to automate configuration by deriving instructions directly from BPMN/*rBPMN* process diagrams.

Since *rBPMN's* original publication in [26], research has been done on expanding the resilience verification from message flows towards complete process paths of a model. A mechanism to evaluate and rank process paths against each other based on their resilience is described in [27]. Since resilience may be an important, but not the only relevant criterion for many business processes, [28] introduces mechanisms to evaluate other process criteria in conjunction with resilient operation. As an example, this allows to automatically identify the process path with highest accuracy at reasonable cost when having multiple resilient paths available.

6 Related Work

BPMN has been in the focus of business process publications since its initial release in 2006. By 2011, it gained even more attention with the second edition release [30]. Several publications extended BPMN's capabilities for various application domains [3]. Many contributions give insights into ongoing research by introducing formal and theoretical concepts. Other contributions provide practical guidelines for process modeling, implementation, and execution in real-world scenarios [18,36,39].

Different activities have extended BPMN for application areas related to unreliable communication environments. Several publications aim to integrate the Internet of Things (IoT) and Cyber-Physical Systems (CPS) into BPMN by extending it for sensors, actors and other physical resources [2,17,22,23]. Other extensions add quality of information and performance aspects [16,20]. Several publications address process, task and resource reliability [1,10,37]. However, none of the extensions is focusing on resiliency aspects of communication and collaboration modeling.

Starting with BPMN 2.0 and associated runtime engines, other approaches for process execution such as the Web Service Business Process Execution Language (BPEL) [43] lost importance. The shifting was accelerated by the rapid dissemination of the microservice and container virtualization paradigms. The microservice approach of provisioning functionality in small, self-sufficient pieces of code and data [24] also gained popularity over Service-Oriented Architectures (SOAs), which often rely on orchestrating numerous modules to be executable. While different technologies and frameworks for the development, deployment, configuration, and execution of microservices exist, none is designed to cope with the consequences of unreliable communication environments on a large scale.

Establishing communication in unreliable communication environments is usually based on adding delay-tolerant capabilities to the network [12]. With data transfers realized by the so-called *custody* principle, participants may communicate even if no continuous communication path exists. Using *custody*, moving participants transfer data bundles on behalf of other participants [5,11]. Since most scenarios apply hybrid networks by combining different communication technologies, the use-case-driven selection and combination of routing algorithms is challenging [19,21]. Various projects and practical implementations performed delay-tolerant research [29,32,38]. Literature provides valuable information to optimize unreliable communication at the network layer, but misses investigation on integrating/extending business processes with delay-tolerant principles.

7 Conclusion

Resilient modeling and execution of business processes in unreliable communication environments is challenging. Connectivity issues may interfere process operation, resulting in delays, failures and complete breakdowns at process runtime.

rBPMN, a BPMN extension supporting resilient modeling, introduces strategies avoiding process failures due to connectivity issues. Opportunistic message flows allow to verify and optimize resilient operation of existing BPMN diagrams. By adding and dynamically deciding on alternatives for message flows, resilience is increased when connectivity failures occur. With movable functionality between participants, a last resort mechanism may be used to guarantee operation in case of communication loss.

Widespread paradigms and technologies such as microservices and container virtualization may be used to implement *rBPMNs* resilience strategies. The paper illustrates concepts for the process configuration, the handling of movable functionality, dynamic service identification and decision making. Existing cloud-based implementations may be adapted with reasonable effort. The proof-of-concept implementation is based on an agricultural slurry process. Evaluation illustrates the ability to dynamically adapt and optimize process operation in case of connectivity issues to avoid process failures at runtime. Concepts and implementation may be adapted and extended to other use cases taking place in unreliable communication environments.

References

1. Bocciarelli, P., D'Ambrogio, A., Giglio, A., Paglia, E.: Simulation-based performance and reliability analysis of business processes. In: Proceedings of the 2014 Winter Simulation Conference, pp. 3012–3023. IEEE Press (2014)
2. Bocciarelli, P., D'Ambrogio, A., Giglio, A., Paglia, E.: A BPMN extension for modeling cyber-physical-production-systems in the context of Industry 4.0. In: 14th International Conference on Networking, Sensing and Control (ICNSC), pp. 599–604. IEEE (2017)
3. Braun, R., Esswein, W.: Classification of domain-specific BPMN extensions. In: Frank, U., Loucopoulos, P., Pastor, Ó., Petrounias, I. (eds.) PoEM 2014. LNBIP, vol. 197, pp. 42–57. Springer, Heidelberg (2014). https://doi.org/10.1007/978-3-662-45501-2_4
4. Braun, R., Schlieter, H., Burwitz, M., Esswein, W.: BPMN4CP: design and implementation of a BPMN extension for clinical pathways. In: 2014 IEEE International Conference on Bioinformatics and Biomedicine (BIBM), pp. 9–16. IEEE (2014)
5. Burleigh, S., Fall, K., Birrane, E.: Bundle protocol version 7 (internet-draft 25). IETF (2020)
6. Camunda: Workflow and Decision Automation Platform (2020). www.camunda.com. Accessed 21 June 2020
7. Christensen, E., Curbera, F., Meredith, G., Weerawarana, S., et al.: Web services description language (WSDL) 1.1 (2001)
8. Clausen, T., et al.: The addition of explicit congestion notification (ECN) to IP. IETF RFC 3626 (2003)
9. Docker Inc. http://www.docker.com/. Accessed 21 June 2020
10. Domingos, D., Respício, A., Martinho, R.: Using resource reliability in BPMN processes. Procedia Comput. Sci. **100**, 1280–1288 (2016)
11. Fall, K., Hong, W., Madden, S.: Custody transfer for reliable delivery in delay tolerant networks. IRB-TR-03-030, July 2003

12. Fall, K.: A delay-tolerant network architecture for challenged internets. In: Proceedings of the 2003 Conference on Applications, Technologies, Architectures, and Protocols for Computer Communications, pp. 27–34. ACM (2003)
13. Fielding, R.T.: REST APIs must be hypertext-driven. https://roy.gbiv.com/untangled/2008/rest-apis-must-be-hypertext-driven/. Accessed 05 Mar 2020
14. Fowler, M.: CircuitBreaker. https://martinfowler.com/bliki/CircuitBreaker.html. Accessed 21 June 2020
15. Fuggetta, A., Picco, G.P., Vigna, G.: Understanding code mobility. IEEE Trans. Softw. Eng. **24**(5), 342–361 (1998)
16. Gounaris, A.: Towards automated performance optimization of BPMN business processes. In: Ivanović, M., et al. (eds.) ADBIS 2016. CCIS, vol. 637, pp. 19–28. Springer, Cham (2016). https://doi.org/10.1007/978-3-319-44066-8_2
17. Graja, I., Kallel, S., Guermouche, N., Kacem, A.H.: BPMN4CPS: a BPMN extension for modeling cyber-physical systems. In: 25th International Conference on Enabling Technologies: Infrastructure for Collaborative Enterprises (WETICE), pp. 152–157. IEEE (2016)
18. Hildebrandt, T., van Dongen, B.F., Röglinger, M., Mendling, J. (eds.): Business Process Management. Springer, Heidelberg (2019)
19. Jain, S., Fall, K., Patra, R.: Routing in a delay tolerant network. SIGCOMM Comput. Commun. Rev. **34**(4), 145–158 (2004)
20. Martinho, R., Domingos, D.: Quality of information and access cost of IoT resources in BPMN processes. Procedia Technol. **16**, 737–744 (2014)
21. Mayer, C.P.: Hybrid Routing in Delay Tolerant Networks. KIT Scientific Publishing (2012)
22. Meyer, S., Ruppen, A., Hilty, L.: The things of the Internet of Things in BPMN. In: Persson, A., Stirna, J. (eds.) CAiSE 2015. LNBIP, vol. 215, pp. 285–297. Springer, Cham (2015). https://doi.org/10.1007/978-3-319-19243-7_27
23. Meyer, S., Ruppen, A., Magerkurth, C.: Internet of Things-aware process modeling: integrating IoT devices as business process resources. In: Salinesi, C., Norrie, M.C., Pastor, Ó. (eds.) CAiSE 2013. LNCS, vol. 7908, pp. 84–98. Springer, Heidelberg (2013). https://doi.org/10.1007/978-3-642-38709-8_6
24. Newman, S.: Building Microservices: Designing Fine-Grained Systems. O'Reilly Media, Inc. (2015)
25. Nordemann, F.: Proof-of-concept implementation - an agricultural slurry scenario. https://github.com/fnordemann/ResilientProcessExecution
26. Nordemann, F., Tönjes, R., Pulvermüller, E.: Resilient BPMN: robust process modeling in unreliable communication environments. In: 8th International Conference on Model-Driven Engineering and Software Development (MODELSWARD). Scitepress (2020)
27. Nordemann, F., Tönjes, R., Pulvermüller, E., Tapken, H.: A graph-based approach for process robustness in unreliable communication environments. In: 15th International Conference on Evaluation of Novel Approaches to Software Engineering (ENASE). Scitepress (2020)
28. Nordemann, F., Tönjes, R., Pulvermüller, E., Tapken, H.: Graph-based multi-criteria optimization for business processes. In: Shishkov, B. (ed.) BMSD 2020. LNBIP, vol. 391, pp. 69–83. Springer, Cham (2020). https://doi.org/10.1007/978-3-030-52306-0_5
29. Nordström, E., Rohner, C., Gunningberg, P.: Haggle: opportunistic mobile content sharing using search. Comput. Commun. **48**, 121–132 (2014)

30. Object Management Group (OMG): Business Process Model and Notation (BPMN) 2.0 Specification (2011). www.omg.org/spec/BPMN/2.0/About-BPMN. Accessed 21 June 2020

31. OpenAPI Initiative (2020). http://coreos.com/rkt/. Accessed 21 June 2020

32. Penning, A., Baumgärtner, L., Höchst, J., Sterz, A., Mezini, M., Freisleben, B.: DTN7: an open-source disruption-tolerant networking implementation of bundle protocol 7. In: Palattella, M.R., Scanzio, S., Coleri Ergen, S. (eds.) ADHOC-NOW 2019. LNCS, vol. 11803, pp. 196–209. Springer, Cham (2019). https://doi.org/10.1007/978-3-030-31831-4_14

33. Perkins, C.E., Bhagwat, P.: Highly dynamic destination-sequenced distance-vector routing (DSDV) for mobile computers. ACM SIGCOMM Comput. Commun. Rev. **24**(4), 234–244 (1994)

34. RAML Workgroup. http://raml.org/. Accessed 21 June 2020

35. Red Hat Inc. RKT. http://coreos.com/rkt/. Accessed 21 June 2020

36. Reinhartz-Berger, I.: 20th International Conference on Business-Process and Information Systems Modeling, Rome, Italy. Springer, Heidelberg (2019)

37. Respício, A., Domingos, D.: Reliability of BPMN business processes. Procedia Comput. Sci. **64**, 643–650 (2015)

38. Schildt, S., Morgenroth, J., Pöttner, W.B., Wolf, L.: IBR-DTN: a lightweight, modular and highly portable bundle protocol implementation. Electron. Commun. EASST **37** (2011)

39. Shishkov, B. (ed.): BMSD 2020. LNBIP, vol. 391. Springer, Cham (2020). https://doi.org/10.1007/978-3-030-52306-0

40. P. Software: Spring Framework (2020). http://spring.io. Accessed 21 June 2020

41. Stroppi, L.J.R., Chiotti, O., Villarreal, P.D.: Extending BPMN 2.0: method and tool support. In: Dijkman, R., Hofstetter, J., Koehler, J. (eds.) BPMN 2011. LNBIP, vol. 95, pp. 59–73. Springer, Heidelberg (2011). https://doi.org/10.1007/978-3-642-25160-3_5

42. Web Application Description Language (WADL). http://javaee.github.io/wadl/. Accessed 21 June 2020

43. Weerawarana, S., Curbera, F., Leymann, F., Storey, T., Ferguson, D.F.: Web services platform architecture: SOAP, WSDL, WS-policy, WS-addressing, WS-BPEL. WS-reliable messaging and more. Prentice Hall PTR (2005)

Model Transformation from CBM to EPL Rules to Detect Failure Symptoms

Alexandre Sarazin[1,2(✉)], Sebastien Truptil[3(✉)], Aurélie Montarnal[2(✉)], Jérémy Bascans[1(✉)], and Xavier Lorca[2(✉)]

[1] APSYS, 36 Rue Raymond Grimaud, 31700 Blagnac, France
alexandre-m.sarazin@mines-albi.fr, jeremy.bascans@apsys-airbus.com
[2] IMT Mines Albi, Centre de Génie Industriel, Allée des Sciences, 81000 Albi, France
{aurelie.montarnal,xavier.lorca}@mines-albi.fr
[3] CEA, CEA Tech Occitanie, 51 Rue de l'Innovation, 31670 Labège, France
sebastien.truptil@cea.fr

Abstract. The increasing complexity of modern systems, cost reduction policies and ever increasing safety requirements are bringing new challenges to the maintenance domain. In many fields, periodic maintenance actions become either insufficient or too expensive. In this context, Condition-Based Maintenance (CBM) strategies, and Prognostics and Health Management (PHM) in particular, are offering an interesting alternative by allowing systems to be maintained only when needed. These strategies rely on a constant monitoring and analysis of the systems operating conditions in order to detect and identify a failure when it occurs and even sometimes beforehand.

Nowadays, two main approaches are explored to detect failures in PHM solutions: one based on machine learning, the other based on expertise and capitalised system knowledge. This work proposes to combine a Complex Event Processing (CEP), to manage incoming data's volumetry and velocity, with an Expert System (ES) in charge of exploiting the capitalized knowledge. This paper focuses on the configuration of a CEP from rules contained in a CBM ES using a Model Driven Architecture (MDA). This configuration is a challenge, especially regarding the management of rules with temporal parameters and the need for intermediate results to deal with the rule's complexity.

Keywords: Maintenance · Knowledge base · Model transformation

1 Introduction

Maintenance is defined as the "combination of all technical, administrative and managerial actions during the life cycle of an item intended to retain it in, or restore it to, a state in which it can perform the required function" [1]. In particular, preventive maintenance describes maintenance action carried out to assess and/or to mitigate the degradation and reduce the probability of failure of an item. Condition-based maintenance (CBM) is a specific kind of preventive

© Springer Nature Switzerland AG 2021
S. Hammoudi et al. (Eds.): MODELSWARD 2020, CCIS 1361, pp. 200–224, 2021.
https://doi.org/10.1007/978-3-030-67445-8_9

maintenance assessing the systems physical conditions and analysing them to identify possible ensuing maintenance actions. Among the many solutions used for CBM data analysis, the two main strategies are data-driven and Expert Systems (ES).

Data-driven strategies, mostly consisting of machine learning algorithms, classify failures from past experience. The drawbacks of these approaches are the difficulty to explain the result and the large amount of reliable and relevant failure records required to train the learning algorithm. In fields like aeronautics where systems reliability is already strong, collecting a large amount of records of the same failure on identical systems is a very challenging task. However, the main advantage is the limited domain knowledge required to implement them.

ES approaches reproduce an expert reasoning by exploiting a base of facts and rules created from capitalised expert knowledge. However, according to [30], ES have "common defects in efficiency, scalability and applicability".

In order to solve the scalability issue, in particular from the data ingestion perspective, [25] proposed to use Complex Event Processing (CEP) to monitor and process the incoming data. The monitoring rules should be provided by the ES base of facts and transformed into generic rules and Event Processing Language (EPL) rules according to the Model Driven Architecture (MDA) methodology. However, the transformations proposed do not manage rules activated over a timeframe observation. For instance, a rule is activated if a condition is fulfilled continuously or repeats itself several times in a predefined timeframe. Yet, these kinds of rules can be written in EPL. In order to integrate these rules, this paper proposes an updated version of the transformations defined in [25].

In Sect. 2, the notions of PHM, ES and CEP will be defined and the motivation behind their combination will be explained. In Sect. 3, the CBM, generic rules and EPL metamodels will be presented. In the 4th section, the model transformations from these models will be detailed according to the MDA methodology. Finally, in Sect. 5, a representative case study is used to illustrate these transformations while stressing the need for considering timeframe based rules.

2   Use PHM Approach to Detect Failure Symptoms

2.1   Prognostics and Health Management

Modern maintenance is confronted to many challenges. Firstly, the systems become more and more complex which raises the difficulty in identifying and preventing failures. Secondly, the safety and availability requirements are getting increasingly demanding. As such, systems reliability is constantly being challenged. Moreover, cost reduction has become a strategic stake in many industrial fields and maintenance is not spared.

In this context, periodic maintenance, also known as time-based maintenance, is becoming insufficient as unnecessary actions become too expensive and unexpected failures affect availability and reliability [17]. In order to tackle these challenges, maintenance needs to be performed only when needed. Consequently, monitoring the systems working conditions in real time should be performed to detect and identify failures the moment they occur or, in best cases, beforehand. Prognostics and Health Management is a CBM strategy defined by [29] as "a method that permits the reliability of a system to be evaluated in its actual life-cycle conditions, to determine the advent of failure, and mitigate the system risks". It is composed of 7 main steps designed to collect, monitor and process sensor data in order to identify failures and estimate the Remaining Useful Life (RUL) of the defective system (Fig. 1). This information can then be processed by a decision support system and displayed to the end user [6,22] .

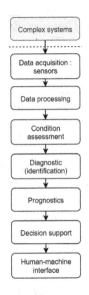

Fig. 1. PHM 7 steps [19].

The first step is to collect data in the system's actual life cycle conditions. This step is critical, as the relevance and quality of the collected data have a major impact on the quality of any further analysis. The second step is the data processing. It is meant to clean and transform collected data into more relevant variables before analysis. The third step is to assess the system's health status through anomaly detection based on the processed data. Next, potential failures and root causes should be identified. Depending on the identified failure, a degradation model should be chosen and applied to estimate the defective systems RUL in the prognostics phase. Finally, this information should be provided to a decision support system and displayed to the end user.

Although PHM architecture addresses modern maintenance issues, it also raises several technical challenges. In particular, ingesting and processing a large amount of incoming sensor data in an acceptable time is no simple task.

2.2 Expert System

In order to assess the system's health and diagnose failures, two main strategies can be adopted: data-driven or Expert Systems (ES). Data-driven technologies mostly rely on learning algorithms to detect anomalies and identify failures from a set of past records. However, this approach has benefits and drawbacks. This approach could detect maintenance needs even if the cause or the reason of the malfunction is unknown or not explainable. Nevertheless, the results obtained from these algorithms are hardly explainable and the confidence on the result depends on the number and the representativeness of the learning dataset. Depending on the observed system, collecting the learning dataset can be challenging, especially in fields like aeronautics where reliability is a major concern.

This work focuses on system without enough learning dataset but with available expert knowledge and safety documentation. To exploit this knowledge, we believe that an Expert System (ES) is interesting as explained in [9,12,17,21,22,28]. An ES is a computer program in which expert knowledge is implemented for a specific topic in order to solve problems or provide some advice [16]. ES are composed of a user interface, an inference engine and a knowledge base [23]. The user interface is meant to allow the user to interact with the system. The knowledge base structures a set of facts and rules describing the monitored system as well as the symptom and failures which can affect it. This component can be implemented using a static and dynamic database. The static database is meant to collect domain expert knowledge on the system. This database is stable, even though facts and rules may be added or modified. It should also be complete, consistent and accurate for the ES to perform acceptable analysis. The dynamic database, however, is used to "store all information obtained from the user, as well as intermediate conclusions (facts) that are inferred during the reasoning" [20]. Its content is lost at the end of each execution. An inference engine processes this knowledge base and reaches a conclusion. It can be used as a "control structure [...] that allows the expert to use search strategies to test different hypotheses to arrive at expert system conclusions" [23]. Using an ES can thus be considered a solution to capitalize and exploit the available knowledge on the system. In the maintenance context, the rules for anomaly detection, diagnostic and prognostic must be applied to the input data in order to identify failures and estimate the RUL.

Although ES offers a good solution for processing maintenance data, this solution has scalability limits and can not easily process a large amount of incoming data [30]. Complex Event Processing (CEP) can be used to fill this gap.

2.3   Complex Event Processing

Managing the inflow of data is one of the main issues in implementing PHM, especially on complex systems. As an acceptable monitoring can only be performed when many sensors of different types are set on the system, the volume and velocity of these inputs are challenging to process. These processing issues share common characteristics with big data problems defined through the 5V [18]: volume of the collected data, velocity of its update, veracity of the information, variety of the sources and value of the information. To process the input data with reduced volume and velocity, a CEP can be used.

As described by [11], a CEP engine aims at processing data efficiently to immediately recognise patterns when they occur. It was first introduced by Luckham and Fransca [24] to process events at multiple levels of abstraction. It enables a system to reach passive context-awareness, however, unlike expert systems, it does not take decisions or recommendations. A CEP engine is based on a set of complex event processing rules. According to [8,10], each rule enables to:

- Detect the occurrence of patterns based on presence or absence of linked events (e.g. incoming data)
- Filter events thanks to conditions;
- Generate new events, called complex events, based on incoming events. These complex events can be processed as new incoming events.

Depending on the language used to describe the complex event processing rules, the condition used to filter conditions could be simple (comparison to a threshold) or more complex with some functionality using temporal windows. Regarding the needs of the PHM approach, the use of temporal windows to detect abnormal situation is a requirement. Thus CEP using rules implementing Event Processing Languages (EPL) is a suitable option. EPLs are SQL-like languages designed support CEP solutions by defining events, conditions and patterns in order to detect interesting behaviors in the data [7]. ESPERTech[1] or Siddhi[2] are some examples of well-known EPL-based solutions.

In conclusion, to support PHM, ES and CEP are both useful and complementary. Indeed, CEP are designed to monitor large amounts of data in real time and detect patterns based on predefined rules whereas ES allow further analysis such as diagnostics or prognostics.

2.4   Using CEP and Expert System to Support PHM Approach

As detailed in [25], CEP can be combined with an ES in a PHM architecture. Indeed, as explained in previous sections, CEP and ES both have advantages and drawbacks. A CEP is designed to monitor large amounts of data in real time and detect patterns. Thus a CEP could reduce the flow of data but it could not

---

[1] http://www.espertech.com/.
[2] https://docs.wso2.com/display/CEP300/Siddhi+Language+Specification.

perform a diagnosis. An ES analyses data (to provide diagnostics or prognostics) and explains the analysis result but the processing could be slow. Therefore, the combination of the two technologies is relevant in a PHM application. To combine the two technologies, the anomaly detection rules implemented in the ES knowledge base should be transformed into EPL rules to be applied by the CEP according to Figure 2.

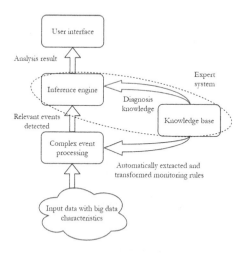

Fig. 2. Relation between CEP and expert system adapted from [25].

In this architecture, incoming sensor data with high velocity and volume should be injected in the CEP. Used as a filter, the CEP then detects the relevant anomalies based on rules extracted from the ES knowledge base. The detected events can then be processed by an inference engine to identify the related failure. This information can then be displayed to the end-user through an interface.

The main issue in combining CEP and ES, is to transform CBM rules into EPL. Moreover, according to [7], one of the downsides of CEP systems is their first hand complexity. In order to ease the domain experts work in implementing CEP solutions despite the lack of EPL knowledge, a meta model for EPL and an automatic model-to-code solution have been designed to implement the rules in commercial solutions. The EPL metamodel proposed by [7] is detailed in Fig.3.

This EPL metamodel is composed of four main types of components: the "SearchConditions","Pattern", "Output" and "Link" elements.

To illustrate these types of components, the following simple examples are used: if x > y then z and if Mean(k,l,m) > y then z.

The "Link" elements are designed to connect the elements of the three other components. It is divided into operands (as x, k, l, m, y and also Mean(k,l,m)) and operators (as >). An operator is an operation performed on one or several operands. Operators can either be Unary, Binary or N-ary depending on the number of operands they can be applied on.

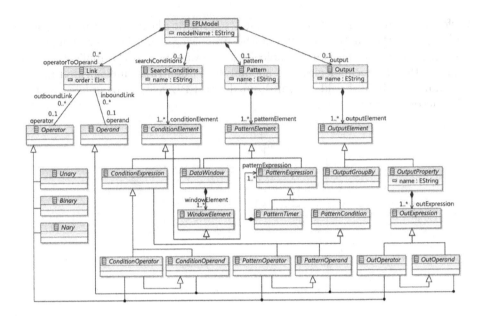

Fig. 3. EPL metamodel [7].

The "SearchConditions" component is a collection of "ConditionsElement". These elements are rules composed of "ConditionExpression" elements (as x > y and Mean(k,l,m) > y). These "ConditionExpression" elements are built from "DataWindow" (as x, y, Mean(k,l,m)), acting as operands, compared with operators. "DataWindow" are transformations of "WindowElement" (as k, l, m and x) which are input data.

The "Pattern" component is defined as "a template specifying conditions which can match sets of related events". It is used to manage sets of events occurring in a timeframe. For instance, a "PatternCondition" can count the occurrence of a specific type of event while the "PatternTimer" specifies the length of a monitoring timeframe. All these elements can be considered in the transformation process and thus leads to extend the work of Sarazin et al. [25].

Finally, the "Output" (as z) component specifies the features of the complex event generated by the rules activation. It can be composed of several events each possessing properties and generated using expressions.

Further details about the elements of this model are available in Boubeta-Puig et al. [7].

3   Proposed Model Driven Architecture

The previous sections aim to argue that the use of CEP combined to ES is relevant to provide a PHM architecture. The combination of the two technologies is based on conditions used to detect relevant anomalies. Indeed, CEP are used to reduce the incoming flow of data to the ES. Therefore, the configuration of the CEP essentially depends on the ES content. This paper's proposal is to automatically configure the CEP from the ES using a model driven architecture (MDA) [26]. This section presents first the concepts as Model, Metamodel and Model Transformation, before proposing a model transformation from CBM to CEP rules based on an MDA methodology.

3.1   Model, Metamodel, Model Transformation

According to [2], a model is a "formal specification of the function, structure and/or behavior of an application or system". It should also be noticed that a single system can be represented by many different models depending on the point of view adopted [4]. The rules used to create and structure a model are defined using a metamodel, which is an "explicit specification of an abstraction" [3]. It defines the concepts manipulated in a model and the relations between them. A model can thus be considered as an instance of a metamodel and all models must conform to their own metamodels, conforming themselves to a metametamodel [5].

In order to differentiate the business concepts manipulated in a system from the technological platform used to implement them, a model-based methodology named Model Driven Architecture (MDA) has been defined [26]. This methodology can be used in software development to separate the design steps based on the formalisation of business logic from the the technical implementation steps. According to the MDA guide, this methodology improves the "portability, interoperability and reusability" of the final result. The MDA methodology relies on four main types of models [2,26]:

- The Computation Independant Model (CIM)
- The Platform Independent Model (PIM)
- The Platform Model (PM)
- The Platform Specific Model (PSM)

The CIM is designed from the formalisation of the business logic by a domain expert with its own vocabulary. According to the MDA methodology, once the CIM is defined, the PIM can be designed to include a first level of specification. The PIM purpose is to make it possible to adapt the CIM to different platforms of the same kind. The PM describes the platform used to implement the model. It describes the concepts manipulated in the platform and the structure binding these concepts together. Finally, the PSM is defined as a "view of a system from the platform specific viewpoint". It is the implementation of the PIM on the platform modeled by the PM. [2].

MDA methodology consists in transforming a CIM to a PIM and a PIM to a PSM. This process is called model transformation [2]. It can also be defined as "a transformation operation Mt taking a model Ma as the source model and producing a model Mb as the target model" [5]. In a model transformation, all concepts may not be commonly shared by the source and target models.

Consequently, the first step of a model transformation is to identify the shared concepts in each model, which correspond to the transformation domain, and the specific concepts which are not shared (Fig. 4). In the transformation domain, the concepts are then converted from the source to the target model using transformation/mapping rules. The specific part of the source model can be considered as capitalized knowledge while the specific concepts of the target model are additional knowledge that should be implemented from external sources [27].

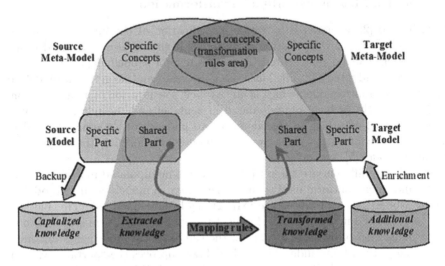

Fig. 4. Model transformation principle [27].

3.2   Model-Driven Architecture from CBM to EPL Rules

To transform CBM rules into CEP rules, an MDA can be implemented. According to the MDA philosophy, the transformation should be performed in two steps: the first step is to transform the CBM model into generic rules and the second step should convert these generic rules into CEP rules. Should alternatives to modern CEP emerge, the generic rules are designed to improve the transformation's adaptability towards new solutions. Consequently, CBM and generic rules refer to CIMs because the rules contain no platform specification even though their respective structures are different. However, EPL rules can be assimilated as a PIM. In [7], a model to code transformation has been presented to convert EPL rules into more specific languages like EQL, CQL, SteamSQL or CCL. These languages could be considered as PMs and the rules implementations in these languages would be PSMs.

In this paper, a metamodel for generic rules will be defined and the transformation rules from CBM to generic rules and from generic rules to EPL will be detailed (Fig. 5).

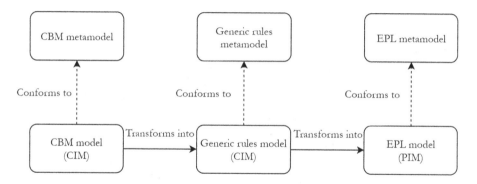

Fig. 5. Model transformation from a CBM to EPL rules [25].

The first transformation should convert CBM rules into generic rules. As such, a metamodel should be used to define and structure the concepts manipulated in a CBM rule. The metamodel chosen has been designed by [13] with concepts defined from ISO standards. This metamodel describes the different parts of a CBM solution (Fig. 6). According to this metamodel, a CBM solution is divided into 5 parts:

- Physical Description
- Functional Description
- Information Sources
- Symptom Analysis
- Maintenance Decision-Making

The "Physical Description" part is composed of all information related to the systems structure. It describes the different components to the maintainable items level which are "the group of parts of the equipment unit that are commonly maintained (repaired/restored) as a whole" [15].

The "Functional Description" part regroups the functions performed by the equipment units. For each function, the related functional failures are also described and the failure modes for each functional failure are provided.

The "Information Sources" block collects all the elements related to information gathering. This block contains monitoring variables generated from sensor data, variables, and measurement techniques. These monitoring variables are meant to be used by the "Symptom Analysis" block for anomaly detection purpose.

The "Symptom Analysis" block defines the descriptors, symptoms and information rules. A descriptor is a "feature, data item derived from raw or processed parameters or external observation" [14]. A descriptor is produced by processing one or several monitoring variables. A symptom is a "perception, made by means of human observations and measurements (descriptors), which may indicate the presence of one or more faults with a certain probability" [14]. An interpretation rule is "the description of how the descriptor values have to be interpreted or treated in order to get the monitoring outputs (detection, diagnosis, prognosis) for a failure mode" [13].

Finally, the "Maintenance Decision-Making" block, regroups several CBM processes divided into three types: anomaly detection, diagnosis and prognosis activities. The detection element is used to calculate the descriptors values and spot abnormal behaviors using interpretation rules. It is a "conclusion or group of conclusions drawn about a system or unit under test" [14]. When an anomaly is detected, it can trigger a diagnosis process in order to identify the related failure and the responsible maintainable item. When an anomaly or a diagnostic process is performed, it can also trigger a prognostics process to estimate the Remaining Useful Life of a maintainable item. The results of these processes are collected by a maintenance decision process meant to help the end-user.

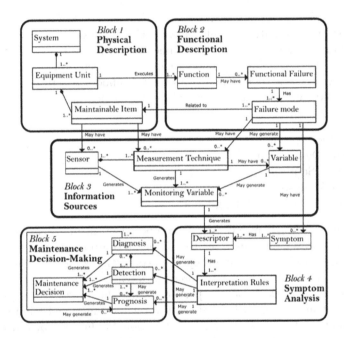

Fig. 6. Basic structure for the CBM solution [13].

4   Model Transformation

Once the motivations to combine ES and CEP in a PHM architecture have been explained, the model transformation from CBM to EPL should be detailed. This transformation is performed in two steps: the CBM rules are first converted into generic rules before being transformed into EPL. In this chapter, the metamodel for generic rules will first be detailed, then the mapping for the first and second transformations will be described.

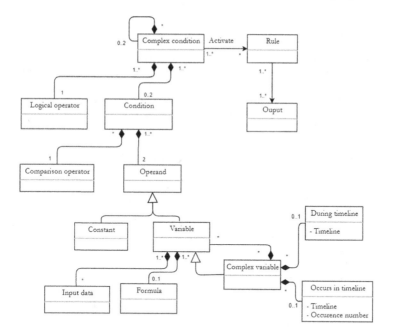

Fig. 7. Generic rules metamodel.

4.1 Generic Rules Metamodel

The first model transformation converts CBM rules into generic rules. As the metamodel for CBM has been previously presented, the generic rules metamodel should now be detailed (Fig. 7). The purpose of designing these generic rules is to improve the transformation adaptability should an alternative to EPL emerge. This metamodel should define a rule general structure while staying at a conceptual level.

According to this metamodel, input data can be transformed into a variable using a formula. This variable can then generate a complex variable which can be created from several variables using a formula and/or by applying timeframe operators. Two timeframe operators are presented in this metamodel: "during timeline" which counts the duration of an event are situation in a predefined timeline and "occurs in timeline" which counts the number of occurrences of an event in a given timeline. These operators and their aggregation in a complex variable can be considered a major modification of the version presented in [25] because it allows the event's chronology to be considered when defining rules activation conditions. The generated complex variable can then be used as a variable. Indeed, a complex variable is a specific kind of variable, which is usually more expensive to create in terms of duration or calculation.

A condition is a comparison operator (e.g. $\leq, \geq, =$) applied to two operands, which can be either a constant value or a variable. A complex condition is an aggregation of two simple or complex conditions related by a logical operator (e.g. AND,

OR). For instance $(a \geq b)OR(c \leq d)$ is a complex condition composed of two conditions $(a \geq b)$ and $(c \leq d)$ related by the logical operator "OR". The highest level complex condition activates a rule which generates an output. This output can potentially be used as an input for an another rule and inserted as a variable. Consequently, a business rule could be converted into several generic rules.

Once the generic rules metamodel has been defined, the mapping rules with the CBM metamodel presented previously can be detailed.

4.2   From CBM Knowledge Base to Generic Rules

As the source and target models for the first transformation, respectively the CBM and generic rules metamodels, have been defined, the mapping rules can be detailed. The first step in performing model transformation is to identify the shared concepts. In the source model, these concepts are:

- the sensor and variables which can be considered as inputs
- measurement techniques as a first input processing
- the monitoring variables which result from input data transformation
- the descriptors which define how the monitoring data should be processed
- the symptoms for rule characterization
- the interpretation rules to define the activation conditions including operators and threshold values
- the detection, diagnosis and prognosis elements to indicate which actions should be triggered by the rule activation

In order to connect these elements to target model concepts, mapping rules should be applied according to Table 1.

Table 1. Transformation rules from a CBM model into generic rules.

CBM model concept	Generic rule model concept
Sensor	Input data
variable	Input data
Measurement technique	Formula
Descriptor	During dimeline
	Occurs in timeline
	Formula
	Variable
	Complex variable
Monitoring variable	Variable
Interpretation rules	Constant
	Comparison operator
	Logical operator
	Condition
	Complex condition
	Rule
	Output
Symptom	Rule
Diagnosis, detection, prognosis	Output

According to this mapping, the source model's sensor and variable concepts can be matched as input data in the target model. These input data are then transformed into a target model variable using a formula. The process is similar to the generation of the source model's monitoring variable from measurement techniques applied to a sensor or variable. As such measurement techniques are matched with a formula and monitoring variable as a target model's variable.

A descriptor is processed from the transformation of one or several monitoring variables using a formula and/or timeline operators. Consequently, a descriptor is mapped to several target model's concepts. Depending on the descriptor's content, formula and variable instances can be generated or even complex variable with "during timeline" and/or "occurs in timeline" instances. Interpretation rules define the conditions applied to a descriptor to trigger a maintenance action.

Similar to descriptors, interpretation rules can be mapped to several target model's concepts depending on their content. Indeed, interpretation rules can be matched with complex conditions and generate the conditions, logical and comparison operators they are composed of. Should an interpretation rule be too complex, an output can be generated to be used as variable in a new rule. One such example will be presented in chapter 5. The symptom component provides business logic on the state of the system depending on the interpretation rule's activation. It can thus be mapped to the target model's rule. The maintenance actions can be triggered by the rule activation and can thus be matched as a rule output.

Once the generic rules are designed, the second transformation into EPL rules can be performed.

4.3   From Generic Rules to EPL

This section aims at presenting the mapping rules, available in Table 2, from generic rules to EPL. In this table, the generic rule model concepts of Table 1 have been factorised to simplify the connection with the EPL model concepts. As a reminder, CEP is designed to monitor large amounts of data in real time and detect patterns thanks to rules which respect the EPL Metamodel. To achieve this purpose, a CEP receives incoming data, named "WindowElement", which has to be combined with others to create a "DataElement". The combination of incoming data could be based on a "PatternExpression" such as the number of occurrences during a timeframe or others aggregation operators as well as the identity function. Once a "DataElement" is generated, a CEP aims to identify a desired pattern referred to as a "SearchCondition" that is a combination of "ConditionElement". More extensive details have been presented in Sect. 2.4.

According to these mapping rules, the source model's input data corresponds to the target model's WindowElement. A WindowElement can be transformed by a PatternExpression, which refers to a formula, in order to provide a DataElement that refers to a variable. Regarding the complex variables, it is obvious that they refer to DataWindow because they are generated based on a combination of variables thanks to aggregation operators. This means that a variable could

Table 2. Transformation rules from generic rules to EPL.

Generic rule model concept	EPL model concept
Input data	WindowElement
Variable	DataWindow or WindowElement
Formula	PatternExpression
Occurs in timeline	PatternCondition
During timeline	PatternTimer
Complex Variable	DataWindow
Constant	Operand
Comparison operator	Operator
Logical operator	Operator
Condition	ConditionElement
Complex condition	SearchConditions
Rule	EPLModel
Output	OutputElement

be a WindowElement. Thus depending on the rule, variables could refers to DataWindow or WindowElement.

The "Occurs in timeline" operator is a pattern condition while the "During timeline" operator is a PatternTimer. A constant is matched as an operand, while the logical and comparison operators are matched as operators. A condition, composed of operands and operators, corresponds to a ConditionElement. A complex condition, composed of several conditions can be assimilated to a SearchCondition element. Finally, the rule, activated by a complex condition and generating a output can be translated as an EPLModel and the source model's output as an OutputElement. In addition, the OutputElement could be used as a new incoming event by CEP as explained in Sect. 2.3. Thus, the generated output element may then be integrated as a WindowElement of another rule.

These rules allow generic rules to be transformed into EPL rules. In the next chapter, examples of such transformations will be presented.

5   Case Study/Illustration

Previously, the motivations behind combining CEP and ES in a PHM solution have been explained. The metamodels for CBM, generic and EPL rules have been presented and the mapping rules have been specified according to the MDA methodology. In this section, a realistic case study with two CBM rules will illustrate how these transformations should be applied. Events chronology management will be displayed to demonstrate the value of these transformations extended from the work of [25].

5.1   System Description

The proposed case study consists in detecting abnormal situations on a system in charge of regulating the airflow in a room. To ensure this functionality the considered system is composed of two actuators A1 and A2 which have to open or close a "panel". A2 can be considered as A1 backup. As such they should be opened and closed at the same time. An abnormal situation is referring to (1) an abnormal opening or closing of the panel and or (2) to an overpressure in the room. In order to detect these abnormal situations, data are gathered by sensors and sent to the PHM architecture. This data is:

- two Boolean variables are used to indicate the actuators position:
  - FO: equals 0 if the actuator is not opened and 1 if opened
  - FC: equals 0 if the actuator is not closed and 1 if closed
- P: the pressure inside the room.

Therefore, the following input data are available to detect abnormal situations: A1_FO, A1_FC, A2_FO, A2_FC and P. Based on these data, the following rules could be used to detect the two kind of abnormal situations:

1. **One of the Two Actuators Has Failed:** This situation occurs when A1 and A2 are in different positions or it can be due to a loss of signal which implies that the Boolean value has not been updated. These abnormal situations could be identified thanks to the following logical expression:

$$\text{If } (A1\_FO \neq A2\_FO) \text{ AND } (A1\_FC \neq A2\_FC)$$

2. **Risk of Overpressure inside the Room Increases:** When the pressure inside the room increases by 0.14psid in a 500 ms timeframe during at least 1s or if this same increase occurs 3 times in 10 s. Figure 8 illustrates the detection of over-pressure in the room. This figure simulates incoming P values each

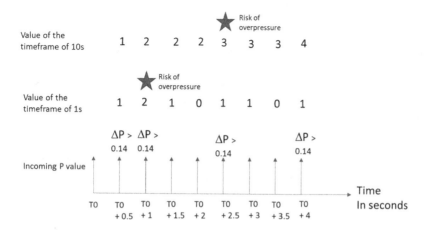

Fig. 8. Illustration of the detection of overpressure in the room.

500ms and the value of the two timeframes (1s and 10s) based on the value of the pressure difference ΔP. If the value of ΔP is over 0.14psi, then each timeframe increases by 1 and if the value of the timeframe is over the threshold, then an alert of risk of over-pressure has to be identified. This figure illustrates also that the timeframe value could decrease if $\Delta P \leq 0.14psi$.

This case study is relevant because the first rule illustrates the transposition of a rule with several monitored variables in the generic rule metamodel and the EPL metamodel whereas the second rule illustrates how to interpret the time windows in the generic and EPL metmamodel.

5.2 Examples of CBM Models

The models of the two previously presented rules are respectively detailed in Fig. 9.

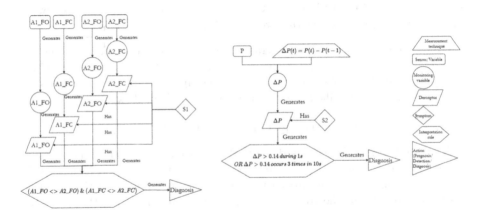

Fig. 9. CBM model for the two rules.

In the first example, A1_FO, A2_FO, A1_FC and A2_FC are being monitored and compared in the interpretation rule $(A1\_FO <> A2\_FO)\,AND\,(A1\_FC <> A2\_FC)$. The related symptom is called "S1" and triggers a diagnosis action when the interpretation rule is activated. This example is meant to detail how to manage several inputs in the transformation process.

In the second example, only the pressure is being monitored. The data generated form the sensor is transformed by the measurement technique Δ into a monitoring variable ΔP. This monitoring variable generates an identical ΔP descriptor which is used in the interpretation rule $(\Delta P > 0.14\ during\ 1s)\ OR\ (\Delta P > 0.14\ occurs\ 3\ times\ in\ 10s)$. The symptom related to this rule is "S2" and triggers a diagnosis action. This example is meant to explain how the "during" and "occurs in timeline" operations are managed in the transformation process.

5.3   Generic Rules Examples

This section focuses on the transformation from the CBM level to the generic rules level of the two rules presented in Sect. 5.1. For each example, the mapping rules will be applied to the source model before presenting the resulting target model.

Regarding the first rule, used to detect that one of the two actuators has failed, the mapping between the CBM model elements and the generic rule model elements is detailed in Table 3. The resulting model is represented in Fig. 10. In this example, it should be noticed that the source model's interpretation rules are transformed into several elements in the target Model. Indeed, the interpretation rule corresponds to a Complex Condition composed of two conditions linked by

Table 3. Application of transformation rules from CBM to generic rules for the first rule.

Source model concept	Source element	Target element	Target model concept
Monitoring variable	A1_FO	A1_FO	Variable
Monitoring variable	A1_FC	A1_FC	Variable
Monitoring variable	A2_FO	A2_FO	Variable
Monitoring variable	A2_FC	A2_FC	Variable
Interpretation rules	$A1\_FO \neq A2\_FO$ and $A1\_FC \neq A2\_FC$	&	Logical operator
		$\neq$	Comparison operator
		$A1\_FO \neq A2\_FO$	Condition (C1)
		$A1\_FC \neq A2\_FC$	Condition (C2)
		C1 & C2	Complex condition
Prognosis	One of the two actuators has failed	One of the two actuators has failed	Output

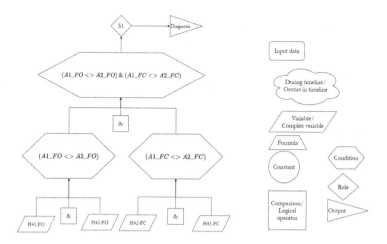

Fig. 10. Generic rule model of the first example.

Table 4. Application of Transformation Rules from CBM to Generic Rules for the second rule (model a).

Source model concept	Source element	Target element	Target model concept
Variable	P	P	Input data
Measurement technique	Δ	Δ	Formula
Monitoring variable	ΔP	ΔP	Variable
Interpretation rules	$\Delta P > 0.14$ during 1 s or $\Delta P > 0.14$ during 3 times in 10 s	0.14	Constant
		>	Comparison operator
		$\Delta P > 0.14$	Condition
		$\Delta P > 0.14$	Complex variable

Table 5. Application of transformation rules from CBM to generic rules for the second rule (model b).

Source model concept	Source element	Target element	Target model concept
Interpretation rules	$\Delta P > 0.14$ during 1 s or $\Delta P > 0.14$ occurs 3 times in 10 s	$\Delta P > 0.14$	Complex Variable
		or	Logical operator
		1 s	During timeline
		3 times in 10 s	Occurs in timeline
		$\Delta P > 0.14$ during 1 s	Condition (C1)
		$\Delta P > 0.14$ occurs 3 times in 10 s	Condition (C2)
		C1 or C2	Complex condition
Diagnosis	Risk of over-pressure	Risk of over-pressure	Output

logical operator. Each condition is composed of two Variables and a Comparison Operator.

Regarding the second rule, which aims to detect a risk of overpressure inside the room, this rule is based on occurrences number of pressure variation above a threshold. If the number of occurrences is greater or equal to 2 in one second or 3 in ten seconds then the risk has to be detected. In this kind of rules, it is necessary to define a complex variable and split the CBM rule into two generic rules at the CIM level in two rules at the PIM level. The first generic rule should generate a complex variable when the pressure variation is above 0.14 psi. The second generic rule should monitor the number of these occurrences over a timeframe to detect the overpressure risk. Table 4 details the mapping from the source model's elements to the target model's element whereas the left part of Fig. 11 corresponds to the part of the target model generating a complex variable.

Once the complex variable $\Delta P > 0.14$ psi is generated, the next part of the second rule could be transformed. Table 5 shows the mapping from the source model elements to the target model elements illustrated by the right part of Fig. 11.

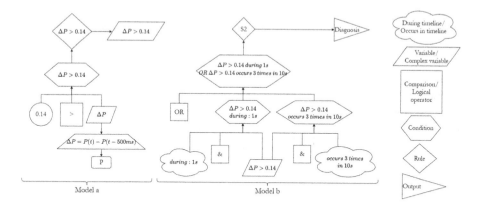

Fig. 11. Generic rule models describing the second example.

5.4   Examples of EPL Models

This section focuses on the transformation from generic to EPL rules of the models presented in Sect. 5.3. These transformations are based on the mapping rules detailed in Sect. 4.3.

A generic rule model of the first rule, referring to an abnormal situation caused by the failure of one of the two actuators, has been described in the previous section. It can now be transformed into an EPL model based on the mapping rules presented in Table 6. The resulting model is detailed in Fig. 12.

Regarding the second Rule, referring to a risk of overpressure in the room, two generic rule models have to be transformed. The generic model which generates the complex variable $\Delta P > 0.14$ psi can be converted in the EPL Model presented in the left part of Fig 13 based on the mapping rules presented in Table 7.

Finally, the model of the second rule detecting a risk of over-pressure in the room is transformed in the EPL model represented in the right part of Fig. 13 according to the mapping rules listed in Table 8.

Table 6. Application of transformation rules from generic rule to EPL for the first rule.

Source model concept	Source element	Target element	Target model concept
Variable	A1_FO	A1_FO	WindowElement
Variable	A1_FC	A1_FC	WindowElement
Variable	A2_FO	A2_FO	WindowElement
Variable	A2_FC	A2_FC	WindowElement
Logical operator	&	&	Operator
Condition (C1)	$A1\_FO \neq A2\_FO$	SearchCondition	
Condition (C2)	$A1\_FC \neq A2\_FC$	SearchCondition	
Complex condition	C1 & C2	C1 & C2	SearchElement
Output	One of the two actuators has failed	One of the two actuators has failed	Output

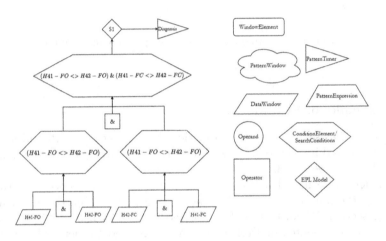

Fig. 12. EPL rule model for the first example.

Table 7. Application of transformation rules from generic rule to EPL for the second rule.

Source model concept	Source element	Target element	Target model concept
Input data	P	P	WindowElement
Formula	Δ	Δ	PatternExpression
Variable	ΔP	ΔP	DataWindow
Condition	$\Delta P > 0.14$	$\Delta P > 0.14$	SearchCondition
ComplexVariable	$\Delta P > 0.14$	$\Delta P > 0.14$	OutputElement

Table 8. Application of transformation rules from generic rule to EPL for the second rule.

Source model concept	Source element	Target element	Target model concept
Complex variable	$\Delta P > 0.14$	$\Delta P > 0.14$	WindowElement
Logical operator	OR	OR	Operator
During timeline	1 s	during: 1 s	PatternTimer
Occurs in timeline	3 times in 10 s	occurs in 10 s	PatternCondition
Condition (C1)	$\Delta P > 0.14$ during 1 s	$\Delta P > 0.14$ during 1 s	ConditionElement
Condition (C2)	$\Delta P > 0.14$ occurs 3 times in 10 s	$\Delta P > 0.14$ occurs 3 times	ConditionElement
Complex condition	C1 or C2	C1 or C2	SearchConditions
Output	Risk of over-pressure	Risk of over-pressure	Output

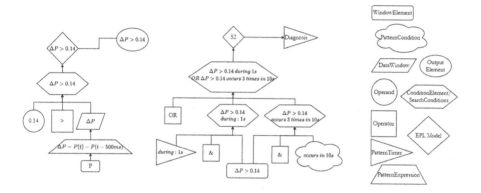

Fig. 13. EPL rule models describing the second example.

6 Summary and Future Work

In the maintenance domain, the multiplication of data sources have boosted the development of condition-based maintenance (CBM) strategies and given birth to new approaches such as Prognostics and Health Management (PHM).

Nowadays, two main approaches are explored to detect failures in PHM solutions: one based on machine learning, the other based on expertise and general domain knowledge. This work focuses on the solutions based on expertise and capitalised knowledge and thus focuses on systems with few records related to failures. In such context, the use of Expert Systems (ES), in charge of exploiting the capitalized knowledge, is relevant. Moreover, unlike machine learning approaches, an ES is able to explain the need for maintenance actions. This aspect is a key stone for decision in the maintenance domain. However, current ES have scalability limits regarding the multiplication of data sources and especially the volumetry and velocity of the incoming data. Therefore, this paper proposes to combine the ES with Complex Event Processing (CEP) to tackle these limits. Indeed, a CEP aims at processing data efficiently to immediately recognise patterns when they occur. Therefore, a CEP can be used in order to filter the incoming data and only requests the ES when it is relevant, in other words a CEP aims to reduce the volumetry and the velocity of the incoming data for the ES.

Even if the idea to combine ES with CEP is promising, it requires that the configuration of the CEP, especially the rules, are always in line with the needs of ES. This requirement implies that the configuration of the CEP has to be automatically generated from the ES. This paper details the proposed Model Driven Architecture (MDA) used to generate the CEP configuration from the ES. This MDA consists in transforming, first, CBM models into generic rules models before transforming these generic rules models into EPL models. Then code, as EQL rules for example, can be generated from these EPL models. This paper focuses on the first two transformations and the need to pass through the generic rules level due to the CBM rule's complexity such as the use of temporal parameters or the need for intermediate results. Due to this complexity, the transformation of descriptors and interpretation rules concepts of the CBM can provide lots of different generic rules concepts.

However, the presented work has limitations which have to be addressed. One of the main challenges in this model transformation is to automatically generate descriptors from documentation. To deal with this issue, exploiting resources in text format may be very helpful. To perform this, using complementary approaches might be necessary to extract and decompose descriptors into generic rules model instances. Consequently, this transformation could be improved by the use of Natural Language Processing (NLP), for example the use of entity named recognition algorithms. In addition, this proposal has, for now, been tested on case studies such as presented here, however the short-term planned perspective is now to implement this architecture on a real complex system.

References

1. AFNOR: NF EN 13306 - Maintenance – Terminologie de la maintenance, January 2018
2. Belaunde, M., et al.: MDA guide version 1.0. 1 (2003)
3. Bezivin, J., Gerbe, O.: Towards a precise definition of the OMG/MDA framework. In: Proceedings 16th Annual International Conference on Automated Software Engineering (ASE 2001), pp. 273–280, November 2001. https://doi.org/10.1109/ASE.2001.989813
4. Bezivin, J., Briot, J.P.: Sur les principes de base de l'ingénierie des modèles. L'OBJET **10**(4), 145–157 (2004)
5. Bézivin, J., Büttner, F., Gogolla, M., Jouault, F., Kurtev, I., Lindow, A.: Model transformations? Transformation models!. In: Nierstrasz, O., Whittle, J., Harel, D., Reggio, G. (eds.) MODELS 2006. LNCS, vol. 4199, pp. 440–453. Springer, Heidelberg (2006). https://doi.org/10.1007/11880240_31

6. Blanchard, B.S., Verma, D.C., Peterson, E.L.: Maintainability: A Key to Effective Serviceability and Maintenance Management. Wiley, New York (1995). https://trove.nla.gov.au/work/30017742
7. Boubeta-Puig, J., Ortiz, G., Medina-Bulo, I.: A model-driven approach for facilitating user-friendly design of complex event patterns. Expert Syst. Appl. **41**(2), 445–456 (2014). https://doi.org/10.1016/j.eswa.2013.07.070, http://www.sciencedirect.com/science/article/pii/S0957417413005575
8. Cugola, G., Margara, A.: Processing flows of information: from data stream to complex event processing. ACM Comput. Surv. (CSUR) **44**(3), 1–62 (2012)
9. DePold, H.R., Gass, F.D.: The application of expert systems and neural networks to gas turbine prognostics and diagnostics. J. Eng. Gas Turbines Power **121**(4), 607–612 (1999). https://doi.org/10.1115/1.2818515
10. Etzion, O., Niblett, P., Luckham, D.: Event processing in action. Manning Greenwich (2011)
11. Flouris, I., Giatrakos, N., Deligiannakis, A., Garofalakis, M., Kamp, M., Mock, M.: Issues in complex event processing: status and prospects in the big data era. J. Syst. Softw. **127**, 217–236 (2017)
12. Gertler, J.: Fault Detection and Diagnosis in Engineering Systems. CRC Press (1998). Google-Books-ID: fmPyTbbqKFIC
13. Guillen, A.J., Crespo, A., Gómez, J.F., Sanz, M.D.: A framework for effective management of condition based maintenance programs in the context of industrial development of E-Maintenance strategies. Comput. Industry **82**, 170–185 (2016). https://doi.org/10.1016/j.compind.2016.07.003, http://www.sciencedirect.com/science/article/pii/S0166361516301178
14. ISO: ISO 13372, Surveillance et diagnostic des machines – Vocabulaire, June 2012
15. ISO: NF EN ISO 14224 - Petroleum, petrochemical and natural gas industries - Collection and exchange of reliability and maintenance data for equipment, October 2017
16. Jackson, P.: Introduction to Expert Systems, 3rd edn. Addison-Wesley Longman Publishing Co. Inc., Boston (1998)
17. Jardine, A.K.S., Lin, D., Banjevic, D.: A review on machinery diagnostics and prognostics implementing condition-based maintenance. Mech. Syst. Sig. Process. **20**(7), 1483–1510 (2006). https://doi.org/10.1016/j.ymssp.2005.09.012, http://www.sciencedirect.com/science/article/pii/S0888327005001512
18. Jin, X., Wah, B.W., Cheng, X., Wang, Y.: Significance and challenges of big data research. Big Data Res. **2**(2), 59–64 (2015). https://doi.org/10.1016/j.bdr.2015.01.006, http://www.sciencedirect.com/science/article/pii/S2214579615000076
19. Jouin, M., Gouriveau, R., Hissel, D., Péra, M.C., Zerhouni, N.: Prognostics and health management of PEMFC – state of the art and remaining challenges. Int. J. Hydrogen Energy **38**(35), 15307–15317 (2013). https://doi.org/10.1016/j.ijhydene.2013.09.051, http://www.sciencedirect.com/science/article/pii/S036031991302274X
20. Kalogirou, S.A.: Artificial intelligence for the modeling and control of combustion processes: a review. Progress Energy Combustion Sci. **29**(6), 515–566 (2003). https://doi.org/10.1016/S0360-1285(03)00058-3, http://www.sciencedirect.com/science/article/pii/S0360128503000583
21. Lee, J., Jin, C., Liu, Z., Ardakani, H.D.: Introduction to data-driven methodologies for prognostics and health management. In: Ekwaro-Osire, S., Goncalves, A., Alemayehu, F. (eds.) Probabilistic Prognostics and Health Management of Energy Systems, pp. 9–32. Springer, Heidelberg (2017). https://doi.org/10.1007/978-3-319-55852-3_2

22. Lee, J., Wu, F., Zhao, W., Ghaffari, M., Liao, L., Siegel, D.: Prognostics and health management design for rotary machinery systems—reviews, methodology and applications. Mech. Syst. Sig. Process. **42**(1), 314–334 (2014). https://doi.org/10.1016/j.ymssp.2013.06.004, http://www.sciencedirect.com/science/article/pii/S0888327013002860

23. Liebowitz, J.: Expert systems: a short introduction. Eng. Fracture Mech. **50**(5), 601–607 (1995). https://doi.org/10.1016/0013-7944(94)E0047-K, http://www.sciencedirect.com/science/article/pii/0013794494E0047K

24. Luckham, D.C., Frasca, B.: Complex event processing in distributed systems. Computer Systems Laboratory Technical Report CSL-TR-98-754. Stanford University, Stanford 28 (1998)

25. Sarazin, A., Truptil, S., Montarnal, A., Lamothe, J., Commanay, J., Sagaspe, L.: Towards model transformation from a CBM model to CEP rules to support predictive maintenance. In: MODELSWARS 2020-The 8th International Conference on Model-Driven Engineering and Software Development, vol. 1, pp. 205–215. SciTePress (2020)

26. Siegel, J.: MDA guide, revision 2.0 (2014)

27. Truptil, S., et al.: Mediation information system engineering for interoperability support in crisis management. In: Popplewell, K., Harding, J., Poler, R., Chalmeta, R. (eds.) Enterprise Interoperability IV, pp. 187–197. Springer, London (2010)

28. Vachtsevanos, G., Lewis, F., Roemer, M., Hess, A., Wu, B.: Systems approach to CBM/PHM. In: Intelligent Fault Diagnosis and Prognosis for Engineering Systems, pp. 13–55. Wiley, Hoboken (2006). https://doi.org/10.1002/9780470117842.ch2, http://onlinelibrary.wiley.com/doi/10.1002/9780470117842.ch2/summary

29. Vichare, N.M., Pecht, M.G.: Prognostics and health management of electronics. IEEE Trans. Components Packag. Technol. **29**(1), 222–229 (2006). https://doi.org/10.1109/TCAPT.2006.870387

30. Xiaoxue, L., Xuesong, B., Longhe, W., Bingyuan, R., Shuhan, L., Lin, L.: Review and trend analysis of knowledge graphs for crop pest and diseases. IEEE Access **7**, 62251–62264 (2019). https://doi.org/10.1109/ACCESS.2019.2915987, conference Name: IEEE Access

Verification and Simulation of Time-Domain Properties for Models of Behaviour

Miguel Carrillo[1]ⓘ, Vladimir Estivill-Castro[2(✉)]ⓘ,
and David A. Rosenblueth[1]ⓘ

[1] Instituto de Investigaciones en Matemáticas Aplicadas y en Sistemas, Universidad Nacional Autónoma de México, Apdo. 20-126, 01000 México D.F., Mexico
[2] School of Information and Communication Technology, Griffith University, Brisbane, QLD 4111, Australia
v.estivill-castro@griffith.edu.au

Abstract. Modelling and simulation are techniques instrumental in the engineering and design of complex systems. The reason is that both these techniques can anticipate possible failures when corrections are less costly to incorporate. Nevertheless, a correct behaviour is no guarantee, especially with software systems and their ubiquitous modelling notation: state machines. Correctness cannot be guaranteed because semantic gaps result from (1) abstractions in modelling and (2) ambiguities in simulation. Formal verification of a model may thus imply little about the correctness of the implementation. This situation is all the more serious with the emergence of Model-Driven Software Engineering and its penetration in the instrumentation of cyber-physical systems, where verification of time-domain properties of systems is now paramount. We use logic-labelled finite-state machines (LLFSMs), a formalism with a precise semantics. We introduce both model-to-model and model-to-text transformations from LLFSMs to either programming languages or formal-specification languages for model checkers with minimal semantic gaps. We describe a transformation in the Atlas Transformation Language (ATL), producing modules of the NuSMV model checker. The time complexity of this transformation is linear in the total number of states of an arrangement of LLFSMs. The transformation is so faithful that the model checker itself can be used as the execution engine of the LLFSMs models.

Keywords: Formal verification · Model-to-model transformations · State machines

1 Introduction

"Systems are inherently complex, and tools such as modelling and simulation are needed to provide the means for gaining insight into aspects of their behaviour" [6].

A previous version of this article appeared in MODELSWARD 2020.

© Springer Nature Switzerland AG 2021
S. Hammoudi et al. (Eds.): MODELSWARD 2020, CCIS 1361, pp. 225–249, 2021.
https://doi.org/10.1007/978-3-030-67445-8_10

With the emergence of Model-Driven Software Development, there is an expectation that, for complex software systems, high-level designs would automatically translate into implementations. The Unified Modeling Language (UML) is possibly the most frequently used language for modelling the behaviour of software systems as arrangements of state machines, and this includes the internet of things (IoT) devices, embedded systems, and smart things [9]. UML state charts adopted and popularised the *Run To Completion (RTC)* event-driven semantics [20,24,39]. Moreover, UML has elaborated (on top of the RTC) the handling of events for all sorts of other compositions with other behaviour models [25]. Unfortunately, such enlargement of UML's artifacts [13,21] has resulted in the widening of semantic gaps (larger discrepancies between modelling languages and their interpretation; both, in the verification or in the execution) and in more elaborate constructs, that many admit they rarely use. For instance, introductory videos [1] on using Papyrus [26] admit ignoring most of the options and elements offered by the modelling tools. In particular, for state machines, it is suggested [23] that the main use of models is their visualisation aspect, ignoring completely the executability.

Simulations that do not exhibit failure are no guarantee of correct behaviour. Hence, there is significant interest to enable formal verification of models. Moreover, with the emergence of Model-Driven Software Engineering and its penetration in the instrumentation of cyber-physical systems, formal verification of time-domain properties [29] (beyond value-domain properties) of systems is now paramount.

In this paper, we report on model-to-model (M2M) transformations and model-to-text (M2Text) transformations directly producing a Kripke structure for model checking in the SMV language [34], which is the core input language to the NuSMV [14] and nuXmv [12] model checkers. The transformation is so faithful that the model checker itself can be used as the execution engine of the LLFSMs models. That is, we minimise the semantic gaps. Moreover, we use SMV's module notation achieving extremely succinct input files for the model checkers. For example, compared with a former implementation [33] of the generation of the input files for the model checker, instead of over 110,000 lines of code, we now generate fewer than 500.

Our contributions are as follows.

1. We detail M2M transformations that reduce the need for sections with states (see Subsect. 5.1).
2. In Subsect. 5.2, we detail M2M transformations that handle the atomicity of actions in states for the semantics of LLFSMs when translated to SMV.
3. We automatically generate verification properties of the model (see Subsect. 7.1).
4. We demonstrate that the transformations are efficient (see Subsect. 7.3).

At mipal.net.au/downloads.php, we release the code for prototype implementation of these transformations. Figure 1 illustrates the M2Text transformations released with the software. An accompanying video[1] illustrates one case study

---

[1] www.youtube.com/watch?v=o2Ut5lAsJe8&feature=youtu.be.

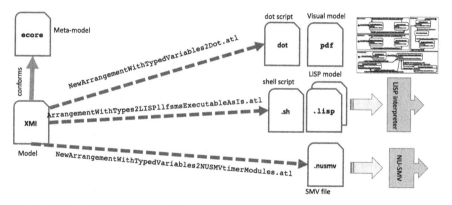

Fig. 1. ATL model-2-text transformations released at mipal.net.au/downloads.php.

where the model is interpreted by the NuSMV model checker and also by our own interpreter written in LISP. Unlike the conference paper [11], this paper offers a direct focus on verifying time-domain properties. In particular, in Section 6 we include a new case study of the garage door controller [2]. This case study has important time-domain aspects. Our transformation in this version can handle integer variables and predefined constants. Most importantly, the model-2-text transformations produce computation-tree logic (CTL) and linear-time logic (LTL) properties about the scheduling of modules and the proper execution of the arrangement (see Subsect. 7.1). This aspect is a fundamental step in proving the model-2-text transformation is in itself correct. With respect to the prototypes of implementing the transformations, we now release the model-2-model transformation in the ATL transformation language that eliminates the need for sections in states (see Sect. 5.1). We also release EMF-Java tools that use the generated classes from the meta-model to produce a graphical user interface (GUI)-enabled emulator of traces produced by the NuSMV [14] and nuXmv [12] model checkers. We hence establish the minimisation of the semantic gap between the verified model and the execution. Moreover, in Sect. 3, we provide a full mathematical definition of LLFSMs, which directly delivers the corresponding meta-model.

2   Adopting Logic-Labelled Finite-State Machines

Despite the attempts to formulate behaviour models as UML state machines, the interpretation of these models still finds semantic variants, so that even in the value domain, properties submitted for formal verification may or may not hold, depending on the particular semantic variant [3]. This discrepancy is a manifestation of a first type of semantic gap, so that the executable model in simulation runs differently from the code generated from the model. A second type of semantic gap occurs when the input for a model checker is produced from the model using simplifying assumptions to ensure that formal verification is feasible (this is the case of translations that assume the execution will always have no bound on the available time to resolve the current event and therefore does not produce the representation of event queues or other mechanisms implied by the RTC semantics). For instance, STP [4, 16] converts STATEMATE's event-driven state-charts into SMV by converting events into Boolean event variables that are true for exactly one time step. In effect, the model being verified is some form of logic-labelled finite-state machine which is no longer equivalent to the original RTC semantics. Other researchers have found ambiguities in UML's semantics [36]. For instance, in cases where several transitions are enabled, some researchers have elected to chose randomly which transition shall fire (which casts serious doubts about the semantics), while others prefer to keep a record of the editing of the model (and assigning priorities to transitions on such invisible criteria as the order of inserted transitions while editing the model [36]). In the time domain, verification with UPPAAL [31] (i.e., timed automata) verifies time bounds once the system starts processing an event. Verification with timed automata does not consider the amount of time that the system has to wait for an event to happen. Thus, verification is limited to best-case scenarios, where, for all the configurations of event queues, the current event is not affected by timing deadlines. We attribute the mismatch between UML being formally verifiable and UML being executable to the original goal of UML to be both human centred and a tool for communication between human designers, allowing a significantly loose semantics, with little intention to be executable [13].

A third semantic gap emerges when the constructs by Model-Driven Software Development are translated by programmers or machines into programming languages with significantly different constructs: the verified model would have even less resemblance with the running program:

> "The only effective way to raise the confidence level of a program significantly is to give a convincing proof of its correctness" [18]

(also cited by Edmund M. Clarke et al. [15]).

We elect here to use arrangements of logic-labelled finite-state machines (LLFSMs) as the constructs to model behaviour. As a first approximation, we can imagine LLFSMs as UML's state charts where transitions are not labelled by events, but only by guards (without side effects). Thus, each transition is labelled only by a Boolean expression. This simple change has profound implications (a summary appears in Table 1).

with the advantage that the computational power is not lost. More precisely, LLFSMs are extended finite-state machines where the user has the liberty to choose the action language. In addition, they can be executed concurrently, but instead of uncontrolled concurrency, the scheduler is predefined ahead of execution. The result is a sequential executable semantics without the earlier semantic problems of the RTC semantics of the event-driven UML modelling tools.

> "The more complex a system is, the more important it is to make it as simple as possible. In complex systems, simplicity isn't achieved by coding tricks. It's achieved by rigorous thinking above the code level" [30].

Table 1. Comparison of behaviour models.

LLFMSs	UML state charts
Transitions labelled by logic expressions	Transitions labelled by events
Analogous to time-triggered (explained in text)	RTC semantics
Sequential semantics (but concurrent)	fUML attempts to produce executable semantics
Executable and verifiable models	Semantic gaps reflected in diverse execution models
Scale up by concurrent execution in arrangement	State nesting is one of the fundamental mechanism for composition
Can produce deliberative system	Usually leads to the confusion between reactive system, event-driven system and real-time system
Communication with control/status messages	send instantaneous semantics

Moreover, for formal verification, the RTC semantics requires model checkers to consider all possible sequences of arrival of events and all possible states of the queue (or queues) that handle(s) the events. Such combinatorial explosion severely limits the potential for model checking of elaborate models.

Logic-labelled state-machines can be considered an alternative to event-driven models in an analogous fashion as time-triggered architectures are an alternative to event-driven systems. However, when timing issues are critical, a time-trigger architecture is fundamental:

> "The safety properties of time-triggered architectures can be formally verified (which is extremely difficult with event-triggered systems)" [22].

Rushby [37,38] showed that time-triggered architectures are resilient and safe in all operating circumstances. Thus, time-triggered architectures guide the design of international safety standards such as IEC 61508 (industrial systems), ISO 26262 (automotive systems), IEC 62304 (medical systems) and IEC 60730 (household goods) [35].

Although LLFSMs can be scheduled as a time-triggered systems, strictly speaking, LLFSMs are not identical to time-triggered systems (see Table 1). The reason is that a "ringlet"s (Definition 8 in Sect. 3) duration is not uniform across different machines. That is, the time it takes to run a scheduler's turn varies depending on (the current state of) the machine in turn. This variation is caused by the fact that some machines may have more statements in their section than others, or that a state may have more transitions than others.

In contrast with both LLFSMs and time-triggered architectures, event-driven systems imply managing queues to store events arriving while handling the current event. Such event-driven architectures exhibit many issues regarding time guarantees [17,28]. But more importantly, in the value domain, all possible orders of events and queue's configurations must be verified (such combinatorial explosion is impractical).

3   Formal Definition of LLFSMs

An *arrangement* of LLFSMs is a sequence of state machines operating in an environment. The order of the state machines in such a sequence defines the execution schedule of such state machines.

Definition 1. *An arrangement $A = (Q, E, W)$ is a triple, where*

1. Q *is a sequence $\langle M_1, M_2, \ldots, M_k \rangle$ of k logic-labelled finite state machines,*
2. $E = E_s \cup E_e \subseteq \mathcal{V}$ *is a set of variables, called external variables, formed of two disjoint sets: the set E_s of sensor (input) variables and the set E_e of effector (output) variables, and*
3. $W \subseteq \mathcal{V}$ *is a set of variables, called shared or whiteboard variables.*

To identify the parts of an arrangement A we use a dot, so $A.Q$ is the sequence of state machines, but if A is understood, we simply write Q.

A *logic-labelled finite state machine* (LLFSM) is a state machine whose transitions are labelled by logic expressions, typically Boolean expressions in an action language. Therefore, as long as there is an effective procedure to evaluate the expressions (even in a multi-valued logic), the formalism applies. (For instance, LLFSMs have been used with defeasible logic [5].) We therefore do not elaborate on the semantics of the logic expressions labelling the transitions, but will refer to them as Boolean expressions.

Definition 2. *A logic-labelled finite-state machine (LLFSM), or machine for short, is a tuple $M = (\mathcal{S}, \mathcal{T}, I, L, \mathcal{F})$, where*

1. $\mathcal{S}$ *is a set of states,*
2. $\mathcal{T}$ *is a partial transition function,*
3. $L \subseteq \mathcal{V}$ *is a set of (local) variables,*
4. $I \in \mathcal{S}$ *is a distinguished initial state, and*
5. $\mathcal{F} \subseteq \mathcal{S}$ *is a set of final or accepting states.*

Definition 3. *The state S of the i-th machine LLFSM in the sequence $A.Q$ is uniquely identified as $M_i.S$.*

States have sections where code of the action language is placed. The sections are of three kinds, in a manner analogous to that of OMT and UML.

Definition 4. *A state S of a machine M_i in an arrangement has the form $M_i.S = (S, Oe_i, Ox_i, Do_i)$, where*

Oe_i, Ox_i, Do_i are respectively called the OnEntry, OnExit, and Internal sections of the state. Each section is a set of legal instructions (commands) in some programming language (for example, assignments)[2] so that $\lambda(E, W, M_i.L).Oe_i$, $\lambda(E, W, M_i.L).Ox_i$, and $\lambda(E, W, M_i.L).Do_i$ have no free variables (that is, all variables occurring in the instructions of a section of a state are either external variables, whiteboard variables, or the local variables of the machine M_i that holds the state S).

For convenience, a partial transition function $\mathcal{T}$ of an LLFSM M is represented as a sequence of triplets (S_s, B, S_t), where

1. S_s, S_t are states in $\mathcal{S}$, the states of M, and S_s is the source state while S_t is the target state (S_s and S_t could possibly be the same),
2. B is a Boolean expression in some logic language, so that $\lambda(E, W, M_i.L).B$ has no free variables (that is, all variables occurring in the Boolean expression B are either external variables, whiteboard variables or the local variables of the machine M_i that holds the state S).

Definition 5. *If two transitions* $T_b = (S_{s_b}, B_b, S_{t_b})$ *and* $T_a = (S_{s_a}, B_a, S_{t_a})$ *in the transitions* $\mathcal{T}$ *of an LLFSM* M*, where*

$$\mathcal{T} = \langle (S_{s_1}, B_1, S_{t_1}), (S_{s_2}, B_2, S_{t_2}), \ldots, (S_{s_t}, B_t, S_{t_t}) \rangle$$

are such that $S_{s_b} = S_{s_a}$ *(that is,* T_b *and* T_a *have the same source state), and* $b < a$ *(that is, transition* T_b *is before* T_a*), then we say that* T_b *has* precedence *over* T_a*.*

When transitions share a source state, they are evaluated in sequence in a shared snapshot of the environment. A transition that shares its source state with others fires only if all transitions that precede it do not fire and its labelling expression evaluates to `true`.

Definition 6. *Let* $T_a = (S_{s_1}, B_a, S_{t_a})$ *be a transition in the transitions* $\mathcal{T}$ *of an LLFSM* M*. If* $\mathcal{T}$ *has transitions* $T_1 = (S_{s_1}, B_1, S_{t_1})$*,* $T_2 = (S_{s_1}, B_2, S_{t_2})$*, ...,* $T_p = (S_{s_1}, B_p, S_{t_p})$ *preceding* T_a *(and thus all have the same source state), then the Boolean expression for* T_a *is*

$$B_A = B_a \wedge \neg(B_1 \vee B_2 \vee \ldots \vee B_p).$$

Definition 7. *A state is* final *when it has no outgoing transition.*

A self-transition (same source and target) is sufficient for a state not to be final. If a self-transition fires, the *OnEntry* is not executed again. Once an LLFSM has reached a final state it will execute its *OnEntry*, its *Internal* once and will be removed from the scheduling in the arrangement. The *OnExit* code of a final state is not executed.

---

[2] For the ATL transformation here we use as the action language an extension of IMP [42] as statements in this language have direct equivalents in CLISP and SMV. However, implementations of LLFSMs have used Simple-C, Java, C++, and Swift.

3.1 Semantics

Depending on the action language, variables may be typed. This just means that the set $\mathcal{V}$ of variables is partitioned. For our implementation, we have at least two types: Boolean variables, and Integer variables since again these are common types between SMV and CLISP. Specifying the type of a variable corresponds to specifying its domain of values. We assume that all domains have a special value $\perp$ which will be the default value for all variables (and represents that the variable has not been assigned a value) [41].

Definition 8. *Given an arrangement* $A = (Q = \langle M_1, \ldots, M_k \rangle, E = E_s \cup E_e, W)$, *a Kripke state is a valuation of*

1. *the external variables* $E = E_s \cup E_e$,
2. *the whiteboard variables* W,
3. *the local variables* L_i, *for each machine* M_i,
4. *the current state* $pc_i \in S_i$, *for each machine* M_i,
5. *a Boolean variable* has_fired$_i$, *for each machine* M_i,
6. *a variable* turn $\in \{1, \ldots, k\}$ *that indicates which machine holds the current token of execution (and performs a ringlet; that is, executes its current state).*

Valuation for variables means that we have a value q_i *(which could be* $\perp$*) for the variable* v_i.

We note that for model checking, systems are categorised as *open* or *closed* [40, Page 88]. Closed systems have no inputs, and are frequently those that are formally verified. But naturally, software operates in interaction with the environment. When dealing with an open system, a corresponding closed system is used by composing the open system with a model of its environment. For the definition of the next Kripke state in computation we adopt the standard convention (of modelling the environment) by allowing the valuation of a sensor variable to remain the same or change non-deterministically to any value in its domain if it is $\perp$, and to remain or change non-deterministically to any value in its domain (except $\perp$) if it is already different from $\perp$. External *sensor* variables will have a subscript s. External *effector* variables will have a subscript e. Whiteboard variables will have a subscript w.

Definition 9. *Given a Kripke state, (that provides (1) a value t for* turn, *(2) for each* M_i, *a current state* pc_i, *and a value for* has_fired$_i$, *and (3) values (or* $\perp$*) for all external variables, all whiteboard variables, all local variables of each LLFSM), the descendant Kripke states (*next *in NuSMV notation) are valuations (new assignment of values to variables) that are obtained as follows. First, all local variables of all other machines besides machine* M_t *retain their values as the only machine which executes a ringlet whose turn it is. That is,*

$$\text{next}(Mj.v_u) \leftarrow \text{value}(Mj.v_u) \ \forall j \neq t.$$

Second, new values are calculated for external variables, whiteboard variables and the local variables of machine M_t *according to the following cases.*

Case has_fired$_i$ = true. *This is the case when a transition fired as the last action of running the ringlet in machine M_t.*

1. *A copy $C = (E, W, M_t.L)$ (recall turn $= t$) (a snapshot is taken) of the valuation defined by the environment variables, the whiteboard variables and the local variables for M_t.*

2. *The current program counter pc_t (points to a state of M_t) of the current state-machine indicated by turn $= t$, is used to select the statements Oe_{pc_t} of OnEntry section of the t-th machine and Oe_{pc_t} is executed in $C = (E, W, M_t.L)$ producing a new valuation C_1*

3. *The set of transitions is analysed resulting in two sub-cases.*
   (a) *If the set of transitions of M_t that have source state pc_t is empty, the machine is removed from the arrangement.*
   (b) *Otherwise, the transitions of M_t that have source state pc_t are evaluated in their precedence order in the same valuation C_1. We have two sub-subcases.*
      i *If a transition $T_a = (S_{pc_j}, B, S_t)$ evaluates to true, then the OnExit section Ox_{pc_t} is evaluated in the context C_1 producing a new context C_2. The next value of the variable has_fired$_t$ is set to true.*
      ii *Otherwise, no transition fired. Then, the Internal section Do_{pc_t} is evaluated in the context C_1 to produce a new context C_2.*

4. *The values of the context C_2 are written back to the corresponding external variables, whiteboard variables and the local variables of M_t.*

Case: has_fired$_i$ = false. *The same steps as in the case when has_fired$_i$ = true are performed except that Step 2 that executes the OnEntry is skipped and thus the context for evaluation transitions is the first snapshot $C = (E, W, M_t.L)$.*

In all cases, the variable turn is updated to turn+1 mod k. In the open execution the sensor variables are executed with sensor values. In the closed system version, several new Krikpe states are produced by generating all possible combinations of the external sensor variables.

3.2   Timed LLFSMs

Timed LLFSMs allow the predicate after (int) as part of the Boolean expression of a transition.

The machines are extended so that the information for a Kripke state about the state of an individual machine is extended. For each machine M_i, besides the current state $pc_i \in S_i$ and $has\_fired_i \in \{\text{true}, \text{false}\}$, we now have a time-stamp t_i which records the time of entering the state pc_i (and before any action in the OnEntry of pc_i runs).

The semantics of the predicate after (int) in a transition B_p with source state S is essentially syntactic sugar for a "less than" comparison between the current time and the time recorded in the time-stamp t_i.

The results should be that, for positive values for the integer argument of after (int), the first time the transition is evaluated, it will evaluate to false.

Every subsequent evaluation while in state S will retrieve the current universal time in the executing hardware as *later-time*. If the later-time is at least `int` seconds later than the time-stamp t_i, then the expression `after (int)` evaluates to `true`; otherwise it evaluates to `false`.

Most importantly, any other transition out of S that fires will reset to a new value the time-stamp t_i as part of the *OnEntry* section of the arrival state.

4   Value-Domain Versus Time-Domain

The common use of model checking is to eradicate value-domain failures. A value-domain failure means that an incorrect value is produced [29, Page 139]. A temporal failure, on the other hand, means that a value is computed outside the intended interval of real time. We already referred to Besnard et al. [3] for the discussion of semantic gaps and the ambivalent semantics of UML. We refer to these authors again because of their case study of the level-crossing train (see Fig. 2). In this case study, a train approaches a level crossing, and presses a first entrance sensor (called the far-entrance sensor). This should activate railway signs and road signs. Closer to the crossing, a second entrance sensor (the near-entrance sensor) activates the lowering down of a gate. Once the train passes, it presses an exit sensor and the gate lifts and the signals stop shining.

Besnard et al. [3] perform model checking (of the closed representation of their executable models) in the value domain. In particular, these authors verify deadlock detection (that the model is deadlock free) as well as four system requirements.

Property 1. The gate is closed when the train is in the level crossing.
Property 2. The light of the road-sign is active when the train is in the level crossing.
Property 3. Eventually, the gate will open after being closed.
Property 4. Eventually, the light of the road-sign will turn off after being activated.

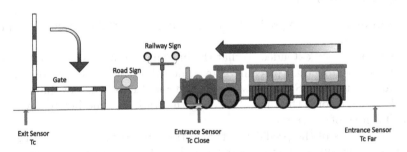

Fig. 2. Scenario of the level-crossing case study [3].

We emphasise that in the work of Besnard et al. [3] there are no time deadlines in the expression and verification of the above properties. A significant contribution of our work is that, in our translation to SMV, we enable integer variables to function as program counters (and a scheduler) for describing the computation progress in the model. Thus, by combining these integer variables and bounded operators of LTL and CTL, we can express and verify properties having explicit time deadlines. Therefore, we can verify the non-existence of temporal failures. For instance, by applying our ATL transformation to the LLFSM model of the level crossing behaviour, we obtain an SMV model where we can verify a variant of Property 4. This variant considers, in addition to the road sign, the train position, and is expressed by the following SMV code.

```
DEFINE
    roadSignIsActive  := (RoadSign.pcRoadSign = 2);
    trainIsPassing    := (Train.pcTrain = 4);
LTLSPEC
   G ((roadSignIsActive & trainIsPassing) ->
      (F[0,8] (!trainIsPassing & (F[0,58] roadSignIsInactive))))
```

These bounded LTL formula and specific naming of LLFSMs program counters state that, if the light of the road sign is active and a train is on the level crossing then, after at most eight Kripke transitions, a train is out of the level crossing and then, after a maximum of 58 additional transitions, the road sign light turns off. From here, by a conversion of state transitions to time units, a worst-case execution time estimate of the statements in *OnEntry* sections of the model results in a verified hard real-time bound Property 4.

5 From LLFSMs to SMV Models via ATL Transformations

We now describe M2Text and M2M transformations that we use to transform an arrangement of LLFSMs into an SMV model (a set of SMV modules).

5.1 LLFSM with Non-sectioned States Through an M2M Transformation

We now describe using standard UML diagrams shown in Fig. 3 (constructed with Papyrus [26]) the algorithm that transforms an LLFSM into an LLFSM where states do not have sections. This condition is equivalent to all statements belonging to the OnEntry section. The version of the code released with this chapter includes an ATL M2M prototype of our transformation, implementing the semantics described in Definition 9. This implementation is similar to those that have removed the nesting of states in UML state machines of depth 2 into UMP state diagrams with no nesting and the Promela language of the Spin model checker [10]. In that setting, the interlingua semantics of hierarchical statecharts [19] unfolds a level-2 nesting into essentially a new statechart without nesting but with states given by the Cartesian product of the container statechart and the contained statecharts.

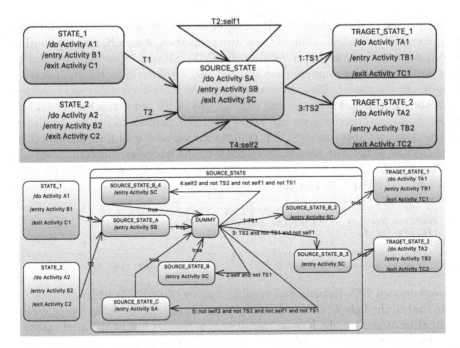

Fig. 3. Schema that defines the M2M transformation that ensures that states do not have sections (or alternatively, all statements are in the OnEntry section).

5.2   M2M Transformation to Handle a State's Section Atomically

Which actions (or code and in which action language) are placed in the sections of the states of LLFSMs is not essential for our discussion. The use of variables and sequences of assignments is a feature common in *extended* state machines, but theoretically, at the cost of having a larger number of states: for every extended state machine there exists an equivalent FSM (or LLFSM) [27].

We also define an M2M transformation that highlights that the semantics of actions (code) in LLFSMs are handled atomically. That is, the intermediate states of the action language inside a state are invisible to all other LLFSMs concurrently executing. Therefore, we can simplify such statements and their translation to SMV's statements. Moreover, this transformation only requires a syntactic analysis of the statements in a state. Figure 4 illustrates the effect of the transformation, which is given by the recursive algorithm in Fig. 5. The algorithm maintains a dictionary that with each variable it associates an expression. When an assignment statement is found for the first time, the variable on the left-hand side (LHS) is inserted as the key in the dictionary with the expression on the right-hand side (RHS) as the associated information. For each new assignment, the RHS has all free occurrences of variables replaced by the values in the dictionary before the LHS is updated with the new expression. Note that the statements are not executed. Instead, they are nested into the resulting expressions.

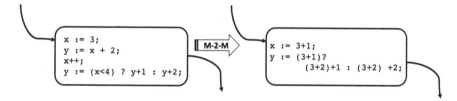

Fig. 4. Since the statements in a section of a state are executed entirely or not at all in each ringlet, they can be considered atomic.

IMP-2-SMV(s : IMP-sequence, d : Dictionary) : String
begin
    if s.isEmpty() **then** **return**''**else**   //The empty string
    if $1 == s$.size() **or not**s.tail.inLHS(s.LHS().variable
    then   //RHS is converted to SMV and free variables appearing in d
                           // replaced by corresponding strings in d
    return 'next(' + s.LHS().variable + ')=' + s.RHS.to-SMV-subs-free(d)
    else return IMP-2-SMV(s.tail(), d.update(s.LHS().variable, s.to-SMV(d))
    fifi
end

Fig. 5. Converting an IMP-sequence of statements to SMV.

5.3 Handling Variables

An arrangement of LLFSMs defines a round-robin schedule for the concurrent execution of the state machines in the arrangement (it is possible to use other schedules, but for now we adhere to Definition 9 where next(turn)←turn+1 mod k). Thus, there are no race conditions; only one state machine is executing its ringlet at a time, so there is no need for mutual exclusion. In our transformation from LLFSMs to modules of SMV, however, some aspects of variables require a special treatment since, in SMV, all variables must belong to a module and must have an explicit value in each state. In the arrangement, all non-local variables are global. A simple solution would be to place all global variables (external and whiteboard variables) in the **main** module in SMV. However, this is not necessary if there is only one LLFSM in the arrangement that is a writer to the variable. Therefore, our M2Text transformation assigns variables in the arrangement to SMV modules as follows:

Variable Is Local to an LLFSM: The variable is declared local in the corresponding SMV module.

Variable Is a Sensor of the Arrangement: The variable is declared global in the main SMV module, no LLFSMs writes to this variable. The open SMV model would manage this variable non-deterministically, taking all possible values in the next Kripke state. This represents the possibility that the environment changes the sensor reading at any time.

Variable Is Written by Only One LLFSM: The variable is declared local in the corresponding SMV module.

Variable is written by more than one LLFSM: The variable is declared global in the main SMV module, but would behave deterministically in the Kripke states.

Because SMV composes modules under synchronous composability, all SMV modules advance simultaneously. Therefore, when producing an SMV module, our M2Text transformation must reflect the LLFSM semantics where a variable is never simultaneously written by more than one LLFSM. We will see in the next section that we use the value of turn, which becomes a variable in the main module of the SMV result, to ensure that only one SMV module would update the LHS of all its statements using next. Moreover, we will use the value of turn to ensure that only one SMV module can have an effect on any sort of variable in the model checker.

5.4   The Transformation When There Are No Temporal Transitions

We illustrate the transformation with an arrangement of two LLFSMs that includes Boolean and arithmetic expression as well as Boolean variables and integer variables. Figure 6 displays the visualisation that appears in our new prototype for emulating traces from model checkers. We describe the transformation from LLFSMs that have no sections in states to SMV modules by a series of rules.

Rule 1: There is an SMV module for each LLFSMs M_i in the arrangement. There is an SMV module main that holds an integer variable turn with domain $\{0, 1, \ldots, k - 1\}$ that serves to indicate the only state machine that will affect values of variables. The SMV module main ensures the round-robin schedule in the Kripke states with transitions such that, for all $i = 0, \ldots, k-2$, $(\text{turn} = i)$ & $(\text{next}(\text{turn}) = i \bmod k)$; while $(\text{turn} = k)$ & $(\text{next}(\text{turn}) = 0)$.

Rule 2: All transitions of the module M_i (besides main) have a test of the form (turn = i) which effectively ensures that only the transitions in M_i advance the Kripke state when indeed the value of turn is i.

Rule 3: The main module instantiates the modules of each M_i in the arrangement for $i = 1, \ldots, k$ with parameters defined by the specification of Sect. 5.3.

For illustration, the corresponding main module for Fig. 6 declares the variable turn with domain $\{0, 1\}$.

```
MODULE main
VAR turn : 0..1;
MonitorCounter : MonitorCounter(turn , Counter.counter);
Counter : Counter(turn , MonitorCounter.GoDown);
TRANS ((turn = 0) & (next(turn) = 1 )) | ((turn = 1) & (next(turn) = 0 ))
```

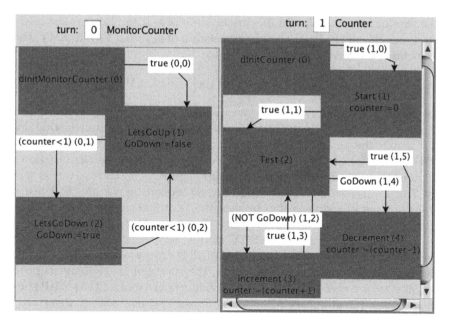

Fig. 6. Arrangement of two state machines with a global (whiteboard) Boolean variable GoDown and a global (whiteboard) integer variable counter.

This SMV code, produced by our ATL M2Text transformation, shows how the SMV module **main** instantiates the two modules for the two LLFSMs in the arrangement. This piece of code also shows that the SMV module **main** schedules the round-robin cycle through the possible values of the **turn** variable.

Rule 4:

1. The i-th SMV module will correspond to machine M_i.
2. The j-th state in machine M_i will be identified as the j-th state in the corresponding SMV module for M_i for $j = 1$ to the number of states in M_i (and an additional 0-th dummy state will be identified as the initial pseudo-state with a transition labelled with **true** to the initial state of M_i).
3. The current state pc_i (see Definition 8) of machine M_i will be identified by a local variable **pc** in SMV module M_i.
4. Moreover, a transition in M_i, whose source state is the j-th state, will be identified with the tuple i, r, where r is the rank of the transition among the transitions in M_i.

Figure 6 shows the use of these identifiers for machines, states, and transitions in our running example. What follows now is the detailed description of how the transformation ensures the running of a ringlet; that is, the effects of the machine whose turn it is.

Rule 5: Each transition $T_{i,r}$ with source state S in M_i will result in a Boolean SMV expression that will guarantee this transition can only fire when it is the turn of machine M_i and its current state is s. If the Boolean expression for $T_{i,r}$ is $b_{i,r}$ and $\text{SMV}(b_{i,r})$ is the translation of $b_{i,r}$ from IMP to SMV, then we defined the SMV condition for $T_{i,r}$ by

$$\text{cond}T_{i,r} := (\textbf{turn} = i) \,\&\, (pc_i = S) \,\&\, \text{SMV}(b_{i,r}) \tag{1}$$

Rule 6: For transition $T_{i,r}$ to fire, no transition with $q \leq r$ should fire (and in the case of the SMV module this could be because the source state does not match the `pc` or because their Boolean expression is `false`), thus the SMV translation for $T_{i,r}$ corresponds to the conjunction of the negation of all $\text{cond}T_{i,q}$ with the affirmation of $\text{cond}T_{i,r}$.

Rule 7: The M_is we are considering have no sections in a state. So when no transition out of a state S fires because the Boolean expressions of all transitions evaluate to `false`, then machine M_i has no effects, and just misses its turn. We represent this in the SMV module for M_i by an SMV expression condDefault_i which is the conjunction of all the negations of all the $\text{cond}T_{i,q}$.

Rule 8: When a transition $\text{cond}T_{i,r}$ fires, the effects of the statements of the target state are encoded by the corresponding translation of those IMP statements (after the atomicity reduction of Subsect. 4) into SMV statements.

The application of these last rules in our ATL transformation results in the following module for the `MonitorCounter` LLFSM from Fig. 6.

```
MODULE MonitorCounter(turn, counter)
VAR pcMonitorCounter : 0..2;
VAR GoDown : boolean;
INIT (pcMonitorCounter    = 0)
DEFINE
condT00 := (((turn = 0) &  (pcMonitorCounter = 0)) & TRUE);
condT01 := (((turn = 0) & (pcMonitorCounter =  1)) & (counter  < 1));
condT02 := (((turn = 0) &  (pcMonitorCounter = 2)) & (counter  < 1));
condDefault0 := (!(condT00) & !(condT01) & !(condT02));
TRANS
(TRUE &
condT00 & (next(pcMonitorCounter)=1) &  (next(GoDown)=FALSE))
|
(!(condT00) &
condT01 & ((next(pcMonitorCounter)=2) &  (next(GoDown)=TRUE)))
|
(!(condT00) & !(condT01) &
condT02 & ((next(pcMonitorCounter)=1) &  (next(GoDown)= FALSE)))
|
(condDefault0 &
TRUE & (turn=0) & ((next(pcMonitorCounter)=pcMonitorCounter)
        & (next(GoDown)=GoDown)))
|
(condDefault0 & TRUE &  (turn !=0)
        & ((next(pcMonitorCounter)=pcMonitorCounter) & (next(GoDown)=GoDown)))
```

Note that all `condT_` ensure that it is this machine's turn (SMV module) and the current state is the source of the transition. Moreover, with the contrasting Fig. 6, observe that the transition from the state `LetsGoUp` (stated ID 1) to the state `LetsGoDown` (state ID 2) is transition with ID $= (0,1)$ as this is the 0-th machine and this is the second transition, but numbering from 0, its numeral is 1. This transition defines `condT01` in the code above (using the Boolean expression that labels this transition). In Fig. 6, we see that if the transition fires, the effect in the target state is for the local variable (as this is the only module that writes on it) `GoDown` to change to `true`. This happens when not `condT00` and `condT01`, and the code above shows that in this case the next Kripke state will have the variable `GoDown` updated accordingly.

5.5   Temporalised Transitions

We now describe the part of our ATL transformation that handles the particular predicate `after` that enables timed LLFSMs. These timed LLFSMs were probably introduced in robotic systems [8,32] as part of the subsumption architecture under the name of *augmented* fine-state machines [7]. If the Boolean expression of a transition T includes the predicate `after`, we say that it is a *temporalised* transition. To translate the semantics of temporalised transition given in Subsect. 3.2, our ATL transformation defines the following rules.

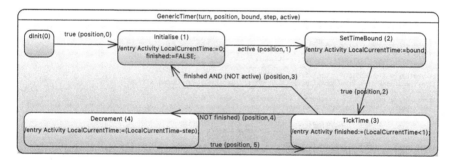

Fig. 7. Chart of the generic timer LLFSM.

Rule 9: For each temporalised transition (a transition whose Boolean expression includes the predicate `after`), there will be an SMV instance of a timer module. For an occurrence of `after(b)` in a transition $T_{i,r}$ with source state S, the corresponding instance of a timer SMV module receives its turn in the round-robin schedule. It also receives as input parameter the bound b and a Boolean variable $M_i\_S\_\text{ACTIVE}$ (recall that $T_{i,r}$ means this is the $(r+1)$-th transition in machine M_i).

Rule 10: For each transition $T_{i,r}$ with source state S, the SMV module corresponding to machine M_i will have the local Boolean variable $M_i\_S\_\text{ACTIVE}$ mentioned before; but also an array of variables $M_i\_S\_\text{BOUND}$ (the array size is equal to the number of temporalised transitions that share S as a source state). It also includes an integer variable $M_i\_S\_\text{STEP}$ that typically has the value 1, but can have a larger value to model the speed of the timers relative to the schedule of LLFSMs in the arrangement.

Rule 11: If an LLFSM M_i has temporalised transitions, its SMV module will have additional parameters, as many as temporalised transitions in M_i, where the corresponding instance of the timer communicates that the time-bound in the corresponding **after** predicate has been reached.

Rule 12: There will be only one SMV module for a timer if any of the LLFSMs in the arrangement has a temporalised transition. The SMV module is the image (by the ATL transformation) of a timer LLFSMs.

```
MODULE Timer(turn, position, bound, step, active)
VAR pcTimer : 0..4;
finished : boolean;
LocalCurrentTime : 0..bound;
INIT (pcTimer=0)
DEFINE
condT50 := (((turn=position)) & (pcTimer=0)) & TRUE);
condT51 := (((turn=position) & (pcTimer=1 )) & (active));
condT52 := (((turn=position) & (pcTimer=2)) & TRUE );
condT53 := ((turn=position) & (pcTimer=3)) & ((finished) & (!(active)));
condT54 := (((turn=position) & (pcTimer=3)) & (!(finished)));
condT55 := (((turn=position) & (pcTimer=4)) & TRUE);
condDefault5 := (!(condT50) & !(condT51) & !(condT52) & !(condT53) & !(condT54) & !(condT55));
TRANS
(TRUE & condT50 & (next(pcTimer)=1) & (next(LocalCurrentTime)=0) & (next(finished)=FALSE ) & TRUE)
|
( !(condT50) & condT51 & ((next(pcTimer)=2) & (next(LocalCurrentTime)=bound)
      & (next(finished)=finished) & TRUE)
|
( !(condT50) & !(condT51) & condT52 &
  ((next(pcTimer)=3) & (next(finished)=(LocalCurrentTime<1)) & TRUE
      & (next(LocalCurrentTime)=LocalCurrentTime))
|
( !(condT50) & !(condT51) & !(condT52) & condT53 &
  ((next(pcTimer)=1) & (next(LocalCurrentTime)=0) & (next(finished)=FALSE) & TRUE)
|
( !(condT50) & !(condT51) & !(condT52) & !(condT53) & condT54 &
  ((next(pcTimer)=4) & (next(LocalCurrentTime)=(LocalCurrentTime-step)) & (next(finished)=finished ) & TRUE)
|
( !(condT50) & !(condT51) & !(condT52) & !(condT53) & !(condT54) & condT55 &
  ((next(pcTimer)=3) & (next(finished) = (LocalCurrentTime<1)) & (next(LocalCurrentTime)=LocalCurrentTime))
|
(condDefault5 & TRUE & ((next(pcTimer)=pcTimer) & (next(firedTimer)=1)
      & (next(LocalCurrentTime)=LocalCurrentTime) & (next(finished)=finished)))))))))
```

Fig. 8. The SMV module for the generic timer for Fig. 7.

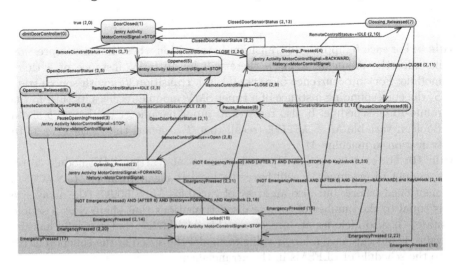

Fig. 9. Chart of the door controller LLFSM in the Garage Door arrangement.

Figure 7 displays the chart of the generic timer and the ATL transformation for it appears in Fig. 8. This illustrates the M2M transformation once more. More importantly, we see that the LLFSMs is parameterised. Since there could be several instances for the same LLFSMs there is a parameter **position** where the instance of the LLFSMs is placed in the arrangement.

To illustrate these rules and the timer, we review a case study of a garage door [2]. The arrangement includes LLFSMs for a sensor that detects when the door is fully open as well as another for when the door is fully closed. A motor that can be pulling forwards (opening), backwards (closing) or halted (holding the door in position). The remote control has three states: idle, commanding a stop, or commanding a close. An emergency button can be pressed or released, while a key is locked or unlocked. For reasons of space, we focus only on the LLFSM for the door controller (Fig. 9). The behaviour is not trivial. Pressing the emergency button halts and locks the door always, and to unlock the garage door, the emergency button must be released and the key unlocked. Such release returns the door to what it was doing at the time of the emergency (for instance, if it was closing, it resumes closing). Also, users can start opening the door by pressing the open button on their remote control. Users can stop the opening by pressing the open button again, and the motor stops. This implies the state machine of the remote control notices the release of the opening button in the remote and the second pressing. Pressing the close button will close the door if it is (partially or completely) open. Closing can be interrupted: by pressing the close button again, the motor stops. Before we pay attention to the time-domain verification with this example, we highlight that the model can use predefined constants for the control signal and the status signal of the motor (such strings as STOP, FORWARD and BACKWARD) and for the control signal and status signal of the remote control (strings such as IDLE, OPEN, CLOSE). These enumerated constants are now generated in a dedicated module of our M2Text ATL transformation to SMV. We also highlight that we have several integer variables in our examples of this paper. The garage-door example also illustrates the capacity to handle a history mechanism in an integer variable.

The LLFSM of Fig. 9 is illustrative of three temporal transitions with the same source state. Therefore, our M2Text transformation produces three instances of the timer form Fig. 7 in the **main** module of the SMV file.

```
Timer_DoorController_Locked_Opening_Pressed_16 :
    Timer( turn ,5 ,  8,  1, DoorController . DoorController_Locked_ACTIVE );
Timer_DoorController_Locked_Closing_Pressed_19 :
    Timer( turn ,6 ,  6,  1, DoorController . DoorController_Locked_ACTIVE );
Timer_DoorController_Locked_PauseReleased_23 :
    Timer( turn ,7 ,  7,  1, DoorController . DoorController_Locked_ACTIVE );
```

6 Verification in the Time Domain

The garage-door example provides several interest requirements whose verification is required in the time domain. We present here some examples where we can bound the delay in the system's reaction. We use an LTL formulation, and define the following SMV-terms for ease of formulation of the properties.

```
DEFINE -- Abbreviations:
doorIsClosed    := !OpenSensor.OpenDoorSensorStatus;
OpenButtonPressed    := (RemoteControl.RemoteControlStatus = 1);
MotorSpinsForward    := (Motor.MotorStatus = 1); MotorSpinsBackwards := (Motor.MotorStatus = 2);
MotorIsStopped    := (Motor.MotorStatus = 0);
CloseButtonPressed    := (RemoteControl.RemoteControlStatus = 2);
DoorIsOpening    := (MotorSpinsForward);
DoorIsClosing    := (MotorSpinsBackwards);
DoorIsMoving    := (DoorIsOpening | DoorIsClosing);
DoorIsStopped    := (! DoorIsMoving);
```

Requirement 1: If the door is closed, and the open button on the remote control is being pressed, then the motor will begin to spin forward.

```
X( (doorIsClosed          -- Excepting the first state, if door is closed
 & G[0,7]                 -- and, during 7 transitions (a round of turns),
   OpenButtonPressed)->   -- the "open" button on the remote is being pressed,
 F[0,8]                   -- then: in a future state, after at most 8 transitions,
 MotorSpinsForward);      -- the motor will begin to move forward to open the door.
```

Requirement 2: If the door is closing, and the "close" button on the remote control is pressed again, then the door will stop.

```
X( (MotorSpinsBackward
 -- Excepting the first state, if the motor is spinning backwards (to close the door),
 & G[0,4]                 -- and, during 4 transitions,
   CloseButtonPressed)->  -- the "close" button on the remote control is being pressed again,
 F[0,8]                   -- then: in a future state, after at most 8 transitions:
 MotorIsStopped);         -- the motor will stop (and the door stops closing)
```

Requirement 3: While the door is moving, pressing the emergency button results in an immediate halt of the door.

```
X( (DoorIsMoving          -- Excepting the first state, if the door is in movement,
 & EmergencyPressed)->    -- and the "emergency" button on the remote control is pressed, then:
 (F[0,7]                  -- in a future state, after at most 7 transitions (a round of turns):
 DoorIsStopped) )         -- the door is stopped (1)
```

We emphasise that these properties show that within a round of turns (that is, each LLFSM receives a turn), the system reacts accordingly.

Naturally, there are reciprocal properties for ensuring that once the emergency button is pressed, the system does not resume immediately, but a minimum amount of time is to occur. This behaviour is what the temporalised transitions are meant to enforce in the model. The formulation of the LTL properties (analogous versions in CTL exist for these requirements) depends on what the door was previously doing at the time the emergency button was pressed. We present one version of these properties.

Requirement 4: If the garage is locked (while stopped) because the emergency button was pressed, it must stay there some specified amount of time before it resumes the movement it was performing when the emergency button was pressed.

```
X( G(
   (DoorControllerAtLockedState    -- Excepting the first state, in all future states:
                                    -- if the DoorController is at state "Locked" (10),
   & TimerFinishedPause             -- and the timer for emergency when door stopped finished
   & (G[0,7] DoorController.KeyUnlock)-- and the key stays unlocked for at least 7 transitions
   & (G[0,7] !EmergencyPressed)
 -- and the emergency button stays unpressed for at least 7 transitions
   & EmergencyWhenStopped)->
 -- and the emergency button was pressed when the door was stopped, then:
   (F[0,8]                          -- in a future state, after at most 8 transitions:
     DoorControllerAtPauseState) )) -- the DoorController will be at state "PauseReleased" (8)
```

For this property we use the timer instances that are produced by the M2Text transformation. And in particular, their local variable indicated they have completed the time counting.

```
DEFINE
 TimerFinishedPause := Timer_DoorController_Locked_PauseReleased_23.finished;
 DoorControllerAtLockedState := (DoorController.pcDoorController = 10);
 DoorControllerAtPauseState := (DoorController.pcDoorController = 8);
```

7   Formal Verification of the SMV Output and Trace Emulation

7.1   Verification of the M2Text SMV Output

One important aspect that we add in this paper is that the M2Text transformation from an arrangement of LLFSMs is not only the corresponding set of SMV modules. We also automatically generate properties that formally verify the correctness of the transformation, and in particular of the scheduling. These properties are generic, but not exactly the same, they depend on the arrangement. For instance, if there are four LLFSMs in the arrangement, the ATL transformation adds the property

```
CTLSPEC
AG ((EF(turn=0)) & (EF(turn=1)) & (EF(turn=2)) & (EF(turn=3)))
```

This property ensures the global condition that from any point in the execution of the arrangement each LLFSM will have its turn. Similarly, for each possible value of the turn, we must have the next value in one more (modulo the number of LLFSMs in the arrangement) in the Kripke structure ensuring the round-robin scheduling. For instance, in an arrangement with four LLFSMs the following code is automatically generated.

```
LTLSPEC
G (  (turn=0 -> X(turn=1)) & (turn=1 -> X(turn=2))
   & (turn=2 -> X(turn=3)) & (turn=3 -> X(turn=0)))
```

7.2   Trace Emulation

To further illustrate the minimisation of the semantic gaps discussed earlier, we have used the EMF generated Java classes for our meta-model for LLF-SMs to produce a tool that enables reading a model (an XMI file) as well as reading a counterexample's trace (the output of a verification exercise where the property is false). The model designer can visualise the execution of the trace in the arrangement of LLFSMs resulting in a more transparent interpretation of the trace and the revision of the behaviour model. The link to a video showing the emulator working on a trace of garage-door example is available at mipal.net.au/downloads.php.

This emulation minimises the semantic gap because it is the model checker that has generated the execution trace. That is, the execution is exactly the execution of the behaviour in the model checker. The trace emulated by our tool is directly visualised in the graphical representation of the XMI file (the model). There are no simplifying assumptions on the model, or any of its constructs.

7.3   Complexity

The size of the resulting SMV file is linear in the number k of LLFSMs in the arrangement since exactly $k + 1$ modules are produced if there are no temporalised transitions and no symbolic constants. One SMV module appears in the output file for each LLFSM and on `main` module. At most one additional module is produced if there are symbolic constants (enumerated types). At most one generic module for the timer is produced if there are t temporalised constants (and t-instances of the timer, one for each temporalised transition in `main`). The size of the SMV file is quadratic in the largest transition out-degree of a state (but this is usually bounded by a small constant). The number of transitions out of a state plays a role because, as specified in Rule 6, for each transition T_i, r, we must explicitly represent that, T_i, r fires when it is true and all previous transitions T_i, s (with $s < r$) have not fired.

8   Final Remarks

Verification in the time domain aims at eradication of time-domain failures. For many cyber-physical systems, it is insufficient to verify that no incorrect value is computed; it is also necessary that the correct value be computed by the required deadline. While event-driven programming has been extremely productive to develop GUI-based applications, this setting has the luxury that (1) human users can usually wait (although many users have noticed occasions when the system becomes less responsive) and (2) human users can hardly generate a shower of events. We have presented here efficient ATL-M2Text transformations that enable time-domain verification of behaviour models. Moreover, we have argued that these transformations support the spirit of model-driven engineering, because the model is executed in an unambiguous semantics. The transformations are so loyal to the model checker itself could be used as the interpreter. Our EMF application is the ultimate illustration of the minimisation of the semantic gap. This application uses the `ecore` generated classes for the meta-model of LLFSMs on one hand, and the trace of the SMV-enabled model checker on the other. This is only possible because there is no semantic gap between how the model checker simulates an arrangement of LLFSMs with no subsection for the states and the semantics of LLFSMs models.

Naturally, we are not arguing that models of behaviour be executed by interpreting them with a model checker. This would imply inefficiencies at run-time and potential limitations to the actions language of the behaviour models. However, the clear and small semantics of LLFSMs facilitates the implementation of compilers that are also loyal to the controlled concurrency of arrangements of LLFSMs and can provide modern constructs of programming (for instance object-orientation). This work here opens the door to new ideas. For instance, test-driven-development suggest building a suite of test that lives along with the development of a system, from requirements engineering to evolution and maintenance. The suite ensures that new features do not incur in regressions. We envisage that we could also have verification-driven development of behaviour models, were the requirements are codified for a model checker and also have a parallel life with the implementation and maintenance.

References

1. Alhaj, M.: UML modeling using Eclipse Papyrus (2018). https://www.youtube.com/watch?v=aMiqJXWfAtQ. Accessed 26 May 2020
2. André, P., El Amin Tebib, M.: Refining automation system control with MDE. In: Hammoudi, S., Ferreira Pires, L., Selic, B. (eds.) Proceedings of the 8th International Conference on Model-Driven Engineering and Software Development, MODELSWARD 2020, pp. 425–432. SCITEPRESS (2020). https://doi.org/10.5220/0009147804250432
3. Besnard, V., Brun, M., Jouault, F., Teodorov, C., Dhaussy, P.: Unified LTL verification and embedded execution of UML models. In: Proceedings of the 21th ACM/IEEE International Conference on Model Driven Engineering Languages and Systems, MODELS 2018, pp. 112–122. ACM, New York (2018). https://doi.org/10.1145/3239372.3239395
4. Bhaduri, P., Ramesh, S.: Model checking of statechart models: Survey and research directions (2004)
5. Billington, D., Estivill-Castro, V., Hexel, R., Rock, A.: Requirements engineering via non-monotonic logics and state diagrams. In: Maciaszek, L.A., Loucopoulos, P. (eds.) ENASE 2010. CCIS, vol. 230, pp. 121–135. Springer, Heidelberg (2011). https://doi.org/10.1007/978-3-642-23391-3_9
6. Birta, L.G., Arbez, G.: Modelling and Simulation – Exploring Dynamic System Behaviour. Springer, Heidelberg (2019)
7. Brooks, R.: A robust layered control system for a mobile robot. IEEE J. Robot. Autom. **2**(1), 14–23 (1986). https://doi.org/10.1109/JRA.1986.1087032
8. Brooks, R.: The behavior language; user's guide. Technical report AIM-1227, Massachusetts Institute of Technology - MIT, Artificial Intelligence Lab Publications, Department of Electronics and Computer Science (1990)
9. Bryce, C.R., Kuhn, R.: Software testing [guest editors' introduction]. IEEE Comput. **47**(2), 21–22 (2014)
10. Caltais, G., Leue, S., Singh, H.: Correctness of an ATL model transformation from sysml state machine diagrams to promela. In: Hammoudi, S., Ferreira Pires, L., Selic, B. (eds.) Proceedings of the 8th International Conference on Model-Driven Engineering and Software Development, MODELSWARD, pp. 360–372. SCITEPRESS (2020). https://doi.org/10.5220/0008968303600372
11. Carrillo, M., Estivill-Castro, V., Rosenblueth, D.A.: Model-to-model transformations for efficient time-domain verification of concurrent models by NuSMV modules. In: Hammoudi, S., Ferreira Pires, L., Selic, B. (eds.) Proceedings of the 8th International Conference on Model-Driven Engineering and Software Development, MODELSWARD 2020, pp. 287–298. SCITEPRESS (2020). https://doi.org/10.5220/0008910202870298
12. Cavada, R., et al.: The nuXmv symbolic model checker. In: Biere, A., Bloem, R. (eds.) CAV 2014. LNCS, vol. 8559. Springer, Cham (2014). https://doi.org/10.1007/978-3-319-08867-9
13. Ciccozzi, F., Malavolta, I., Selic, B.: Execution of UML models: a systematic review of research and practice. Softw. Syst. Modeling **18**(3), 2313–2360 (2018). https://doi.org/10.1007/s10270-018-0675-4

14. Cimatti, A., Clarke, E., Giunchiglia, F., Roveri, M.: NUSMV: a new symbolic model checker. Int. J. Softw. Tools Technol. Transf. **2**(4), 410–425 (2000). https://doi.org/10.1007/s100090050046
15. Clarke, E.M., Henzinger, T.A., Veith, H.: Introduction to model checking. In: Clarke, E.M., Henzinger, T.A., Veith, H., Bloem, R. (eds.) Handbook of Model Checking, pp. 1–26. Springer, Cham (2018). https://doi.org/10.1007/978-3-319-10575-8_1
16. Clarke, E., Heinle, W.: Modular translation of statecharts to SMV. Technical report, School of Computer Science, Carnegie Mellon University, Pittsburg, PA 15213 (2000). Sponsored by General Motors Corp
17. Damm, W., Jonsson, B.: Eliminating queues from RT UML model representations. In: Damm, W., Olderog, E.R. (eds.) Formal Techniques in Real-Time and Fault-Tolerant Systems, pp. 375–393. Springer, Heidelberg (2002). https://doi.org/10.1007/3-540-45739-9_22
18. Dijkstra, E.W.: The humble programmer. Commun. ACM **15**(10), 859–866 (1972). https://doi.org/10.1145/355604.361591
19. Drusinsky, D.: Modeling and Verification Using UML Statecharts: A Working Guide to Reactive System Design. Runtime Monitoring and Execution-based Model Checking. Newnes, Newton, MA, USA (2006)
20. Eriksson, H.E., Penker, M., Lyons, B., Fado, D.: UML 2 Toolkit. Wiley, Hoboken (2003)
21. Evans, A., Bruel, J.M., France, R., Lano, K., Rumpe, B.: Making UML precise. In: Andrade, L., Moreira, A., Deshpande, A., Kent, S. (eds.) OOPSLA 1998 Workshop on "Formalizing UML. Why and How?", October 1998. www.se-rwth.de/publications
22. Furrer, F.: Future-Proof Software-Systems: A Sustainable Evolution Strategy. Springer, Berlin (2019). https://doi.org/10.1007/978-3-658-19938-8
23. Grischa, L.: Papyrus 2.0: State machine diagrams (2016). www.youtube.com/watch?v=xEC8bQ27lBk. Accessed 26 May 2020
24. Group, T.O.M.: Precise Semantics of UML State Machines (PSSM). OMG, May 2019
25. Group, T.O.M.: Precise Semantics of UML Structure (PSCS). OMG, June 2019
26. Guermazi, S., Tatibouet, J., Cuccuru, A., Seidewitz, e., Dhouib, S., Gérard, S.: Executable modeling with fUML and Alf in Papyrus: tooling and experiments. In: Mayerhofer, T., Langer, P., Seidewitz, E., Gray, J. (eds.) Proceedings of the 1st International Workshop on Executable Modeling co-located with ACM/IEEE 18th International Conference on Model Driven Engineering Languages and Systems (MODELS 2015). CEUR Workshop Proceedings, vol. 1560, pp. 3–8. CEUR-WS.org (2015)
27. Kang, I., Lee, I.: A state minimization algorithm for communicating state machines with arbitrary data space. Technical report MS-CIS-93-07, Department of Computer & Information Science, University of Pennsylvania, January 1993
28. Knapp, A., Merz, S., Rauh, C.: Model checking timed UML state machines and collaborations. In: Damm, W., Olderog, E.R. (eds.) Formal Techniques in Real-Time and Fault-Tolerant Systems, pp. 395–414. Springer, Heidelberg (2002). https://doi.org/10.1007/3-540-45739-9_23
29. Kopetz, H.: Real-Time Systems: Design Principles for Distributed Embedded Applications, 2nd edn. Springer, Heidelberg (2011). https://doi.org/10.1007/978-1-4419-8237-7
30. Lamport, L.: The TLA$^+$ home page, 6th December 2018. lamport.azurewebsites.net/tla/tla.html. Accessed 20 Apr 2020

31. Larsen, K.G., Pettersson, P., Yi, W.: Uppaal in a nutshell. Int. J. Softw. Tools Technol. Transf. **1**(1–2), 134–152 (1997). https://doi.org/10.1007/s100090050010, https://doi.org/10.1007/s100090050010

32. Mataric, M.: Integration of representation into goal-driven behavior-based robots. IEEE Trans. Robot. Autom. **8**(3), 304–312 (1992). https://doi.org/10.1109/70.143349

33. McColl, C., Estivill-Castro, V. Hexel, R.: An OO and functional framework for versatile semantics of logic-labelled finite state machines. In: Lavazza, L. (ed.) ICSEA : The Twelfth International Conference on Software Engineering Advances, pp. 238–243. Int. Academy, Research, and Industry Association (IARIA), Curran, 8th–12th October 2017

34. McMillan, K.L.: Symbolic Model Checking – An approach to the state explosion problem. Ph.D. thesis, Carnegie Mellon University, 5000 Forbes Ave, Pittsburgh, PA 15213, United States, May 1992. cMU-CS-92-131

35. Obermaisser, R., Kopetz, H.: Chapter 3: properties of time-triggered communication systems. In: Obermaisser, R. (ed.) Time-Triggered Communication. CRC Press Inc., USA (2011)

36. Pham, V.C., Radermacher, A., Gérard, S., Li, S.: A framework for UML-based component-based design and code generation for reactive systems. In: Pires, L.F., Hammoudi, S., Selic, B. (eds.) MODELSWARD 2017. CCIS, vol. 880, pp. 300–327. Springer, Cham (2018). https://doi.org/10.1007/978-3-319-94764-8_13

37. Rushby, J.M.: Systematic formal verification for fault-tolerant time-triggered algorithms. IEEE Trans. Softw. Eng. **25**(5), 651–660 (1999). https://doi.org/10.1109/32.815324

38. Rushby, J.: Bus architectures for safety-critical embedded systems. In: Henzinger, T.A., Kirsch, C.M. (eds.) EMSOFT 2001. LNCS, vol. 2211, pp. 306–323. Springer, Heidelberg (2001). https://doi.org/10.1007/3-540-45449-7_22

39. Samek, M.: Practical UML Statecharts in C/C++, Second Edition: Event-Driven Programming for Embedded Systems, 2nd edn. Newnes, Newton (2008)

40. Seshia, S.A., Sharygina, N., Tripakis, S.: Modeling for verification. In: Clarke, E.M., Henzinger, T.A., Veith, H., Bloem, R. (eds.) Handbook of Model Checking, pp. 1–26. Springer, Cham (2018). https://doi.org/10.1007/978-3-319-10575-8_1

41. Weise, C.: An incremental formal semantics for PROMELA. In: Proceedings of the Third SPIN Workshop, SPIN 1997 (1997)

42. Winskel, G.: The Formal Semantics of Programming Languages: An Introduction. MIT Press, Cambridge (1993)

Domain-Driven Architecture Modeling and Rapid Prototyping with Context Mapper

Stefan Kapferer[✉] and Olaf Zimmermann[✉]

University of Applied Sciences of Eastern Switzerland (OST),
Oberseestrasse 10, 8640 Rapperswil, Switzerland
stefan@kapferer.ch, olaf.zimmermann@ost.ch

Abstract. Strategic Domain-driven Design (DDD) has become an established practice for system decomposition and service identification in recent years. The trend towards microservices increased the popularity of DDD patterns such as Subdomain, Bounded Context, Aggregate and Context Map. In our previous work, we presented a Domain-Specific Language (DSL) providing a clear and concise interpretation of the DDD patterns and their combinations. As a machine-readable description of DDD, the DSL establishes a foundation for systematic service decomposition and DDD-based architecture descriptions that can be refactored and refined by model transformations. The DSL and supporting tools are implemented in the open source project Context Mapper. In this extended version of our previous paper we enhance the DSL grammar to allow domain-driven designers to prototype applications rapidly: they can specify user stories and/or use cases in the DSL, and model transformations can then derive Sub-domains and Bounded Contexts automatically. The Context Mapper tool chain supports the continuous, iterative specification and evolution of Context Maps and other service design artifacts. Our validation activities included prototyping, action research, and case studies. This paper illustrates such a transformation chain on the basis of one of our case studies.

Keywords: Domain-driven design · Domain-specific language · Microservices · Model-driven software engineering · Service-oriented architecture

1 Introduction

Domain-driven Design (DDD) was introduced in a practitioner book in 2003 [10]. Since then, the DDD patterns, especially tactical ones such as Entity, Value Object, Aggregate, and Repository, have been used in software engineering to model complex business domains. However, strategic DDD has gained even more attention during the last few years in the context of microservices and enterprise application integration [30]. A second generation of DDD experts such as Vernon [39] or Tune and Millet [38] provides advice how to apply the patterns of Evans book in practice.

The decomposition of an application into appropriately sized services is challenging. Achieving high cohesion within the services and loose coupling between them is

© Springer Nature Switzerland AG 2021
S. Hammoudi et al. (Eds.): MODELSWARD 2020, CCIS 1361, pp. 250–272, 2021.
https://doi.org/10.1007/978-3-030-67445-8_11

crucial to keep the application scalable and maintainable. It is not well understood yet how service interfaces can be identified and which patterns and practices are suitable to analyze and design service-oriented systems. DDD can play a key role in answering this question: with patterns such as Bounded Context (an abstraction of systems and teams developing them) and Context Map, it provides an approach for decomposing a domain. Context mapping patterns such as Customer-Supplier, Shared Kernel or Open Host Service can define the relationships between the units of decomposition. However, the strategic patterns come with a certain ambiguity and different interpretations of how they shall be applied. The question how concrete (micro-)services shall be derived from a DDD-based model (and then composed into applications) has only been answered partially so far [31].

2   Context and Previous Work

How to decompose software systems into cohesive modules (or components and services) that are loosely coupled is one of the classic questions and challenges in software engineering. For instance, Parnas [29] already wrote about how to decompose software systems into modules in 1972. Research questions that have not been answered satisfyingly yet include a) which criteria are relevant to find good module boundaries and b) which patterns and practices can be applied to identify the modules or services? [30]. Practitioners in the microservices community suggest to apply the strategic DDD patterns to tackle the problem. They propose to model complex business domains in terms of Bounded Contexts – a sub-system or module that implements a specific part of the domain. A Bounded Context establishes a boundary around a domain model that consist of so-called Aggregates: a set of objects/classes such as Entities or Value Objects. While the terms of the domain may have different meanings outside that boundary, they are clearly defined within the boundary (the so-called "ubiquitous language"). As we described in our previous paper [23], the identification of suited Bounded Contexts is still challenging. Context Maps and context mapping as a practice shall support this process of finding Bounded Contexts. The strategic DDD patterns are used on Context Maps to define the relationships between the Bounded Contexts.

Our experience in the industry has shown that a clear understanding of how these patterns shall work together is often missing, and different stakeholders have different opinions on how these patterns shall be applied and combined. Based on this observation, we derived the following hypothesis [23]:

Software engineers and service designers benefit from a precise interpretation of – and advice on how to apply and combine – the strategic DDD patterns.

We further consider a Context Map an artifact that evolves iteratively. Software architects and DDD adopters develop a Context Map by increasing their knowledge about the problem domain step-by-step. This is why we believe that Context Maps written in a formal language such as our Context Mapper DSL (CML) can be beneficial, since we can offer automated transformation tools that support the evolution of the models. It is further possible to generate other representations such as Unified Modeling Language (UML) diagrams or graphical Context Maps. This has already led us to our second hypothesis [23]:

Adopters of DDD benefit from a tool which supports the creation of DDD pattern-based models in a rigorous and expressive way. They want to transform and evolve such models iteratively.

In our previous paper [23] we presented a meta-model based on the DDD patterns and our CML language that implements that model. We illustrated how Context Mapper users can represent Domains, Subdomains, and Bounded Contexts in CML. We further proposed a set of semantic rules that reflect our interpretation of how the strategic DDD patterns can be combined. Those semantic rules have been implemented as validators for the CML language.

In this paper, we present an extended version of the CML Domain-specific Language (DSL) [23] that allows to prototype Domains and Bounded Contexts rapidly on the basis of use cases [8] and/or user stories [2]. Furthermore, we demonstrate how we validated the usefulness of the language and our hypothesis above by implementing model transformations that support the rapid prototyping. This paper illustrates such a process on an exemplary case.

The remainder of the paper is structured in the following way. Section 3 explains important DDD concepts briefly. It further introduces the meta-model behind the CML language [23] and discusses related work. Section 4 explains our first contribution: the DSL syntax including the latest extensions for feature modeling with use cases and user stories. In Sect. 5 we introduce a set of model transformations that support rapid prototyping of Domains and Bounded Contexts explained with an exemplary case. This section does a) suggest transformations to derive Bounded Contexts automatically with tool-support, and b) validate whether our language can serve as a foundation for evolving DDD Context Maps step-by-step. Section 6 discusses further validation activities and outlines pros and cons of the presented approach. Section 7 concludes and outlines future work.

3   Domain-Driven Design (DDD) Essence, Meta-model

Since Evans has published his original DDD book [10], other – mostly gray – literature on this topic has been published. Our analysis and interpretation of the patterns is based on the books of Evans [10] and Vernon [39]. Our personal professional experience [20] has influenced the meta-model as well. Additional patterns of Evans' DDD reference [11], which has been published a fews years after his first book, were also considered. We further studied publications of context mapping experts such as Brandolini [5] and Plöd [31,32].

3.1   Motivating Example

Strategic Domain-driven Design (DDD) can be used to decompose the problem domain of a software system into multiple Subdomains and the so-called *Bounded Contexts*. It also allows architects to define the relationships between Bounded Contexts, e.g., how they work together. To explain pattern concepts (and also, in Sect. 4, the DSL syntax) we use a fictitious insurance software scenario. Figure 1 illustrates the Context Map of the scenario inspired by the visualizations of Vernon [39], Brandolini [5] and Plöd [31].

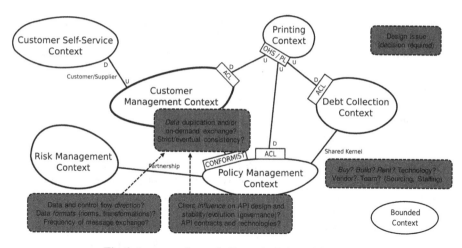

Fig. 1. Insurance Scenario Example Context Map [21].

Figure 1 also highlights a number of design issues that arise when refining the Context Map and domain design. For instance, for each component (or context), it has to be decided whether to buy a software product (or install free software), rent the desired functionality as a cloud service offered by a cloud provider or build it. Connectors (here: relationships between contexts) may have a direction and require integration technologies such as message exchange formats and protocols (such as JSON over HTTP, XML over a mesage queue, etc.). Many data management decisions are required as well (copy or access patters, ownership, update frequencies, etc.). DDD and Context Maps can help identify the need for such decisions, and can also document the decision outcome.

3.2 DDD Patterns

A Bounded Context defines an explicit boundary within which a particular domain model, implementing parts of Subdomains, applies. This boundary affects team organization as well as physical manifestations such as code bases and database schemata. The internal design of a Bounded Context is specified with the tactic DDD patterns, including the *Aggregate* pattern. An Aggregate is a cluster of domain objects (such as *Entities*, *Value Objects*, and *Services*) which is kept consistent with respect to specific invariants and typically also represents a unit of work regarding system (database) transactions. A *Context Map* provides a global view over all Bounded Contexts which are related to the one a team is working on.

The DDD relationship patterns allow modelers to describe how two Bounded Contexts and their development teams work together. The *Partnership* relationship describes an intimate mutual relationship between two Bounded Contexts, since the resulting product of the two can only fail or success as a whole. A *Shared Kernel* relationship indicates that two contexts are very closely related and the two domain models overlap at many places. This pattern is often implemented as a shared library that is maintained by both teams.

Upstream-downstream relationships are marked with a *U* for upstream and a *D* for downstream in our illustration in Fig. 1. The terms *upstream* and *downstream* are used to describe relationships in which only one Bounded Context influences the other; the upstream influences the downstream. Thus, the downstream Bounded Context depends on the domain model of the upstream Bounded Context, but not vice versa. A *Customer-Supplier* relationship is given if the downstream Bounded Context in an upstream-downstream relationship has power regarding the implementation decisions of the upstream. The supplier respects the requirements of the downstream in its development plans.

The patterns *Published Language (PL), Open Host Service (OHS), Anticorruption Layer (ACL)* and *Conformist (CF)* are used to describe the interaction between Bounded Contexts in an upstream-downstream relationship. Figure 1 shows them as labels of relationship ends. A Bounded Context can offer an OHS to grant access to a subsystem as a set of open APIs if multiple other Bounded Contexts require access to the same functionality. The PL pattern advises to use a well-documented shared language for communication and translation. Serving as a wrapper, an ACL protects the domain model of a Bounded Context from changes to another one it depends on. In contrast to an ACL, a context applying CF decides to simply conform to the domain model of the other context and must therefore always adjust its model to follow changes of the other context. Due to space limitations we do not explain all pattern details here, but refer the reader to the literature [10, 11, 31, 39].

3.3   DDD Meta-model for Context Mapper

The meta-model presented in this section is based on the previously explained DDD patterns and our own analysis and understanding regarding how they can be combined. The model is illustrated in Fig. 2. It is implemented by our DSL and the Context Mapper tool introduced in Sect. 4.

The most central element in our meta-model is the Context Map. A Context Map shows Bounded Contexts and their relationships. A Bounded Context implements parts of one or many Subdomains, which can be *Core Domains, Supporting Domains* or *Generic Subdomains*. Both a Subdomain and a Bounded Context benefit from a statement regarding the vision and purpose of their own part of the domain. Hence, we apply the *Domain Vision Statement* pattern. We further include the *Knowledge Level* pattern on the level of a Bounded Context. The *Responsibility Layers* pattern is implemented by assigning single responsibilities to Bounded Contexts.

We distinguish between *symmetric* and *asymmetric* relationships between Bounded Contexts: We call asymmetric relationships *upstream-downstream* relationships in our meta-model. This is in line with the terminology in the DDD literature. In an upstream-downstream relationship only one context depends on the other. Likewise, only one Bounded Context influences the other; the upstream-downstream metaphor indicates an *influence flow* between teams and systems as discussed by [31]. The Partnership and Shared Kernel patterns, on the other hand, describe symmetric relationships. The Bounded Contexts involved in such relationships are mutually dependent on another.

The remaining patterns Published Language (PL), Open Host Service (OHS), Anticorruption Layer (ACL) and Conformist (CF) are roles taken by the upstream or

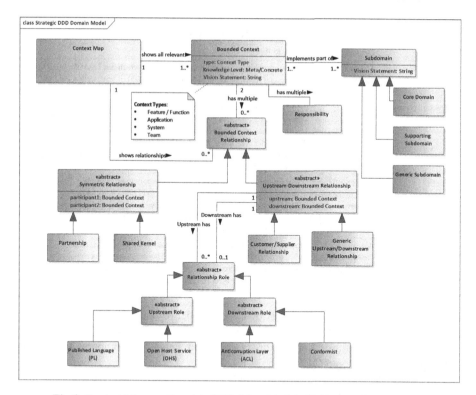

Fig. 2. Context Mapper: Strategic DDD Meta-Model (UML class diagram) [23].

downstream context within an upstream-downstream relationship. OHS and PL are patterns implemented by the upstream, which exposes parts of the model to be used by the downstream. The CF and ACL patterns are implemented by the downstream, which decides to either conform to the model exposed by the upstream or protect itself from changes (ACL).

According to our analysis, the Customer-Supplier pattern is a special case of upstream-downstream. We indicated this in Fig. 2 by distinguishing between Customer-Supplier and *generic* upstream-downstream relationships.

In addition to this meta-model we presented a set of semantic rules in our previous paper [23]. Those rules reflect our own interpretation of the DDD patterns and state which combinations are allowed and which are not allowed according to this interpretation.

3.4 Architectural Viewpoints

Bounded Contexts are created for different reasons and can be seen from different perspectives. Brandolini [5] presents a comprehensive introduction into context mapping and explains different scenarios for the evolution of Bounded Contexts. In our DSL we implemented an additional attribute *context type* to reflect different reasons for creation. We see these types as different viewpoints corresponding to the 4+1 view model

Table 1. FAST Context Types.

Type	Description and Mapping to Related Work
Feature or Function	This is a Bounded Context representing a feature or requirement which has been identified by the Object-oriented Analysis (OOA). In terms of the 4+1 model [25], it represents a context from the *Scenario* viewpoint. The system context view (level 1) of the C4 model shows such contexts and their relationships
Application	Such a Bounded Context represents a certain application. It is evolved by Object-oriented Design (OOD) and from our understanding reflects the *Logical* and *Development* viewpoint in terms of 4+1 [25]. The C4 model does not differentiate between features or applications. Therefore *application* contexts map to the system context view as well (level 1). Its tactic DDD content (Aggregates with their Entities, Services, etc.) can be seen as C4 components
System	A Bounded Context representing an physical system, container, or application tier. This type maps to the *physical* and/or *process* viewpoint in the 4+1 model [25]. The latter perspective is concerned with the way systems communicate and integrate with each other, for example by implementing Enterprise Integration Patterns (EIP) [18]. *System* Bounded Contexts correspond to the containers in the container diagram of C4
Team	A Team context represents a small organisational unit. A new context of this type might be created when a team has to be split to scale the company. This cross-cutting perspective is inspired by Conway's Law [9], stating that a systems design copies the communication structures of an organization. There are no corresponding concepts in 4+1 or C4

of software architecture [25]. Simon Brown's C4 model [6] is another but very similar approach to visualize software architecture from different perspectives. Table 1 lists the four context types, Feature, Application, System and Team and compares them with the perspectives of 4+1 and C4.

The model transformations presented in Sect. 5 make use of the types *Feature* and *System*; the design of *Application* contexts remains manual work (requiring creativity and problem solving skills). The rapid prototyping process leads from user requirements to a Feature Bounded Context first. Later, the context specifications get more detailed and we switch the perspective to systems. Section 5 explains the process in detail.

3.5   Related Work

Decomposing monolithic systems into microservice architectures [42] is a topic with a huge attention within the last years not only in the industry but in the academic field as well [4, 13, 14, 17, 19, 28]. Furthermore, DDD with its Bounded Contexts promises to ease this challenging task [13, 19, 26, 28, 30, 33]. However, there are not many tools which support modeling and specifying a system formally in terms of the strategic DDD patterns in order to decompose it in a structured manner.

Rademacher [34] presents a formal modeling language based on UML. The UML profile which extends meta-classes with stereotypes for DDD patterns shall be used for modeling microservice architectures. They further aim to derive code from their UML models in future projects. However, the profile seems to focus on modeling Bounded Contexts with the tactical DDD patterns. The strategic patterns concerning the relationships between the contexts are not mentioned explicitly.

Le et al. [27] propose a DDD approach using meta-attributes to capture domain-specific requirements. The meta-attributes are implemented as Java annotations. Their aim is to overcome gaps between different domain models of different stakeholders such as domain experts, designers and programmers. This approach mainly aims to support the software designing process on a tactical level as well. Furthermore, it differs from our approach in the sense that it does not explicitly expresses DDD patterns.

A few projects implementing DSLs for tactic DDD patterns exist, such as *Sculptor*[1], *fuin.org's DDD DSL*[2] and *DSL Platform*[3]. Further approaches and projects based on annotations exist as well. None of these covers the strategic DDD patterns concerning the relationships between Bounded Contexts.

Informal graphical representations of Context Maps and the strategic DDD patterns were introduced by Brandolini [5] and Vernon [39]. Plöd proposed a formal graphical notation for Context Maps [31], which has not been implemented in a tool yet.

A less formal approach towards the identification of Bounded Context is "Event Storming", invented by Brandolini[4]. In our online documentation[5] we discuss how event storming results can be formalized with Context Mapper. More advice how to decompose a system into Bounded Contexts can be found in the gray literature[6,7,8]. However, the authors of these online resources focus on providing advice, best practices and heuristics, but do not offer formal approaches and concrete transformation tools as Context Mapper does.

4   Context Mapper DSL (CML)

We implemented the *Context Mapper*[9] tool that allows software architects to model systems according to the DDD meta-model introduced in the previous section. The following DSL examples are based on the insurance scenario introduced in Sect. 3. The complete example can be found in our examples repository[10].

4.1   Domains and Subdomains

Before thinking in terms of Bounded Contexts, DDD practitioners typically start discovering and analyzing a domain by decomposing it into Subdomains. As we explain in Sect. 5, we call this the *domain analysis* phase.

Domains and Subdomains in CML are declared as illustrated in Listing 4.1. A Subdomain is of the type *Core Domain*, *Supporting Subdomain* or *Generic Subdomain* according to our meta-model and [10].

---

[1] http://sculptorgenerator.org/.

[2] https://github.com/fuinorg/org.fuin.dsl.ddd.

[3] https://docs.dsl-platform.com/dsl-concepts.

[4] https://ziobrando.blogspot.com/2013/11/introducing-event-storming.html.

[5] https://contextmapper.org/docs/event-storming/.

[6] https://leanpub.com/ddd-by-example/.

[7] https://medium.com/nick-tune-tech-strategy-blog/.

[8] https://github.com/ddd-crew/.

[9] https://contextmapper.org/.

[10] https://github.com/ContextMapper/context-mapper-examples/.

Listing 4.1. Subdomain Syntax in CML.

```
Domain Insurance {
  Subdomain CustomerManagementDomain {
    type = CORE_DOMAIN
    domainVisionStatement = "Customer-related entities..."

    Entity Customer
    Entity Address
    Service CustomerService {
      createCustomer;
      changeAddress;
    }
  }

  Subdomain PolicyManagementDomain {
    type = CORE_DOMAIN

    Entity Contract
    Entity Policy
  }

  Subdomain PrintingDomain {
    type = SUPPORTING_DOMAIN
  }
}
```

The CML language allows users to specify which Entities (domain objects) are part of which Subdomains. With Services it is further already possible to declare operations that will be required.

4.2 Bounded Contexts

From the *domain analysis* with the Subdomains as result we typically move onto the *stratgic DDD* phase where the models become more concrete and organized within Bounded Contexts. Listing 4.2 shows the declaration of the *CustomerManagementContext* as an example for a Bounded Context in CML. A Bounded Context has a type as already explained in Sect. 3. The following attributes are implementations of the Domain Vision Statement and the Responsiblity Layers patterns. The user can further specify the implementation technology of a Bounded Context. A Bounded Context consists of one or more Aggregates. Inside the Aggregates the language supports the usage of all tactical DDD patterns to fully specify the domain model of the Bounded Context. The implementation of CML inside the Aggregates is based on the Sculptor[11] project.

Listing 4.2. Bounded Context Syntax in CML.

```
BoundedContext CustomerManagementContext implements CustomerManagementDomain {
  type = FEATURE
  domainVisionStatement = "The customer context ..."
  responsibilities = "Collects and exposes customer data",
                     "Manages the customers addresses"
  implementationTechnology = "Java, JEE Application"

  Aggregate Customers {
    Entity Customer {
      aggregateRoot
```

---

[11] http://sculptorgenerator.org/.

```
        String firstname
        String lastname
      }
    }
}
```

With the *implements* keyword we refer back to the analysis part and specify which Subdomains are implemented by a specific Bounded Context. Note that a Bounded Context not necessarily implements a complete Subdomain.

4.3   The Context Map

The central and most important structure of CML is the Context Map which specifies the relationships between Bounded Contexts. Listing 4.3 shows a small example of a Context Map written in CML. The *contains* keyword indicates the Bounded Contexts that are added to the Context Map. They can then be used to declare relationships.

Listing 4.3. Context Map Syntax in CML.

```
ContextMap {
  contains CustomerManagementContext, PolicyManagementContext

  CustomerManagementContext [U,OHS,PL]->[D,CF] PolicyManagementContext {
    implementationTechnology = "RESTful HTTP"
  }
}
```

Listing 4.3 also features an exemplary upstream-downstream relationship. The endpoints of this relationship apply three more patterns, Open Host Service (OHS), Published Language (PL) and Conformist (CF).

4.4   Relationship Syntax

For symmetric relationships the syntax uses an arrow directing to both Bounded Contexts ($< - >$), whereas asymmetric relationships use an arrow ($- >$ or $< -$) pointing from the upstream towards the downstream. In all cases, the relationship roles are declared within brackets as illustrated in Listing 4.3. Note that the declaration of the implementation technology is optional and we omit it in the following examples.

Partnership. Listing 4.4 shows an example for the Partnership (P) pattern, which is a symmetric relationship.

Listing 4.4. Partnership Pattern Syntax in CML

```
RiskManagementContext [P]<->[P] PolicyManagementContext
```

Shared Kernel. The second symmetric relationship is the Shared Kernel (SK). The syntax is identical to the Partnership. Listing 4.5 illustrates an example.

Listing 4.5. Shared Kernel Pattern Syntax in CML.

```
PolicyManagementContext [SK]<->[SK] DebtCollection
```

Generic Upstream-Downstream Relationship. As already mentioned, the upstream-downstream (or asymmetric) relationships use an arrow from the upstream towards the downstream, expressing the influence flow. This syntax states which Bounded Context is upstream and which one is downstream in an expressive way. The arrowhead can be placed either on the left or on the right. Thus, the declaration examples in Listings 4.6 and 4.7 are semantically equal.

Listing 4.6. Upstream-Downstream Relationship in CML (1).

```
PrintingContext [U]->[D] PolicyManagementContext
```

Listing 4.7. Upstream-Downstream Relationship in CML (2).

```
PolicyManagementContext [D]<-[U] PrintingContext
```

Upstream-Downstream Roles. The upstream and downstream roles Open Host Service (OHS), Published Language (PL), Anticorruption Layer (ACL) or Conformist (CF) are listed within the brackets after the upstream (U) and downstream (D) specification. Listing 4.8 illustrates an example with the OHS and PL patterns on the upstream side and the ACL pattern on the downstream side.

Listing 4.8. Upstream-Downstream Relationship with Roles.

```
PrintingContext [U,OHS,PL]->[D,ACL] PolicyMgmtContext
```

Customer-Supplier Relationship. The customer-supplier relationship is a special case of an upstream-downstream relationship in which the upstream is called supplier and the downstream is called customer. The syntax is therefore almost identical to the generic upstream-downstream relationship; to state that the upstream-downstream relationship is a customer-supplier relationship the user has to add the abbreviations S for supplier and C for customer. These abbreviations must appear behind the U/D, but before the relationship roles, as shown in Listing 4.9.

Listing 4.9. Customer-Supplier Relationship in CML (1).

```
SelfServiceContext [D,C,ACL]<-[U,S,PL] CustomerMgmtContext
```

However, since the upstream in a customer-supplier relationship is always the supplier and the downstream is always the customer, it is also possible to omit the U and D abbreviations in this case. Thus, the declaration in Listing 4.10 is semantically equal to the one in Listing 4.9.

Listing 4.10. Customer-Supplier Relationship in CML (2).

```
SelfServiceContext [C,ACL]<-[S,PL] CustomerMgmtContext
```

4.5 Expressing User Requirements

In addition to the CML concepts presented above and in our previous publication [23], we enhanced Context Mapper to express features in the form of use cases [8] or user stories [2]. This grammar feature allowed us to realize the rapid prototyping process introduced in Sect. 5.

Listing 4.11 illustrates a user story written in CML. The syntax corresponds to the "role-feature-reason" format invented at Connextra in the UK and published by the Agile Alliance [2]. Note that we extended the template with the "with its" and "for a" parts so that one can model attributes and references to other entities. These elements are not part of the original template [2]. However, they are optional in CML; we hypothesize that both domain experts and software designers can adopt such an extension (which is subject to validation).

Listing 4.11. User Story in CML.

```
UserStory ManageCustomers {
  As an "Insurance Employee"
    I want to "create" a "Customer" with its "firstname", "lastname"
    I want to "update" an "Address" for a "Customer"
    I want to "create" a "Contract" for a "Customer"
  so that "I am able to manage the customer data and offer them contracts."
}
```

In addition, to reduce code duplication CML allows modellers to add multiple "I want to" parts per user story as shown in Listing 4.11. This is a slight deviation from the original template [2] as well. Listing 4.12 illustrates how the same user requirement can be formulated as a use case in CML.

Listing 4.12. Use Case in CML.

```
UseCase ManageCustomers {
  actor "Insurance Employee"
  interactions
    "create" a "Customer" with its "firstname", "lastname",
    "update" an "Address" for a "Customer",
    "create" a "Contract" for a "Customer"
  benefit "Being able to manage the customers data and offer them contracts."
  scope "Insurance Application"
  level "Summary"
}
```

The attributes *actor*, *interactions*, and *benefit* cover the same information as the user story format seen before. With the additional attributes *scope* and *level* we support expressing use cases according to the brief or casual format suggested by A. Cockburn [8].

We have shown the core concepts of CML Context Maps above. Due to space limitations we cannot present all abilities of our language. CML currently also supports an alternative syntax to declare relationships for A/B testing purposes. All language features are documented online[12] and the complete insurance example can be found in our examples repository[13]. In the next section we introduce one approach how we validated our modeling language and our hypothesis by providing transformation tools that allow users to prototype an application in terms of DDD patterns rapidly.

---

[12] https://contextmapper.org/docs.

[13] https://github.com/ContextMapper/context-mapper-examples.

5 Language and Tool Extension: Rapid Prototyping

The Context Mapper DSL (CML) is based on the Xtext[14] language framework. The models behind the textual representation are Eclipse Modeling Framework (EMF) [37] models. Therefore, we can support the evolution of CML models by providing model transformations [22]. Starting from the user story [2] or use case [7] syntax introduced in Sect. 4, we designed and implemented three novel model transformations that support rapid prototyping. The transformations do not aim at replacing human design work but capture some proven analysis and design heuristics from the literature and online resources.

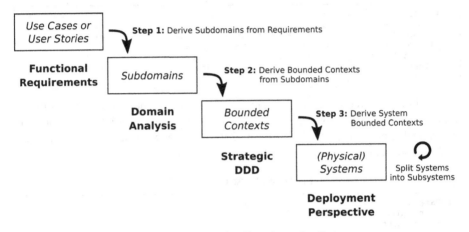

Fig. 3. Rapid Prototyping Transformation Steps.

Figure 3 illustrates the steps and provided transformations. A domain modeler can specify requirements in the form of user stories [2] or use cases [8] as an initial step. The following model transformations support him/her in deriving Subdomains and Bounded Contexts from these requirements. Hence, the CML language is able to represent all stages of the process: requirements (use cases and/or user stories), Subdomains, and Bounded Contexts (of the different architectural viewpoints explained in Sect. 3).

The Exemplary Case. In order to validate our use case grammar we modeled a case of A. Cockburn's book [8] in CML. The following Listing 5.1 shows the use case "Get paid for car accident" (we stay in the insurance domain) written in our DSL. The interactions in the CML use case correspond to the six steps described by Cockburn [8].

Listing 5.1. "Get paid for car accident" in CML.

```
UseCase Get_paid_for_car_accident {
  actor "Claimant"
  interactions
    "submit" a "Claim" with its "date", "amountClaimed", "desc" for a "Policy",
    "verifyExistanceOf" "Policy" with its "startDate", "endDate" for a "Contract",
    "assign" an "Agent" with its "personalID", "firstName", "lastName" for "Claim"
```

---

[14] https://www.eclipse.org/Xtext/.

```
    "verify" "Policy" for a "Contract",
    "pay" "Claimant" with its "firstName", "lastName",
    "close" "Claim" for "Claimant"
  benefit "Claimant submits claim and and gets paid from the insurance company."
  scope "Insurance company"
  level "Summary"
}
```

Step 1: Derive Subdomains from Requirements. Context Mapper offers a model transformation that produces a Subdomain definition given a set of requirements or features as shown in Listing 5.1 as input. From the use case in Listing 5.1 the transformation creates the Subdomain illustrated by Listing 5.2.

Listing 5.2. Subdomain Derived From Use Case.

```
Domain Insurance_Application {
  Subdomain ClaimsManagement {
    domainVisionStatement "Aims at promoting: A claimant submits a claim and ..."
    Entity Claim {
      Date date
      Double amountClaimed
      String description
      - Agent agent
    }
    Entity Policy {
      Date startDate
      Date endDate
      - List<Claim> claims
    }
    Entity Contract {
      - List<Policy> policies
    }
    Entity Agent {
      Long personalID
      String firstName
      String lastName
    }
    Entity Claimant {
      String firstName
      String lastName
      - List<Claim> claims
    }
    Service AccidentService {
      submitClaim;
      verifyExistanceOfPolicy;
      assignAgent;
      verifyPolicy;
      payClaimant;
      closeClaim;
    }
  }
}
```

The transformation uses the verbs, Entity names, and attributes mentioned in the interactions to derive the elements of the Subdomain. The user selects the use cases and user stories that will be jointly mapped to a single Subdomain, thereby controlling the placement of Entities and Services. This makes it possible to group by high cohesion, low coupling criteria at an early stage, while still analyzing the domain and the requirements. These placement decisions can be revised later on. The goal of this step is to break the domain down into sets of Entities and operations that belong together according to the business/domain. For example: typical Subdomains in the insurance domain are customers, contracts/policies, claims.

The mapping of the transformation from Listing 5.1 to Listing 5.2 (Step 1) is trivial. Figure 4 illustrates it more explicit. The single interactions contain a *verb*, an *entity name*, *entity attributes*, and optionally a *reference to another Entity*. Based on this information we derive Entities with attributes and references, and Services with operations for the Subdomain. For example, the interaction shown in Fig. 4 leads to the Entity called *Claim* and the Service operation called *submitClaim* in the resulting Subdomain.

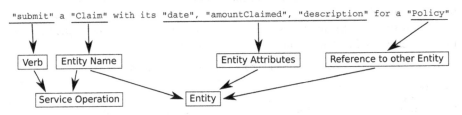

Fig. 4. Model transformation mapping: Use Case to Subdomain (Entities and Services).

Step 2: Derive Feature Bounded Context. This step is performed by application designers and software architects when transitioning from analysis to design. Context Mapper can derive a Bounded Context of the type *Feature* (see Architectural Viewpoints in Sect. 3) automatically from the Subdomain illustrated above (Step 2).

In this transformation step the user can select a set of Subdomains to be mapped into one Bounded Context; one Bounded Context can implement parts of multiple Subdomains [39]. In case multiple Subdomains are involved, we map each Subdomain into one Aggregate of the Bounded Context. The transformation further increases the level of detail in the Service operations and introduces parameters and return types. The resulting Bounded Context for our example use case is shown in Listing 5.3. Thus, the input of the transformation are multiple Subdomains and the output is one Bounded Context. The user is in control again and decides which Subdomains shall be implemented as one Bounded Context. The purpose of this step is to organize the implementation of the Subdomains.

Listing 5.3. Bounded Context (Feature) Derived From Subdomain.

```
BoundedContext ClaimsManagement implements ClaimsManagement {
  domainVisionStatement "Realizes the following subdomains: ClaimsManagement"
  type FEATURE
  /* Contains the entities and services of the 'ClaimsManagement' subdomain.
   * TODO: You can now refactor the aggregate, for example by ...
   * TODO: Add attributes and operations to the entities.
   * TODO: Add operations to the services.
   * Find examples and further instructions on our website:
   * https://contextmapper.org/docs/rapid-ooad/ */
  Aggregate ClaimsManagementAggregate {
    Service Get_paid_for_car_accidentService {
      boolean submitClaim (@Claim claim);
      boolean verifyExistanceOfPolicy (@Policy policy);
      boolean assignAgent (@Agent agent);
      boolean verifyPolicy (@Policy policy);
      boolean payClaimant (@Claimant claimant);
      boolean closeClaim (@Claim claim);
    }
```

```
Entity Claim {
  String date
  String amountClaimed
  String description
  ClaimId claimId
  - List<Agent> agentList
}
Entity Policy {
  String startDate
  String endDate
  PolicyId policyId
  - List<Claim> claimList
}
Entity Contract {
  ContractId contractId
  - List<Policy> policyList
}
Entity Agent {
  String personalID
  String firstName
  String lastName
  AgentId agentId
}
Entity Claimant {
  String firstName
  String lastName
  ClaimantId claimantId
  - List<Claim> claimList
}
}
}
```

The generated Bounded Context contains "TODO" hints/comments that help the modeler to refine and detail the design. Note that the transformation produces generic parameter and return types in case they cannot be mapped to Entities automatically. Context Mapper users can indicate that they refined the Bounded Context setting its type to *Application*. The transformation in the next step supports contexts of the type *Feature* as well as *Application* as input.

Given such a Bounded Context of the type *Feature*, Context Mapper is already able to generate a running Java application in a few steps. We do not discuss code generation in this paper, but we documented how users can generate a Java application using Context Mapper and JHipster[15] in our online tutorial[16]. The tool generates one Microservice for each Bounded Context in the CML model.

Step 3: Derive System Bounded Contexts. Bounded Contexts of the type *Feature* represent a boundary around specific features as already explained in Sect. 3. In this chain described here, we map Bounded Contexts of the type *Feature* one-to-one to Bounded Contexts of the type *Application*. Therefore, Step 3 in our transformation process already changes the architectural viewpoint to physical systems; Bounded Contexts of the type *System*. Currently, Context Mapper offers a transformation to transform a *Feature* Bounded Context (or *Application* Bounded Context) into two *System* Bounded Context: a frontend and a backend system. Listing 5.4 illustrates the result for our use case. Note that we do not repeat the contents of the Aggregates to save space at this

---

[15] https://www.jhipster.tech/.

[16] https://contextmapper.org/docs/jhipster-microservice-generation/.

point. Based on the domain model seen in Listing 5.3 this transformation generates an Aggregate in the backend context and a view model (technically an Aggregate as well) in the frontend context. The transformation takes one Bounded Context as input and produces two new Bounded Contexts. The goal of this step is to break an application down into its deployment units, tiers, or technical building blocks.

Listing 5.4. Bounded Context (System) Derived From Feature Context.

```
ContextMap {
  contains ClaimsManagementFrontend, ClaimsManagementBackend

  ClaimsManagementBackend [ PL ] -> [ CF ] ClaimsManagementFrontend {
    implementationTechnology "RESTful HTTP"
    exposedAggregates ClaimsManagementAggregate
  }
}

BoundedContext ClaimsManagementBackend implements ClaimsManagement {
  domainVisionStatement "Realizes the following subdomains: ClaimsManagement"
  type SYSTEM
  implementationTechnology "Java, Spring Boot"
  Aggregate ClaimsManagementAggregate {
    // removed contents to save space
  }
}

BoundedContext ClaimsManagementFrontend implements ClaimsManagement {
  domainVisionStatement "Realizes the following subdomains: ClaimsManagement"
  type SYSTEM
  implementationTechnology "Angular"
  Aggregate ViewModel {
    // removed contents to save space
  }
}
```

In addition, the transformation in Step 3 creates a Context Map with a relationship that illustrates the information flow between the frontend and the backend system.

Steps 4 to N: Continue Decomposing into Subsystems. Finally, we offer a transformation "Split System Context Into Subsystems" that allows users to further decompose a system into more subsystems or deployment units. The input for this transformation is always one Bounded context, and the output are two Bounded Contexts (split one into two). For example: one could split the backend tier into a *domain logic* and a *database* tier.

Besides the transformations presented above we realized a set of Architectural Refactorings (ARs)[17] [36] that support the continuous improvement of the design. They allow Context Mapper users to further *split* or *merge* Bounded Contexts and Aggregates, or *extract* parts of the domain model into new Bounded Contexts. We discuss our ARs in a separate paper [24] in more detail. All these transformation tools supported us in applying the presented modeling language in case studies and self experiments with the goal to validate the practicability of the DSL. The next section lists all our validation activities in more detail and discusses strengths and weaknesses of the approach.

---

[17] https://contextmapper.org/docs/architectural-refactorings/.

6   Validation and Discussion

Goals and Techniques. We validated our approach according to Shaw's recommendations [35] with the goal to demonstrate correctness, usefulness and effectiveness according to the validation type "experience" [35]. Having designed our meta-model we implemented a prototype, the first version of our DSL, to validate the model. We made the tool available for download allowing practitioners to evaluate it (including ourselves when working in industry projects). To validate the implementation we applied empirical validation techniques such as prototyping, case study [40], and action research [3].

Conducted Validation Activities. The prototypical *implementation* of the tools allowed us to evaluate the language, its abilities, and our hypothesis that the DSL can provide a foundation for service design and system decomposition.

We conducted several self-experiments and *action research*, including modeling Cockburn's sample use case [8] explained in the previous Sect. 5. We also demonstrated the tool to DDD thought leaders [39], peers and interested practitioners; one of the authors demonstrated another end-to-end example of the rapid prototyping chain at ICWE 2020[18]. Feedback from these demonstrations was continuously incorporated into our research cycles and development sprints. Since November 2018 we published 50 Context Mapper releases.

Next, the rapid OOAD/DDD toolchain was used in a two-hour service design workshop with five software architects with multiple years of experience in professional services (enterprise application development and integration); they were familiar with strategic and tactic DDD. One of the authors received a list of three service design questions (also outlining one user story/use case) two days before the workshop: a) should services be flexible and generic/broad or specific and narrow? b) how does database design and the service autonomy tenet influence service granularity? c) should system or business transactions (sagas) be used? He was able to model the story and sample DDD designs for a) and b) within one hour (supported by the transformations). Question c) was also discussed but pertains to the service implementation rather than the API, so was deemed out of scope. The draft model was shown in the workshop and another story modeled. This helped ground the discussion and focus on a concrete example.

During the implementation of the Context Mapper tool we also applied action research to validate and improve the DSL iteratively and with short feedback cycles. One of the authors modeled the *Lakeside Mutual*[19] project, an example application for microservice API patterns (MAP) [43], with CML to validate the tool with a practical application. As another case study we modeled the "Cargo Tracking" sample application [10] to validate the tool and its compatibility with the original DDD concepts. Furthermore, we conducted a *case study* on a real-world project in the health-care sector [16]. The hardened syntax was also used to model another case, the microservices in an existing production system for document management. An architect of the system and one of the paper authors cooperated for this validation activity. Previous models were updated to feature and re-validate the revised syntax. We further used the tool as part

---

[18] https://ozimmer.ch/practices/2020/06/10/ICWEKeynoteAndDemo.html.

[19] https://github.com/Microservice-API-Patterns/LakesideMutual.

of an exercise accompanying the DDD lesson of the software architecture course at our institution and collected the feedback of the nearly 20 exercise participants. Thereby we were able to evaluate the simplicity of the DSL and improve the syntax and tooling. The observations conducted by modeling these applications influenced the improvements of our DSL substantially. The CML syntax introduced in Sect. 4 is a revised version which improved *writability, readability* and *consistency with meta-model and DDD patterns* in comparison to the first version [21].

In addition to our own validation activities, we made the Context Mapper tool available to the DDD community and collected feedback via issues on GitHub. Context Mapper is available for the Eclipse IDE[20] as well as for Visual Studio Code[21]. Via Gitpod[22], Eclipse Theia[23], and the Visual Studio Code extension, we can even offer a Web IDE running in the browser. According to the Eclipse marketplace Context Mapper has been installed over 40 times per month in the last three months (March, April, and May 2020). We only released the Visual Studio Code extension recently but already had 40 downloads within the first two weeks, according to the marketplace statistics.

Validation Results. The five architects in the service design workshop challenged whether a graphical representation would be better suited, whether application services (DDD pattern) should be placed inside or outside aggregates, whether such a tool could be used as an excuse for not engaging with end users (the whole point of DDD: establish a conversation and a common language). The conclusion from this validation activity was that the general approach can be useful in education and early project stages, but should not replace careful business analysis and coding in Java or other languages. Support for roundtripping and a careful synchronization of manual and tool supported steps in agile (iterative, incremental) practices were seen to be critical success factors for a broader adoption. Attendees appreciated the representation of the patterns in the DSL; the story extension with attributes and relationships was accepted.

In general, our intermediate validation activities so far suggest that both our hypothesis mentioned in Sect. 2 hold true. Discussions with DDD experts have further confirmed that controversial debates regarding the original pattern definitions and how the patterns can be combined exist among the practitioners, which supports our first hypothesis stating that architects and adopters benefit from a precise interpretation. The validation results gained from our case studies also support our second hypothesis that a modeling language such as CML can be helpful to model (micro-)service-oriented architectures with strategic DDD.

Threats to Validity. Regarding *construct validity* [40] there might be a risk that questions in our workshops or exercise lessons were misinterpreted by the participants. We tried to mitigate this threat by selecting experienced architects that are familiar with the

---

[20] https://marketplace.eclipse.org/content/context-mapper.

[21] https://marketplace.visualstudio.com/items?itemName=contextmapper.context-mapper-vscode-extension.

[22] https://www.gitpod.io/.

[23] https://theia-ide.org/.

topic and DDD. However, in our exercise lessons with the less experienced students there might be a risk for misunderstandings. We consider it unlikely that the opinions of the workshop participants, exercise participants, and DDD experts were influenced by factors unrelated to our approach (*internal validity* [40]). Threats to *external validity* [40] do exist, since we mainly relied on feedback of users that are familiar with DDD. Therefore, the validation results could vary in case we validate with other potential users (not familiar with DDD). We mitigated this threat a bit by using the tool with students at our university. However, future validation activities should include even more potential users that are experienced with software architecture but not DDD specifically. In addition, many of our experiments were self-experiments; since Context Mapper is an open source project, we do not know all our users, but have received direct feedback from six companies and teaching institutions located in different European countries (so we can consider the diversity threat and possible interest bias to be mitigated somewhat).

Analysis of Validation Results: Pros and Cons of DSL and Tools. We consider the conformance of the language and our terminology with the original DDD patterns to be a strength of the proposed approach. DDD adopters can familiarize themselves with the language easily. Our validation activities further indicate that the tool can increase the productivity in context mapping, especially when the map has to be improved iteratively. The model transformations can improve such a process in comparison to drawing by hand. This support for iterative model evolution is also a reason why we consider the approach conform with agile practices [1]. However, members of the agile community may argue that the approach is non-conforming with "working software over comprehensive documentation" [1]. Therefore, we can consider this a weakness and strength at the same time. Another strength is that we are able to generate architecture visualizations on different levels of abstraction out of the DSL-based models. Communicating software architecture always requires different perspectives and levels of abstraction depending on the audience. The "model-code" gap [12] can be considered a weakness of DSL- and generator-based approaches is general. Generated code typically changes and the original architecture descriptions tend to become outdated quickly. In addition, the approach requires an Integrated Development Environment (IDE) with editor support. This can be costly, especially if multiple IDEs have to be supported. However, we still consider the approach based on DDD future-proof, since technology-independent domain modeling is always relevant in software engineering. The presented approach is independent of any programming languages, architectural styles, or frameworks.

7   Summary and Outlook

In our previous paper [23] we presented Context Mapper, our approach to describe integration architectures and service decompositions in terms of strategic DDD patterns. As our research contributions, we proposed a) a meta-model and semantic rules based on the DDD patterns aiming for a concise interpretation of the patterns and how they can be combined, and b) a DSL and supporting tools to model Bounded Contexts and their relationships as well as Aggregates.

This extended version of the original paper introduced language improvements and enhancements that allow users to start modeling on the level of use cases and user stories. Additionally, we introduced model transformations that a) support Context Mapper users in modeling DDD Subdomains and Bounded Contexts rapidly, and b) illustrate how the Context Mapper DSL (CML) can be used as a foundation for systematic service decomposition approaches. The Context Mapper tool further allows to generate code, visual Context Maps and other architecture diagrams (not presented in this paper). In addition, the rapid prototyping transformations demonstrate how we apply and validate the DSL in practical cases.

Besides the rapid prototyping transformations we implemented several Architectural Refactorings (ARs)[24] (discussed in another paper [24]) that support the users in improving the architecture models iteratively.

Validation results collected via implementation, action research, and case studies suggest that Context Mapper can support architects in their modeling work and decision making effectively and efficiently. The existing results and user feedback further led to the syntax enhancements presented in this paper. However, additional validation activities will be required to finally confirm our hypothesis that Context Mapper can be beneficial in agile architecting and modeling environments.

In our future work we plan to further improve the language and tool so that software architects can evolve their designs with additional transformations and architecture refactorings [41] in an iterative and incremental manner. A reverse engineering library shall close the "model-code" gap [12] and provide model generation from existing or generated source code. This shall ease the application of the tool in brownfield projects that plan to refactor monoliths to microservices and/or migrate to the cloud. The integration of a systematic service decomposition approach similar to Service Cutter [15] shall propose new decompositions (Context Maps) that improve coupling and cohesion between contexts automatically.

References

1. Agile Alliance: Agile Manifesto (2001). https://www.agilealliance.org/agile101/the-agile-manifesto/
2. Agile Alliance: User story template (2001). https://www.agilealliance.org/glossary/user-story-template/
3. Avison, D.E., Lau, F., Myers, M.D., Nielsen, P.A.: Action research. Commun. ACM **42**(1), 94–97 (1999). https://doi.org/10.1145/291469.291479. http://doi.acm.org/10.1145/291469.291479
4. Baresi, L., Garriga, M., De Renzis, A.: Microservices identification through interface analysis. In: De Paoli, F., Schulte, S., Broch Johnsen, E. (eds.) ESOCC 2017. LNCS, vol. 10465, pp. 19–33. Springer, Cham (2017). https://doi.org/10.1007/978-3-319-67262-5_2
5. Brandolini, A.: Strategic domain driven design with context mapping (2009). https://www.infoq.com/articles/ddd-contextmapping
6. Brown, S.: The C4 model for visualising software architecture: context, containers, components and code (2018). https://www.infoq.com/articles/C4-architecture-model/

---

24 https://contextmapper.org/docs/architectural-refactorings/.

7. Cheesman, J., Daniels, J.: UML Components: A Simple Process for Specifying Component-Based Software. Addison-Wesley Longman Publishing Co., Inc. (2000)
8. Cockburn, A.: Writing Effective Use Cases. Agile Software Development Series. Addison-Wesley (2001)
9. Conway, M.: Conway's law (1968)
10. Evans, E.: Domain-Driven Design: Tackling Complexity in the Heart of Software. Addison-Wesley (2003)
11. Evans, E.: Domain-driven design reference: definitions and pattern summaries (2015). https://domainlanguage.com/ddd/reference
12. Fairbanks, G.: Just Enough Software Architecture: A Risk-Driven Approach. Marshall & Brainerd (2010)
13. Francesco, P.D., Lago, P., Malavolta, I.: Migrating towards microservice architectures: an industrial survey. In: 2018 IEEE International Conference on Software Architecture (ICSA), pp. 29–2909, April 2018. https://doi.org/10.1109/ICSA.2018.00012
14. Gouigoux, J., Tamzalit, D.: From monolith to microservices: lessons learned on an industrial migration to a web oriented architecture. In: 2017 IEEE International Conference on Software Architecture Workshops (ICSAW), pp. 62–65, April 2017. https://doi.org/10.1109/ICSAW.2017.35
15. Gysel, M., Kölbener, L., Giersche, W., Zimmermann, O.: Service cutter: a systematic approach to service decomposition. In: Aiello, M., Johnsen, E.B., Dustdar, S., Georgievski, I. (eds.) ESOCC 2016. LNCS, vol. 9846, pp. 185–200. Springer, Cham (2016). https://doi.org/10.1007/978-3-319-44482-6_12
16. Habegger, M., Schena, M.: Cloud-Native Refactoring in a mHealth Scenario. Bachelor thesis, University of Applied Sciences of Eastern Switzerland (HSR FHO) (2019)
17. Hassan, S., Ali, N., Bahsoon, R.: Microservice ambients: an architectural meta-modelling approach for microservice granularity. In: 2017 IEEE International Conference on Software Architecture (ICSA), pp. 1–10, April 2017. https://doi.org/10.1109/ICSA.2017.32
18. Hohpe, G., Woolf, B.: Enterprise Integration Patterns: Designing, Building, and Deploying Messaging Solutions. Addison-Wesley Longman Publishing Co. Inc., Boston (2003)
19. Josélyne, M.I., Tuheirwe-Mukasa, D., Kanagwa, B., Balikuddembe, J.: Partitioning microservices: a domain engineering approach. In: Proceedings of the 2018 International Conference on Software Engineering in Africa, SEiA 2018, pp. 43–49. ACM, New York (2018). https://doi.org/10.1145/3195528.3195535
20. Kapferer, S.: Architectural Refactoring of Data Access Security. Semester thesis, University of Applied Sciences of Eastern Switzerland (HSR FHO) (2017). https://eprints.hsr.ch/564
21. Kapferer, S.: A Domain-specific Language for Service Decomposition. Term project, University of Applied Sciences of Eastern Switzerland (HSR FHO) (2018). https://eprints.hsr.ch/722
22. Kapferer, S.: Model Transformations for DSL Processing. Term project, University of Applied Sciences of Eastern Switzerland (HSR FHO) (2019). https://eprints.hsr.ch/819/
23. Kapferer, S., Zimmermann, O.: Domain-specific language and tools for strategic domain-driven design, context mapping and bounded context modeling. In: Proceedings of the 8th International Conference on Model-Driven Engineering and Software Development - Volume 1: MODELSWARD, pp. 299–306. INSTICC, SciTePress (2020). https://doi.org/10.5220/0008910502990306
24. Kapferer, S., Zimmermann, O.: Domain-driven service design - context modeling, model refactoring and contract generation. In: Dustdar, S. (ed.) SummerSOC 2020. CCIS, vol. 1310, pp. 189–208. Springer, Cham (2020). https://doi.org/10.1007/978-3-030-64846-6_11
25. Kruchten, P.: The 4+1 view model of architecture. IEEE Softw. **12**(6), 42–50 (1995). https://doi.org/10.1109/52.469759

26. Landre, E., Wesenberg, H., Rønneberg, H.: Architectural improvement by use of strategic level domain-driven design. In: Companion to the 21st ACM OOPSLA, OOPSLA 2006, pp. 809–814. ACM, New York (2006). https://doi.org/10.1145/1176617.1176728

27. Le, D.M., Dang, D.H., Nguyen, V.H.: Domain-driven design using meta-attributes: a DSL-based approach. In: 2016 Eighth International Conference on Knowledge and Systems Engineering (KSE), pp. 67–72, October 2016. https://doi.org/10.1109/KSE.2016.7758031

28. Mazlami, G., Cito, J., Leitner, P.: Extraction of microservices from monolithic software architectures. In: 2017 IEEE International Conference on Web Services (ICWS), pp. 524–531, June 2017. https://doi.org/10.1109/ICWS.2017.61

29. Parnas, D.L.: On the criteria to be used in decomposing systems into modules. Commun. ACM **15**(12), 1053–1058 (1972). https://doi.org/10.1145/361598.361623

30. Pautasso, C., Zimmermann, O., Amundsen, M., Lewis, J., Josuttis, N.: Microservices in practice, part 1: reality check and service design. IEEE Softw. **34**(1), 91–98 (2017). https://doi.org/10.1109/MS.2017.24

31. Plöd, M.: DDD Context Maps - an enhanced view (2018). https://speakerdeck.com/mploed/context-maps-an-enhanced-view

32. Plöd, M.: Hands-on Domain-driven Design - by example. Leanpub (2019)

33. Rademacher, F., Sorgalla, J., Sachweh, S.: Challenges of domain-driven microservice design: a model-driven perspective. IEEE Softw. **35**(3), 36–43 (2018). https://doi.org/10.1109/MS.2018.2141028

34. Rademacher, F., Sachweh, S., Zündorf, A.: Towards a UML profile for domain-driven design of microservice architectures. In: Cerone, A., Roveri, M. (eds.) SEFM 2017. LNCS, vol. 10729, pp. 230–245. Springer, Cham (2018). https://doi.org/10.1007/978-3-319-74781-1_17

35. Shaw, M.: Writing good software engineering research papers: minitutorial. In: Proceedings of the 25th International Conference on Software Engineering, ICSE 2003, pp. 726–736. IEEE Computer Society, Washington (2003). http://dl.acm.org/citation.cfm?id=776816.776925

36. Stal, M.: Software architecture refactoring. In: Tutorial in the International Conference on Object Oriented Programming, Systems, Languages and Applications (2007)

37. Steinberg, D., Budinsky, F., Merks, E., Paternostro, M.: EMF: Eclipse Modeling Framework. Eclipse Series, Pearson Education (2008)

38. Tune, N., Millett, S.: Designing Autonomous Teams and Services: Deliver Continuous Business Value Through Organizational Alignment. O'Reilly Media (2017)

39. Vernon, V.: Implementing Domain-Driven Design, 1st edn. Addison-Wesley Professional (2013)

40. Wohlin, C., Runeson, P., Hst, M., Ohlsson, M.C., Regnell, B., Wessln, A.: Experimentation in Software Engineering. Springer, Heidelberg (2012). https://doi.org/10.1007/978-3-642-29044-2

41. Zimmermann, O.: Architectural refactoring for the cloud: a decision-centric view on cloud migration. Computing **99**(2), 129–145 (2017). https://doi.org/10.1007/s00607-016-0520-y. https://link.springer.com/article/10.1007/s00607-016-0520-y

42. Zimmermann, O.: Microservices tenets. Comput. Sci. - Res. Dev. 301–310 (2016). https://doi.org/10.1007/s00450-016-0337-0

43. Zimmermann, O., Stocker, M., Lübke, D., Pautasso, C., Zdun, U.: Introduction to microservice API patterns (MAP). In: Cruz-Filipe, L., Giallorenzo, S., Montesi, F., Peressotti, M., Rademacher, F., Sachweh, S. (eds.) Joint Post-proceedings of the First and Second International Conference on Microservices (Microservices 2017/2019). OpenAccess Series in Informatics (OASIcs), vol. 78, pp. 4:1–4:17. Schloss Dagstuhl-Leibniz-Zentrum fuer Informatik, Dagstuhl, Germany (2020). https://doi.org/10.4230/OASIcs.Microservices.2017-2019.4. https://drops.dagstuhl.de/opus/volltexte/2020/11826

Abstract Test Execution for Early Testing Activities in Model-Driven Scenarios

Reinhard Pröll$^{(\boxtimes)}$ ⓘ, Noël Hagemann ⓘ, and Bernhard Bauer ⓘ

Software Methodologies for Distributed Systems, University of Augsburg,
Augsburg, Germany
{reinhard.proell,noel.hagemann,bauer}@informatik.uni-augsburg.de

Abstract. The continuous improvement of the performance of computing units makes it possible to cope with increasingly complex tasks.
This results in more complex software systems. However, the development of such highly complex systems is difficult to achieve using traditional approaches. Concepts like model-driven software development can
weaken this problem in these constructive phases. However, new challenges arise for the testing of development artifacts. In order to be able to
perform a real shift left of verification and validation tasks towards early
phases of development, we present a semi-formal approach that enables
users to execute test cases against the system under development (SUD)
on the model-level. Grounded on an Integrated Model Basis which is created and maintained during development, test reports are automatically
derived. This opens up a wide range of possibilities for early and targeted
troubleshooting.

Keywords: Test execution · Model-based testing · Domain-specific
modeling · Integrated model basis · Model-driven software development

1 Introduction

Due to the rapid development of hardware, more and more complex tasks can
be mastered. As the complexity of the tasks steadily increases, the complexity
of the software that handles these tasks is growing. In order to handle this
increased complexity of the software development, a new trend has emerged in
development practices.

In contrast to purely code-based approaches, many development tasks are
nowadays handled by model-based ones. These techniques are characterized by
the concepts of abstraction and automation, thus reducing complexity for the
user. Considerable progress has been made in the areas of executable models,
especially in the formal verification of suitable models, and in model-based testing. This gives insights into the planned system in early phases of development
and enables developers to take appropriate and possibly early (counter-) mea-
sures, since defects introduced into the system in early phases of development
usually cause significantly higher costs for elimination (time and money) [5,23].

© Springer Nature Switzerland AG 2021
S. Hammoudi et al. (Eds.): MODELSWARD 2020, CCIS 1361, pp. 273–297, 2021.
https://doi.org/10.1007/978-3-030-67445-8_12

Further, Jones et al. [13] show how the worst-case scenario of very late discovery of such defects is the rule rather than the exception. Thus, verification in early phases of development is significant.

1.1 Problem Statement

The mentioned approaches in the model context either place high demands on the modeling languages used or work effectively on code artifacts derived from models or even platform specific artifacts. If one tries to put this into the context of Model-Driven Architecture (MDA), instances of the Platform-Specific Model (PSM) or Implementation-Specific Model (ISM) level are usually used for this purpose [15]. Especially for semi-formal test activities no effective shift left towards early development phases can be achieved, due to missing execution or simulation concepts.

We want to achieve this kind of functionality by implementing an approach to perform tests against the system based on model artifacts associated with the Platform-Independent Model (PIM). This enables the possibility to detect certain types of defects even earlier and thus reduce the overall costs. In contrast to purely specification-based tests (black-box), information about the implementation can be used at this point, allowing more targeted testing in the sense of gray-box testing. This can be seen as a kind of guidance for the modeler in addition to classical test results.

Up to our knowledge, there is no semi-formal approach that offers such functionalities. Based on an integrated set of model artifacts of different domains, like system development and testing, our *Abstract Test Execution (ATE)* approach is implemented. Therefore, the modeling expert specifies correlations between elements of the system model and the test model. From this *Integrated Model Basis*, an analysis-specific representation can be derived by using Model-to-Model (M2M) transformations. On the basis of these transformed model representations as well as the updated mapping information captured by the Integration Model, the concept of ATE is applied. Similar to classical testing, reports are created for the test runs, documenting the results of the execution to support troubleshooting.

In contrast to the related conference paper [10], the following sections draw a holistic picture of the concepts around the ATE approach. Furthermore, the ATE itself is more detailed and reworked with a lightweight formalization. This is followed by a critical discussion.

1.2 Outline

Following the previously presented introduction and problem statement, the remaining contents are structured as follows. In the course of Sect. 2 the foundations are described. This includes the introduction of our running example (Sect. 2.1) which demonstrates the details of our approach. Further, the *Integrated Model Basis (IMB)* is presented throughout Sects. 2.2 and 2.3, using the running example to give a more intuitive understanding of the concepts. The main contribution, namely the *Abstract Test Execution*, is introduced in Sect. 3. Thereby, the structure of Subsects. 3.2 to 3.6 reflects the overall structure of the underlying process. Following Sect. 3, a mixed qualitative evaluation/discussion of concepts is presented in Sect. 4. In order to set our approach in context to other research, related work is discussed in Sect. 5. Finally, a conclusion is drawn and a road map for future topics is elaborated.

2   Foundations

In order to detail the approach outlined in the previous chapter, the necessary foundations, including the running example, are presented. In particular, the different model artifacts which are part of the concept are explained. An overview is given in Fig. 1.

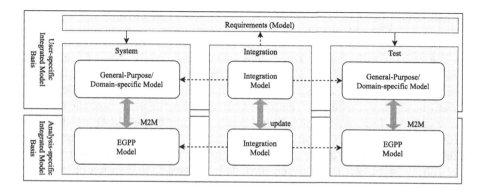

Fig. 1. Model artifacts in the context of abstract test case execution.

In the upper part of the figure the *Requirements Model* is shown, representing the starting point of any development. In the context of Model-Driven Software Development (MDSD), both *System* and *Test Models* are built upon this basis. Different types of modeling languages can be applied to create these artifacts, such as General Purpose Modeling Languages (GPML) or Domain-Specific Modeling Languages (DSML). In this case, the use of two separate model artifacts is considered to support the automation of subsequent processing steps. Therefore, it is necessary to define a well-formed relation between these model artifacts, achieved by the integration component placed in the middle of the figure, namely the *Integration Model*. All of these models represent possible interaction points with the user (*User-Specific Integrated Model Basis*) For details see Sect. 2.2.

In addition, derived from the *User-Specific Integrated Model Basis* through Model-to-Model (M2M) transformations, a so-called *Analysis-specific Integrated Model Basis* is introduced (for details see Sect. 2.3). Essentially, the System and Test Models are mapped to an internal metamodel, which was designed for the subsequent automated processing (for details see Sect. 2.3).

2.1   Running Example - Automatic Door Control System

As already mentioned, the running example serves for illustrating the different aspects of our approach. In order to keep this intuitively understandable and clear, we have chosen a simple example from everyday life. Due to its simplicity, there are no structural artifacts of the System Model. It is a door control system, where its control logic is represented by the state machine in Fig. 2.

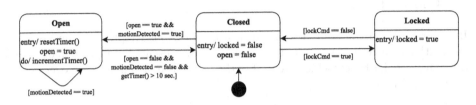

Fig. 2. Behavior system model for the automatic door control syste.

The control logic defines three different states, namely Open, Closed and Locked. The door is able to query the status of a sensor, which reveals if the door is open or closed (open). This is supplemented by a sensor for detecting movement at close range (motionDetected). Besides the sensors of the system, a conventional lock is provided for manually locking of the door, which sends a lockCmd to the door control unit on actuation. Apart from the event-driven points of interaction, a time-triggered component is part of the door control unit. Precisely, as soon as a timer of ten seconds has elapsed, the closing of the door is initiated, unless motion is detected by the sensor.

Starting with this System Model artifact, the proposed running example is extended and constantly used in the following sections to illustrate certain aspects of our contributions.

2.2   User-Specific Integrated Model Basis

As already mentioned above, the so-called *User-specific Integrated Model Basis* (*Omni Model* for short) represents the data side of the approach. In particular, this combination of model artifacts represents the action point for the users of the subsequent automated processing chain. In principle, any development model can be integrated, provided their metamodels are completely available. This approach forces the separation of concerns on the model-level, which has a positive impact on the significance of the resulting tests [25]. An essential role and the minimal amount of model information is given by the System Model, the Test Model and the integration of these two artifacts modeled within the Integration Model. In this context, most of the relevant aspects of these artifacts have already been introduced in earlier publications by Rumpold and Pröll (for details see [27,28]).

System Model. In the context of MDSD, this model covers both structural and behavioral aspects of the SUD. Different modeling languages can be used, depending on the application domain and the expertise of the developers. E.g. GPMLs such as the SysML [19] or DSMLs used in the context of the embedded MDSD tool radCase [7] from IMACS can be used.

Test Model. The same applies to the model artifacts concerning test modeling. The choice of the metamodel should be based primarily on aspects such as expertise of the test engineers and sufficient tool support. E.g. GPML-based approaches such as the UML Testing Profile [21] or proprietary modeling languages can be used.

Other Domain-Specific Development Models. The combination of different models is not limited to the two domains already mentioned. If information about e.g. temporal behavior, safety or security of the SUD is considered in separate DSMLs, it can be linked to the Integrated Model Basis. Even if this information has no direct influence on the processing and thus results of the ATE, such information can be included in the context of post-processing. For subsequent troubleshooting, correction and, under certain circumstances, transitive defect effects can be determined.

Integration Model. This model artifact provides the link between the sets of different domain-specific models. In order to map the relationships between the models, the structural decomposition of the instantiated SUD is primarily modeled. This enables purely structural mappings between instance- and component-related parts of the different models. Beyond the structural mappings, additional information on elements of the structural decomposition can be added to the Integration Model (see aspects concept in [26]).

In addition, these mappings between models participating in the Integrated Model Basis can be specified for behavioral model elements. These mappings represent a key concept in the implementation of the ATE, since this enables the synchronization of different types of models of the same behavioral aspect. I.e. a series of synchronization points (so-called `IMSyncPoints`) is defined for each behavior model, which are connected to elements of the System Model as well as the Test Model. Furthermore, different types of synchronization points are distinguished. Besides the conventional `IMSyncPoints` there are `IMSyncEntryPoints` and `IMSyncExitPoints` representing the entry and the exit of a synchronization sequence respectively. The level of detail or completeness of these mappings has a decisive influence on the test results determined in the context of the ATE. Therefore, careful modeling must be carried out to avoid deducing false conclusions from the corresponding results.

Application to the Running Example. In order to illustrate the concepts of the Integrated Model Basis, the concrete instances of the models in the context of the Automatic Door Control System will be discussed below.

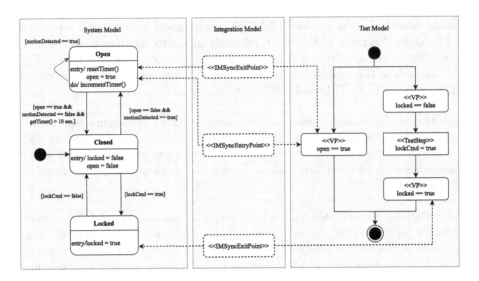

Fig. 3. Excerpt of the user-specific integrated model basis for the automatic door control system.

Figure 3 shows the relationships between the individual model instances. On the left side of the figure, the state machine previously introduced in Fig. 2 represents the behavioral model of the SUD. The model elements arranged in the middle of this figure show synchronization points and thereby specify the behavioral mappings across the development domains. On the right side, a activity chart based Test Model consisting of *Test Steps* and *Verification Points (VP)* is conducted. In principle, two different test cases can be derived (see right side of Fig. 7) from this model, which are evaluated against the system as part of the ATE.

2.3   Analysis-Specific Integrated Model Basis

In Fig. 1 the user-specific and the analysis-specific view of the model basis was shown. Basically, the analysis-specific representation of the Integrated Model Basis decouples the algorithmic implementation from the specifics of the respective application context. In contrast to the manual modeling of the model artifacts, the analysis-specific variant is derived automatically. This is done by a set of transformation steps describing a model transformation. These steps are specified on the metamodel-level. The components of this target metamodel, relevant for ATE as well as the concepts of the transformations, are explained in the following.

Analysis-Specific Metamodel. In order to be able to map multiple models in the context of model-centric testing, the *Execution Graph ++* (EGPP) metamodel was developed. In the context of Pröll et al. [26] the metamodel simultaneously representing the structure, control flow and data flow information of a system, was introduced. Basically, the control flow information is described by nodes (EGPPNode) and edges (EGPPTransition). In addition, structure information can be modeled by nesting these control flow structures, since special nodes

(`EGPPGraph`) can contain control flow (sub-)graphs. The data flow information (`EGPPTaggedData`) completes the information set and annotates nodes and edges of the model. In particular, the annotated data are atomic with regard to the included expressions, such that only one expression is captured per node/edge.

In general, an instance of the EGPP describes behavior by sequences of states, which can be applied to both a Test Model and a System Model. Each of these states consists of an active node of the control flow and a set of variable assignments. A variable state is updated by the assignments of the active node, assuming the intermediate guards could be fulfilled. If an assignment is made in the node, it is further identified by a `EGPPInputNode`, if only a condition is checked, a `EGPPOutputNode` is modeled. The latter type of node is used when mapping Test Models, particularly to check the current state from a data flow perspective. In case of the control flow perspective, `IMSyncPoints` concept of the Integration Model is evaluated. If such a connection between `EGPPNodes` of a Test Model and a System Model is specified, an additional condition is imposed on the control flow. Especially in case of `IMSyncEntryPoints` or `IMSyncExitPoints` this means that the evaluation of the test case against the system has to start or end at the referenced points of the control flow.

Model-to-Model Transformations. As shown in Fig. 1, both the original System and the Test Model are transformed into the EGPP metamodel by a horizontal exogenous M2M transformation. Different patterns are implemented such that a uniform representation is created for both aspects independent of the user-specific metamodel. The basic concepts of these patterns are shown in Fig. 4. Further, it is crucial that the transformation rules defined for this purpose do not change the semantics of the original models, but at best refines them.

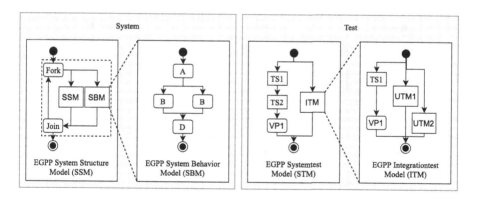

Fig. 4. EGPP model patterns for system and test context.

On the left side of Fig. 4, the System Model is considered. In case of purely structuring model elements of the original model, a construct is created in the EGPP context, which cyclically embeds all included components (SSM) and behavioral models (SBM) in its flow. In contrast, the behavioral models are not enriched with any synthetic control structures, as long as the original model already provides a defined initial and final state. At this point, it is important to preserve the original specification of system states.

In contrast, the right side of the graph shows the pattern for the Test Model. Here, the different test levels are aligned to the integration levels of the System Model. In this hierarchy the highest level model is the *System Test Model (STM)*, which specifies consistent test cases at the integration level, but can include lower integration levels, such as an *Integration Test Model (ITM)*. This is done through all the integration levels considered down to the unit level, which is illustrated in the right-hand part of Fig. 4.

In addition to the control flow and structure-giving patterns, the data flow is transformed realized in the form of a pseudo-code-like language, which is out of scope for this contribution. According to this language the `EGPPTaggedData` elements are filled with information during the transformation.

In addition to the M2M transformations of the System and Test Models, the mapping information is updated between artifacts of these modeling domains captured by the integration model. This update includes the creation of new mappings between transformed model elements of the respective EGPP instances, provided that their original model elements are already part of a mapping relation specified by the Integration Model. Normally, no manual intervention is necessary, provided that the M2M transformations are specified completely regarding the conventions mentioned above.

Application to the Running Example. The application of these transformation rules converts the Integrated Model Basis already introduced in Fig. 3 into the following variant (see Fig. 5).

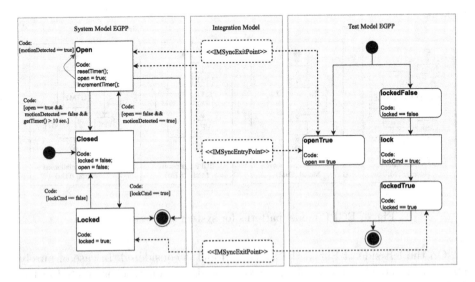

Fig. 5. Excerpt of the analysis-specific integrated model basis for the automatic door control system.

Basically, the two graphs are very similar, since the original model elements have been transformed into `EGPPNodes`. Model elements with sharp corners represent `EGPPInputNodes` and round corners represent `EGPPOutputNodes`. Exceptions are the dashed model elements of the Integration Model, arranged in the middle of this figure. The annotated data flow information is stored in the code fragments, which reflects the `EGPPTaggedData`. Furthermore, an explicit final state was added to the original System Model, which can be reached by all original states.

3   Abstract Test Execution

Several input artifacts are required to perform the process of *Abstract Test Execution*. These input artifacts are given by the Analysis-Specific Integrated Model Basis. As mentioned in Sect. 2.3, this model basis mainly consists of two model artifacts which are interconnected by a third model artifact, namely the Integration Model.

3.1   Overall Process

Both main artifacts, namely the System Model and the Test Model, are instance models of the EGPP metamodel. The System Model describes the structure and behavior of the system, while the Test Model represents the intended behavior of the system. The Integration Model can be used to define so called `IMSyncPoints` and is based on a corresponding metamodel. `IMSyncPoints` are used to define entry points and exit points of the execution of abstract test cases.

The test cases are derived from the Test Model. The process is detailed in the following Sect. 3.2.

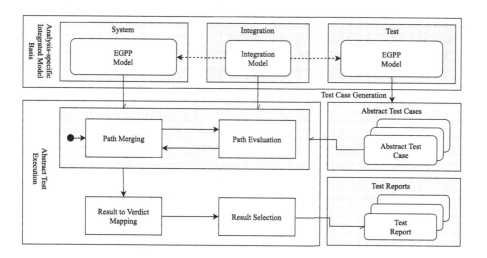

Fig. 6. Overall ATE process.

The process of ATE uses the System Model, the Integration Model and the generated set of abstract test cases to perform testing. The general approach is visualized in Fig. 6. Every abstract test case contained in the generated set is evaluated one after the other. This evaluation process of each abstract test case consists of multiple steps, which ultimately result in a test report.

At first, the abstract test case is merged into the System Model. Different cases for the merging exist which results in a vast range of different paths describing the majority of all possible data flows and control flows. We identify some basic merging rules, which are described in Sect. 3.3. Besides the merging process, the data flow and the control flow of these paths are assessed. Therefore, basic data flow specific faults are taken into account as well as control flow specific characteristics. This baseline is detailed in Sect. 3.4. In addition, the preliminary results gathered by this analysis are collected and classified. The result classes are described in Sect. 3.5.

Then, one of these preliminary results is chosen to be the representative result of the ATE. Finally, a human-readable test report is generated from the representative result. These steps are detailed in Sect. 3.6. For further understanding, all the mentioned process steps are illustrated along the running example.

3.2   Preprocessing and Derivation of Abstract Test Cases

A model is viewed as a graph consisting of nodes and edges. A Test Model comprises two kinds of nodes and unidirectional edges. As described in Sect. 2.2, such models are structurally based on activity diagrams that can preserve a chain of events by transforming them into a fixed sequence of nodes enclosed by an initial and a final node. Contained nodes are connected by unidirectional edges. Generally, a distinction is made between nodes that contain instructions which either send stimuli to the SUT or check whether certain outputs of the system meet predefined conditions. Due to the abstract nature of the ATE approach, we distinguish between instructions that modify variables of the SUT or check for certain variable values. Nodes included in a Test Model can either contain one instruction that is capable of modifying exactly one system variable or any number of conditions to challenge the system state. The former are called *Test Steps* while the latter are referred to as *Verification Points*. During transformation from the user-specific input model to its analysis-specific EGPP-based form, it is ensured that non-atomic nodes are transferred into an atomic form. Furthermore, nodes of type *Test Step* are transformed into `EGPPInputNodes` while *Verification Points* are converted into `EGPPOutputNodes` as described in Sect. 2.3. Depending on the Test Model as an EGPP-based artifact, a data flow analysis is performed which is able to mimic combinations of structural as well as data flow coverage metrics to derive sets of abstract test cases.

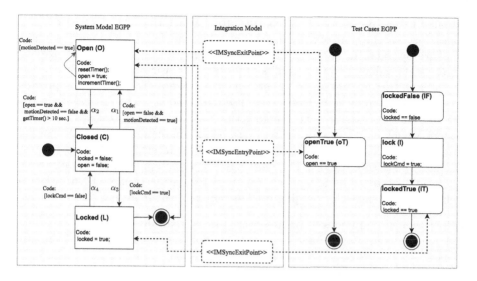

Fig. 7. EGPP representation of running example.

In the context of the running example, two test cases are extracted from the Test Model (see Fig. 5) and presented in Fig. 7. The test case on the left hand side checks whether the internal system variable open is set to true while the system state is initialized as Open. The other test case determines whether the system switches correctly into the Locked system state after initializing the system to the Closed state and sending the lockCmd = true stimulus to it.

3.3   Path Merging Based on Integrated Model Basis Mappings

Like the Test Model described in Sect. 3.2, the System Model supports different model elements. Generally speaking, the System Model can have nodes that contain instructions that modify the system state and conditional transitions that restrict the change of system states (referred to as *Guards*).

Nodes of the System Model and Test Steps of the Test Model contain instructions capable of altering the system state. Verification Points of a Test Model and instructions of guarded transitions of the System Model share the same kind of instructions to validate the system state. Overall, the Test Model and the System Model contain two different kinds of instructions which represent the basic blocks of the merging process.

Furthermore, the EGPP-based structure of the System Model and Test Model is defined by an initial node and a final node. This common structure of the models naturally specifies the entry point and exit point for ATE. However, due to the potentially multi-layered structure of the input models (cf. Sect. 2.3) more than two entry and exit point pairs may exist. Therefore, we introduce the possibility to specify explicit connections between both models to determine the entry point as well as the exit point of the ATE to restrict the number of model artifacts taken into account. In contrast to the fact that end connections are mandatory for the control flow analysis of ATE, the definition of entry connections are optional. In addition, entry connections can be used to initialize the system state different to the initial system state as visualized in Fig. 7.

After the determination of an entry point for the ATE, the merging process is carried out step by step. Every step inserts one node of the test case into the system. The process starts by merging the first node of the test case into the System Model and ends with the test case being completely merged. Depending on the System Model, several possibilities exist for inserting a node of the test case into the System Model. The most basic merging approach is to take every permutation into account but this can lead to a state explosion. In order to tackle this challenge, the merging process performs the following rules:

1. The sequence of nodes of the test case and System Model is kept.
2. Incoming transitions of a system node are not separated by nodes of the test case
3. Verification Points are inserted after nodes of the System Model
4. Test Steps of a segment are inserted directly after the leading Verification Point

Generally speaking, these rules limit the set of permutations without loss of generality on the final result of the ATE. The effect of the rules is discussed in Sect. 4. Moreover, we name the set of all permutations the path space P and the subset of permutations created by applying the rules as the limited path space P_{lim}.

The first rule ensures that the control flow of the system is maintained by keeping the general structure of the test case during merging. Subsequently, nodes of the test case can only be inserted into the System Model, if the given order of test nodes is preserved, which represents the first step of limiting the path space.

The second rule is used to imitate more classical testing approaches. From a classical testing point of view, stimuli are sent to the system to initialize a change of system state. In more detail, the stimuli are used to satisfy some condition which guard the change of system state. From our abstract testing point of view, nodes of the test case can be inserted directly before a node of the System Model or before an incoming transition of a node of the System Model. In order to preserve the behavior of classical testing, rule two allows the insertion of nodes of the test case before an incoming transition of the system model which is used to imitate the classical testing approach.

The third rule aligns with entrenched code-based testing activities. From a classical testing point of view, a test case must interact with the SUT to verify its functionality. In consequence, if the test case does not interact with the SUT, the test case fails. Due to the abstract nature of this approach, test cases may be defined that rely on induced variables by the test cases rather than variables induced by the system. This could potentially lead to a test case that is falsely successful. To reduce the risk of such test cases, rule three is defined (cf. Sect. 4).

The last rule leads to a significant reduction of the path space. Two aspects come into play. First, due to the abstract nature of this approach, time-dependent variables are out of scope. As a result, the sequence of Test Steps of a Segment can be ignored since Test Steps represent stimuli to the system which are affected by timing. Here, a *Segment* refers to all nodes between two successive Verification Points. Second, stimuli to the system are bound to a change of system state. Therefore, if more than one node of the System Model is contained in a Segment, the test may fail by mistake. To cope with this problem, we allow the over-assignment of variables to declare all assignments of variables induced by Test Steps of a Segment as valid. A more in-depth description of the over-assignment of variables and the resulting effect can be found in Sect. 4.

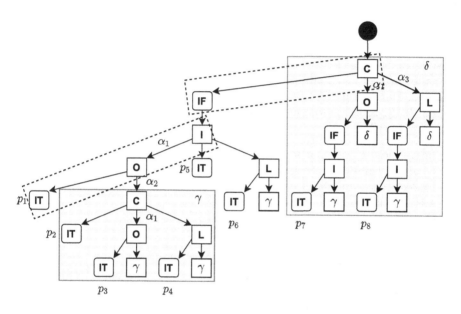

Fig. 8. Limited tree of paths of the running example.

To visualize the merging process, a tree can be formed which contains the limited subset of permutations P_{lim}. Figure 8 shows the path tree of the running example. For better understanding, the Segments of the path p_1 are visualized by dashed boxes. In addition, nodes of the System Model and Test Model are visualized by squares which have rounded or sharp corners. The former represent nodes that contain instructions which verify the system state. The latter illustrates nodes that consist of instructions which modify the system state. The naming refers to Fig. 7 while the following sections utilize the abbreviations in brackets. Guarded transitions are referenced by their respective identifier α_x, which can also be found in Fig. 7. Due to loops in the representative System Model, the tree of paths contains an infinite number of paths. Therefore, nodes labeled with γ or δ can be substituted by nodes enclosed by the box with the same label.

3.4 Evaluation of Path Space

In reality, paths are not evaluated as a whole. Instead, the evaluation process is triggered after a new Segment is formed by injecting a Verification Point into the System Model.

The analysis of such a segment is carried out with the help of a combination of data flow and control flow analysis. The former is used to determine whether the instructions of guarded transitions and Verification Points can be fulfilled. The latter is used to check if the test case is solvable from a structural point of view and if the final system state is reached after the data flow is completely analyzed.

Generally, data flow analysis is an approach of collecting information about possible values of system variables. We use this analysis to execute and evaluate the instructions contained in the nodes of the segment currently being analyzed. During this process, several faults can be detected. We define $D :=$ $\{d_1, d_2, d_3, d_4, d_5, d_6\}$ as the set of data flow based faults. In the following, these cases are described.

d_1 Instruction of node not solvable
d_2 Guard of transition not solvable
d_3 Undeclared or uninitialized variable
d_4 Missing end point for data flow analysis
d_5 Guard contains time-dependent variable
d_6 Guard fulfilled by over-assigned variable

As previously detailed, several paths emerge which are likely to solve the test case. Test cases contained in the resulting P_{lim} consists of nodes of the EGPP Test Model and nodes and transitions of the EGPP System Model. The merging process removes the boundaries between these models, which causes the evaluation to distinguish only between variable-verifying instructions (VVI) and variable-modifying instructions (VMI). Such verifying instructions are Boolean expressions which can be evaluated to `true` or `false`. On the one hand, we consider the latter result as unwanted behavior and register a fault in the event of such a case. On the other hand, if the Boolean expression results in `true`, the associated Guard or Verification Point is successfully solved.

Algorithm 3.1 presents the procedure to evaluate a Segment which is detailed in the following. However, one of the requirements for the ATE is that an end connection is specified in the Integration Model that defines the desired exit point as specified in Sect. 3.3. If no end connection is defined, the fault d_4 is reported and the segment evaluation of the path is skipped.

If a variable-verifying instruction fails as part of a transition, the fault d_2 is registered, otherwise if it is part of a node, the fault d_1 is registered. However, as a first step of evaluating instructions, affected variables need to be resolved. If they are not initialized or undeclared, the fault d_3 is listed.

Algorithm 3.1: EVALSEGMENT(s.)

procedure EVALSEGMENT(s)
  for each $e \in$ GETELEMENTS(s)
    do $\begin{cases} \textbf{if } \text{INSTANCEOF}(\text{GETINST}(e), VMI) \\ \quad \textbf{then } \text{STOREVALUESOFELEMENT}(e) \\ \quad \textbf{else if } \text{INSTANCEOF}(\text{GETINST}(e), VVI) \\ \quad \textbf{then } \text{VERIFYELEMENT}(e) \end{cases}$
  PERSISTLASTSTOREDVARIABLEVALUES()

procedure VERIFYELEMENT(e)
  if NEWFAULTSREGISTERED(CHECKPRECONDITIONS(e))
    then return
  if INSTANCEOF($e, node$)
    then $\begin{cases} \textbf{if } ! \text{ VERIFYINST}(\text{GETINST}(e)) \text{ XOR } \text{ISOVERASSIGNED}(\text{GETINST}(e)) \\ \quad \textbf{then } \text{REGISTERFAULT}(d_1, e) \end{cases}$
    else if INSTANCEOF($e, edge$)
    then $\begin{cases} \textbf{if } \text{VERIFYINST}(\text{GETINST}(e)) \\ \quad \textbf{then } \begin{cases} \textbf{if } \text{ISOVERASSIGNED}(\text{GETINST}(e)) \\ \quad \textbf{then } \text{REGISTERFAULT}(d_6, e) \end{cases} \\ \quad \textbf{else } \text{REGISTERFAULT}(d_2, e) \end{cases}$

procedure CHECKPRECONDITIONS(e)
  for each $v \in$ GETVARIABLES(GETINST(e))
    do $\begin{cases} \textbf{if } \text{ISTIMEDEPENDENTVARIABLE}(v) \\ \quad \textbf{then } \text{REGISTERFAULT}(d_5, e) \\ \textbf{if } \text{SIZE}(\text{GETSTOREDVALUES}(v)) == 0 \\ \quad \textbf{then } \text{REGISTERFAULT}(d_3, e) \end{cases}$

procedure ISOVERASSIGNED(i)
  for each $v \in$ GETVARIABLES(i)
    do $\begin{cases} \textbf{if } \text{SIZE}(\text{GETSTOREDVALUES}(v)) > 1 \\ \quad \textbf{then return } (\textbf{true}) \end{cases}$
  return (**false**)

procedure STOREVALUESOFELEMENT(e)
  if INSTANCEOF($e, node$)
    then STORE(GETLHS(GETINST(e)),
        EVAL(GETRHS(GETINST(e)),
        GETPERMUTATEDVARIABLEASSIGNMENTS(GETINST(e)))))

procedure VERIFYINST(i)
  for each $va \in$ GETPERMUTATEDVARIABLEASSIGNMENTS(i)
    do $\begin{cases} \textbf{if } \text{EVAL}(i, va) \\ \quad \textbf{then return } (\textbf{true}) \end{cases}$
  return (**false**)

Due to the fact that this approach is based on data flow and control flow analysis, time-dependent variables are out of scope. In general, however, there are test cases that rely on such variables. In order to be able to evaluate such test cases, the over-assignment of variables within a segment is allowed, which leads to multiple valid values at a time. However, after a segment is evaluated, only the value last-set remains valid, while the others are invalidated. Further, the usage of over-assigned variables is only allowed to evaluate verifying instructions of transitions, but in any case a fault is logged. If the instruction can be fulfilled by over-assigned variables, the fault d_6 is noted, otherwise the fault d_5 is captured. If an over-assigned variable is used to solve such an instruction of a node, the fault d_1 is added to the set of registered data flow faults for this path. As presented, the topic of over-assigned variables is addressed in detail in Sect. 4.

On the one hand the data flow of the path is analyzed, on the other hand control flow analysis is used to structurally evaluate the path. Due to the end connections contained in the Integration Model, it can be distinguished if the system has reached the desired system state after the last node of the test case is merged into the System Model. The result is categorized into one of four fault classes. The set of the characteristics based on control flow is defined as $C := \{c_1, c_2, c_3, c_4\}$.

c_1 All verifying instructions of path are fulfilled and the last verification point is solved by the instructions of one of the marked system nodes

c_2 All verifying instructions of the path are fulfilled and the last verification point could be satisfied using the instructions of one of the marked system nodes

c_3 At least one verification point of the path could not be fulfilled, but a system node marked as exit point is part of the path

c_4 At least one verification point of the path is not solvable and no system node marked as exit point is part of the path

In general, we distinguish between test cases that can or cannot be fulfilled. If the test case can be fulfilled, it is differentiated whether the last verification point and the instruction of the system node used to fulfill the VP are connected by an end connection. If the test case is not solvable, it is determined whether an end node is generally found or not. These cases result in the four control flow specific fault classes listed above.

Overall, a set $O := \{R_1, \ldots, R_{|P_{lim}|}\}$ is iteratively formed containing result sets $R := D_H \cup C_{NI}$ derived from the segments of the paths p included in the limited path space P_{lim}. The set R consists of the set $D_H := D \times H$ containing the detected data flow faults D combined with hints H on their cause and a set $C_{NI} := C \times \{NI\}$ of control flow characteristics C with the symbol NI as a pair. This symbol signals the absence of a hint resulting in the extended set $H_{NI} := H \cup \{NI\}$. Generally, hints can be instructions or variables of the System Model and Test Model.

$$R_1 = \{(d_2, \alpha_1), (d_1, lT), (c_4, NI)\}$$
$$R_2 = \{(d_2, \alpha_1), (d_2, \alpha_2), (d_1, lT), (c_4, NI)\}$$
$$R_3 = \{(d_2, \alpha_1), (d_2, \alpha_2), (d_2, \alpha_1), (F1, lT), (c_4, NI)\}$$
$$R_4 = \{(d_2, \alpha_1), (d_2, \alpha_2), (d_1, lT), (c_3, NI)\}$$
$$R_5 = \{(d_1, lT), (c_4, NI)\}$$
$$R_6 = \{(c_1, NI)\}$$
$$R_7 = \{(d_2, \alpha_1), (d_1, lT), (c_4, NI)\}$$
$$R_8 = \{(d_2, \alpha_3), (d_1, lT), (c_3, NI)\}$$

In context of the running example, the set of detected faults and characteristics stated above are based on the paths p_x given by Fig. 8. In this case, the set of hints is defined as $H = \{O, C, L, \alpha_1, \alpha_2, \alpha_3, \alpha_4, oT, lF, l, lT\}$. The result sets R_x are directly derived from their respective paths by their identifier $p_x \rightarrow R_x$ with $x \in \{1, \ldots, 8\}$.

For Example, the set R_1 consist of three elements. The first elements gives information that the guard `open == false && motionDetected == true` could not be satisfied. The second element can be interpreted in that way that the Verification Point `locked == true` is not solvable. The last element marks the evaluation of this path as finished and states that at least one Verification Point could not be fulfilled and the test case could not be solved structurally, since an end connection exits which connects the Verification Point `lockedTrue` with the system state `Locked`, but this system state is not part of the analyzed path.

3.5 Result to Verdict Mapping

The next step covers the classification of the result sets $R \in O$. For this purpose, we define the set of verdicts $V := \{v_1, v_2, v_3, v_4\}$. In general, we distinguish between the four verdicts *Passed* (v_1), *Probably Passed* (v_2), *Inconclusive* (v_3) and *Failed* (v_4). The test verdicts *Passed, Inconclusive* and *Failed* are based on TTCN-3's verdict set [8], extended by the new test verdict *Probably Passed*. We justify the extension of the classical verdict set to signal the existence of aspects which cannot be evaluated due to the abstract nature of this approach.

A path that is classified as *Passed* fulfills all variable-verifying instructions contained in the path based on its data flow. The classifications *Probably Passed* and *Inconclusive* indicate that some information is missing. In the case of *Inconclusive*, these information can be added to the source models by the modeler. Otherwise, this information cannot be provided in the case of *Probably Passed*, as the exact runtime behavior of the system cannot be determined by the ATE. We leave this feature over to code-based testing mechanisms. The last verdict marks paths where the evaluation of variable-verifying instructions leads to a negative result (`false`).

$$M : R \to V \begin{cases} v_1, & \text{if } \exists (f, h) \in R.\ f = c_1 \wedge |R| = 1 \\ v_2, & \text{if } \exists (f, h) \in R.\ f = d_i \text{ such that } i \in \{5, 6\} \wedge \\ & \quad \forall (f, h) \in R.\ f \neq d_j \text{ such that } j \in \{1, 2, 3, 4\} \\ v_3, & \text{if } \exists (f, h) \in R.\ f = d_i \text{ such that } i \in \{3, 4\} \wedge \\ & \quad \forall (f, h) \in R.\ f \neq d_j \text{ such that } j \in \{1, 2\} \\ v_4, & \text{otherwise} \end{cases}$$

The presented verdicts are concluded by the cases of the function shown above. It is used to derive a verdict from a result set. Generally, a pessimistic approach is chosen for the determination of verdicts. For example, a missing end connection d_4 does not necessarily lead to a failing test case, but considering the displayed function, it is marked as Inconclusive, although the missing connection has no effect on the data flow on the one hand. On the other hand, this feature can significantly impact the runtime of the ATE, which may result in the test case not being able to be analyzed by the ATE in the worst case. To prevent such behavior, the classification process is based on very strict and pessimistic rule set, in the sense that the worst possible result is always expected which reflects the core classical testing approaches.

Table 1. Mapped results of the running example.

R_x	R_1	R_2	R_3	R_4	R_5	R_6	R_7	R_8
$M(R_x)$	v_1	v_1	v_1	v_1	v_1	v_4	v_1	v_1

Table 1 shows the results of determining the verdicts of the result sets of the running example. Here, seven out of eight result sets are classified as *Failed*. The remaining result set R_6 derived from the path p_6 is marked as *Passed*.

3.6   Result Selection and Test Report

The last step of the ATE is the selection of one result set as the final result of the ATE. In contrast to the pessimistic approach of the verdict determination, the process of result selection follows a more optimistic approach. Here, the best result set is selected based on their classification. The best case describes result sets that are identified as *Passed*, in contrast to the worst case, which is a result set marked as *Failed*. In addition, test cases rated as *Inconclusive* can be improved by enriching the model in that way that the test case may pass later. Furthermore, test cases assessed as *Probably Passed* cannot be improved by adding information. Therefore, we define that the verdict *Probably Passed* represents a better case than the verdict *Inconclusive*. As a result, the verdicts are weighted as follows: $v_4 > v_3 > v_2 > v_1$.

$$\Sigma : O \to O_{best} := \{R_i - \exists R_i \forall R_j.\ i, j \in \{1, \ldots, |P_{lim}|\}$$
$$\text{such that } i \neq j \wedge M(R_i) \geq M(R_j) \wedge |R_i| < |R_j|\}$$

In general, the selection of the best result set as the final test report for the test case is performed in two steps. For this purpose, the function Σ is defined to select in the first step the happy cases $O_{best} \subseteq O$. Second, if $|O_{best}| > 1$ the result sets $R \in O_{best}$ which represents the path with the least steps is chosen as the test report. In context of the running example $O = O_{RE}$, $\Sigma(O_{RE}) = \{R_6\}$ with $M(R_6) = v_4$ which indicates that the test case presented as the running example passed.

Subsequently, the test report reflects the faults and characteristics derived by the ATE to give the modeler hints on possible causes. Therefore, our approach can be seen as Gray-Box Testing as detailed in Sect. 1.

4 Qualitative Evaluation and Critical Discussion

Following the introduction of basics and implementation of the Abstract Test Execution, the approach will be further evaluated qualitatively and critically discussed in the course of this chapter. At the beginning the evaluation of Hagemann et al. [10] should be mentioned, which has already been carried out in the context of the conference contribution. In the course of that evaluation, excerpts from the Automotive Light Control System, originally utilized by Peleska et al. [22], were used to demonstrate the proof of concept. There, a wide variety of defects were introduced into the model through a mutation analysis. Then test cases capable of detecting these defects were tested against the mutated system models using our approach. As a result, this demonstrated the ability of the approach to verify test cases against the system model in an abstract way. This was subsequently done for other parts of the system model, which supports the drawn picture. The same approach was applied to the Ceiling Speed Monitoring model of the University of Bremen, again showing the same possibilities and limitations [3].

In order to provide a meaningful extension of the previous findings on our approach to *Abstract Test Execution*, a qualitative evaluation is carried out. Here, the results gathered so far are compared to the state of the art and put in relation to the technical background of the approach. In order to be able to conduct such a discussion in a reasonable manner, a brief overview of the state of the art is given in advance, which should be seen in relation with the content of the section on related work.

In today's software development, different kinds of tests are performed depending on the applied development process and the desired level of integration of the software. Depending on the integration level, different knowledge bases are assumed and usually special techniques are used to derive possible test cases from development artifacts. The palette here ranges from black box to white box procedures. In order to execute such test cases, the SUT must be available in a (partially) executable version. Depending on the test level, concepts such as mocking or stubbing are often used to simulate system parts which are missing or lie outside the development context. In contrast to this, the concept of *Abstract Test Execution*, where only model artifacts are used to derive the test results, is used.

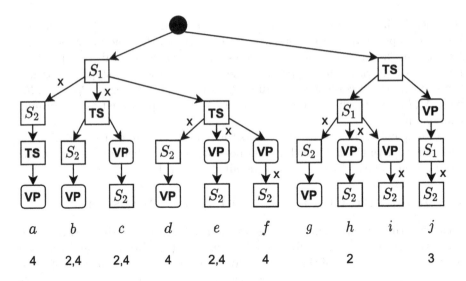

Fig. 9. Path space limited by rule one.

Based on the findings in Sect. 3, we identify that the limitation of path space by merging rules and subsequently their potential impact on the test report needs to be discussed. For better understanding, a path space is generated from the minimal System Model $Init \rightarrow [S_1] \xrightarrow{x} [S_2]$ and Test Model $Init \rightarrow [TS] \rightarrow (VP) \rightarrow End$. The System Model consists of the two system nodes S_1 and S_2 with the exception that S_2 is guarded by x. The Test Model includes the node TS as a Test Step and the node VP as a Verification Point. The representative and slightly limited tree of paths is shown in Fig. 9. It is derived by taking merging rule one into account. This fundamental tree of paths represents all cases that could come into play. The included paths can be identified by a letter attached to the end node of each path. In addition, paths that violate the remaining rules are flagged by the numerical identifier of the violated rule. Since the first rule guarantees the consistency of the test cases, the importance of this rule does not need to be discussed further.

The second rule is another approach to reduce the level of abstraction and to bring the approach of ATE more in line with classical testing approaches. Unlike rule one which focuses on the sequence of nodes, this rule focuses on the sequence of edges or guarded edges in particular. From the viewpoint of classical testing, stimuli applied to the system are used to trigger a change of the system state. In case of ATE, such stimuli are expressed as Test Steps. Furthermore, the change of system state is usually bound to conditions. The Test Steps are then used to fulfill the conditions bound to a specific system state to change the system state to that state. Such conditions are modeled by enriching edges of the System Model with instructions. Previously, we referred to such enriched edges as guarded transitions or Guards. Unguarded edges can therefore be ignored, since the change of system state is not bound to any condition. Subsequently, if a guarded edge is inserted before the Test Step that simulates stimuli required to satisfy the guard of the edge, the path can never be fulfilled as represented by the paths b and c. In addition, paths e and h exist where the guarded edge is inserted before the Verification Point VP. In this case, the paths are able to meet the requirements of the test cases, since instructions contained in guards generally cannot change the data flow. However, the paths g and i exists which are not excluded by appliance of rule two. As a result, the paths e and h can be excluded without harming the final result of ATE.

Since test cases in which a Verification Point can be fulfilled without the use of system nodes can be considered a bad test design, such test cases can be excluded. Structurally, this can be done by forced insertion of Verification Points after nodes of the System Model. For this purpose, rule three is conducted. The enforcement of this rule prevents verification points from being injected between the initial node and the first system node during merging process. Generally, this leads to the path space always being shortened by exactly one path. In case of the generic path space, the path j is therefore excluded.

The fourth and last merging rule excludes the most paths from the path space shown in Fig. 9, but may affect the outcome of the ATE as described in Sect. 3.4. In this context, this rule has the power to exclude six of the represented ten paths. In general, rule four is used to dictate the structure of segments. A segment consists of system nodes and Test Steps followed by a Verification Point. This rule forces test steps of a segment to be inserted before the system nodes of the segment. This results in the structure that a segment starts with Test Steps followed by system nodes and ends with a Verification Point. This change is generally not problematic and mimics a more natural approach of testing. However, if more than one guarded system node is included in the segment the analysis may inadvertently fail. We justify this rule with the abstract character of this approach and the resulting incompatibility with time-dependent system states. Since Test Steps simulate stimuli to trigger system changes that are inseparably linked to time aspects, the concept of the over-assignment of variables is introduced to overcome the incapability of temporal considerations. Here, variables can have more than one valid value during segment analysis as presented in Sect. 3. This solves the problem of temporal incompatibility, since the needed stimuli to solve a test case are delivered at the right time, but due to the uncertainty factor, test cases solved with the help of such variables are marked to maintain the pessimistic evaluation of the ATE approach.

In conclusion, the limited path space P_{lim} of the generic Test Model and the generic System Model holds the two paths g and h which underlines the possibility that the instruction of the Verification Point VP verifies either the system state S_1 or the system state S_2.

5   Related Work

In the context of test execution at model level, the execution of the modeled functionality itself plays a central role. This was originally applied in the engineering context and is known as Model-In-The-Loop Testing [24]. Furthermore, it is important to be able to manipulate the execution of the model with stimuli, as well as to verify the system state (internal or external). In literature, there are many ways of doing this, but there are some parts that differ significantly from our approach.

First, approaches are discussed that consider the model artifacts as input and convert the model into code for execution. For example, this is the basis for the simulation/execution of Matlab/Simulink models, which are therefore converted into C code [6,14]. The same applies to the approach of Anlauf et al., which is based on so-called Extensible Abstract State Machines [1]. In comparison to the approach presented, however, this type of execution is not applicable to other original models. Zentai et al. have implemented this in a similar way in the context of the MDA-oriented test methodology using the IBM Rhapsody tool and its simulation capabilities [29]. This mitigates the above mentioned problem of input models, but still requires the detour via code representation.

A similar variant for the execution of model artifacts is given by the Foundational Subset for UML (fUML), which represents a subset of UML that has been substantiated with clean semantics [18,20]. In particular, execution engines have been implemented for this modeling language, which no longer requires upstream translation into code artifacts [9]. This was implemented by Arnaud et al. and extended by more formal concepts like symbolic execution [2]. Similarly, Iftikhar et al. introduced a virtual machine for the execution of timed automata [12]. The disadvantages of such approaches are the same as those mentioned above.

In the context of execution engines, there are approaches that rely on model interpreters. In most cases, a internal model artifact is created for this purpose, which is derived from the input model. Within the MoMuT::UML project, for example, UML models are translated into Object Oriented Action Scripts (OOASs) for the purpose of mutation analysis, which in turn are animated by an interpreter [16]. The test cases are evaluated in this context by means of conformance checks on these representations. This evaluation is realized in particular by formal approaches, which in turn entails limitations.

In contrast to these approaches are the formal verification approaches, which are not the same as executing and testing a SUT, but have a similar goal. In particular, such approaches place special demands on the input models, which usually severely limits their applicability. Various model checking approaches have been presented for decades, but most of them are strongly optimized for the respective application context [4,11,12,17]. At this point, again, our presented approach is much more flexible and does not require the detailed knowledge of formal technologies.

6   Conclusion and Outlook

Within the scope of this work, we have presented a promising approach to the challenges initially displayed. Especially the ability to perform tests in early phases of model-centric software development represents a significant improvement. Based on the presented foundations regarding modeling and analysis-specific constructs, the concept of *Abstract Test Execution* was presented, which performs a comprehensive analysis of the System Model in the context of previously generated test cases. In particular, the concept behind the integrated evaluation of control and data flow properties was presented in detail. The results of this analysis can be compared to a classical test report. In contrast, the range of verdicts has been extended to explicitly represent novel evaluation results in the modeling context and to introduce no room for interpretation within the set of possible results. In the course of the discussion on the presented approach, the meaningfulness of the concept as well as its limitations were particularly emphasized.

At the same time, these limitations indicate possible starting points for improvements and extensions of the current approach. On the one hand, the approach could be extended by concepts that allow time considerations to be carried out on the basis of runtime estimates. For this purpose, however, the model has to be enriched with information or at least given access to data about execution times on the target platform or target technology used. However, this is in some ways contradictory to our overarching goal of applying the approach as early as possible in order to receive early and automated feedback.

On the other hand, the approach could be improved in such a way that not only a set of test cases is evaluated against the System Model, but a complete test model. From a technical point of view, this could result in a significant performance gain, since test sequences that appear in several test cases could be evaluated once.

An abstract view on the presented approach could be a possible development towards an automated decision support for model-centric software development approaches. Based on the collected test results of the *Abstract Test Execution*, this could for example include concrete suggestions for improving or extending the current model.

Acknowledgements. The research in this paper was funded by the German Federal Ministry for Economic Affairs and Energy under the Central Innovation Program for SMEs (ZIM), grant numbers 16KN044137.

References

1. Anlauff, M.: XASM-an extensible, component-based abstract state machines language. In: Gurevich, Y., Kutter, P.W., Odersky, M., Thiele, L. (eds.) ASM 2000. LNCS, vol. 1912, pp. 69–90. Springer, Heidelberg (2000). https://doi.org/10.1007/3-540-44518-8_6
2. Arnaud, M., Bannour, B., Cuccuru, A., Gaston, C., Gerard, S., Lapitre, A.: Timed symbolic testing framework for executable models using high-level scenarios. In: Boulanger, F., Krob, D., Morel, G., Roussel, J.-C. (eds.) Complex Systems Design & Management, pp. 269–282. Springer, Cham (2015). https://doi.org/10.1007/978-3-319-11617-4_19
3. Braunstein, C., et al.: Complete model-based equivalence class testing for the ETCS ceiling speed monitor. In: Merz, S., Pang, J. (eds.) ICFEM 2014. LNCS, vol. 8829, pp. 380–395. Springer, Cham (2014). https://doi.org/10.1007/978-3-319-11737-9_25

4. Cimatti, A., Clarke, E., Giunchiglia, F., Roveri, M.: NuSMV: a new symbolic model checker. Int. J. Softw. Tools Technol. Transf. **2**(4), 410–425 (2000)
5. Galin, D.: Software Quality Assurance: From Theory to Implementation. Pearson Education India (2004)
6. Gambarotta, A., Morini, M., Saletti, C.: Development of a model-based predictive controller for a heat distribution network. Energy Proc. **158**, 2896–2901 (2019)
7. GmbH, I.: radCase - Model-Driven Generation (2020). http://www.radcase.com/
8. Grossmann, J., Serbanescu, D.A., Schieferdecker, I.: Testing embedded real time systems with TTCN-3. In: ICST, pp. 81–90. IEEE Computer Society (2009)
9. Guermazi, S., Tatibouet, J., Cuccuru, A., Dhouib, S., Gérard, S., Seidewitz, E.: Executable modeling with fUML and alf in papyrus: tooling and experiments. Strategies **11**, 12 (2015)
10. Hagemann, N., Pröll, R., Bauer, B.: Towards abstract test execution in early stages of model-driven software development. In: Hammoudi, S., Pires, L.F., Selić, B. (eds.) Proceedings of the 8th International Conference on Model-Driven Engineering and Software Development - Volume 1: MODELSWARD, 25–27 February 2020, Valletta, Malta (2020). DOIurl10.5220/0008934802160226
11. Henzinger, T.A., Ho, P.-H., Wong-Toi, H.: HyTech: a model checker for hybrid systems. In: Grumberg, O. (ed.) CAV 1997. LNCS, vol. 1254, pp. 460–463. Springer, Heidelberg (1997). https://doi.org/10.1007/3-540-63166-6_48
12. Iftikhar, M.U., Lundberg, J., Weyns, D.: A model interpreter for timed automata. In: Margaria, T., Steffen, B. (eds.) ISoLA 2016. LNCS, vol. 9952, pp. 243–258. Springer, Cham (2016). https://doi.org/10.1007/978-3-319-47166-2_17
13. Jones, C.: Applied Software Measurement: Global Analysis of Productivity and Quality, 3rd edn. McGraw-Hill Education Group, New York (2008)
14. Khalesi, M.H., Salarieh, H., Foumani, M.S.: Dynamic modeling, control system design and MIL-HIL tests of an unmanned rotorcraft using novel low-cost flight control system. Iran. J. Sci. Technol. Trans. Mech. Eng. **44**, 707–726 (2020). https://doi.org/10.1007/s40997-019-00288-x
15. Kleppe, A.G., Warmer, J., Warmer, J.B., Bast, W.: MDA Explained: The Model Driven Architecture: Practice and Promise. Addison-Wesley Professional, Boston (2003)
16. Krenn, W., Schlick, R., Tiran, S., Aichernig, B., Jobstl, E., Brandl, H.: MoMuT: UML model-based mutation testing for UML. In: 2015 IEEE 8th International Conference on Software Testing, Verification and Validation (ICST), pp. 1–8. IEEE (2015)
17. Clarke, E., McMillan, K., Campos, S., Hartonas-Garmhausen, V.: Symbolic model checking. In: Alur, R., Henzinger, T.A. (eds.) CAV 1996. LNCS, vol. 1102, pp. 419–422. Springer, Heidelberg (1996). https://doi.org/10.1007/3-540-61474-5_93
18. Mellor, S.J., Mellor, S., Balcer, M.J.: Executable UML: A Foundation for Model-driven Architecture. Addison-Wesley Professional, Boston (2002)
19. OMG: OMG Systems Modeling Language (OMG SysML), Version 1.3 (2012). http://www.omg.org/spec/SysML/1.3/
20. OMG: About the Semantics of a Foundational Subset for Executable UML Models Specification Version 1.4 (2018). https://www.omg.org/spec/FUML/About-FUML/
21. (OMG), O.M.G.: UML Testing Profile 2 (UTP 2), Version 2.0, December 2018. https://www.omg.org/spec/UTP2/2.0/PDF

22. Peleska, J., et al.: A real-world benchmark model for testing concurrent real-time systems in the automotive domain. In: Wolff, B., Zaïdi, F. (eds.) ICTSS 2011. LNCS, vol. 7019, pp. 146–161. Springer, Heidelberg (2011). https://doi.org/10.1007/978-3-642-24580-0_11

23. Planning, S.: The economic impacts of inadequate infrastructure for software testing. National Institute of Standards and Technology (2002)

24. Plummer, A.R.: Model-in-the-loop testing. Proc. Inst. Mech. Eng. Part I: J. Syst. Control Eng. **220**(3), 183–199 (2006)

25. Pretschner, A., Philipps, J.: 10 methodological issues in model-based testing. In: Broy, M., Jonsson, B., Katoen, J.-P., Leucker, M., Pretschner, A. (eds.) Model-Based Testing of Reactive Systems. LNCS, vol. 3472, pp. 281–291. Springer, Heidelberg (2005). https://doi.org/10.1007/11498490_13

26. Pröll, R., Bauer, B.: A model-based test case management approach for integrated sets of domain-specific models. In: O'Conner, L., Feldt, R., Yoo, S. (eds.) Proceedings of the 2018 IEEE International Conference on Software Testing, Verification and Validation Workshops (ICSTW), ICSTW 2018, 9–13 April 2018, Västerås, Sweden (2018). https://doi.org/10.1109/icstw.2018.00048

27. Pröll, R., Rumpold, A., Bauer, B.: Applying integrated domain-specific modeling for multi-concerns development of complex systems. Commun. Comput. Inf. Sci. **880**, 247–271 (2018). https://doi.org/10.1007/978-3-319-94764-8_11

28. Rumpold, A., Pröll, R., Bauer, B.: A domain-aware framework for integrated model-based system analysis and design. In: Pires, L.F., Hammoudi, S., Selic, B. (eds.) Proceedings of the 5th International Conference on Model-Driven Engineering and Software Development, 19–21 February 2017, in Porto, Portugal (2017). https://doi.org/10.5220/0006206301570168

29. Scippacercola, F., Pietrantuono, R., Russo, S., Zentai, A.: Model-in-the-loop testing of a railway interlocking system. In: Desfray, P., Filipe, J., Hammoudi, S., Pires, L.F. (eds.) MODELSWARD 2015. CCIS, vol. 580, pp. 375–389. Springer, Cham (2015). https://doi.org/10.1007/978-3-319-27869-8_22

A Methodological Assistant for UML and SysML Use Case Diagrams

Erika Rizzo Aquino[1,2], Pierre de Saqui-Sannes[1(✉)],
and Rob A. Vingerhoeds[1]

[1] ISAE-SUPAERO, Université de Toulouse, Toulouse, France
`erika.rizzo-aquino@student.isae-supaero.fr`,
`{pdss,rob.vingerhoeds}@isae-supaero.fr`
[2] ITA, São José dos Campos, Brazil

Abstract. Use case driven analysis is the corner stone of software and systems modeling in UML and SysML, respectively. A use case diagram identifies the main functions to be offered by the system and showcases the interactions between in-system use cases and out-system users. Identifying and organizing use cases requires good abstraction skills. Therefore, many students and industry practitioners face methodological problems in writing good use cases. Many books and tutorials have addressed the subject. Nevertheless, integration of use case elaboration principles into a UML or SysML tool still remains an open issue. This paper proposes solutions and discusses implementation in a methodological assistant named UCCheck. The latter helps use case diagrams designers to rely on formalized rules and reuse of previous diagrams to create and review their use case diagrams. Implemented in Python, UCCheck is interfaced with the free SysML software TTool and with Cameo Systems Modeler, leaving doors open for other UML or SysML tools.

Keywords: SysML · UML · Use case diagram · Model design assistant

1 Introduction

Adoption of Model-Based Systems Engineering approaches is a challenging issue for systems and software manufacturers. Implementing a MBSE approach requires working on a triptych (language, tools, method). Ranging from formal methods to diagrammatic notations such as UML [28] and SysML [27], many papers have discussed model simulators, formal verification tools, and code generators. By contrast, little work has been published on tools that may assist UML and SysML diagrams designers in implementing a method.

Experience in teaching UML and SysML [9,24,37] has confirmed that modeling requires good abstraction skills. Considering traditional V life cycle, this statement particularly applies to analysis when the 'What the system should

First author acknowledges support from CAPES and Brafitec program.

S. Hammoudi et al. (Eds.): MODELSWARD 2020, CCIS 1361, pp. 298–322, 2021.
https://doi.org/10.1007/978-3-030-67445-8_13

do' question must be answered. The question remains unanswered as long as the high level functions and services to be offered by the system are not defined at the right abstraction level. This is a challenging issue for use case diagram designers.

The art of writing good use case diagrams has been discussed by many authors (see, *e.g.*, [2,6,9,14,21]). A use case diagram could be good from a syntactic semantic point of views in regards of its compliance with the UML or SysML standard. The soundness of use case may further be assessed in regards of methodological guidelines applied by the team in charge of elaborating the UML or SysML models. Use case diagrams additionally impact other diagrams, particularly sequence and activity diagrams that enable documenting use case using scenarios and a flow-chart fashion, respectively.

How to assist SysML and UML diagram designers in writing good use case diagrams is the subject of this paper. Contributions include a set of rules for writing good use cases, solutions for constructing use case diagrams relying on formalized rules and repositories of previously designed use case diagrams, and solutions for checking use case diagrams a posteriori. A methodological assistant named UCCheck [30] implements the proposals elaborated in this paper. UCCheck is coded in Python and interfaced with free software TTool [36] from Telecom Paris and Cameo Systems Modeler from Dassault Systems [4].

This paper extends [30] to provide the reader with a more exhaustive list of guidelines for use case diagram construction. This paper further details the structure of the methodological assistant, and provides a complete depiction of the functions implemented by UCCheck.

This paper is organized as follows. Section 2 identifies difficulties in writing good use case diagrams. Section 3 discusses the design and implementation of UCcheck. Section 4 discusses a case study. Section 5 surveys related work. Section 6 concludes the paper and outlines future work.

2   Design Guidelines for Use Case Diagrams

OMG (Object Management Group) and INCOSE (International Council on Systems Engineering) have jointly defined SysML, a System Modelling Language that is now an international standard at OMG [27] and one of the pillars of Model-Based Systems Engineering (MBSE). The SysML standard at OMG defines a notation, not the way of using it, leaving doors open for application to various domains, *e.g.* real-time systems, and to the methods or processes practitioners of these application domains are familiar with.

The way of using SysML has therefore regularly questioned in the literature. Surveying all contributions goes beyond the scope of this paper, which focuses discussion on use case diagrams. The latter are the corner stone of use case driven analysis, a fundamental step in the method associated with UML and SysML.

Despite of its early introduction in the UML standard [28], use case diagrams have often remained misunderstood, as testimonied by teaching experiences [24].

This is partly not surprising. Unlike state machines diagrams that can be animated by a simulator and therefore debugged, use case diagrams are indeed developed in context of uncertainty. UML and SysML tools usually check use case diagrams against elementary syntax errors but do not supply any assistance for appreciating the abstraction level and pertinence of the functions modeled by the use cases. Nor these UML and SysML tools help appreciating the relevance of associations linking pairs of use cases or associations linking use cases to actors modeling the environment of the system.

The need therefore exists for guidelines and tool assistance. These issues are discussed by the remainder of the paper.

2.1   Use Case Diagrams

A SysML (resp. UML) use case diagram identifies the main functions and services to be offered by a system (resp. a piece of software). A use case defines the interactions between a system (resp. software) to be developed and a role external to that system (a human or another external system). Use case analysis ([19]) plays an important role in requirement analysis in modern software and systems engineering.

A box defines the boundary of the system or software, and names it. On Fig. 1 the system is named **Real-Time System Controller**. The ellipses depict the use cases that contain the names of the functions or services to be offered. On Fig. 1, **Perform Computation** is a use case.

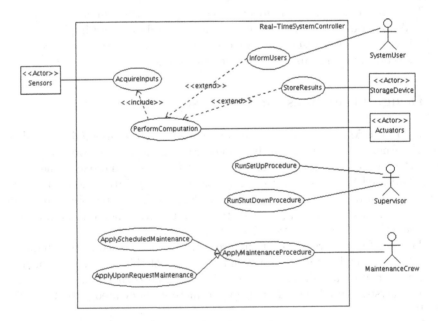

Fig. 1. Source [30]: Use Case Diagram for real-time systems.

A use case diagram defines relations between pairs of use cases. On Fig. 1, the `extend` relation makes `InformUsers` and `StoreResults` an option of `PerformComputation`. The `include` relation from `PerfomComputation` to `AcquireInputs` states each computation demands to acquire values from sensors.

A use case diagram also shows the system or software interacts with its environment, the latter being depicted by a set of actors. On Fig. 1, a link connects use case `AcquireInputs` to actor `Sensors`.

2.2   Rules and Guidelines for SysML/UML Use Case Diagrams

This section summarizes the rules and guidelines that will be addressed by the methodological assistant.

Meaning of Actors and Use Cases. Actors and use cases should respect the following semantic rules [16, 22, 28]:

- Actors represent a particular role that interacts with the system, not a specific physical entity. Thus, a physical instance can play multiple roles.
- Actors must belong to the external environment, that is, they cannot be part of the system being developed.
- Use cases must represent a high-level functionality, defined as a function that produces an observable result to the actor.
- Use cases should state the functions performed by the system, not the functions performed by the actors.

Names of Actors and Use Cases. According to SySML/UML specification, actors and use cases names must obey the following characteristics [28]:

- Names must start with a capital letter.
- Names must be unique and not duplicated in the diagram.
- Actors name must contain a common noun since they represent roles.
- Use cases name must start with a verb since they represent functionalities.

Layout. To maintain consistency with the definitions presented in Sect. 2.2, the layout and position of the elements on the diagram must observe the following principles [8, 16, 23]:

- The diagram should have a border to distinguish what is part of the system and what is not.
- Actors must be positioned outside the border, as they are external to the systems.
- Use cases must be positioned inside the border, as they represent functions performed by the system.
- Primary actors, whose goals are directly fulfilled by the system, should be positioned to the left of the border.
- Secondary actors, who support the system or who indirectly benefit from it, should be positioned to the right.

Relationships Between Elements. Elements are linked by relationships, which can be of four types: association, include, extend and generalization. Globally, relations in the diagram must comply with the subsequent rules [18, 28]:

- There cannot be isolated elements in the diagram.
- Elements cannot be related to themselves, that is, self relationships are not allowed.
- Between two elements, there must be only one relation, that is, double relationships are not allowed.
- Each relationship can only connect elements of a certain type:
  - Association relationship can only be defined between one actor and one use case.
  - Include and Extend relationships can only be defined between two use cases.
  - Generalization can be defined between two actors or between two use cases.
- Generalization must be acyclical, irreflexive and transitive.

Meaning of Relationships. In order to model a correct use case diagram, it is essential to properly understand the difference in meaning of the three relationships that can occur between two use cases [28]:

- Include relationships link one base use case, called including use case, to an included use case. The latter represents part of the behavior of the base use case. Consequently, the functionality expressed by the base use case always needs the functionality of the included use case to happen.
- Extend relationships links one extending use case to an extended use case. The former represents an additional behavior of the extend use case, that is necessary under certain conditions. Therefore, the extended functionality can happen without the extending one.
- Generalization relationships links one general use case to generalized use cases. The latter inherit all the behavior of the general use case and is expanded by supplementary information. The additions express a way that the base functionality can be performed.

Unnecessary Relationships. Due to the transitive nature of the relationships between use cases and of the generalization between actors, one should be careful not to add unnecessary relationships to the diagram. This increases the diagram's complexity and the difficulty of understanding. With respect to unnecessary relations, guidelines are as follows: [18].

- An actor that is associated to a use case does not need to be associated to its refined use cases (included, extending or generalized). The communication is implicitly stated.

- Based on previous item, if an actor is associated to all refined use cases of a base use case, it is recommended to associate the actor to the base functionality instead.
- A generalized actor does not need to be associated to the use cases already linked to the general actor from whom he inherits his behavior.

Warning Patterns. Holt [16] presents three patterns that may indicate incompleteness or incorrectness in a use case diagram and should be observed carefully.

- An actor associated to use cases may be too high level, perhaps representing multiple rules. It is suggested to decompose its roles and replace it with the new actor.
- Two actors associated to the same set of use cases may be representing the same interaction with the system. Perhaps, specific instances of stakeholders were used. If this is the case, they must be replaced by generic roles.
- A use case associated to all actors may be too high level, representing on its own the whole functionality of the system. It is suggested to decompose it into other use cases.

Coherence. One of the benefits of the model-centric approach is the ability to keep a traceability across the different levels of abstraction of a model, from the requirements to the final product. The traceability is ensured with coherence rules. For the use case diagram, the following has to be observed [16]:

- Each use case must be documented by at least one associated scenario, either by means of a textual description, a sequence diagram or an activity diagram.

Combining the previous rule with the possible relationships between use cases, the following can be proposed:

- Included use cases should participate in all sequence and activity diagrams used to document the including use case, since they represent part of the behavior.
- Extending use cases, on the other, have an optional behavior. Therefore, there must be at least one scenario for the extended use case where conditions are not satisfied, and the extending use case will not take part in.
- Refined use cases (included, extending or generalized) not be documented without their based use cases.

2.3 Generic Use Case Diagram

To create a generic use case diagram for a large variety of systems, one needs to keep in mind that:

- A system has a nominal behavior.
- A system may enter downgraded modes.

– A system must run a set up procedure before starting its execution.
– A system must run a shutdown procedure before being moved or updated, and more generally maintained and serviced.
– Maintenance is a normal concern when one is designing a system.

Relying on previous principles, Fig. 1 depicts a generic use case diagram for a real-time system controller that receives inputs from sensors and triggers output devices, part of the latter being in charge of informing the user and the supervisor of the system.

The use case diagram in Fig. 1 depicts the set-up, shutdown and maintenance phases that are usually concealed by the use case diagrams presented in papers or books addressing real-time systems modeling. One may note that Fig. 1 does not mention degraded modes: they will be addressed in sequence or activity diagrams associated with the use case diagrams. These documentation-purpose sequence and activity diagrams are not presented in this paper. Discussion is limited on use case diagrams for themselves.

2.4 Difficulties for Beginners

SysML textbooks and tutorials usually recommend a four-step process to create a use case diagram:

1. Define the boundary of the system;
2. Identify the actors as external entities that interact with the system;
3. Identify the use cases from the actors' goals;
4. Establish the connections between actors and use cases, and set up relations between pairs of use cases.

This methodology is usually explained through an example for a simple system [38]. Such explanations help beginners to see clearer, but often when in front of a screen or in front of a white piece of paper, beginners have difficulties to get things started. Studies conducted with students allowed to identify difficulties with choosing the right type of relationship, defining the direction of the `extend` relationship and proper naming of elements [6,16,21]. These results were confirmed by our own experience.

Maintaining the use cases at the right level and not confusing high-level functions and elementary actions is a major difficulty. When thinking of a hot drink distribution system, for example. One may think of high-level functions such as 'selection of hot drink' with lower-level functions such as 'establish contact with the credit card server at the company'. Indeed such a confusion might lead to an unbalanced design of the system, on one hand looking at main functions and at the other hand looking at implementation details. The structure of the use case diagram induces functional decomposition and consequent insertion of low-level functions that do not generate value for the actors [16].

Another important problem for the students is to appreciate what is supposed to be in the box and what is supposed to be outside of the box (*i.e.* what is part of the system to be developed and what is an external role). Thinking again of the hot drink distribution system, typically the preparation of a hot drink may be part of the design, but the way the credit card company accepts or not the requested payment is not. This notion has shown to be a real blocking point, since students sometimes feel that they need to be able to design all in the same diagram. This point is related to the basics of design, but the abstraction level may pose problems of understanding, in particular if different subsystems are developed. In such cases, a beginner may mix up internal and external roles.

Other common beginners' errors may include the absence of verbs in use case names and the use of proper names for actors rather than a common name representing a role.

With experience, the identification of use cases becomes easier as the designer can rely on past models. One way therefore to help beginners is to provide various examples of use case diagrams. However, the number of examples needed to cover multiple domains may be very large. A better solution is to provide generic diagrams, which can be adapted to similar systems. These diagrams can be designed by experts based on experience, and then be provided to beginners to serve as guides. An assistant for use case diagrams should manage a repository of example diagrams, helping to retrieve and customize them. In addition, an assistant for use case diagrams should not only guide the identification of actors and use cases, but also verify the diagram compliance with SysML/UML syntax or semantics, and systems engineering guidelines.

3 Methodological Assistant

3.1 Overview

This section describes the two assistance strategies that were explored in order to help the design of better use case diagrams.

The first proposition is named *a posteriori*, since it focuses on improving use case diagrams previously designed in an external SysML modeling tool. The *a posteriori* assistant is built onto the *verification* module. It checks diagram compliance with SysML/UML rules and modelling guidelines. In addition to the basic checks typical of Type Checkers, the assistant manages to address semantic compliance through a user interface. In other words, the assistance helps the user to decide whether the modeled elements comply with SysML definitions or not. The goal was to address the most common errors committed by SysML practitioners, in particular by beginners.

The *a posteriori* assistant helps to reinforce SysML/UML concepts and improves an previously made diagram. However, it does not address difficulties that arise when creating a diagram from scratch. One of the main difficulties for beginners is to identify the actors and use cases at a good level of abstraction, that is, use cases that provide value to actors.

The second proposition, named *a priori*, supports the creation of correct use case diagrams. The *a priori* assistant attempts to reproduce the analogical reasoning employed by experienced system architects. The user departs from a generic diagram, created by experts, and only has to identify the corresponding elements for a particular system. The program is built onto the *creation* module and uses continuous checking to prevent errors during design. Additionally, the *insertion* module was developed to store the generic diagrams in a database.

The methodological assistant is developed using Python and the `Tkinter` library for user interfaces. The rest of this section details the different modules of the tool, where each module corresponds to a specialized user interface. Figure 2 summarizes the main steps of each module and the common functionalities between them.

3.2 Verification Module

The *Verification* module takes a selected use case diagram in XML format. It identifies its elements and verifies them against SysML rules and guidelines.

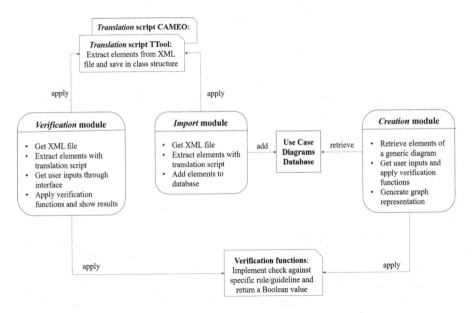

Fig. 2. Structure of the methodological assistant.

A first procedure before analysis is to extract the diagram elements from the XML file and store the relevant information in an object-oriented structure. In the structure conceived, the diagram is represented as a class that possesses components and connectors. Components have as attribute: name, type and position in the diagram, given by Cartesian coordinates. Actors and use cases, for example, are represented as components. Connectors, on the other hand, have name, type and references to each one of the two components being linked. They represent association, include, extend and generalization relationships. The name of the diagrams in the model and their respective types is also extracted. They will be used to ask the user about the linkage between use cases and scenarios.

The objective of the pre-processing step is to achieve independence from the modelling tool. Up to now, the module accepts XML files generated by two modeling tools: TTool [36], a free software developed by Telecom Paris, and CAMEO Systems Modeler [4], a tool developed by NoMagix, now a subsidiary of Dassault Systèmes. To extend the assistant to a new SysML/UML, one needs only to write the script that translates the XML file to the class structure.

Rules and guidelines addressed by the *verification* module are summarized in Sect. 2.2. Some of the aforementioned items can be verified automatically using only the information available in the diagram and in Python libraries. Each of these points was addressed by its proper function. Other rules require extra user information, which is requested through an interface. The interface is also used to exhibit the analysis results and improvement suggestions. The verification strategy for each group is detailed below.

Initial checks of actors and use cases names are performed automatically by the assistant through Python build-in string functions. These include verifying that names begin with capital letters and that they do not appear more than once in the same diagram.

With the help of Python libraries for natural language processing, it is possible to inspect the grammatical class of elements names. Actors should be named by common nouns. Use cases should start with a verb. The possible word class is obtained through `nltk` library, that uses `Wordnet` lexical database as reference. For actors' names, only the last word is analyzed, since we suppose that the others are qualifiers. Besides, this procedure helps to identify the possible use of proper nouns to nominate actors. Generally, these words will not be found in the `Wordnet` database.

Furthermore, the lexical database can be exploited to evaluate the semantic uniqueness of the actors' names. First, the assistant shows the possible definitions offered by the library for each actor's last word. Then, the user selects the most appropriate one. Finally, the assistant calculates the semantic closeness of the definitions though the Leacock-Chodorow similarity function. Hence, it is possible to warn about the presence of actors who perform the same role, or similar roles, even if their names are not identical.

Only with the information available in the diagram, it is not possible to verify if actors and use cases follow the meaning expected by the modeling language, that is, whether actors represent external roles and use cases represent high-level functions of the system. These points require external user confirmation through checkbox on the interface. Although prone to errors, the questions encourage user reasoning and reinforce SysML language concepts.

Likewise, initial checks on relationships structure is done automatically only with the information available in the diagram. These include detection of isolated elements, self/double relations, type improperness, cyclic dependence (suggest unnecessary relationships) and the mentioned warning patterns. The verification functions exploit the similarity between a use case diagram and a graph. It thus becomes possible to employ `network`, a Python library to analyze graphs and networks, to identify cycles and obtain the descendants of a certain node.

The semantic check of the relationships is also user-dependent. The strategy consists in asking the user what idea he/she wanted to convey with the relationship. For each pair of refined use case to base use case, the user is asked if the refined one is needed every time the base use case happens, is optional or is a specialization, or type, of the base use case. These ideas correspond respectively to the include, extend and generalization relationship. The assistant compares the user's response with the type used and warns in the event of a mismatch. The rationale of the proposed strategy is to not use directly the SysML/UML nomenclature, which poses problems for beginners. Instead, the questions explore to idea behind the relationship type, which is less prone to confusion and helps to reinforce nomenclature learning.

The layout inspection follows a similar approach. By comparing the position values in Cartesian coordinates, it is possible to automatically check if actors and use cases are positioned correctly in relation to the border. However, aspects related to meaning, to mention the positioning of primary or secondary actors, require asking the user what the classification of each actor is. The assistant then checks the consistency between the position and the classification and warns in case of mismatch.

Lastly, the coherence rules state that, for a complete model, each use case must be documented in at least one scenario. Automatically, it is possible to identify the other diagrams available in the model. Then, the user is required to link the use case to the corresponding documentation, which can be a sequence diagram, an activity diagram or a textual description. Additionally, the connection must be coherent with the relations between pairs of use cases. For example, an included use case should appear in all the scenarios of the including use case, because there is a necessary relation between the two. On the other hand, an extended use case should only appear in some specific scenarios. Together, these checks reinforce the completeness of the model and the meaning of the relationships between use cases.

In general, the points that demand user information are those that analyze semantic aspects. The assistant considers the user's responses to update the status of each check, so that the user can know what remains to be verified and where the error is. The details of the interface and the observations made by the assistant are presented through a case study in Sect. 4.1.

3.3 Import Module

The *Import* module receives a use case diagram in XML format and stores its elements into a relational database. First, the same pre-processing script described in Sect. 3.2 is applied to interpret the XML file. Then, the queries to add new diagrams to the database are based on the class structure, and thus inherit the modeling tool independence. Similarly to Sect. 3.2, the module accepts, by now, files from TTool and from CAMEO Systems Modeler. Any new transcription script will be compatible with both the *Verification* module and the *Insertion* module.

A graphical interface asks the user whether the inserted files are references or examples. A reference is defined as a general diagram for a group of similar systems and can be used to guide the conception of new diagrams. An example is a diagram for a specific system, which must be associated with the name of a general group.

The Python library `sqlite3` is used to build the database and execute queries. The communication with the database uses the Structured Query Language (SQL). The queries are used to insert a new file to the database, and to recovers its elements when requested. Moreover, the benefits of working with database are scalability, *i.e.* a relation database is able to handle a large number of diagrams, and the opportunity to execute more complex queries. For instance, it is easy to state queries to find diagrams that contain certain actors or use cases.

3.4   Creation Module

The *Creation* module guides the user on the identification of actors, use cases and relationships based on a reference use case diagram chosen from the database. A graph is then used to represent the new diagram designed.

In the first place, the user must select a reference diagram from the database. To help with the selection, the interface displays the name of the example systems stored in the database and associated with each generic group.

The assistant automatically retrieves the elements (actors and use cases) in the reference diagram. After that, the user must choose which elements he/she wants to reuse and shall rename them according to the system being modeled. The new name is inputted in an entry widget and checked against the naming conventions detailed in Sect. 3.2 before being accepted.

One actor in the reference diagram can give rise to multiple actors in the new diagram. In addition, the user can enter other actors that he/she considers not to be on the suggestion list. Regarding use cases, each suggestion can only generate one new element. In particular, the use case suggestion list is optimized based on to the chosen actors. Only use cases that communicate with at least one of the selected actors are suggested to the user.

After actors and use cases identification, the program recovers the existing relationships in the reference diagram between the selected elements. Then, it depicts a graph representation of the designed diagram, with its elements and connections. The user may add other connections manually, and the figure will be automatically refreshed. Only relationships that respect the rules detailed in Sect. 3.2 are allowed by the assistant.

Next to the graph representation, the assistant points out improvement suggestions and errors to be revised. This may happen when an element is created without referencing any other in the diagram. As a consequence, no relationship may be automatically recovered. The wizard shall warn isolation and request manual connection. Another example occurs when the assistant identifies two actors associated with the same group of use cases. It then asks whether they cannot be grouped into one common general actor.

4   Case Study

4.1   A Posteriori Assistance

In this section, the functionalities and benefits of the verification module are illustrated through a case study for an agricultural drone. The first version of its use case diagram, which is submitted for examination by the module, is shown in Fig. 3. It contains purpose-made errors that will by identified by the assistant.

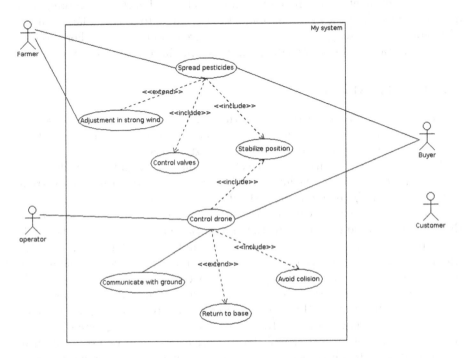

Fig. 3. Source [30] - Initial use case diagram for an agricultural drone.

Figure 3 depicts a system with two main functions: control drone and spread pesticides. These main use cases are refined with extending and included use cases. The actor Buyer is interested in the two main functions. The actor Farmer is interested in pesticide application. The actor operator is responsible for controlling the drone. An actor named Customer can be seen isolated in the diagram.

To initiate the verification process, the first step is to select the XML file that contains the diagram to be analyzed. Only files in which the assistant was able to identify a use case diagram are accepted. It will then extract the relevant elements. In the case of multiple use case diagrams in the model, only one can be checked at once. Section 3.2 explains how to extend the assistant for unsupported modelling tools.

The interface of the verification assistant is organized into tabs, as shown in Fig. 4, each tab for one group of rules. The **General** tab overviews the use case diagram and the points to be verified. These points are structured in a checklist that delineates the step-by-step verification and helps to quickly locate the mistake. Additionally, a table summarizes the quantities of each element in the diagram, among actors, use cases and relationships. This table helps the user the level of abstraction of the diagram. Having more than 20 use cases may indicate the representation of too low-level functions.

The next two tabs are focused on actors and use cases. Figure 4 depicts the interface designed to collect user information and show the results of the actor's checks. Initial checks mentioned at Sect. 3.2 are performed automatically by the assistant and non-conformities are indicated with **X marks**. The checkboxes on the right are used to ask the user if the elements comply with the language definition – actors should represent external roles and use cases should express high-level functions that produce an observable result to an actor. The assistant warns if one of the checkboxes is not selected. Finally, the **Check correlation** button launches the semantic correlation analysis based on **Wordnet** database. The use case check tab follows a similar structure, without the correlation functionality.

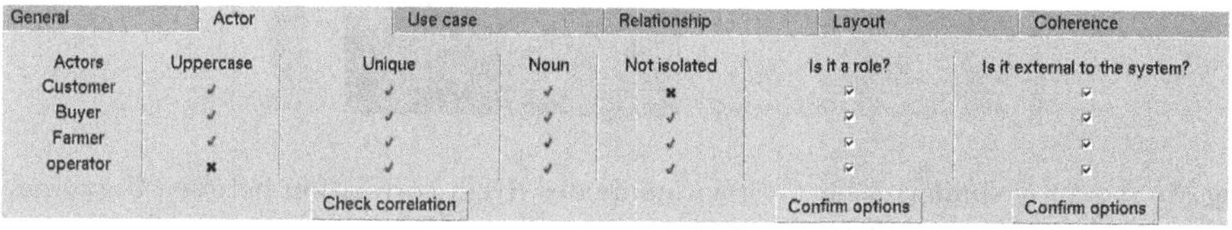

General	Actor	Use case		Relationship	Layout	Coherence
Actors	Uppercase	Unique	Noun	Not isolated	Is it a role?	Is it external to the system?
Customer	✓	✓	✓	✗	☑	☑
Buyer	✓	✓	✓	✓	☑	☑
Farmer	✓	✓	✓	✓	☑	☑
operator	✗	✓	✓	✓	☑	☑
		Check correlation			Confirm options	Confirm options

Fig. 4. Source [30]: Extract of *Actor* Tab for verifying the name and meaning of the actors.

For our case study, it was possible to identify syntactical errors. For instance, actor **operator** does not start with a capital letter. Further, use case **Adjustment in strong wind** must be rephrased with the verb **Adjust**. The program also pointed out that the actor **Customer** is isolated in the diagram.

Besides, through answering the questions, the user noticed some incorrect use cases: **Control valves** was too low-level and could be removed, and **Control drone** was in the point of view of the user and should be rewritten as the real function performed by the drone, which is **Change direction by remote control**. An interface with guided questions allows the assistant to go beyond a type checker.

The result of the semantic analysis of actors' names is presented through a heatmap and colors should be interpreted qualitatively. The more intense the color, the more similar the two words. Results in the principal diagonal are not relevant, because they represent the correlation of a word to itself. For our case study, a high correlation is seen between the names **Customer** and **Buyer** in Fig. 5. Since the actor **Customer** is also isolated, one could hypothesize that the user changed the name of actor from Customer to Buyer but forgot to delete the old one. In this case, the correction applied is to remove the isolated actor from the diagram. However, in other situations, the problem may be a missing relationship. The user must decide the appropriate actions to be taken, supported by the assistant's information.

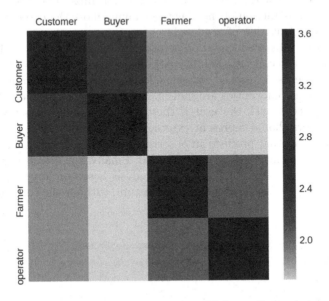

Fig. 5. Semantic similarity between actors names. High correlation between Customer and Buyer indicate that they may represent the same role.

The Relationships tab addresses the correctness of the relationships between elements of the use case diagram. It is possible to automatically verify some basic properties, such as no double linkage between the same pair of elements, no cycles, and correct type of elements for each type of relationship (for example, an association can only be defined between one actors and one use case). These checks guarantee no relationship was left unintentionally and enable further verification.

For our case study, it was identified the incorrect use of an association to link two use cases. This relation needs to be changed to either an include, an extend or a generalization relationship - the only possibilities between use cases. The user chooses to change the association to an include relationship. Then, he/she must correct the diagram on the modeling tool and resubmit the new XML file to the assistant.

The correctness of the basic properties allows verifying whether the type of relationships between use cases agrees with the desired meaning. The interface designed for this analysis is portrayed in Fig. 6. Each relationship is written from the main use case to the refined use case. For each pair, the user must answer whether it is a necessary, an optional or a specialization relation, and the assistant warns in case the answer does not correspond respectively to `include`, `extend` or `generalization` relationship in the diagram. The user is also asked if the relation is written in the correct direction or not, that is, from the broad one to the specific one. If the user identifies that the use cases names do not follow the desired order, it implies that the corresponding relationship was drawn in the wrong direction.

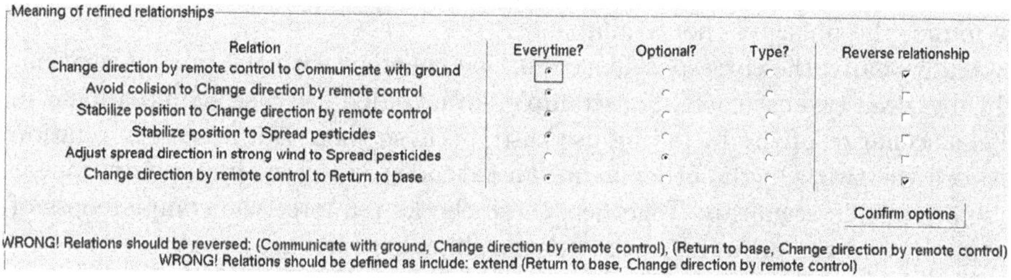

Relation	Everytime?	Optional?	Type?	Reverse relationship
Change direction by remote control to Communicate with ground				
Avoid colision to Change direction by remote control				
Stabilize position to Change direction by remote control				
Stabilize position to Spread pesticides				
Adjust spread direction in strong wind to Spread pesticides				
Change direction by remote control to Return to base				

Confirm options

WRONG! Relations should be reversed: (Communicate with ground, Change direction by remote control), (Return to base, Change direction by remote control)
WRONG! Relations should be defined as include: extend (Return to base, Change direction by remote control)

Fig. 6. Source [30]: Extract of *Relationships* Tab for verifying connection properties.

For the diagram in Fig. 3, the user identifies two reverse relations, and one incorrect meaning: the use case `Return to base` should be rewritten to represent an optional action, performed only in case of bad weather conditions. With the right set of questions, the assistant reinforces inspection on commonly misunderstood points.

Furthermore, the tool contributes for a cleaner diagram by identifying automatically the unnecessary relations described in Sect. 2.2. No unnecessary relationship was found in our case study.

Finally, by analyzing relationships, the assistant may identify the warning patterns explained in Sect. 2.2. Actors and use cases that are connected to all elements may be too high-level. Actors that are associated to the same set of use cases may be redundant, which means they represent similar roles.

For our case study, the assistant identified that actor `Buyer` is a too high-level one. This means that either the diagram conveys the point of view of `Buyer` and the latter should not appear, or that `Buyer` represents multiple roles and should be decomposed, or that some use case is missing. A decomposition of actor `Buyer` would lead to actors that are either similar to `Farmer` or to `Operator`, in the sense that they would be connected to the same set of use cases. Thus, the user finds out that actor `Buyer` actually combines two roles already in the diagram and can be removed.

The `layout` tab checks for the presence of a border. Moreover, it verifies whether the actors are positioned according to categorization into primary actors, whose goal is fulfilled by the system, and secondary actors, who support the system. Although this actors' classification is not a language standard, it is a common practice among SysML/UML community that conveys additional information. This classification requires user input: for each actor, the user must select whether they are primary or secondary actors. No error was identified for our case study.

The `coherence` tab certifies that each use case is documented by at least one scenario. This is accomplished by asking the user to associate each use case to the corresponding detailed description, which can be done through a textual description, a sequence diagram or an activity diagram. The names of the sequence and activity diagrams comprised in the same XML file of the use case diagram are retrieved automatically by the assistant. When no diagrams are found, the linkage is not available.

Additionally, the correspondence must be coherent with the type of relationships between two use cases. For example, an included use case should appear in all the scenarios of the including use case, because there is a necessary relation between the two. On the other hand, an extended use case should only appear in some specific scenarios. Together, these checks reinforce the completeness of the model and the meaning of the relationships between use cases.

In summary, the case study demonstrated the assistant's ability to improve the diagram. Syntactical errors are fixed and unnecessary relationships are removed. The meaning of actors, use cases and relationships are reinforced through the questions proposed by the tool. The warning patterns (one element related to all the others, and actors associated to the same use cases) contribute to identify possible missing elements or too high-level and unnecessary ones. Finally, the coherence matching helps to ensure that each use case is documented in at least one scenario.

One limitation of the *verification* module is the dependence on user's inputs, which may be not correct. Further work should explore how to automate the user-dependent checks. One idea is to use information from other diagrams. For instance, the context diagram could be used to verify whether an actor is an external entity to the system. Analysis of sequence diagrams could be used to verify association between actors and use cases. Another research axis consists in employing artificial intelligence techniques, notably natural language processing, to analyze semantic compliance. For instance, some words may identify the optional character of extending use cases.

4.2   A Priori Assistance

The functionalities of the creation assistant and its potential benefits for beginners will be demonstrated through a case study for a mobile phone camera. This system will use as a starting point the generic use case diagram for real-time systems, shown in Fig. 1.

The first step in the creation module consists in filling up basic information about the model (author, date and system's name) and choosing the use case diagram to use as reference. The generic diagram for real-time systems was previously inserted into the database through the `insertion` module.

The user proceeds to actor identification using the interface presented in Fig. 7. The list of suggestions corresponds to the actors in the reference diagram. Based on the suggestions, the user must identify the corresponding actors in the context of the system being modeled and name them accordingly. The given name must start with a capital letter, be unique and contain a common noun.

To insert a new actor to the diagram, the user first selects one actor from the suggestion list; then, he/she gives a new name appropriate to the context and clicks on "Add actor" button; when the button is pressed, the assistant checks the name against naming rules before accepting it. The user is informed of the error in case of noncompliance.

For a cellphone camera, the following actors are identified: **Touch Screen** takes the role of the sensor that receives capture order and triggers the "Take photograph" functionality; in its turn, the "Take photograph" function is executed by the **Camera Module**, which corresponds to the actuator. Two storage devices are possible: the cellphone's **Internal Memory** and **External Memory**. The user of the system plays the role of taking and visualizing the photo: it will be called **Photographer**. The supervisor performs the role of starting and closing the application and will be identified as the **Cellphone Owner**. Often, these two different roles are performed by the same person in the physical world. No maintenance actor was added, since it is not of interest to the part of the system being conceived.

Having a list of suggestions from a generic use case diagram simplifies actor identification, by transforming it to an analogy exercise, and helps to achieve diagram completeness. By combining insertion with a verification procedure, the assistant guarantees the syntactic correctness of actors' names.

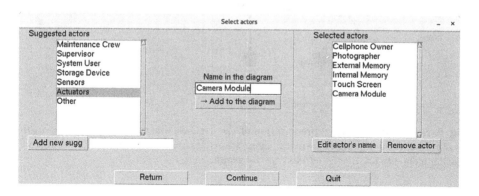

Fig. 7. Source [30]: Selecting actors relying on a generic diagram.

Next, the user proceeds to use case identification. The process is similar to that used for actors, except that each suggestion only derives one use case. For each suggested use case, the user must choose whether or not to add it to the diagram, and by what name. The name must start with capital letter, be unique and start with a verb. The suggestion list is optimized based on the actors added. In our case study, since no maintenance actor was chosen, the use cases related to maintenance will not be suggested to the user.

For the cellphone camera system, the following adaptations were made. The use case Run Set Up Procedure became Open Camera App. Similarly, Run Shut Down Procedure became Close Camera App. The use case Acquire Inputs was adapted to Get image, Perform Computation to Take Photograph, Inform Users to Show Image and, lastly, Store Results became Store Photo.

Automatically, the program retrieves the existing relationships in the reference file and draws a graph corresponding to the new diagram. Blue nodes represent actors, red nodes represent use cases, and relationships are given by edges. Next to the graph, the assistant displays errors and suggestions for possible improvements, such as isolated elements or too high-level ones, according to the warning patterns in Sect. 2.2. Figure 8 exhibits the use case diagram representation generated by the assistant for the case study.

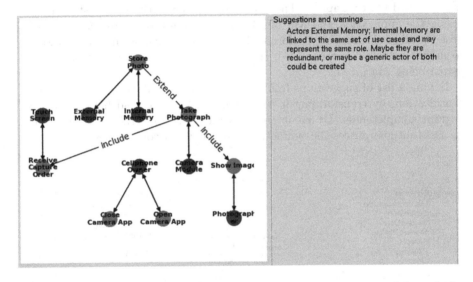

Fig. 8. Source [30]: Graph representation of the use case diagram created through the assistance for the cellphone camera. Suggestions for improvements and warnings of missing elements are displayed next to the graph.

Relationships may be managed through three tables: the first one for relations between actors, the second one for relations between use cases, and the third one for associations between actors and use cases. The tables may be understood as matrices that display all the possible pairs of elements of the comprised types.

For the first two, the rows represent the main elements (base use case or general actor) and the columns, the refined ones. The cell corresponding to the intersection of two elements stores the type of relationship between them. For example, if there is an extension relationship between two use cases, the cell whose row corresponds to the extended use case (base one) and whose column corresponds to the extending use case stores the value *is extended by*, and the reciprocal cell stores the value *extends*. Thus, one can read the table from rows to columns, e.g. *the base use case is extended by the extending use case*. For the association table, actors are listed in the rows, and use cases in the columns. The association relationship is indicated by a checkbox.

These tables are automatically semi-filled by the assistant based on the existing relationships in the reference diagram. The user should criticize the relationships set out and modify them according to the system in consideration. For example, functions that are optional for some real-time systems may be systematically executed in particular ones. Then, the user manually changes from `extend` to `include` relationship. For a cellphone camera, the use case `Show image` will always happen, even if for other types of cameras it may be optional.

The facilities offered by the creation assistant includes guiding identification of actors and use cases through analogical reasoning, and minimizing deviations from SysML/UML rules by means of on-going checking. Nonetheless, a drawback of the procedure is to rely on the existence of a generic diagram. Future work may address how to obtain generic diagrams automatically from a series of example diagrams using case-based reasoning and ontologies.

Up to now, it is not possible to export the graph representation of the use case diagram to an XML file compatible with modelling tools due to the positioning problem. The library used to build the graph applies an automatic positioning algorithm to improve readability. However, an automatic layout of use case diagrams, compliant with SysML/UML standards, is a complex problem and is a research subject on its own [12].

5   Related Work

5.1   Experiences with Use Case Diagrams

In [24], Moisan and Rigault discuss an experience in teaching object-oriented modeling and UML in academia and industry. The authors identify a risk with use cases: to go too far in the functional decomposition, entering into low level system details, forgetting about the external actors. In [9], Costain and McKenna report difficulties encountered by their students in using use case diagrams. First identified difficulty is possible confusion between `include` and `extend` relations. Main problems are related with actors: distinguishing between primary and secondary actors, determining the associations between actors and use cases, and determining the granularity of use cases.

In [11], Dolques *et al.* discuss a Relational Concept Analysis approach to refactor a use case diagrams by introducing generalized actors and use cases to factorize relations. In [15], Fauzan *et al.* combine structural information and lexical information for measuring similarities among use case diagrams. The authors use Wordnet, WuPalmer, and Cosine Similarity to semantically measure lexical information based on text extracted from actors and use cases.

In [2], Beimel and Kedmi-Shahar discuss experiences in encouraging students to develop a Conceptual Mental Model (CMM) before developing the use case diagram itself. A CMM is a tangible visual representation of the user's beliefs and expectations (in other words, the user's mental model) about the system to be developed. The authors particularly discuss a controlled experiment testing whether creation of a CMM prior to the creation of a use case diagram improves identification of functional system requirements, relations, and actors in terms of correctness, completeness, and non redundancy of the use case diagram. Participants who produced a use case diagram after producing a CMM performed significantly better in defining system requirements, relations and actors, as expressed in their use cased diagrams, compared to participants who produced a use case diagram without first producing a CMM.

Several studies have been conducted on verification of UML/SysML diagrams. Unfortunately, research has tended to focus on analysis of scenarios rather than of use case diagrams. Scenarios can be either modeled by sequence or activity diagrams, or documented by a textual explanation of the use case. Analysis techniques include graph transformation [20,39], logical verification [20] and grammar formalization [5,7].

In [39] and [20], the authors focused on verifying the correctness and completeness of a scenario, but they did not address a syntactical verification of UML standards. On the other hand, Chanda [5] investigated the use of formalization to verify syntactical rules, however no computational tool is proposed. The study in [7] complements the prior by proposing the use of natural language techniques to transform a use case description in the formal model. Deep natural language analysis is not necessary for the proposed assistant, since it works with use case diagrams, in which phrases are simpler and follow a structure - for example, to identify the verb of a use case, extracting the first word of the sentence should be enough.

Some modeling tools have incorporated basic checks for use case diagrams. For example, verification of double relationships and of repeated elements is available in Cameo System Modeler. The assistant discussed in this paper is different from Cameo by the broader spectrum of points to be verified, and by the dialogue with the user of the assistant, asking him or her questions such as "Is this actor really an external entity?"

Many attempts have been made on how to automate the creation of use case diagrams. Certain studies proposed its derivation from other textual documents through natural language processing. The transformation process has been applied to requirement [33], use case descriptions [13] and user stories [14]. The drawback of these proposals is that the quality of the use case diagram highly depends on the quality of the textual documents. Additionally, in a system engineering logic, these documents are supposed to be conceived from the use case diagram, and not the opposite.

Other studies proposed the reuse of previous diagrams using case base reasoning (CBR) [35] or ontology [3] approaches. From an initial draft of a use case diagram, it was possible to retrieve the most similar diagram from a database. CBR was developed starting from the idea that human beings think and reason using analogies and examples [1]. The use of CBR for assisting designers for use cases refers back to the suggestion made in Sect. 2.4, the use of examples of use case diagrams. It was noted that the number of examples needed to cover multiple domains might be very large, which is certainly a blocking point. However, having these examples being used in the form of cases by a case-based reasoning system takes this blocking point away.

Finally, some authors examined the problem of UML design from the educational point of view. In [6] and [21] the authors point out the common mistakes made by students in SysML/UML courses. In [29], Ramollari proposed an object-oriented modelling tool suitable for students. The tool, called StudentUML, includes design and verification of some UML diagrams, as the sequence and class diagram. Particularly, the use case diagram is not addressed. Verification is only available for diagrams drawn in the platform. With respect to creation, the assistant proposed in this article differs from Ramollari's tool by the guidance functionality that is provided to beginners. Actually, StudentUML works like other modelling tools, but it offers a simpler interface and further verifications.

6   Conclusions

A MBSE approach relies on a triptych (language, tool, method). In terms of language, this paper focuses on use case diagrams and more precisely on the version of them supported by the OMG-based languages UML and SysML. In terms of tool and method, the authors of this paper make a 3-fold statement: (1) use case diagrams have been existing for many years; (2) their use is the cornerstone of the use case driven analysis step of the methods associated with UML and SysML, and (3) Nevertheless, many people still have difficulties in writing good use cases.

Previous three statements provide the rationale behind the design and prototyping of a methodological assistant that help UML and SysML model designers to create and review their use case diagrams. The tool named UCcheck helps constructing use case diagrams relying on formalized rules and repositories of previously designed use case diagrams. It also check use case diagrams a posteriori and suggests improvements.

UCcheck is a free software coded in Python. UCcheck was first interfaced with TTool, the free software from Telecom Paris that we used to draw the use case diagrams in Fig. 1 and Fig. 3. TTool has further been applied for teaching, enhancing the expression power of SysML [31], and for tooling the first steps of the life cycle of systems [10,32]

The use of UCcheck is not restricted to TTool. Indeed, UCcheck stores use case diagrams using an intermediate form that is not specific to one particular UML or SysML tool. An interface exists for Cameo Systems Modeler, a tool from Dassault Systems. Similarly, UCcheck can be interfaced with other SysML tools such as Enterprise Architect [34] and Rhapsody [17].

UCcheck nowadays supports current versions of UML and SysML uses case diagrams. A new version of SysML is in preparation at OMG. Known as 'SysML 2' [26], next version of SysML is claimed to be less dependent on UML and globally more compliant with system engineers needs. At the time of writing this paper, there is no clear evidence that SysML use case diagrams will evolve in terms of syntax or semantics. Would this happen, UCCheck will be updated accordingly at the condition the tools UCCheck is interfaced with evolves too.

In Sect. 5 the use of case base reasoning (CBR) was mentioned. Reusing previous experience is an interesting option for guiding through design (see for example [25]). Case-based reasoning tries to contribute by solving a new problem by remembering a previous similar situation and by reusing information and knowledge of that situation, and this approach looks promising for extending the work on guiding designers through the earliest phases of setting up use-cases.

Acknowledgements. Baptiste Labarthe has contributed to UCcheck software development.

References

1. Aamodt, A., Plaza, E.: Case-based reasoning: foundational issues, methodological variations, and system approaches. AI Commun. **7**(1), 39–52 (1994)
2. Beimel, D., Kedmi-Shahar, E.: Improving the identification of functional system requirements when novice analysts create use case diagrams: the benefits of applying conceptual mental models. Requir. Eng. **24**, 483–502 (2019). https://doi.org/10.1007/s00766-018-0296-z
3. Bonilla-Morales, B., Crespo, S., Clunie, C.: Reuse of use cases diagrams: an approach based on ontologies and semantic web technologies. IJCSI Int. J. Comput. Sci. Issues **9**(2), 1–6 (2012)
4. Casse, O.: SysML in Action with Cameo Systems Modeler. ISTE Press, Elseiver, London (2018)
5. Chanda, J., Kanjilal, A., Sengupta, S., Bhattacharya, S.: Traceability of requirements and consistency verification of UML use case, activity and class diagram: a formal approach. In: 2009 Proceeding of International Conference on Methods and Models in Computer Science (ICM2CS), pp. 1–4. IEEE (2009)
6. Chren, S., Buhnova, B., Macak, M., Daubner, L., Rossi, B.: Mistakes in UML diagrams: analysis of student projects in a software engineering course. In: Proceedings of the 41st International Conference on Software Engineering: Software Engineering Education and Training, pp. 100–109. IEEE Press (2019)
7. Christiansen, H., Theil, C., Tveitane, K.: From use cases to UML class diagrams using logic grammars and constraints. In: RANLP, vol. 7, pp. 128–132 (2007)
8. Cockburn, A.: Structuring use cases with goals. J. Object-Orient. Program. **10**(5), 56–62 (1997)
9. Costain, G., McKenna, B.: Experiencing the elicitation of user requirements and recording them in use case diagrams through role-play. J. Inf. Syst. Educ. **22**(4), 367–380 (2019)
10. Daigmorte, H., de Saqui-Sannes, P., Vingerhoeds, R.A.: A SysML method with network dimensioning. In: 5th IEEE International Symposium on Systems Engineering (ISSE 2019) (2019)
11. Dolques, X., Huchard, M., Nebut, C., Reitz, P.: Fixing generalization defects in UML use case diagrams, Sevilla, Spain, pp. 247–258 (2010)
12. Eichelberger, H.: Automatic layout of UML use case diagrams. In: Proceedings of the 4th ACM Symposium on Software Visualization, pp. 105–114. ACM (2008)

13. El-Attar, M., Miller, J.: Producing robust use case diagrams via reverse engineering of use case descriptions. Softw. Syst. Model. **7**(1), 67–83 (2008). https://doi.org/10.1007/s10270-006-0039-3
14. Elallaoui, M., Nafil, K., Touahni, R.: Automatic transformation of user stories into UML use case diagrams using NLP techniques. Proc. Comput. Sci. **130**, 42–49 (2018)
15. Fauzan, R., Siahaan, D., Rochimah, S., Triandini, E.: Use case diagram similarity measurement: a new approach, pp. 3–7, July 2019
16. Holt, J., Perry, S.: SysML for systems engineering, vol. 7. IET (2008)
17. IBM-Rhapsody (2020). https://www.ibm.com/ca-en/marketplace/architect-for-systems-engineers
18. Ibrahim, N., Ibrahim, R., Saringat, M.Z., Mansor, D., Herawan, T.: On well-formedness rules for UML use case diagram. In: Wang, F.L., Gong, Z., Luo, X., Lei, J. (eds.) WISM 2010. LNCS, vol. 6318, pp. 432–439. Springer, Heidelberg (2010). https://doi.org/10.1007/978-3-642-16515-3_54
19. Jacobson, I.: Object-Oriented Software Engineering - A Use Case Driven Approach. Addison-Wesley, Boston (1992)
20. Klimek, R., Szwed, P.: Formal analysis of use case diagrams. Comput. Sci. **11**, 115–131 (2010)
21. Kruus, H., Robal, T., Jervan, G.: Teaching modeling in SysML/UML and problems encountered. In: 2014 25th EAEEIE Annual Conference (EAEEIE), pp. 33–36. IEEE (2014)
22. Lilly, S.: Use case pitfalls: top 10 problems from real projects using use cases. In: Proceedings of Technology of Object-Oriented Languages and Systems-TOOLS 30 (Cat. No. PR00278), pp. 174–183. IEEE (1999)
23. Marchese, F.: Use Case Diagrams Tutorial. Pace University. http://csis.pace.edu/~marchese/CS389/L9/Use%20Case%20Diagrams.pdf
24. Moisan, S., Rigault, J.-P.: Teaching object-oriented modeling and UML to various audiences. In: Ghosh, S. (ed.) MODELS 2009. LNCS, vol. 6002, pp. 40–54. Springer, Heidelberg (2010). https://doi.org/10.1007/978-3-642-12261-3_5
25. Netten, B., Vingerhoeds, R., Koppelaar, H., Boullart, L.: Expert assisted discrete optimization of composite structures. In: European Simulation Symposium, pp. 143–148 (1993)
26. Object-Management-Group: Systems modeling language (SysML) v2 RFP (2017)
27. OMG: OMG Systems Modeling Language. Object Management Group (2017). https://www.omg.org/spec/SysML/1.5
28. OMG: OMG Unified Modeling Language (OMG UML) Version 2.5. Object Management Group (2018). https://www.omg.org/spec/UML/2.5/PDF
29. Ramollari, E., Dranidis, D.: StudentUML: an educational tool supporting object-oriented analysis and design. In: Proceedings of the 11th Panhellenic Conference on Informatics, pp. 363–373 (2007)
30. Rizzo Aquino, E., de Saqui-Sannes, P., Vingerhoeds, R.A.: A methodological assistant for use case diagrams. In: 8th MODELSWARD: International Conference on Model-Driven Engineering and Software Development (2020)
31. de Saqui-Sannes, P., Apvrille, L.: Making modeling assumptions an explicit part of real-time systems models. In: The 8th European Congress Embedded Real Time Software and Systems (ERTS2) (2016)
32. de Saqui-Sannes, P., Vingerhoeds, R.A., Apvrille, L.: Early checking of SysML models applied to protocols. In: 12th International Conference on Modeling, Optimisation and Simulation, MOSIM 2018, Toulouse, France (2018)

33. Seresht, S.M., Ormandjieva, O.: Automated assistance for use cases elicitation from user requirements text. In: Proceedings of the 11th Workshop on Requirements Engineering, WER 2008, vol. 16, pp. 128–139 (2008)
34. SparkSystems: Entreprise-architect (2019). https://www.sparxsystems.com/products/ea/
35. Srisura, B., Daengdej, J.: Retrieving use case diagram with case-based reasoning approach. J. Theoret. Appl. Inf. Technol. **19**(2), 68–78 (2010)
36. TTool: An open-source UML and SysML toolkit (2020). https://ttool.telecom-paris.fr
37. Vacharajani, V., Pareek, J.: A proposed architecture for automated assessment of use case diagrams. Int. J. Comput. Appl. **108**(4), 1–6 (2019)
38. Weilkiens, T.: Systems Engineering with SysML/UML: Modeling, Analysis, Design. Elsevier, Amsterdam (2011)
39. Zhao, J., Duan, Z.: Verification of use case with petri nets in requirement analysis. In: Gervasi, O., Taniar, D., Murgante, B., Laganà, A., Mun, Y., Gavrilova, M.L. (eds.) ICCSA 2009. LNCS, vol. 5593, pp. 29–42. Springer, Heidelberg (2009). https://doi.org/10.1007/978-3-642-02457-3_3

Model-Based Static and Runtime Verification for Ethereum Smart Contracts

Shaun Azzopardi$^{(\boxtimes)}$ (iD), Christian Colombo (iD), and Gordon Pace (iD)

Department of Computer Science, University of Malta, Msida, Malta
{shaun.azzopardi,christian.colombo,gordon.pace}@um.edu.mt

Abstract. Distributed ledger technologies, e.g. blockchains, are an innovative solution to the problem of trust between different parties. Smart contracts, programs executing on these ledgers present new challenges given their non-traditional execution context – blockchains. The immutability of smart contracts once they are deployed makes their pre-deployment correctness essential. This can be achieved through verification methods, which attempt to answer conclusively whether the code respects some specification. Another approach is model-driven development, where the specification is used directly to create a correct-by-const-ruction implementation. A specification may however still need to be verified to ensure it satisfies some properties. Verifying properties pre-deployment is ideal, however it may not always be possible to do completely, depending on the complexity of the smart contract. Traditionally upon failure of a verification attempt the only option is to attempt a different verification method. Recent approaches instead enable the transformation of the verification problem into a smaller problem, reducing the load of subsequent verification attempts. We have previously proposed an automata-theoretic approach to reason systematically about this kind of *residual analysis* for (co-)safety properties, while we have implemented an intraprocedural data-flow approach for Java programs. In this paper we extend our approach for Solidity smart contracts, present a corresponding tool, evaluate the approach with several new case studies, and compare it with existing approaches.

Keywords: Smart contracts · Verification · Partial verification · Residual analysis · Static analysis · Runtime verification

1   Introduction

Distributed ledger technologies (DLTs), including blockchains, present new challenges for programming. DLTs act as immutable ledgers which several mutually untrusting entities can use as a single source of truth. DLTs can also act as both a store and execution context for programs (e.g. on the Ethereum blockchain [30]), usually called *smart contracts*. These public programs can be used to regulate some business process or the interaction between multiple parties in an

© Springer Nature Switzerland AG 2021
S. Hammoudi et al. (Eds.): MODELSWARD 2020, CCIS 1361, pp. 323–348, 2021.
https://doi.org/10.1007/978-3-030-67445-8_14

open, transparent, automatic, and deterministic manner. An important issue is then the well-behaviour of these smart contracts, especially since they are usually *immutable* when deployed. Smart contracts that behave in an undesirable way can lead to loss in terms of real-world value (see [5] for a survey). Ensuring well-behaviour of smart contracts is an important new area of study. Focusing on Ethereum [30], a popular blockcahin aiming to operate as a "world computer", we find two main strands of approaches to well-behaviour of smart contracts: (i) model-driven development (MDD); and (ii) verification techniques.

Smart contracts in Ethereum are deployed as Ethereum VM bytecode, however they are generally programmed in Solidity[1], a Javascript-like language. Although smart contracts are limited in size, they tend to get complicated quickly, especially due to certain non-traditional aspects of the semantics of the language (e.g. reverting of transactions upon gas being exhausted, and calls to external functions that can act on the local state). One approach to handle the complexity of programming smart contracts is to take an abstraction step further and specify models instead of writing code directly [23,24,29,31]— model-driven development (MDD). These kind of approaches allow for a specification model to (semi-)automatically be used to produce an implementation, ensuring correctness by construction. Other approaches instead verify a specification against manually written Solidity code to identify violations or confirm compliance [11,12,19,26–28]. This can both be done by analysing the code or by instrumenting the code to identify (and possibly reverting) violations at runtime.

These two approaches are not independent of each other. A model may need to be verified to satisfy other properties, for example to ensure compliance of a modelled business process with some regulations. The runtime verification approach of instrumenting smart contracts with monitors can also be used to enforce a property at runtime, adapting smart contracts to be correct-by-construction, similar to MDD.

In this paper we are interested in model-based analysis of smart contracts, remaining agnostic of whether these are extracted automatically from smart contract code or used for MDD. Ideally we want to perform this analysis before deployment. However, sound and complete analysis can be too expensive, in terms of memory and/or time, especially since a smart contract may have dynamic dependencies on data and code in other blockchain locations. When static analysis does not scale up to the problem at hand we can instead perform runtime verification or enforcement of the property. This is however not ideal, since instrumenting a smart contract adds more code that needs to be deployed to the blockchain and adds computation to be performed at runtime, which can be costly on Ethereum. Our solution here is to a hybrid approach to verification: *use runtime verification only on the part of the program not proven safe statically* [7,18].

We take an automata-based approach, using symbolic automata to model both the program and the property being verified. Similar symbolic automata have been used in Ethereum in the context of MDD [23,24] and verification [11],

---

[1] https://solidity.readthedocs.io/.

and thus our approach here is applicable to optimise existing work almost out of the box. We consider correctness conditions for how static analysis can be used to reduce both the monitor logic and the required event instrumentation. We consider several such reduction, or *residual*, operations. Furthermore we have implemented this work in the `solidClarva`[2] tool.

This paper is an extension of [9]. The contributions of this paper, going beyond our previous work, include: (i) a version of the model language used in [9] that reflects the semantics of transaction failure in Solidity smart contracts; (ii) a tool implementing thee analysis for Solidity; (iii) a more extensive evaluation of the approach; and (iv) a comparison of this work with existing approaches to the verification of smart contracts.

```
1 contract SmartAuctionHouse{
2   address owner;
3   bool ongoing;
4   mapping(int => uint) offers;
5   ...
6
7   modifier isOwner(){
8       require(owner == msg.sender);
9       _;
10  }
11
12  function startAuction(int itemID, uint startOffer) public isOwner{...}
13  function bid() public payable{...}
14  function declareWinner() public isOwner{...}
15  function callBid() public isOwner{...}
16 }
```

Listing 1.1. Auction smart contract implementation extract (full version in [9]).

In Sect. 2 we describe formally our approach to smart contract verification. In Sect. 3 we discuss the way we combine static and runtime verification through creating residual problems, describe a tool implementing this in Sect. 4, and evaluate the approach in Sect. 5. We discuss this work in Sect. 6, contrast it with related work in Sect. 7, and conclude in Sect. 8.

2 Smart Contract Verification

There are several approaches one can take in verifying smart contracts. Here we take an *automata-theoretic* approach, where smart contracts and properties are all specified as automata, with the objective being to check that the model refines the required property.

Traditional approaches to represent models and properties use finite-state automata, with transitions triggered by events (corresponding to program actions). Here instead we use *symbolic automata*, where in addition to a finite set of explicit states, we consider a possibly infinite set of implicit states. Symbolic automata are more succinct and expressive than finite-state automata, e.g. with

---

[2] https://www.github.com/shaunazzopardi/solidity-static-analysis.

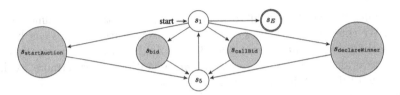

Fig. 1. Automata modelling the interface of the smart contract, with shaded states marking call states [9].

symbolic automata we can give a finite representation of an automaton that accepts the language $a^n b^n$ for any n, which is impossible to do with finite-state automata.

We will be representing smart contracts in terms of *control-flow automata* (CFAs) and their properties in terms of *dynamic event automata* (DEAs). These automata are complementary: a CFA produces events that are processed by a DEA. We keep the implicit states of the symbolic automata abstract since their structure is tangential to our analysis here, however they can be thought of as being a set of variable bindings.

We describe formally these automata in the rest of this section. Throughout, we will be using the example of a smart contract implementing the business process of an auction house. A high-level view of this smart contract is given in Listing 1.1, with the low-level implementation of two of its functions given in Listing 1.2 and Listing 1.3.

The definitions in this section are largely from [9], but optimised for smart contracts.

2.1 Control-Flow Automata

We represent Solidity smart contracts in terms of control-flow automata (CFAs). These automata simply encode the control-flow of the program in the structure of the automaton, with program step-wise logic encoded in transition labels, and function calls through state labels.

Transition labels are triples of: (i) a condition that must hold for the transition to be taken; (ii) a statement that transforms the implicit variable state; and (iii) a monitor event triggered after the statement executes, written: *condition* ▷ *statement* ▶ *event*.

Another feature of CFAs is the possibility to *call* other CFAs. Calls may be of two types: (i) a normal call; or (ii) a delegate call. In Solidity a delegate call executes another smart contract's function on the caller's variable state, while a normal `call` executes another smart contract's function on the state of the callee. This is also relevant to the notion of *reverting* of a call. In Solidity, calls can fail—if a delegate call fails, then the original transaction also fails, however if a normal call fails, execution continues in the original CFA [30]. We handle this logic in the semantics we give to CFAs.

```
1 function startAuction(int itemID,
          uint startOffer) public
          isOwner{
2    require(!ongoing);
3    require(!finished[id]);
4    offers[itemID] = startOffer;
5    id = itemID;
6    ongoing = true;
7 }
```

Listing 1.2. `startAuction` implementation [9].

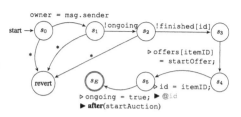

Fig. 2. `startAuction` CFA [9].

```
1 function bid() public payable{
2    require(ongoing);
3
4    if(offers[id] < msg.value &&
           winner[id] != address(0)){
5        winner[id].transfer(offers[id
             ]);
6        winner[id] = msg.sender;
7        offers[id] = msg.value;
8    }
9 }
```

Listing 1.3. `bid` implementation [9].

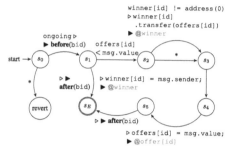

Fig. 3. `bid` CFA [9].

Definition 1. *A CFA, of type **CFA**, is a tuple* $\langle \Omega, S, s_0, E, \text{calls}, \text{dcalls}, \rightarrow \rangle$, *where:*

(a) Ω *is a set of implicit variable states;*
(b) S *is the set of explicit states;*
(c) $s_0 \in S$ *is the initial explicit program state;*
(d) $E \subseteq S$ *is the set of end states, we use* s_E *as a variable ranging over this set;*
(e) calls, dcalls $: S \nrightarrow (\Omega \rightarrow \textbf{CFA})^3$ *identify states associated, respectively, with normal calls and delegate calls; and*
(f) $\rightarrow: S \times \textbf{Cond} \times \textbf{Stmt} \times \Sigma \rightarrow S$ *is the deterministic transition relation (where* $\textbf{Cond} = \Omega \rightarrow \textbf{Bool}$, *and* $\textbf{Stmt} = \Omega \rightarrow \Omega$*).*

We write $s \xrightarrow{c \triangleright st \blacktriangleright e} s'$ for $(s, c, st, e, s') \in \rightarrow$. We use P or M for CFAs. We use the function methods : $\textbf{CFA} \rightarrow 2^{\textbf{CFA}}$ for the set of methods transitively called by M^4.

Figure 2 and Fig. 3 give an example encoding of two Solidity functions as CFAs (gray events will be removed by the analysis we define in Sect. 3.2). In turn, Fig. 1 encodes the interface of a smart contract, allowing its functions to be called in any sequence.

---

^{3} $\nrightarrow$ is used to denote a partial function.
^{4} In this paper we will be limiting our analysis to when this is finite, which is sufficient for smart contracts.

We give CFAs an operational semantics with configurations as a pair of a sequence of states and the current variable state.

States are tagged with either $\uparrow$ or $\downarrow$ ($S^{\uparrow\downarrow} \stackrel{\text{def}}{=} S \times \{\uparrow,\downarrow\}$). A directed state $s^{\downarrow}$ denotes that if s state is a call state, then its call is yet to be executed, dually $s^{\uparrow}$ denotes that any call pf s has already been entered and exited from.

Transitions in the semantics are tagged by pairs of events and variable states, denoting the triggered monitored events and the variable state at that point in time. In the semantics we give to CFAs we only consider the traces that reach end configurations. Then we ignore infinite loops, that would never be recorded to the blockchain.

Definition 2. *The operational semantics of a CFA is given with configurations as pairs of directed states and implicit states ($S^{\uparrow\downarrow} \times \Omega$), transitions labeled by pairs of events, and implicit states ($\Sigma \times \Omega$), and characterised by:*

(i) *Given a transition $s_1 \xrightarrow{c \triangleright st \triangleright e} s_2$, with c holding on ω, and s_1 not being an end state, then a configuration $(s_1^{\uparrow}, \omega)$ transitions to $(s_2^{\downarrow}, st(\omega))$ with $\langle e, st(\omega) \rangle$:*

$$\frac{s_1 \xrightarrow{c \triangleright st \triangleright e} s_2 \qquad s_1 \notin E \qquad c(\omega)}{(s_1^{\uparrow} : ss, \omega) \xrightarrow{\langle e, st(\omega) \rangle} (s_2^{\downarrow} : ss, st(\omega))}$$

(ii) *A call is recorded by the semantics if it reaches an end state:*

$$\frac{s \in dom(calls) \qquad M = calls(s)(\omega) \qquad \exists s_E \in E_M, \omega' \in \Omega \cdot (s_{0_M}^{\downarrow}, \omega) \Rightarrow (s_E^{\uparrow}, \omega')}{(s^{\downarrow} : ss, \omega) \xrightarrow{\langle \epsilon, \omega \rangle} (s_{0_M}^{\downarrow} : (s^{\uparrow} : ss), \omega)}$$

(iii) *Delegate calls are always entered:*

$$\frac{s \in dom(dcalls) \qquad M = dcalls(s)(\omega)}{(s^{\downarrow} : ss, \omega) \xrightarrow{\langle \epsilon, \omega \rangle} (s_{0_M}^{\downarrow} : (s^{\uparrow} : ss), \omega')}$$

(iv) *Upon an end state being reached with any associated call being resolved, and the state being part of a nested call, then execution continues from the calling state:*

$$\frac{s_E \in E \qquad ss \neq \langle \rangle}{(s_E^{\uparrow} : ss, \omega) \xrightarrow{\langle \epsilon, \omega \rangle} (ss, \omega)}$$

(v) *If the state is not associated with a call or delegate call, or if a call cannot reach an end state, then the state is marked with $\uparrow$[5]:*

$$\frac{otherwise}{(s^{\downarrow} : ss, \omega) \xrightarrow{\langle \epsilon, \omega \rangle} (s^{\uparrow} : ss, \omega)}$$

---

[5] Here we use the *otherwise* condition for simplicity to denote the situation when no other rule applies.

We use s⁻ for an element of $S^{\uparrow\downarrow}$. We write (s^-, ω) for $(\langle s^- \rangle, \omega)$, and use $\Rightarrow$ for the transitive closure of $\rightarrow$.

Then we can identify the prefixes of a smart contract's behaviour, which will be the object of verification.

Definition 3. *The behaviour of CFA P starting with implicit state ω of length $i \in \mathbb{N}$ is the trace $t_{P,\omega,i}$ defined formally as follows:*

$$t_{P,\omega,i} \stackrel{\text{def}}{=} \begin{cases} pre(ews, i) & (s^{\downarrow}_{0_P}, \omega) \stackrel{ews}{\Rightarrow} (s^{\uparrow}_{E_P}, \omega') \wedge i < len(ews) \\ \langle\rangle & otherwise \end{cases}$$

where $pre(ews, i)$ gives the prefix of ews with length i if defined, otherwise it is the empty trace, and $len : (\Sigma \times \Omega)^* \rightarrow \mathbb{N}$ gives the length of a trace.

2.2 Dynamic Event Automata

A control-flow automaton defines the behaviour of a smart contract. However, when doing verification, we are not generally interested in the exact low-level semantics, but rather that the program obeys some high-level specification (e.g. the input-output behaviour of functions). For this purpose we use dynamic event automata (DEAs). These are structurally similar to CFAs, but semantically they differ in that DEAs instead characterise the set of traces *that should not be exhibited*. DEAs abstract over behaviour of the program that is irrelevant to the specification, allowing specifications that do not unduly limit the low-level implementation.

Instead of an end state, DEAs have bad states. As an optimisation, DEAs also have accepting states which are used to identify prefixes that cannot have a violating continuation. These can be used to abort monitoring early, avoiding waste of resources.

Transitions are also tagged by three labels: (i) an event; (ii) a guard on the CFA and DEA variable state; and (iii) an action on the DEA variable state, represented with *event | guard $\mapsto$ action*. A transition is taken if the CFA triggers the corresponding event and the guard holds on the variable states, after which the action transforms the current DEA variable state.

Figure 4 illustrates DEA properties we require out of Listing 1.1.

Definition 4. *A DEA is then a tuple $\pi \stackrel{\text{def}}{=} \langle \Theta, \Omega, q_0, \theta_0, B, A, \rightarrow \rangle$, where:*

(a) Θ is a set of implicit variables states;
(b) Ω is the set of explicit state;
(c) $q_0 \in Q$ is the initial explicit monitor state;
(d) $\theta_0 \in \Theta$ is the initial implicit monitor state;
(e) $B, A \subseteq Q$ are respectively the set of explicit bad and accepting states, we use q_B for a bad state; and
(f) $\rightarrow: Q \times (\Sigma) \times Guard \times Act \rightarrow Q$ is the deterministic transition function (where $Guard = \Theta \times \Omega \rightarrow Bool$, and $Act = \Theta \times \Omega \rightarrow \Theta$).

We write $q \xrightarrow{e|g \mapsto a} q'$ for $(q, e, g, a, q') \in \rightarrow$.

We give an operational semantics to DEAs in terms of configurations as pairs of DEA states and variable states. These configurations evolve according to the DEA transitions until an end or accepting state is reached.

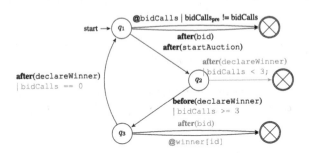

(a) *The business process of an auction smart contract: (i) no bids can be made before an auction is started; (ii) during an auction the winner cannot be declared before the bid being called thrice; (iii) no bid can be made the winner cannot be changed the winner is declared; and (iv) after the auction has been declared the* `bidCalls` *variable reset.*

(b) *When a bid is made during an ongoing action and the item being auctioned is changed, no winner is set until the auction starts.*

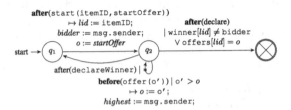

(c) *Whenever the current winning bid for an item is modified, the new value must be larger than the old value.*

(d) *Keep track of the current highest bid. This should be the winning bid at the end of an auction.*

Fig. 4. Several properties expected of the auction smart contract, with bad states marked with a cross[9], and grey labels which will be removed by the analysis presented in Sect. 3.2.

Definition 5. *The operational semantics of a DEA is given with configurations of type $Q \times \Theta$, with transitions labeled by elements of $\Sigma \times \Omega$, and characterised by:*

(i) A configuration (q, θ), given a transition $q \xrightarrow{e|g \mapsto a} q'$, evolves to a configuration $(q', a(\omega, \theta))$ only if the guard g holds on θ:

$$\frac{q \xrightarrow{e|g \mapsto a} q' \qquad q \notin A \cup B \qquad g(\omega, \theta)}{(q, \theta) \xrightarrow{\langle e, \omega \rangle} (q', a(\omega, \theta))}$$

(ii) if a bad or accepting state has been reached, or there is no outgoing transition with a guard that holds on the current implicit state, the configuration does not evolve:

$$\frac{q \in A \cup B}{(q, \theta) \xrightarrow{\langle e, \omega \rangle} (q, \theta)} \qquad \frac{\nexists g, q, a \cdot q \xrightarrow{e|g \mapsto a} q' \wedge g(\omega, \theta)}{(q, \theta) \xrightarrow{\langle e, \omega \rangle} (q, \theta)}$$

We overload $\Rightarrow$ for the transitive closure of $\rightarrow$.

We use DEAs to identify the set of traces that reach a bad state.

Definition 6. *The* bad traces *of property π are those traces that reach a bad state in π: $B(\pi) \stackrel{\text{def}}{=} \{t \in \Sigma \times \Omega \mid \exists q_B \in B, \theta \in \Theta \cdot (q_0, \theta_0) \stackrel{t}{\Rightarrow} (q_B, \theta)\}$.*

Note that traces reaching accepting states cannot be in $B(\pi)$, however there can still be traces that do not reach accepting states that are not bad states.

We shall be assuming that DEAs are in a structurally optimal form. Any DEA can simply and efficiently be reduced to optimal form through structural analysis. The ability to do this is essential for the reduction operators we define in Sect. 3.

Definition 7. *A DEA is in* optimal form *if: (i) it has no states unreachable from the initial state: $\nexists q \in Q \cdot q_0 \nrightarrow q$; and (ii) any state that cannot reach a bad state is accepting with no outgoing transition: $\forall q \in Q, q_B \in B \cdot q \nrightarrow q_B \implies (q \in A \wedge q \nrightarrow)$.*

The verification problem can then be framed in terms of whether the CFAs produces any bad traces of the DEA.

Definition 8. *A CFA P is said to satisfy a property π if every execution prefix it generates is not a bad trace of π: $P \vdash \pi \stackrel{\text{def}}{=} \forall \omega \in \Omega, i \in \mathbb{N} \cdot t_{P, \omega, i} \notin B(\pi)$.*

3   Synergy of Static and Runtime Verification

Sound and complete verification is ideal, since it can ensure the absence of all specified errors. Here we are interested in the situation where this is not an option, for example when it is undecidable or when time and memory resources are limited.

In this case we have two options that scale up better: sound static analysis and runtime verification (RV). Sound static analysis does not attempt to be complete, resulting in an analysis that does not analyse the program state space at a fine-grained level, avoiding the need for large time and memory resources. RV instead may be both sound and complete however only with respect to a single execution trace at runtime. Moreover it compares favourably with other techniques in terms of time and memory since the focus is only on one execution trace rather than all the possible traces [20].

Using only static analysis is not viable, since sound techniques can fail to prove compliance. On the other hand, assuming monitorable properties (like DEAs), RV can always prove compliance, while it can also be used to enforce specifications (e.g. by canceling violating transactions). The issue with runtime enforcement is that it requires synchronous monitoring, where the smart contract is instrumented with the analysis logic to ensure events are dealt with as they occur. This instrumentation (and any added storage costs) can cause overheads at runtime, both in terms of gas added to the smart contract deployment, and to the cost of executing transactions at runtime.

Our approach here is not just to choose one or the other, but to exploit the benefits of both. We attempt sound static analysis to show the required property, accepting that this can fail. Instead of expecting that a failing static analysis simply returns an unknown verdict we take a *partial verification* or *residual analysis* approach and expect the static analysis to return a *residual* verification problem. This residual problem (containing a reduced property and/or reduced instrumentation) is then proven or enforced using RV. This kind of approach follows the principle *use runtime verification only on the part of the program not proven safe statically*. It ensures that if a property can be proven before deployment then it is not left to runtime, while it can reduce the runtime effort required to prove properties that are not fully verifiable pre-deployment.

In this section we consider residual analysis in the context of CFAs and DEAs, discussing and formally identifying a correctness condition for residual problems, and giving some residual analyses for CFAs and DEAs. The definitions and theorems here are largely from [9], proofs can be found in [6].

3.1   Residual Correctness

A verification problem is a program-property pair: (P, π). A residual verification problem in turn is a transformation of the original program: (P', π'). Such a residual technique is sound if a proof of (P', π') implies that (P, π) holds. The weakest such soundness condition is that $P' \vdash \pi' \implies P \vdash \pi$.

This condition however has limitations, especially using RV. Consider that this condition does not ensure that if a trace satisfies the residual property it also satisfies the original. For example, consider that the original property π has the set of bad states $B(\pi) = \{t_1, t_2\}$ (and their continuations), while the residual property π' has bad traces $B(\pi') = \{t_2\}$. If the program exhibits both traces, then the sufficiency condition holds. However, if the trace exhibited at runtime is t_1 with monitoring for π', then no violation will be caught. Thus, we want to ensure that the condition holds at the level of traces instead of simply at the level of the program.

Table 1. State invariants for the `bid` CFA in Fig. 3 [9].

State	Data abstraction
s_1, s_E	`ongoing`
s_2, s_3	`ongoing & offers[id] < msg.value`
s_4, s_5	`ongoing & offers[id] < msg.value & winner[id] == msg.sender`

We also want violations to be caught by the residual monitor at the same point in time the original monitor would have caught it, so as not to add to the execution costs associated with a transaction. These concerns are characterised by the notion of *lockstep equivalence*, which essentially requires that the original and residual property give the same verdict to execution prefixes of the same length (and same initial variable states).

Definition 9. *(P, π) is said to be in* lockstep *with the pair (P', π') iff execution traces of P and P' from the same implicit state ω are given the same verdict by π and π' for every prefix length i:* $\forall \omega \in \Omega, i \in \mathbb{N} \cdot t_{P,\omega,i} \in B(\pi) \iff t_{P',\omega,i} \in B(\pi')$.

We shall be using this as the correctness condition we require out of the residual operations we shall be defining.

3.2 Residual Analysis

The residual analysis we present is based on composing a CFA with a DEA. Through analysing this composition, at a certain level of abstraction, we are then able to prune some DEA features (transitions and guards), and silence some CFA events. To enable reasoning about DEA guards against the CFA implicit (variable) state, we consider *state invariants*, which can be computed easily through data-flow propagation algorithms.

We consider conditions required out of the data-flow analysis required to produce state invariants, after which we describe our control-flow analysis based on synchronous composition of CFAs and DEAs. We can then characterise some residual operators based on this composition artifact.

Data-Flow Analysis. We are interested in abstracting each possible runtime state of the program, since analysing each possible state can lead to state explosion problems. One choice is to simply abstract each runtime configuration (s, ω) with state s. However this ignores any data aspects of the runtime behaviour. Instead, we can abstract each runtime configuration with a pair (s, c) where $c \in$ Cond and c is true for every variable state associated with s at runtime. Such a condition is said to be a *state invariant* of s. Recall also we are only interested in configurations that reach an end configuration (i.e. that are part of a successful transaction).

Definition 10. *A condition c is said to be a* state invariant *of state s if it holds on each variable state associated with a state of s in a successful runtime execution:*

$$\forall \omega_0, \omega, \omega_E \in \Omega, s^- \in S^{\uparrow\downarrow} \cdot (s_0^\downarrow, \omega_0) \Rightarrow (s^- : ss, \omega) \Rightarrow (s_E^\uparrow, \omega_E) \implies c(\omega).$$

We use $\sigma : S \to$ Cond as a function that associates states with state invariants.

For example, Table 1 illustrates some state invariants of Fig. 3 that can be inferred easily from a simple condition and statement propagation algorithm.

Consider that a DEA transition (e.g. $q \xrightarrow{e|g \mapsto a} q'$) triggers after a certain CFA transition (e.g. $s \xrightarrow{c \triangleright st \blacktriangleright e} s'$) emits an event. In our analysis we can then check whether the state invariant of s' allows the DEA guard g to be true or not. However, s' may have multiple incoming transitions, leading to a weaker state invariant. Instead, since a DEA transition executes immediately after a CFA transition executes, we are only interested in the runtime configurations the CFA transition induces. To abstract these we can consider the state invariant of s updated with condition and statement associated with a CFA transition, which correspond to the configurations that the DEA guard will be checked against at runtime. We define the condition required out of such an update function.

Definition 11. *A procedure that updates a condition with the effects of a statement, update : Cond $\times$ Stmt $\to$ Cond, returns a condition that holds on each variable state that respects the original condition: $\forall \omega \in \Omega \cdot c(\omega) \implies update(c, st)(st(\omega))$*

On the concrete side we can compute $g(\theta, \omega)$ to check whether DEA guard g is true for ω and θ. Abstractly we are ignoring θ, but abstracting each ω with a condition c. To check whether a guard can be true for a condition we require an appropriate satisfiability checking procedure. We define appropriate conditions for such a function. We also assume that the function can fail, returning the unknown verdict ?.

Definition 12. *A satisfaction procedure sat : Guard $\times$ Cond $\to \{\top, \bot, ?\}$ is a procedure that satisfies the following conditions:*

(i) *Satisfiability implies that if the condition is true on an implicit state, the guard is also true on the same state: $sat(g, c) = \top \implies (\forall \omega \in \Omega, \theta \in \Theta \cdot c(\omega) \implies g(\theta, \omega))$; and*

(ii) Unsatisfiability implies that if the condition is true on an implicit state, the guard is false on the same state: $sat(g, c) = \bot \implies (\forall \omega \in \Omega, \theta \in \Theta \cdot c(\omega) \implies \neg g(\theta, \omega))$.

Control-Flow Analysis. We are interested in over-approximating the executions of the smart contract, and moreover in whether they satisfy or violate the required property.

As an abstract interpretation of the execution traces we can take the CFA itself annotated with state invariants: a state and invariant pair (s, c) correspond to the set of configurations associated with the state at runtime $\{(s^-, \omega_1), (s^-, \omega_2), ...\}$.

On function calls we have two choices: (i) we can flatten the CFA and do an intraprocedural analysis; or (ii) we can over-approximate outside the CFA and perform an intraprocedural analysis. Here we the latter approach. We analyse each function CFA separately, and join the results together to remain sound over the whole smart contract. Each CFA will be extended implicitly to be an abstract interpretation of the smart contract traces that pass through it. This will be composed with a DEA, and the paths in this composition then correspond to the monitored traces at runtime.

We tag transitions in the composition by the respective CFA and DEA transition labels. Due to intraprocedurality we have to consider the possibility that (almost) any event can occur before the CFA is entered, after a trace exits from it, and during a call. In this case, and the case that there is no matching DEA transition, we mark the respective place in the composition transition with the empty symbol $\square$.

Definition 13. *The* abstract intraprocedural composition *of a CFA M and a property π is the transition system with states of type $S \times Q$, transitions labeled by pairs of CFA and DEA transition labels, with possibly one label missing represented by the $\square$ symbol:* $((\text{Cond} \times \text{Stmt} \times \Sigma) \cup \{\square\}) \times ((\Sigma \times \text{Guard} \times \text{Action}) \cup \{\square\})$, *and characterised by the following rules:*

1. *(s, q) transitions to (s', q') if there are transitions between the respective states in the CFA and DEA, with the same event, and if the abstraction of s updated with the CFA transition is not incompatible with the DEA guard:*

$$\frac{s \xrightarrow{c \triangleright st \blacktriangleright e} s' \quad q \xrightarrow{e|g \mapsto a} q' \quad sat(update(\sigma(s) \wedge c, st), g) \neq \bot}{(s, q) \xrightarrow[e|g \mapsto a]{c \triangleright st \blacktriangleright e} (s', q')}$$

2. *(s, q) transitions to (s', q) if there are transitions between the respective CFA states, and if the invariant of s updated with the CFA transition is not incompatible with the conjunction of the negation of each guard associated with a transition from q:*

$$\frac{s \xrightarrow{c \triangleright st \blacktriangleright e} s' \quad sat(update(\sigma(s) \wedge c, st), \bigwedge_{q \xrightarrow{e|g' \mapsto a} q'} \neg g') \neq \bot}{(s, q) \xrightarrow[\square]{c \triangleright st \blacktriangleright e} (s', q)}$$

3. *Any configuration with a program state with an outgoing ϵ-transition asynchronously transitions with that CFA transition:*

$$\frac{s \xrightarrow{c \triangleright st \blacktriangleright \epsilon} s'}{(s,q) \xrightarrow[\square]{c \triangleright st \blacktriangleright \epsilon} (s',q)}$$

4. *Initial, end, and call configurations take any available DEA transition with events used outside of M[6]. End and call configurations may transition into M and back:*

$$\frac{s \in \{s_0\} \cup E \cup dom(calls) \qquad e \in out(M) \qquad q \xrightarrow{e|g \mapsto a} q'}{(s,q) \xrightarrow[e|g \mapsto a]{\square} (s,q')}$$

$$\frac{s \in E \cup dom(calls) \qquad q,q' \in Q}{(s,q) \xrightarrow[\square]{\square} (s_0,q) \qquad (s_E,q') \xrightarrow[\square]{\square} (s,q')}$$

We overload $\Rightarrow$ as its transitive closure and we use $\boxslash$ for a label that is not $\square$.

The paths in the composition we are interested in are those that start at an initial state and end in a bad end configuration. These paths abstract exactly those traces of the program that violate the property. We define formally a transition relation that captures composition transitions used by or to avoid such violating paths.

Definition 14. *We write $(s,q) \xrightarrow[y]{x} (s',q')$, when:*

(i) *the transition is in the composition: $(s,q) \xrightarrow[y]{x} (s',q')$; and*

(ii) *(s,q) is reachable from the initial configuration and can reach a bad end configuration: $(s_0,q_0) \Rightarrow (s,q) \Rightarrow (s_E,q_B)$.*

We say a CFA transition $s \xrightarrow{x} s'$ is used on the way to a violation when $(s,q) \xrightarrow[y]{x} (s',q')$, and similarly for DEA transitions.

Note how we require that only (s,q) can reach a violating configuration, and not (s',q'). Any such transitions are in fact transitions that help *avoid a violation*. Identifying these transitions will be useful when considering our residual operators, to avoid removing needed property transitions and/or instrumentation.

A clear result is that if there is no path to a bad configuration in any CFA then we can conclude that the property is satisfied. We can check for this by checking if there is a path in a composition that transitions from a good configuration to a bad one.

---

[6] $out : \textbf{CFA} \rightarrow 2^{\Sigma}$ is the function that returns the set of events used shallowly in CFAs of P that are not the input CFA.

Theorem 1. $\nexists M \in functions(P), s, s' \in S_M, q_B \in B, q \in Q \setminus B \cdot (s, q) \xrightarrow[\boxtimes]{\boxtimes} (s', q_B) \implies P \vdash \pi.$

However, since our approach is only sound, the composition will have paths that are not realizable at runtime. By making our analysis more exact we can make the composition more complete, and decrease the incidence of such paths. Here we are considering the case that the composition is not sound and complete, and thus there are cases for which we cannot determine compliance. For these cases we want to focus the verification effort on the part of the program that cannot be proven safe, and the part of the property that has not been proven.

The first residual we define concerns reductions of DEAs.

Consider that any concrete trace can be associated with the set of DEA transitions it activates at runtime. If we consider only the set of violating traces, then we can identify the set of DEA transitions used by at least one violating trace. The sub-DEA created with only these transitions is enough to give a verdict for these violating traces.

However, we want to ensure that the residual monitor gives a correct verdict also to compliant traces. Consider that compliant traces either: (i) use a subset of the DEA transitions used by the violating traces, but simply succeed in not using transitions whose destination state is a bad state; or (ii) end up in a part of the DEA that is not used by a violating trace (e.g. a transition towards an accepting state). To ensure equivalent verdicts for compliant traces we can create a sub-DEA made of all the DEA transitions of the first kind (i), along with the DEA transitions that transition into the part identified in (ii). Note, we do not need all the transitions in this second part, since entering it ensures eventually a satisfying verdict will be given.

To create an appropriate sub-DEA that monitors equivalently both violating and compliant traces we can simply consider the sub-DEA created with the union of transitions of both the above identified sub-DEAs. Here we can simply characterise this with our notion of a transition being used on the way to a violation (Definition 14).

Definition 15 (Control-Flow Residual). $\pi \backslash P$ *is the property with the transitions of* π *used on the way to a violation in a method of* P:

$$\rightarrow_{\pi \backslash P} \overset{def}{=} \left\{ q \xrightarrow{e \mid g \mapsto a} q' \mid \exists M \in functions(P), s, s' \in S_M \cdot (s, q) \xrightarrow[e \mid g \mapsto a]{\boxtimes} (s', q') \right\}.$$

s Greyed out transitions in Fig. 4 represent guards removed with this residual. For example, for Fig. 4a we are able to show that the `declareWinner` function cannot be called successfully immediately after `startAuction`.

Dually we can reduce a program's event instrumentation by removing those events not used on the way to a violation.

Definition 16. $P \backslash \pi$ *is the CFA with the union of:*

(i) the transitions of P *used on the way to a violation:*

$$\rightarrow_0 \overset{def}{=} \left\{ s \xrightarrow{c \triangleright st \blacktriangleright e} s' \mid \exists M \in functions(P), s, s' \in S_M \cdot (s, q) \xrightarrow[\boxtimes]{c \triangleright st \blacktriangleright e} (s', q') \right\}; \ and$$

(ii) the rest of the transitions of P silenced: $\rightarrow_1 \stackrel{\text{def}}{=} \left\{ s \xrightarrow{c \triangleright st \blacktriangleright e} s' \mid (s, c, st, e, s') \in \rightarrow_\pi \setminus \rightarrow_0 \right\}.$

The reduction applies transitively to calls.

Grey events in Fig. 2 and Fig. 3 represent events removed with this residual operator. For example in Fig. 2 we are able to show that the modification event of variable id can be turned off in Listing 1.2, since the **after**(startAuction) event always occurs after it. This means that in the monitor corresponding to Fig. 4b the transition between q_3 and q_1 is always taken, and thus there is never a violation.

By applying these dual reductions we can produce a reduced verification problem that is still equivalent to the original one. We can show that the verification problem reduced with these operators is in lockstep with the original, since (i) the residual DEA is exactly the part of the original DEA exercised by violating traces, and simply allows for early satisfaction verdicts for some compliant traces; and (ii) the removed events could not have participated in a violation.

Theorem 2. *$(P\setminus\pi, \pi\setminus P)$ is in lockstep with (P, π).*

Another residual operator we consider is one that identifies property transition guards that can be determined to always hold true at runtime. This can be done by inspecting the compositions: if whenever a property transition is used in the composition there is no alternative, then its guard always holds at runtime.

Definition 17 (Guard Residual). *$\pi \,\|\, P$ is the property with the union of:*

(i) the DEA transitions that are not always activated:

$$\rightarrow_0 \stackrel{\text{def}}{=} \left\{ q \xrightarrow{e \mid g \mapsto a} q' \mid \begin{array}{l} \exists M \in functions(P), s, s', s'' \in S_M, q'' \in Q \cdot (s, q) \xrightarrow[e \mid g \mapsto a]{c \triangleright st \blacktriangleright e} (s', q') \\ \wedge \exists l \neq (e, g, a) \cdot (s, q) \xrightarrow[l]{c \triangleright st \blacktriangleright e} (s'', q'') \end{array} \right\}$$

and

(ii) the DEA transitions that are always activated with silenced guards:

$$\rightarrow_1 \stackrel{\text{def}}{=} \left\{ q \xrightarrow{e \mid true \mapsto a} q' \mid (q, e, g, a, q') \in \rightarrow_{\pi\setminus P} \wedge (q, e, g, a, q') \notin \rightarrow_0 \right\}.$$

Transitions labels with only transition guards greyed out in Fig. 4 represent guards removed with this residual. For example, for Fig. 4b we are able to show that any successful trace entering the bid will always satisfy the **ongoing** condition, which is trivially implied the statement on line 2 in Listing 1.3.

This residual satisfies our required correctness condition, since it is assured that any removed guard evaluates positively when used at runtime.

Theorem 3. *$(P, \pi \,\|\, P)$ is in lockstep with (P, π).*

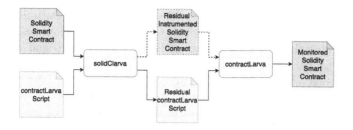

Fig. 5. Workflow with `solidClarva` and `contractLarva` (Dashed lines denote not yet implemented flows).

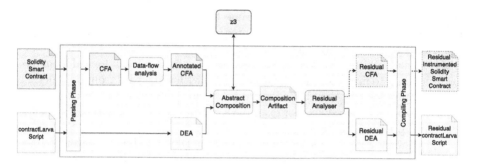

Fig. 6. Architecture of `solidClarva` (Dashed lines denote not yet implemented flows).

4   Tool

The principles and algorithms described in this chapter have been implemented in the `solidClarva` tool[7], implemented in Haskell.

This tool is meant to be used as a pre-processor for the `contractLarva` Solidity runtime verification tool [11,19], as illustrated in Fig. 5.

We have not yet implemented the flow to produce residual-instrumented smart contracts. This can be implemented by performing the analysis of `solidClarva` as part of the instrumentation process of `contractLarva`. Otherwise, to keep the two tools separate, another choice, illustrated in Fig. 5 with dashed lines, is to produce a smart contract with points that should not be instrumented but rather appropriately annotated and ignored by `contractLarva`.

4.1   Architecture and Flow

The architecture of `solidClarva` is illustrated in Fig. 6.

`solidClarva` uses the Solidity and DEA script parsing modules of `contractLarva` to parse the input text files into appropriate intermediate data structures.

---

[7] https://www.github.com/shaunazzopardi/solidity-static-analysis.

The CFA data structure is further analysed with a simple data-flow analysis, that considers the effect of statements on transitions. For example, if a state s is only accessible through a transition with condition $x == 0$ and a statement $y = 1$, then we can determine that $x == 0 \land y == 1$ is an appropriate state invariant for s. If s is accessible from multiple transitions, then the propositions generated in this manner for each transition can be combined disjunctively to produce an appropriate state invariant. In a similar manner we propagate state invariants of the previous states. A limitation of our simple analysis is that we propagate invariants only up to statements that affect them, and avoid dealing with issues related to loop invariants and variable updates.

The abstract composition module implements the logic of Definition 13, and exploits the generated invariants to prune the abstract state space to explore. This requires *satisfiability checking* of program conditions against DEA guards. In `solidClarva` this is implemented using a *satisfiability modulo theories* (SMT) solver: z3 [25]. Essentially z3 is able to check the satisfiability of logical formulas, corresponding to first-order logic with equality, with some background theory. To use z3 we provide functionality to represent Solidity statements and expressions as SMT-Lib [13] expressions. For example a condition $x = 0$ would be translated into the expression (`assert (= x 0)`).

The residual analyser module implements the DEA residual operators defined in Definitions 15 and 17, producing a residual DEA taken from applying both of these. Currently we have not implemented the instrumentation residual. Its utility for Solidity smart contracts needs to be re-visited. We have implemented this in the case of analysis of Java programs [10] in the `clarva` tool. There, for each function call event (e.g. entering a function) we created a version of the function that is unmonitored, and used that version in call sites we wanted to uninstrument. `contractLarva` performs instrumentation in a different manner, placing events inside of a function itself instead of at call sites. This makes perfect sense in the context of Solidity, since the functions are triggered by external users and not necessarily with known code. Then, in this case we can only determine that, for example, a function start event is not needed when we dually can determine that all transitions in the DEA that correspond to that event are also not needed. DEA reductions are then enough for DEAs with only function events.

In Solidity we are however also interested in another kind of event: *variable change events*. If a DEA has a transition on such an event, e.g. $x@(x == 1)$ (which triggers whenever variable x is changed and the new value is 1), then each location in the smart contract where the mentioned variable, x, changes is instrumented. Our analysis can help identifying locations that do not need to be instrumented, e.g. by identifying that the variable change condition will never hold or by concluding that the event can never occur at the source state of a DEA transition triggered by a corresponding event. We leave integration of this analysis into our tool for future work.

Finally, upon production of a residual DEA, `solidClarva` simply uses again the `contractLarva` parsing modules to compile the intermediate DEA data structure into a corresponding `contractLarva` monitor script.

Table 2. Evaluation of analysis with different case studies.

Case study		Added gas cost for monitoring as % of original gas		Added gas cost for residual monitoring as % of original gas	
		Deployment cost	Transaction average cost	Deployment cost	Transaction average cost
Auction	Fig. 4a	54.89%	33.71%	38.52%	27.78%
	Fig. 4b	41.49%	22.49%	0%	0%
	Fig. 4c	48.42%	17.59%	0%	0%
	Fig. 4d	52.42%	33.66%	52.42%	33.66%
Courier	v1-comp	181.5%	55.26%	103.21%	26.49%
	v1-viol	185.12%	66.1%	124.76%	62%
	v2-comp	120.5%	44.67%	107.32%	21.02%
	v2-viol	198.94%	29.69%	108.55%	30.71%
Ether-wallet	comp	114.14%	43.57%	0%	0%
	viol	114.36%	43.57%	43.83%	31.83%
Token-wallet	comp	28.67%	71.36%	0%	0%
	viol	77.76%	71.37%	39.38%	31.59%

5   Evaluation

We evaluated our approach and tool with a number of example smart contracts and specifications[8]. The motivation behind our analysis is to identify the parts of the DEA that the program satisfies, reducing the amount of computation that has to be done at runtime for verification. Then we wish to measure how much of the property was proven. This could be done by counting the numbers of property transitions and guards removed. However, this does not necessarily tell us how lighter computation-wise the residual is compared to the original one. For this we need a measure of computation.

Ethereum comes with a native measure of computation, *gas*. Each transaction in Ethereum in fact costs a pre-determined amount of gas [30], paid in *ether* (the Ethereum native token). The cost depends on the type of computation. This concept is useful since it ensures that any computation in Ethereum eventually ends (when the gas is all spent).

For our evaluation we then characterise the computation costs of a smart contract in terms of the needed gas to deploy it, and the (average) cost of executing its functions. Then, we calculate the extra computation costs induced by instrumenting a smart contract by a monitor of the original property, and

---

[8] Available at https://www.github.com/shaunazzopardi/solidity-static-analysis.

contrast this with that needed for the residual property. The results of our evaluation of twelve smart contract and property pairs is illustrated in Table 2. As can be noted, our analysis can both succeed in proving a property fully and fail in proving any of the property. In the case that the property is proven partially the reduced gas cases can be quite significant, even reducing the added costs of monitoring by almost half that of the original.

6   Discussion

The approach presented here is generally applicable. It is not limited to smart contracts, in fact we have implemented a similar earlier approach to residual analysis for symbolic typestate properties of Java programs [8,10]. Moreover, the effectiveness of the residual operators is only dependent on how complete the composition is. This means that future efforts can be focused on making the composition more complete, and the residual operators re-used. The composition can also be used in the future to identify actual violations, by considering transitions that are necessarily taken as in Definition 17.

It bears noting that the approach we consider here can be framed as a partial approach to verification. Verification techniques can be characterised as functions that determine whether a program satisfies a property, possibly failing: $ver : \mathbb{P} \times \Pi \to \{\top, \bot, ?\}$. A partial verification instead returns a reduced verification problem: $partialVer : \mathbb{P} \times \Pi \to \mathbb{P} \times \Pi$. If the returned property is the always-satisfied property (e.g. a DEA without any bad state), or the program has no event instrumentation, then satisfaction can be determined. If instead the always-violating property (e.g. a DEA with a bad initial state) is returned, then violation can be determined. Partial verification then merely generalises verification techniques by returning a verification problem that is at least sufficient to prove the original problem. Some further conditions may be useful to give, to ensure that the resulting problem is 'easier' to prove than the original. In our case this is self-evident, since the reduced problem is structurally smaller than the original.

The approach we give is intraprocedural (as is our implementation), however this approach can be easily extended to the interprocedural case. This can be done by inlining called methods in the caller CFA, with appropriate call and return transitions. Another method could be to simply adapt our algorithm to collect the transitions and instrumentation of the residual verification problem while analysing the smart contract through a depth-first search on-the-fly of the interprocedural composition. Intraprocedural analysis is however still useful. Consider that it can be used in the middle of development, when not all the functions of the smart contract have been implemented yet. It is also relevant that not all calls to external smart contracts may be statically determinable, preventing a full interprocedural representation.

The semantics of Ethereum bytecode depends on the notion of gas, which our formalism to model smart contracts fails to take into account. Each function call in Ethereum is executed with a certain amount of gas, and each computation or storage of values costs a pre-defined amount of gas [30]. This means that a function may be executed without the requisite amount of gas, leading to transaction failure and reversion of its effects. In our approach we are abstracting away from gas, and simply soundly modeling the effects of a smart contract.

7   Related Work

7.1   Verification Methods for Smart Contracts

We describe approaches to verifying Ethereum smart contracts, for a more complete survey see [4].

Albert et al. present SAFEVM, a tool that exploits existing robust verification tools through a translation from smart contracts as EVM bytecode into C programs [3]. This is done through an intermediate translation of the bytecode into a control-flow graph representation. SAFEVM verifies assertions in the smart contract (i.e. reverts and asserts) and array accesses. This approach is limited since the truth of assertions may depend on the input variables, and thus have to be enforced at runtime. There is similar work that proposes the use of existing tools through appropriate translations of Solidity code, e.g. Osterland and Rose translate Solidity code into PROMELA models and verifies their assertions using the SPIN model checker [26], and Ahrendt et al. propose translating Solidity into Java and exploiting the KeY theorem prover [1].

Zhang et al. also present the SMARTSHIELD approach that analyses bytecode, to identify pre-defined insecure patterns [32]. They also go one step further and transforms the code to correct the identified errors. There are three kinds of possibly insecure patterns considered: (i) modifying the variable state after an external call (which has been associated with ill-behaviour because of re-entrancy); (ii) no checks for out-of-bounds arithmetic operations; and (iii) not dealing with the possibility of failed external calls. This tool is focused on only these three properties, unlike our general approach.

A notable general approach for verification of EVM bytecode is that of Park et al. who present a model checker [27] exploiting KEVM, an executable complete semantics of the Ethereum virtual machine [21]. This approach allows the specification of functional correctness properties of smart contract functions. This approach may require some manual introduction of lemmas to aid verification. Our approach on the other hand is automated, where instead of requiring manual input in the case of failure we simply enforce or verify the unproven part of the property at runtime.

Permenev et al. describe VerX, an approach that verifies temporal properties of smart contracts, by projecting these into reachability properties, and through symbolic execution and predicate abstraction [28]. VerX considers smart contracts that are free of re-entrancy (or callbacks) from external smart contracts while in the middle of local function execution for scalability. In our approach we do not have such a limitation.

Li et al. present Solythesis, a tool for runtime validation of smart contracts [22]. Properties in this approach are quantified invariants on smart contract variables. Static analysis is employed to determine the set of variables that can be modified in a way that violates the required invariant. Only the points at which this can happen are then instrumented code to check and revert in case of misbehaviour at runtime. The runtime verification tool that we use for the runtime phase of our workflow has a more general specification language [11], however with no guarantees of better performance.

Mavridou et al. describe VeriSolid, a model-driven approach to verification of smart contracts specified as transition systems using state space exploration and properties defined in computation tree logic [24]. The model language used has guarded transitions, similar to ours, however we keep ours at a more abstract level for simplicity and general applicability to other languages. As opposed to our approach Mavridou et al. also consider liveness and properties about time variables.

7.2 Partial Verification

For smart contracts we then only find two tools that take a partial verification approach [22,32] (described above). In literature we also find partial verification approaches applied to different contexts, which we describe here briefly. These can be classified generally in terms of whether they deal with *event-based* or *state-based* approaches to verification. The former correspond to methods with specification languages corresponding to automata with transitions triggered by program events, while the latter consider instead properties as assertions at different points in the program.

On the event-based side, an early work that inspired ours is that of Bodden and Lam with the Clara tool [16]. This tool analyses properties as finite-state automata (with transitions tagged by events) against Java programs, by identifying points in the program that do not need to be instrumented. This is done intraprocedurally by identifying sequences of instrumentation points that together have no effect on the property, e.g. two instrumentation points may be removed if the event induced by the second cancels out the effects of the first. A different approach is taken by Dwyer and Purandare, where sequences of instrumentation that always have the same effect on the property are summarised [17]. The work presented here takes a different direction in that we remove property transitions and event instrumentation that cannot contribute to identifying or avoiding a violation. We also consider both control-flow and data concerns'.

For symbolic automata, in previous work we extended some of Clara's analyses for properties as symbolic automata [8]. Like Clara, that work ignored data aspects of the program. StaRVOOrS is an approach for symbolic automata that takes into account some data concerns but ignores the property control-flow [2]. This approach is complementary to ours, since the property automata considered by StaRVOOrS are syntactic extensions of ours, with states tagged by Hoare contracts. Essentially, the analysis considered proves Hoare contracts required of functions (i.e. whether a post-condition follows from a pre-condition and the function implementation). When it fails to do so, it strengthens the pre-condition with what is already known about the function.

On the state-based side, a main approach is that of Beyer et al., where the model checking problem is modified to transform the property with a predicate that characterises the states of the program that are left to prove to satisfy the property [14]. Then further analysis can be focused on the smaller state space. This work is further extended to be able to slice from a C program, the part of the program proven compliant [15]. This allows the approach to be used with out-of-the-box model checkers. This work has a similar approach to ours, where verification is focused on smaller parts of the program, however they do not consider the use of runtime verification.

8   Conclusions and Future Work

We have described an approach to combine inconclusive static analysis steps with runtime verification in the context of verification of Solidity smart contracts. Our approach – embodied in `solidClarva` – is model-based, where the smart contract is not verified directly but through a corresponding model. The specification we use is a form of symbolic automaton that consumes program events and variable state, while maintaining its own variable state.

In the future we intend on implementing an interprocedural approach to this residual analysis, by flattening the control-flow model we use. Moreover, we intend on adding a notion of gas in our modeling language, which can be useful in avoiding the analysis of paths that can be determined to always need more gas than the allowed gas limit. The runtime verification tool we consider `contractLarva` also has room for optimisation. For example, properties that simply correspond to pre- and post-conditions of a certain function could be detected and simply implemented with `require` and `assert` statements, rather than the more expensive general instrumentation approach.

References

1. Ahrendt, W., et al.: Verification of smart contract business logic - exploiting a Java source code verifier. In: Hojjat, H., Massink, M. (eds.) Fundamentals of Software Engineering - 8th International Conference, FSEN 2019, Tehran, Iran, May 1–3, 2019, Revised Selected Papers. Lecture Notes in Computer Science, vol. 11761, pp. 228–243. Springer, Heidelberg (2019). https://doi.org/10.1007/978-3-030-31517-7_16
2. Ahrendt, W., Pace, G.J., Schneider, G.: A unified approach for static and runtime verification: framework and applications. In: Margaria, T., Steffen, B. (eds.) Leveraging Applications of Formal Methods, Verification and Validation - 5th International Symposium, ISoLA 2012, Heraklion, Crete, Greece, Proceedings, Part I. LNCS, vol. 7609, pp. 312–326. Springer, Heidelberg (2012). https://doi.org/10.1007/978-3-642-34026-0_24
3. Albert, E., Correas, J., Gordillo, P., Román-Díez, G., Rubio, A.: SAFEVM: a safety verifier for Ethereum smart contracts. In: Proceedings of the 28th ACM SIGSOFT International Symposium on Software Testing and Analysis, ISSTA 2019, pp. 386–389. Association for Computing Machinery, New York (2019). https://doi.org/10.1145/3293882.3338999

4. Angelo, M.D., Salzer, G.: A survey of tools for analyzing Ethereum smart contracts. In: IEEE International Conference on Decentralized Applications and Infrastructures, DAPPCON 2019, Newark, CA, USA, April 4–9, 2019, pp. 69–78. IEEE (2019). https://doi.org/10.1109/DAPPCON.2019.00018

5. Atzei, N., Bartoletti, M., Cimoli, T.: A survey of attacks on Ethereum smart contracts SoK. In: Proceedings of the 6th International Conference on Principles of Security and Trust, vol. 10204, pp. 164–186. Springer, Heidelberg (2017). https://doi.org/10.1007/978-3-662-54455-6_8

6. Azzopardi, S., Colombo, C., Pace, G.: A technique for automata-based verification with residual reasoning. Tech. rep. CS-2019-02, Department of Computer Science, University of Malta (2019). https://www.um.edu.mt/ict/cs/ourresearch/technicalreports

7. Azzopardi, S., Colombo, C., Pace, G.J.: A model-based approach to combining static and dynamic verification techniques. In: Margaria, T., Steffen, B. (eds.) Leveraging Applications of Formal Methods, Verification and Validation: Foundational Techniques - 7th International Symposium, ISoLA 2016, Imperial, Corfu, Greece, October 10–14, 2016, Proceedings, Part I. Lecture Notes in Computer Science, vol. 9952, pp. 416–430. Springer, Cham (2016). https://doi.org/10.1007/978-3-319-47166-2_29

8. Azzopardi, S., Colombo, C., Pace, G.J.: Control-flow residual analysis for symbolic automata. In: Francalanza, A., Pace, G.J. (eds.) Proceedings Second International Workshop on Pre- and Post-Deployment Verification Techniques, Torino, Italy, 19 September 2017. Electronic Proceedings in Theoretical Computer Science, vol. 254, pp. 29–43. Open Publishing Association (2017). https://doi.org/10.4204/EPTCS.254.3

9. Azzopardi, S., Colombo, C., Pace, G.J.: A technique for automata-based verification with residual reasoning. In: Model-Driven Engineering and Software Development - 8th International Conference, MODELSWARD 2020, Valletta, Malta, February 25–27, 2020 (2020)

10. Azzopardi, S., Colombo, C., Pace, G.J.: CLarva: model-based residual verification of java programs. In: Model-Driven Engineering and Software Development - 8th International Conference, MODELSWARD 2020, Valletta, Malta, February 25–27, 2020 (2020)

11. Azzopardi, S., Ellul, J., Pace, G.J.: Monitoring smart contracts: contractLarva and open challenges beyond. In: Colombo, C., Leucker, M. (eds.) Runtime Verification, pp. 113–137. Springer, Cham (2018). https://doi.org/10.1007/978-3-030-03769-7_8

12. Azzopardi, S., Pace, G.J., Schapachnik, F.: On observing contracts: deontic contracts meet smart contracts. In: Palmirani, M. (ed.) Legal Knowledge and Information Systems - JURIX 2018: The Thirty-first Annual Conference, Groningen, The Netherlands, 12–14 December 2018. Frontiers in Artificial Intelligence and Applications, vol. 313, pp. 21–30. IOS Press (2018). https://doi.org/10.3233/978-1-61499-935-5-21

13. Barrett, C., Stump, A., Tinelli, C.: The SMT-LIB standard: version 2.0. In: Gupta, A., Kroening, D. (eds.) Proceedings of the 8th International Workshop on Satisfiability Modulo Theories, Edinburgh, UK (2010)

14. Beyer, D., Henzinger, T.A., Keremoglu, M.E., Wendler, P.: Conditional model checking: a technique to pass information between verifiers. In: Proceedings of the ACM SIGSOFT 20th International Symposium on the Foundations of Software Engineering, FSE 2012, pp. 57:1–57:11. ACM, New York (2012). https://doi.org/10.1145/2393596.2393664

15. Beyer, D., Jakobs, M.C., Lemberger, T., Wehrheim, H.: Reducer-based construction of conditional verifiers. In: Proceedings of the 40th International Conference on Software Engineering, ICSE 2018, pp. 1182–1193. ACM, New York (2018). https://doi.org/10.1145/3180155.3180259

16. Bodden, E., Lam, P.: Clara: partially evaluating runtime monitors at compile time. In: Barringer, H., et al. (eds.) Runtime Verification. RV 2010. Lecture Notes in Computer Science, vol. 6418. Springer, Heidelberg (2010). https://doi.org/10.1007/978-3-642-16612-9_8

17. Dwyer, M.B., Purandare, R.: Residual dynamic typestate analysis exploiting static analysis: results to reformulate and reduce the cost of dynamic analysis. In: Proceedings of the Twenty-Second IEEE/ACM International Conference on Automated Software Engineering, ASE 2007, pp. 124–133. ACM, New York (2007). https://doi.org/10.1145/1321631.1321651

18. Dwyer, M.B., Purandare, R.: Residual checking of safety properties. In: Havelund, K., Majumdar, R., Palsberg, J. (eds.) Model Checking Software. SPIN 2008. Lecture Notes in Computer Science, vol. 5156. Springer, Heidelberg (2008). https://doi.org/10.1007/978-3-540-85114-1_1

19. Ellul, J., Pace, G.J.: Runtime verification of Ethereum smart contracts. In: 14th European Dependable Computing Conference, EDCC 2018, Iaşi, Romania, September 10–14, 2018, pp. 158–163. IEEE Computer Society (2018). https://doi.org/10.1109/EDCC.2018.00036

20. Falcone, Y., Krstić, S., Reger, G., Traytel, D.: A taxonomy for classifying runtime verification tools. In: Colombo, C., Leucker, M. (eds.) Runtime Verification. RV 2018. Lecture Notes in Computer Science, vol. 11237. Springer, Cham (2018). https://doi.org/10.1007/978-3-030-03769-7_14

21. Hildenbrandt, E., et al.: KEVM: a complete formal semantics of the Ethereum virtual machine. In: 31st IEEE Computer Security Foundations Symposium, CSF 2018, Oxford, United Kingdom, July 9–12, 2018, pp. 204–217. IEEE Computer Society (2018). https://doi.org/10.1109/CSF.2018.00022

22. Li, A., Choi, J.A., Long, F.: Securing smart contract with runtime validation. In: Proceedings of the 41st ACM SIGPLAN Conference on Programming Language Design and Implementation, PLDI 2020, pp. 438–453. Association for Computing Machinery, New York (2020). https://doi.org/10.1145/3385412.3385982

23. Mavridou, A., Laszka, A.: Designing secure Ethereum smart contracts: a finite state machine based approach. In: Meiklejohn, S., Sako, K. (eds.) Financial Cryptography and Data Security - 22nd International Conference, FC 2018, Nieuwpoort, Curaçao, February 26–March 2, 2018, Revised Selected Papers. Lecture Notes in Computer Science, vol. 10957, pp. 523–540. Springer, Heidelberg (2018). https://doi.org/10.1007/978-3-662-58387-6_28

24. Mavridou, A., Laszka, A., Stachtiari, E., Dubey, A.: VeriSolid: correct-by-design smart contracts for Ethereum. In: Goldberg, I., Moore, T. (eds.) Financial Cryptography and Data Security, pp. 446–465. Springer, Cham (2019). https://doi.org/10.1007/978-3-030-32101-727

25. de Moura, L., Bjørner, N.: Z3: an efficient SMT solver. In: Ramakrishnan, C.R., Rehof, J. (eds.) Tools and Algorithms for the Construction and Analysis of Systems. TACAS 2008. Lecture Notes in Computer Science, vol. 4963. Springer, Heidelberg (2008). https://doi.org/10.1007/978-3-540-78800-3_24

26. Osterland, T., Rose, T.: Model checking smart contracts for Ethereum. Pervasive Mob. Comput. **63**, 101129 (2020). https://doi.org/10.1016/j.pmcj.2020.101129

27. Park, D., Zhang, Y., Saxena, M., Daian, P., Roşu, G.: A formal verification tool for Ethereum VM bytecode. In: Proceedings of the 2018 26th ACM Joint Meeting on European Software Engineering Conference and Symposium on the Foundations of Software Engineering, ESEC/FSE 2018, pp. 912–915. Association for Computing Machinery, New York (2018). https://doi.org/10.1145/3236024.3264591

28. Permenev, A., Dimitrov, D., Tsankov, P., Drachsler-Cohen, D., Vechev, M.: VerX: safety verification of smart contracts. In: 2020 IEEE Symposium on Security and Privacy (SP), pp. 414–430. IEEE Computer Society, Los Alamitos (May 2020)

29. Tran, A.B., Lu, Q., Weber, I.: Lorikeet: a model-driven engineering tool for blockchain-based business process execution and asset management. In: van der Aalst, W.M.P., et al. (eds.) Proceedings of the Dissertation Award, Demonstration, and Industrial Track at BPM 2018 Co-located with 16th International Conference on Business Process Management (BPM 2018), Sydney, Australia, September 9–14, 2018. CEUR Workshop Proceedings, vol. 2196, pp. 56–60. CEUR-WS.org (2018)

30. Wood, G.: Ethereum: a secure decentralised generalised transaction ledger. Ethereum Proj. Yellow Pap. **151**, 1–32 (2014)

31. Xu, X., Weber, I., Staples, M.: Model-driven engineering for blockchain applications. In: Architecture for Blockchain Applications. Springer, Cham (2019). https://doi.org/10.1007/978-3-030-03035-3_8

32. Zhang, Y., Ma, S., Li, J., Li, K., Nepal, S., Gu, D.: Smartshield: automatic smart contract protection made easy. In: 2020 IEEE 27th International Conference on Software Analysis, Evolution and Reengineering (SANER), pp. 23–34 (February 2020). https://doi.org/10.1109/SANER48275.2020.9054825

A Novel Family of Queuing Network Models for Self-adaptive Systems

Davide Arcelli[(✉)]

Department of Information Engineering, Computer Science and Mathematics,
University of L'Aquila, via Vetoio 1, 67100 L'Aquila, Italy
davide.arcelli@univaq.it,davide.arcelli@gmail.com

Abstract. A Self-adaptive System (SaS) consists of an autonomic manager which is able to adapt the system's behavior by operating on a managed sub-system that perceives and affects the environment through its sensors and actuators, respectively. Self-adaptation may occur at different levels, devising a number of knobs that the autonomic manager can properly regulate in order to produce actuation in response to environment sensing.

This paper is an extension of our previous work introducing a generalized QN model that allows performance modeling and assessment of SaSs. We here extend previous work by defining modeling patterns and controller selection policies to conform to during the instantiation of the generalized model, resulting into a novel family of QN models aimed at representing the different parts of the system and the dynamics occurring over and among them.

A controlled experiment addressing a realistic SaS for emergency handling shows that, by adhering to the defined patterns and controller selection policies, QN models behave as expected, and that the latter can be immersed into a performance optimization context that opens to the development of automated solutions to support the identification of efficient system configurations.

Keywords: Self-adaptive systems · Software architecture · Modeling patterns · Performance · Queuing networks · SMAPEA QNs

1 Introduction

In the last 15 years, new IT technologies have appeared and many applications of them have been proposed, where a hw/sw system is immersed in a dynamic environment subject to uncertainty [14,33]. In this context, the need to face such an uncertainty has brought to *Self-adaptive Systems* (SaSs). A SaS is composed by a *managed* and a *managing* sub-system: the former directly interacts with the environment by perceiving and affecting it by means of sensing and actuating

Supported by the Italian Ministry of Education, University and Research – MIUR, L. 297, art. 10.

S. Hammoudi et al. (Eds.): MODELSWARD 2020, CCIS 1361, pp. 349–376, 2021.
https://doi.org/10.1007/978-3-030-67445-8_15

components; the latter sub-system implements an autonomic manager which provides self-adaptation capabilities, that are the ability to adapt the system's behavior based on its awareness about the current environmental conditions. To this aim, the coupling between managed and managing sub-systems usually takes the form of *MAPE-K feedback loop(s)* [23], i.e. "an architecture model that divides the process of adaptation into four phases: Monitor (M), Analyze (A), Plan (P), and Execute (E). Data that is collected and used during adaptation is stored in the so-called Knowledge base (K)" [9].

Much work has been done to devise autonomic managers implementing self-adaptation mechanisms. With this regard, most of existing approaches exploit Model-Driven Architecture (MDA) principles [25] to abstract the system and its self-adaptation capabilities. In addition, other kind of notations have been exploited to model and analyze non-functional attributes – e.g. performance, reliability and energy [35] – of the managing sub-system and its adaptation mechanisms.

Among non-functional attributes, performance has gained importance, as from several literature studies [9,34,35]. Hence, Performance Engineering approaches have been proposed for modeling and assessing performance of the managing sub-system, by either coupling MDA and performance modeling notations or directly working onto a non-functional representation of the SaS – i.e. adaptation is enabled onto the performance model[1].

Besides, techniques of different nature have been leveraged in order to devise efficient adaptation mechanisms, especially by approaches working directly on performance models. For instance, Control Theory has been used to introduce local [5,6] or global [21] MAPE loops for providing formal performance guarantees in the context of Queuing Networks (QNs) [27]. Furthermore, Machine Learning allowed to introduce different forms of performance-driven automated reasoning aimed at deciding about adaptation [7,8,13,17,20,22,26,28].

This paper extends our previous work [3], where we have illustrated how to cast a SaS to a QN, thus to be able to leverage QN analysis tools and methods for assessing the performance of such systems, in ways that were not previously possible. In particular, a generalized QN performance model has been introduced in previous work [3] that, differently from existing approaches, abstracts both sub-systems of a SaS, widening the focus of performance analysis from the self-adaptation mechanisms (in charge of the managing subsystem only) to the whole SaS. QN *stations* represent system's components and are properly visited by *job classes* corresponding to the different types of tasks (jobs) they perform, i.e. Sensing, Actuating and MAPE activities. These latter tasks, whose execution is in charge of control components within the managing sub-system, are involved in a MAPE loop implemented by exploiting advanced QN constructs, i.e. class switches, which enable dynamic job class transformation conforming to the system's mode profile [32].

---

[1] As highlighted in previous work [4], the expressiveness of the architectural notation, as well as the available degree of tool support, heavily affect approach potential in terms of "what and how" to adapt.

Previous work is here extended by defining a set of modeling patterns that allow to instantiate the different parts of the generalized model, thus defining a novel family of QNs, namely SMAPEA QNs. By conforming to these patterns, it is possible to model SaSs in terms of their managing and managed subsystems, and to enable performance analysis based on specific parameters such as workload, components service demands, mode-adaptation probabilities and controller selection policy. The latter define the criteria for routing MAPE jobs to controllers, which are also devised in this paper.

SMAPEA QNs have been preliminarily evaluated in previous work [3] by showing that they allow to model and assess the performance of a realistic SaS for emergency handling and they can help in identifying controller selection policies that may enhance performance. Such preliminary evaluation is here extended by: (i) matching the considered SaS to the defined modeling patterns and showing that the corresponding SMAPEA QN behaves as expected under controlled conditions; (ii) considering several controller selection policies, with the main goal of opening to the development of optimization techniques (e.g. search-space exploration with genetic algorithms [16]) that might overcome the human in devising efficient system configurations, thus providing valid support to performance modeling, assessment and optimization of SaSs.

The paper is structured as follows: Sect. 2 illustrates a motivating scenario which needs a SaS with efficient performance. Section 3 firstly illustrates the generalized SMAPEA QN model and the underlying reference self-adaptation model and then it describes modeling patterns to instantiate the former. Section 4 provides an experimentation aimed at showing that SMAPEA QNs can be successfully applied to performance modeling and assessment of SaSs and they can provide valid support to performance optimization of such systems. Section 5 reviews existing approaches exploiting the QNs as performance notation for SaSs. Section 6 concludes the paper and points out future research intents.

2 Motivating Scenario

Figure 1 shows a motivating scenario in the context of emergency handling, designed for a real exhibition venue in Alan Turing Building – Department of Information Engineering, Computer Science and Mathematics – L'Aquila, Italy, and used to evaluate SMAPEA QNs.

The scenario addresses the problem of monitoring people in a public *area* (i.e. a building room), while keeping track of environment temperature and CO_2 level, in order to intervene in case an evacuation of the area shall be needed due to fire detection. People position and movements are detected by CCTV cameras, whilst date concerning temperature and CO_2 levels are measured by specific sensors. Sensed data are forwarded to an autonomous manager which is required to be continuously aware of the area and to properly react by affecting the environment through actuation, based on the situation. To this aim, the autonomous manager aggregates and analyzes sensed data, in order to establish if safety thresholds are overcame, thus causing a *switching* from *normal* to *critical* operational mode.

In normal mode, actuation consists of displaying a dynamic 2D-representation of the area on a dashboard, while periodically estimating the time needed to empty the area through usual exits.

In critical mode, people evacuation is needed. Hence, as a fire is detected, the autonomous manager contrives an optimal evacuation plan as soon as possible, resulting into the activation of evacuation signs which indicate the best evacuation routes while an acoustic alarm alerts people. In addition, the 2D-representation the dashboard is augmented with additional information useful to security assistants and, eventually, rescue teams.

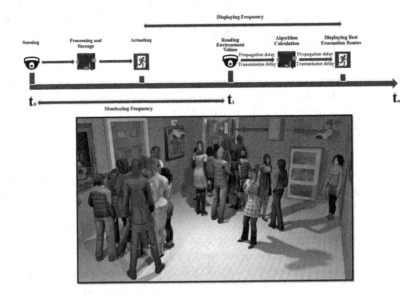

Fig. 1. Infrastructure for emergency response [1].

The motivating scenario devises a SaS with a number of Sensing and Actuating components within the managed sub-system (i.e. CCTV cameras, temperature and CO_2 sensors, dashboard, acoustic alarm and evacuation signs) interacting with the autonomous manager in the managing sub-system; the latter implements a MAPE control loop by exploiting a number of control components performing Monitor, Analyze, Plan and Execute activities.

As can be understood from the description above, the scenario is very challenging, because it requires the SaS to react quickly, as the latter is immersed in a safety-critical context. In such a context, performance become a key-aspect, thus requiring to leverage performance modeling notations and assessment techniques that may help in identifying efficient system configurations. This is the main goal of SMAPEA QNs, which represent a novel family of QN models for modeling and assessing the performance of SaSs, by considering both their managed and managing sub-systems, as well as the activities executed by the latter, i.e. Sense/Actuation and MAPE, respectively.

3 SMAPEA Queuing Networks

As mentioned before, the goal of this paper is to introduce a novel family of QN models to support performance modeling and analysis of SaSs, in terms of both managing and managed subsystems. To this aim, prior to the definition of a pattern-based generalized QN model which allows to address a plethora of SaSs, the underlying reference model for self-adaptation is described.

3.1 Reference Self-adaptation Model

Figure 2 illustrates the self-adaptation model SMAPEA QNs rely on, which comes from a reworking on the autonomic control loop model proposed by Weyns et al. [36] and which has been firstly introduced in previous work [3].

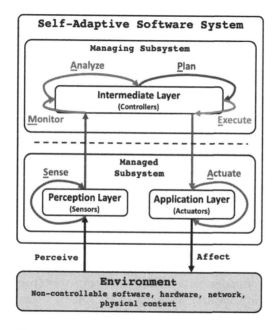

Fig. 2. Reference model for self-adaptation [3].

The SaS can perceive the *environment* by means of sensing components deployed to a conceptual macro-component named *Perception Layer* (PL) located into the *managed subsystem*. The latter contains another macro-component as well, namely *Application Layer* (AL), which contains actuating components through which the system can affect the environment.

Actuation results from a complex interpretation of what has been perceived by the system and is aimed at implementing an adaptation of the latter's behavior. This is in charge of the *managing subsystem*, which contains the so-called *Intermediate Layer* (IL) where a number of control components are deployed to.

Due to the fact that the managed and managing subsystems operate in synergy, they are connected by network(s) (see the dashed line).

Conforming to Weyns et al. [36], the adaptation logic is realized through the four sequential activities of MAPE control loops [23], namely *Monitor* (M), *Analyze* (A), *Plan* (P) and *Execute* (E).

Table 1. MAPE Vs. SMAPEA control loops [3].

Order	Activities	
	Weyns et al. [36]	Our approach
0	-	Sense (measure)
1	Monitor (collect)	Monitor (collect)
2	Analyze (determine)	Analyze (determine)
3	Plan (prepare)	Plan (contrive)
4	Execute (act)	Execute (prepare)
5	-	Actuate (act)

As from Table 1, two additional activities are devised, namely (0) *Sense* and (5) *Actuate*, both taking place at the managed subsystem, thus widening the scope of performance modeling and analysis to system boundaries, i.e. where interactions with the environment occur.

Sense is associated to the term "measure" to distinguish raw data retrieval from their subsequent aggregation performed during *Monitor* ("collect"). *Plan* is associated to the term "contrive" rather than "prepare", in order to better distinguish between conceiving an adaptation and preparing the sequence of actions needed to *Execute* the adaptation. The term "act" naturally shifts to *Actuate*, that is in charge of the managed subsystem.

SMAPEA activities are thus performed spanning among sensors (responsible for *Sense*), controllers (responsible for MAPE) and actuators (responsible for *Actuate*). This brings to a natural mapping of (i) system's components onto QN *stations* and (ii) activities onto QN *job classes*, resulting into the generalized model described in the next section. Distinguishing system topology and the dynamics occurring into the latter represents an improvement compared to the work by Weyns et al. [36], where MAPE activities are directly mapped to ad-hoc components, resulting into an inextricable binding between static and dynamic aspects of the system.

Concerning the self-adaptation itself, SMAPEA QNs ground on *mode-adaptation*. The has been used since more than a decade to devise different configurations among which a system may transit for self-adaptation [30], based on a mode profile represented by a set of predefined probabilities [32]. For instance, Fig. 3 shows a mode profile for the motivating scenario.

The system can *switch* between *normal* and *critical* modes with 12% and 88% probability, respectively. Based on the latter, *Sense* jobs are trans-

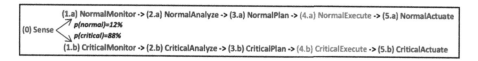

Fig. 3. Example of self-adaptation within SMAPEA Queuing Networks [3].

formed into mode-specific *Monitor* jobs, corresponding to the adoption of a particular mode. MAPE jobs, as well as *Actuate* ones, shall be thus "instantiated" modulo those two modes, resulting into 10 MAPEA instances, i.e. {*Normal, Critical*} × {*Monitor, Analyze, Plan, Execute, Actuate*}.

In addition, *Actuate* instantiation also depends on the specific type of actuation. For example, the SaS for the motivating scenario has three actuating components, namely *Dashboard, Alarm* and *EvacuationSigns*; hence, six *Actuate*-instances shall be devised, i.e. {*Normal, Critical*} × {*DashboardActuate, Alarm Actuate, EvacuationSignsActuate*}. Similarly, *Sense* instantiation depends on the specific type of sensing. For example, the considered SaS has three sensing components, namely *CCTVs*, CO_2 and *Temperature*; hence three *Sense* instances might be devised, i.e. *CameraSense*, CO_2Sense and *TemperatureSense*.

3.2 Generalized Queuing Network Model for SaSs

Figure 4 depicts the generalized QN conforming to the reference self-adaptation model of Sect. 3.1, i.e. in terms of PL, AL and IL, their connections and the job classes visiting them while flowing through the QN.

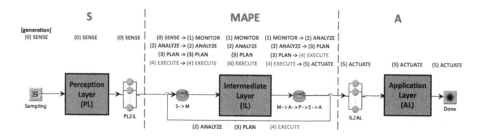

Fig. 4. Generalized SMAPEA queuing network model [3].

The QN is partitioned in three parts, namely **S**, **MAPE** and **A**, containing PL's sensors, IL's controllers and AL's actuators, respectively. Such system components are mapped onto (properly connected and parameterized) *stations*, whilst SMAPEA activities naturally map onto *job classes* visiting those stations.

As PL and AL are at the boundaries, they are connected to source and sink nodes, namely *Sampling* and *Done*, respectively. The latter realize Perceive and

`Affect` interactions of Fig. 2, as follows: At the **S**-side, *Sampling* emulates environmental stimuli by generating $SENSE$ jobs, based on a certain probability distribution to be specified; At the **A**-side, *Done* represents that actuation has been performed and the environment has been (possibly) affected.[2]

Notice that a single workload source is illustrated in Fig. 4, meaning that sensors have the same sampling rate, however more workload sources can be introduced for the different areas of the system.

Both PL and the AL are connected to the IL through $PL2IL$ and $IL2AL$ delay stations, respectively, representing the network(s) between the two sub-systems.

The `SMAPEA` control loop is implemented by two *class-switch*es, namely $S{\to}M$ and $M{\to}A{\to}P{\to}E{\to}A$, placed before and after the IL, respectively. $S{\to}M$ transforms $SENSE$ jobs into $MONITOR$ to realize mode-based adaptation, whilst $M{\to}A{\to}P{\to}E{\to}A$ transforms each `MAPEA` job into a job of the subsequent type to progress along the `MAPE` loop.

Mode-adaptation grounds on the mode-switching probabilities mentioned in Sect. 3.1 and exemplified in Fig. 3. Mode-specific $MONITOR$ jobs (e.g. *Normal* and *CriticalMonitor*) are generated from $SENSE$ jobs with certain probabilities and then forwarded to the controllers, spending their demands before visiting $M{\to}A{\to}P{\to}E{\to}A$. The latter transforms them into $ANALYZE$ jobs, which are routed back to $S{\to}M$. The loop is further iterated by producing the subsequent mode-specific $PLAN$, $EXECUTE$ and $ACTUATE$ jobs. $ACTUATE$ jobs are finally forwarded to the **A**-side for actuation.

When a `MAPE` job is forwarded to the IL, one controller among the ones in the latter must be chosen to serve that job. This choice is referred as *Controller Selection Policy* (CSP), and is in charge to $S{\to}M$. Hence, specifying a CSP for a `SMAPEA` QN corresponds to the specification of $S{\to}M$ routing strategies for each job class. Several other routing strategies are available, such as random, round-robin, and others which consider controllers' metrics at the time the routing is performed (e.g. forwarding to the controller with the shortest queue length). However, in this paper we consider probability-based routing strategies only, leaving other strategies as future work without jeopardizing paper contribution. In fact, a probability-based strategy for $S{\to}M$ could be exploited to devise different system configurations, as shown later in Sect. 4.

3.3   Modeling Patterns for SMAPEA QNs

We describe in the following several ways to "instantiate" **S**-, **MAPE**- and **A**-parts of the generalized SMAPEA QN model, by defining modeling patterns that allow to introduce: (i) sensing and actuating components within the managed sub-system (Sect. 3.3), (ii) controllers within the IL and CSP for $S{\to}M$ (Sect. 3.3). To this aim, we define *Logical Decomposition Units* (LDUs) for each of the three parts. An LDU characterizes configurations of system components within a specific part of the

---

[2] By uppercase words we denote all *Sense, Monitor, Analyze, Plan, Execute* and *Actuate* job classes. E.g., with respect to Fig. 3, $MONITOR = \{NormalMonitor, CriticalMonitor\}$.

SMAPEA QN and the dynamics occurring in that part. Hence, LDUs can be *instantiated* and properly *connected* in order to specify SMAPEA QNs for specific SaSs.

Managed Sub-system. LDUs for **S**- and **A**-parts allow to model – respectively – sensing and actuating components of the managed sub-system by organizing them into *areas*. In particular, each LDU devises an area where a *cluster* of one or more sensing/actuating components is deployed. For example, a building may be divided into several areas (e.g. rooms), each equipped with a cluster of sensing components, i.e. a CCTV, a temperature sensor and a CO_2 sensor, and a cluster of actuating components, i.e. a dashboard, an alarm and evacuation signs.[3]

Figure 5 illustrates the LDU for **S**-part. It contains a number of sensing components surrounded by a fork and a join aimed at properly splitting (i.e. fork) *Sense* jobs and distributing them among those components. Those jobs arrive at the fork – see the dashed arrow in Fig. 5 – either directly from a workload source or indirectly, from a preceding fork (not shown in the figure), which also determine the sampling of sensing components.[4]

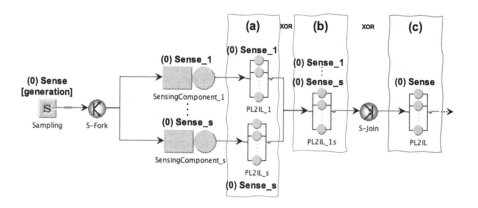

Fig. 5. LDU for **S**-part.

Figure 5 devises three mutually exclusive positions for delay stations representing networks between PL and IL. In particular, each sensing component may have a separate network (case a) or, alternatively, only one delay station may be exploited – either before (case b) or after the join (case c) – meaning that all the sensing components within that area use the same network. Choosing among those alternatives strictly depends on the particular system and available data. In fact, as can be noticed from Fig. 5, different job classes result from the three alternatives, hence different service demands must be specified.

---

[3] Notice that, in general, the number of areas which sensing and actuating components are deployed to can be different.

[4] In the particular case of a cluster with only one sensing component, fork and join can be omitted, thus making (b) and (c) equivalent.

Figure 6 shows a generic example with a areas in the **S**-part, each having a cluster with a number i of sensing components. Delay stations are placed conforming to case (c) of Fig. 5.

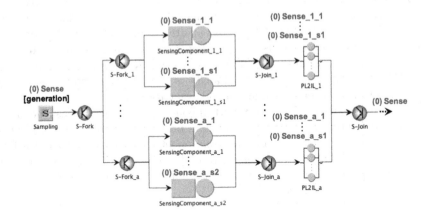

Fig. 6. LDU instantiation for **S**-part.

Concerning the LDU for **A**-part, we refer to Fig. 7. Similarly to the **S**-part, a number of actuating components are surrounded by a fork and a join, aimed at properly splitting (i.e. fork) $ACTUATE$ jobs (i.e. fork) and distributing them among those components.[5]

Moreover, delay stations representing networks between IL and AL can be positioned in two mutually exclusive ways, i.e.: (a) before the fork, in case all the actuating components of the cluster use the same network or (b) each actuating component is on a separate network.

Figure 8 shows a generic example with a areas in the **A**-part (possibly corresponding to the ones in Fig. 6), each having a cluster with a number a_j of actuating components. Delay stations are placed conforming to case (a) of Fig. 7.

Managing Sub-system. The LDU for **MAPE**-part allow to model control components of the managing sub-system in terms of *local* and *remote* controllers, with respect to the autonomous system realizing the MAPE control loop.

As from Fig. 9, remote controllers are included between delay stations representing a network (e.g. a cloud). Instead, no delay nodes are introduced while specifying local controllers.

The *Controller Selection Policy* (CSP) that has been previously mentioned in Sect. 3.2 defines the strategy adopted by $S{\rightarrow}M$ to forward incoming jobs to its outgoing paths. While defining a CSP, a number of routing strategies must be specified for $S{\rightarrow}M$, i.e. one for each MAPE job class flowing through the latter. In particular,

---

[5] As for the **S**-part, in the particular case of a cluster with only one actuating component, fork and join can be omitted.

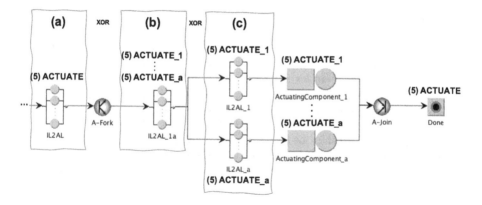

Fig. 7. LDU for **A**-part.

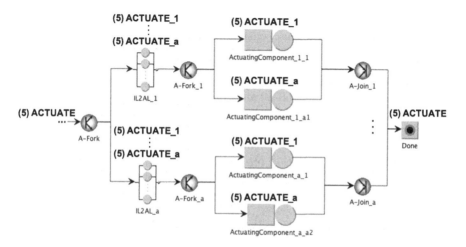

Fig. 8. LDU instantiation for **A**-part.

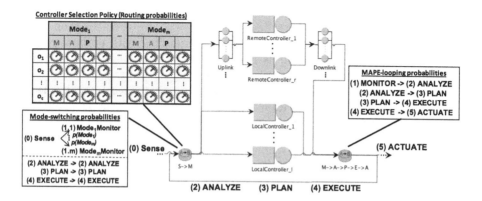

Fig. 9. LDU for **MAPE**-part.

it corresponds to a $o \times 4m$ matrix, where o is the number of $S{\rightarrow}M$ outgoing paths and m is the number of system modes. Hence, each column of the matrix defines the routing strategy for a MAPE job class related to a specific mode, with respect to $S{\rightarrow}M$ outgoing paths (o_i).

By reasoning at different level of abstraction, jobs can be routed based on two dimensions: (i) the MAPE activities they belong to and (ii) the system modes they refer to. This results into the following four possible combinations:

(1) CSP.equality. All the jobs follow the same (unique) strategy. In other words, there is no distinction based on the corresponding system modes or MAPE activities.
(2) CSP.activities. Jobs belonging to the same MAPE activity (e.g. $MONI$-TOR) follow the same routing strategy, independently from system modes.
(3) CSP.modes. Jobs referring to the same system mode (e.g. normal or critical) follow the same routing strategy, independently from the MAPE activity they belong to.
(4) CSP.diversity. Each job follows its own routing strategy, independently from any other class. This means considering both the MAPE activity and the system mode it corresponds to, at the same time.

As noticed before, several routing strategies are available and some of them allow to introduce run-time self-adaptation, but we only consider probability-based routing strategies in this paper. We limit the scope with respect to CSP in order to avoid further complexity needing a deep investigation of possible side-effects and solutions to overcome them.

At this point, an optimization problem can be defined, concerning the CSP specification, namely *CSP problem*. The CSP problem consists in identifying optimal $S{\rightarrow}M$ routing strategies for incoming MAPE jobs. The term "optimal" refers to some performance indices of interest, that usually are the mean system response times of the different system modes (i.e. $ACTUATE$ jobs). In fact, system modes are "concurrent", as the probabilities that the system is operating in each mode always sum to 100%. Consequently, performance optimization in this context is a matter of trade-off modulo system modes.

The CSP problem may exist at design- and/or run-time, introducing a further dimension (i.e. the CSP) for self-adaptation beside the mode-based one. The aim at design-time is the identification of system designs with optimal performance; instead, the aim at run-time is dynamic system reconfiguration by adapting $S{\rightarrow}M$ routing strategies.

The definition of the CSP problem opens to its automated resolution by means of, e.g., multi-objective optimization meta-heuristics such as genetic algorithms [16], as highlighted by the experimentation of Sect. 4.

3.4   Limitations

The SMAPEA QN family in its current form presents a number of limitations.

The most significant one concerns the fact that the **MAPE**-part implements a single MAPE loop where IL components control all the sensing and actuating components. On the one hand, this allows to assume that the information which is typically shared among control components – i.e. the *Knowledge* – is implicit within the model, since there is one overall control flow that is managed by the (unique) **MAPE**-part. On the other hand, having a single MAPE loop would not allow to model decentralized architectural patterns, such as the ones introduced by Weyns et al. [36], where different MAPE loops or part of them interact each other and participate to the adaptations concerning other portions of the system.

Enabling decentralization within SMAPEA QNs would mean being able to "compose" **MAPE**-parts of different SMAPEA QNs, each responsible for a set of sensing and actuating components. Such a composition might result into very large and complex models where the different ILs interact by routing their corresponding jobs among themselves. For this reason, we plan to address decentralized MAPE loops in the future.

Moreover, although sensing components within the **S**-part may be clustered with respect to different areas that the SaS spans over, a unique sampling rate shared by those components can be specified, which limits SMAPEA QNs modeling potential. The definition of ad-hoc sampling rate for specific clusters of sensing components shall be enabled in the future, however this requires a deep investigation aimed at identifying additional patterns.

Another important limitation is that SMAPEA QNs are multi-class models containing class-switches and fork/join. For this reason, they cannot be solved with exact analytical techniques [15], but only by simulation. In practical terms, those constructs are currently supported by JMT tool-suite [11] only, which thus represents a "single-point-of-failure". However, although JMT represents a standard de-facto, its adoption implies a number of limitations due to absence/inadequacy of some features that – realistically – might be implemented/enhanced in the future. For instance, JSimGraph currently lacks features enabling sensitivity (*what-if*) analyses with respect to variations of class-switch routing probabilities (i.e. $S{\rightarrow}M$ mode-switching probabilities). Furthermore, the what-if analyses that are currently available are not adequate to conduct significant sensitivity analyses with respect to variations of service demands, because they address one component at a time.

Finally, like most of related work exploiting QN as performance modeling notation [9], our approach suffers from the neglect of reconfiguration times and costs, due to the fact that only steady states of the system are analyzed.

4 Experimentation

In this section, a controlled experiment is conducted with respect to a realistic case study from previous work [3], aimed at answering the following Research Questions (RQs):

RQ_1: *Can SMAPEA QNs be successfully applied to performance modeling and assessment of SaSs?* To this aim, the SMAPEA QN for the considered case study is firstly matched to the patterns illustrated in Sect. 3.3; then we show that, by adhering to those patterns, the obtained performance model behaves as expected.

RQ_2: *Can SMAPEA QNs provide valid support to performance optimization of SaSs?* With this regard, a number of system configurations (in terms of different CSPs) are considered: some of those represent configurations that a human may easily conceive, whilst others represent more complex configurations which are very hard for a human to devise. By showing that at least one of the latter configurations overcome the former ones, we demonstrate that SMAPEA QNs have the potential for introducing significant added-value to performance optimization of SaSs.

4.1   Subject of the Experimentation

A SMAPEA QN representing a SaS performance model for the motivating scenario described in Sect. 2 is illustrated in Fig. 10.

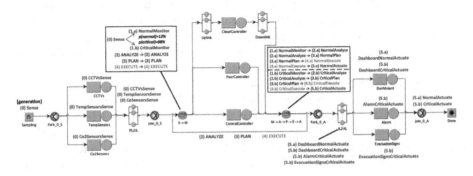

Fig. 10. SMAPEA QN for the considered case study [3]. For sake of illustration $S \rightarrow M$ routing probabilities are not reported, as they vary during the experiment.

The QN model conforms the patterns introduced in Sect. 3.3 as follows:

- Both **S**- and **A**-part devise only one area (i.e. one cluster of components), since just one room of the building (i.e. the main hall) is considered. We remark that (shared) sampling is modeled by a deterministic distribution, denoted by det(k), as the latter describes a constant flow of customers, arriving exactly every k time units [12].
- **S**-part has been modeled conforming to case (b) of Fig. 5, whilst the **A**-part conforms to case (b) of Fig. 7.
- **MAPE**-part has been modeled by instantiating the pattern of Fig. 9 with two local controllers – namely *CentralController* and *PeerController* – and a remote controller – namely *CloudController* – deployed at the cloud by placing it between *Uplink* and *Downlink* delay stations.

4.2   QN Parameterization

Like any other QN, a SMAPEA QN must be parameterized, i.e. a set of input parameters has to be provided. Among those, some depend on the specific system, thus representing a sort of "control variables" around which experiments can be devised. In particular, the input must be characterized in terms of:

- **Workload** distribution and corresponding mean values for each source node.
- **Service demand** distribution and corresponding mean values for each station (i.e. service centers and delay nodes).
- **Class-switching** probabilities for $S{\rightarrow}M$, each representing the probability for the system to operate in a certain mode.
- **Routing** probabilities for $S{\rightarrow}M$, i.e. a CSP matrix defining how incoming jobs are forwarded to outgoing paths based on the class they belong to.

Several experimental settings can be thus devised with respect to the input parameters above. For example, one could be interested in analyzing different mode-switching probabilities while varying controllers' service demands; As another example, given fixed service demands and mode-switching probabilities, a sensitivity analysis modulo different workload intensities could be conducted, aimed at studying different CSPs. The latter setting is adopted for the controlled experiment, in particular increasing intensities for the (deterministic) workload distribution are considered, i.e. 2.5 (minimum intensity), 2.25, 2, 1.75, 1.5, 1.25, 1, 0.75, 0.5 (maximum intensity).

Components' service demands are fixed in the experiment, as well as $S{\rightarrow}M$ class-switching probabilities. Concerning the former, they are all exponential distributions; transmission and propagation delays for sensing, actuating and networking components, as well as controllers' processing times for the different MAPE activities, have been obtained by means of CAPS [31] simulation tool and the well-known CPLEX.[6]

We do not detail here the service demand definition, however it must be remarked that all the controllers have the same service demands for MAPE job classes, i.e. they have identical CSP matrices. On the one hand, this allows to perform the experimentation in a "controlled environment", i.e. an experimental setting that is suitable to prove that the SMAPEA QN is correct and behaves as expected. On the other hand, it avoids unnecessary complexity that may harden reasoning about the quality of experimental results.

Moreover, it is worth to notice that *CriticalPlan* has the highest magnitude, thus making the critical mode crucial in determining a physiological lower bound to system performance. For this reason, we set mode-switching probabilities of 12% for *Normal* and 88% for *Critical*, respectively, which allow to stress the system during emergencies.

Finally, performance indices of interest have to be defined. For a certain type of performance index, e.g. mean response time, mean throughput, SMAPEA QNs allow to address it at system level, modulo system modes. In the controlled experiment,

---

[6] http://www.cplex.com/.

we consider the mean system response time for each mode, i.e. for *NormalActuate* and *CriticalActuate* job classes.

4.3 Methodology

The experimentation is divided into two phases.

Phase 1. By means of probability-based CSP.equality, three types of system configurations are devised, namely centralized, collaborative and hybrid, as reported in Table 2. Centralized forwards any $S{\rightarrow}M$ incoming job to the same controller; Collaborative equally distributes the load between two out of three controllers; *Hybrid* equally distributes the load between all the controllers. Local and remote versions exist for centralized and collaborative: the former versions exploit local controllers only (i.e. *CentralController* and/or *PeerController*), whilst the latter – that represent additions with respect to previous work [3] – involve the remote controller (i.e. *CloudController*).

Table 2. Human-conceived system configurations (CSP.equality).

Pattern		Routing Probabilities							
		Normal				Critical			
Name	Destination	M	A	P	E	M	A	P	E
Centralized. local	CentralController	1	1	1	1	1	1	1	1
	PeerController	0	0	0	0	0	0	0	0
	CloudController	0	0	0	0	0	0	0	0
Centralized. remote	CentralController	0	0	0	0	0	0	0	0
	PeerController	0	0	0	0	0	0	0	0
	CloudController	1	1	1	1	1	1	1	1
Collaborative. local	CentralController	0.5	0.5	0.5	0.5	0.5	0.5	0.5	0.5
	PeerController	0.5	0.5	0.5	0.5	0.5	0.5	0.5	0.5
	CloudController	0	0	0	0	0	0	0	0
Collaborative. remote	CentralController	0.5	0.5	0.5	0.5	0.5	0.5	0.5	0.5
	PeerController	0	0	0	0	0	0	0	0
	CloudController	0.5	0.5	0.5	0.5	0.5	0.5	0.5	0.5
Hybrid	CentralController	0.334	0.334	0.334	0.334	0.334	0.334	0.334	0.334
	PeerController	0.333	0.333	0.333	0.333	0.333	0.333	0.333	0.333
	CloudController	0.333	0.333	0.333	0.333	0.333	0.333	0.333	0.333

The five system configurations defined above can be seen as typical configurations that a human could conceive as, in general, it is very hard for the latter to devise more complex configurations when service demands are very heterogeneous (i.e. non-controlled environment), that is what happens in real contexts. However, being in a controlled environment allows to point out some hypotheses that shall be met after experiment execution, thus allowing to conclude that SMAPEA QNs behave as expected (RQ_1), i.e.:

H_1. Mean response times for *CriticalActuate* shall be greater than *NormalActuate*, mostly due to the fact that *CriticalPlan* service demand has the highest magnitude.

H_2. Pattern shall saturate in the following order, as the workload intensity increases: centralized, collaborative, hybrid, as they involve an increasing number of controllers (i.e., 1, 2 and 3, respectively).

H_3. Remote versions of the patterns shall be always worse than the corresponding local versions, as the former involve the additional delay introduced by *Uplink* and *Downlink*.

H_4. As consequences of H_2 and H_3:

> H_{4a}. Centralized.remote shall be the worst pattern, as it involves one controller only (i.e. the minimum) that is the remote one.
>
> H_{4b}. Excluding hybrid, Collaborative.local shall be the best pattern, as it involves the maximum number of controllers and they are all local.

Phase 2. Further system configurations potentially bringing to performance enhancement may be identified, by exploiting different probability-based CSPs.

For example, let us suppose that saturation shall be avoided. We thus look for hybrid alternatives, as the one that has been devised during Phase 1 by exploiting CSP.equality is expected to be the configuration able to manage more workload intensities than the other ones (H_2). Table 3 reports three hybrid alternatives – namely hybrid.modes, hybrid.activities and hybrid.diversity – each adopting a different probability-based CSP. The human-conceived hybrid pattern – namely hybrid.equality – is reported as well.

Table 3. Alternative system configurations (rows 2–4).

Pattern		Routing Probabilities							
		Normal				Critical			
Name	Destination	M	A	P	E	M	A	P	E
Hybrid. equality	CentralController	0.334	0.334	0.334	0.334	0.334	0.334	0.334	0.334
	PeerController	0.333	0.333	0.333	0.333	0.333	0.333	0.333	0.333
	CloudController	0.333	0.333	0.333	0.333	0.333	0.333	0.333	0.333
Hybrid. activities	CentralController	1	0.334	0.334	1	1	0.334	0.334	1
	PeerController	0	0.333	0.333	0	0	0.333	0.333	0
	CloudController	0	0.333	0.333	0	0	0.333	0.333	0
Hybrid. modes	CentralController	0	0	0	0	0.334	0.334	0.334	0.334
	PeerController	1	1	1	1	0.333	0.333	0.333	0.333
	CloudController	0	0	0	0	0.333	0.333	0.333	0.333
Hybrid. diversity	CentralController	0.792	0.693	0.399	0.853	0.735	0.981	0.294	0.921
	PeerController	0.158	0.02	0.097	0.011	0.196	0.004	0.372	0.062
	CloudController	0.05	0.287	0.504	0.137	0.069	0.015	0.334	0.017

The three alternative configurations have been devised as follows:

- Hybrid.activities equally distributes the most demanding MAPE activities, i.e. *Analyze* and *Plan*, whilst the remaining ones – that are less demanding – are routed like centralized.local.
- Hybrid.modes equally distributes jobs belonging to the most demanding system mode, i.e. *critical*, whilst the ones belonging to *normal* mode – that is less demanding – are routed like centralized.local.
- Hybrid.diversity has very heterogeneous routing probabilities and it has been obtained by running a prototype multi-objective optimization tool relying on NSGA-II genetic algorithm for search-space exploration [16], aimed at suggesting sub-optimal system configurations.

Differently from phase 1, no particular hypotheses can be formulated in this phase. However, in case at least one of the alternative configurations will result to a performance improvement, it would be possible to conclude that SMAPEA QNs can provide a valid support to performance optimization of SaSs (RQ₂).

In order to evaluate performance results for alternative system configurations, we need some criteria to compare the latter to hybrid.equality. To this aim, we define the concepts of *ameliorative, non-ameliorative, non-pejorative* and *pejorative* configuration, by taking into account the confidence interval of 0.9 (i.e. 90%) that has been used during SMAPEA QNs simulation.[7]

Denoting by c a system configuration and by $rt(c, m, w)$ its mean response time for a certain system mode m and a workload intensity w, we have that:

- c' is *ameliorative* for mode m and workload intensity w with respect to c if $1.1 \times rt(c', m, w) < 0.9 \times rt(c, m, w)$.
- c' is *non-pejorative* for mode m and workload intensity w with respect to c if $0.9 \times rt(c, m, w) \leqslant 1.1 \times rt(c', m, w) \leqslant rt(c, m, w)$.
- c' is *non-ameliorative* for mode m and workload intensity w with respect to c if $rt(c, m, w) \leqslant 0.9 \times rt(c', m, w) \leqslant 1.1 \times rt(c, m, w)$.
- c' is *pejorative* for mode m and workload intensity w with respect to c if $0.9 \times rt(c', m, w) > 1.1 \times rt(c, m, w)$.

The definitions above can be graphically represented as in Fig. 11, where the two factors 0.812 and 1.222 have been respectively obtained by solving the corresponding equations:

$$rt(c', m, w) + 0.1 \times rt(c', m, w) = rt(c, m, w) - 0.1 \times rt(c, m, w) \qquad (1)$$

$$rt(c', m, w) - 0.1 \times rt(c', m, w) = rt(c, m, w) + 0.1 \times rt(c, m, w) \qquad (2)$$

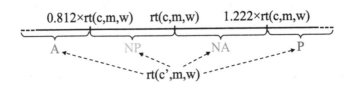

Fig. 11. Classification in terms of ameliorative (A), non-pejorative (NP), non-ameliorative (NA) and pejorative (P) system configurations.

---

[7] Simulation confidence interval can be seen as the fuzziness degree of the obtained performance indices. For example, 90% confidence interval means that multiple simulations of the same QN model may bring performance indices to "oscillate" within a range of ±10%.

4.4   Execution

All the QN models have been developed and simulated within the JSimGraph tool available within JMT 1.0.3, running onto a machine equipped with an Intel Core i5 CPU and 16 GB of DDR3 RAM at 1867 MHz. Configuration parameters for QN simulation can be found within the JSimGraph file (.jsimg) within the GitHub project available at https://github.com/davewilsonfbc/smapeaqn.moo (i.e. `CCIS-replication-package` folder). The latter also provides the prototypal implementation that has been developed to obtain `hybrid.diversity`, as well as experimental results and instructions for replication.

4.5   Results

Phase 1. Table 4 reports the mean response times for the five human-conceived system configurations devised during Phase 1, under the considered workload intensities. Results are also plotted in Fig. 12.

Table 4. Performance results for human-conceived system configurations.

mode →	Response time (s)									
pattern →	Normal Actuate					Critical Actuate				
Workload	Centr. local	Centr. remote	Coll. local	Coll. remote	Hybrid	Centr. local	Centr. remote	Coll. local	Coll. remote	Hybrid
det(0.5)	10000	10000	100	100	8.1585	10000	10000	100	100	11.4902
det(0.75)	1000	10000	5.0495	7.5993	4.0206	1000	10000	8.2972	10.9237	7.2027
det(1)	100	1000	2.2040	4.7983	2.9869	100	1000	5.4959	8.0355	6.2358
det(1.25)	3.2591	10.3364	1.2977	3.8097	2.5666	6.3914	12.8426	4.5673	7.1380	5.6665
det(1.5)	1.4774	7.5616	0.9215	3.4017	2.2624	4.7167	11.0367	4.1554	6.7308	5.5407
det(1.75)	0.9382	6.5429	0.7149	3.1559	2.1336	4.0771	9.9997	3.9295	6.5361	5.3789
det(2)	0.6362	6.0588	0.5242	2.9543	2.1024	3.8854	9.3890	3.7195	6.2205	5.2000
det(2.25)	0.5302	5.7261	0.4884	2.8957	1.9391	3.8029	9.0929	3.7257	6.0155	5.2550
det(2.5)	0.4828	5.4406	0.4313	2.7643	1.9206	3.6604	8.7343	3.6488	6.0488	5.1792

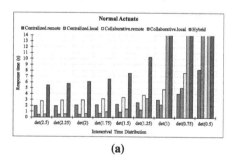 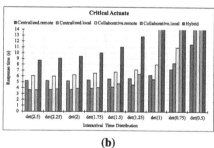

Fig. 12. Mean response times for (a) normal and (b) critical mode. Values overcoming the maximum y value denote saturation.

It can be noticed that the obtained results confirm all the hypotheses devised in Sect. 4.3. In fact:

H_1. For each pattern and workload intensity, the mean response time for *CriticalActuate* is always greater than *NormalActuate*.

H_2. As the workload intensity increases, `centralized` patterns saturate before `collaborative` ones (det(1) Vs. det(0.5)). Instead, `hybrid` never saturates.

H_3. `Centralized.remote` always performs worse than `centralized.local`. Similarly, `collaborative.remote` always performs worse than `collaborative.local`. In such `remote` patterns, any job spends positive delays at *Uplink* and *Downlink*; these delays make `centralized.remote` (resp. `collaborative.remote`) "dominated" by `centralized.local` (resp. `collaborative.local`) by construction.[8]

H_4. As a result,

H_{4a}. `Centralized.remote` actually is the worst pattern.

H_{4b}. Excluding `hybrid`, `collaborative.local` actually is the best pattern.

> RQ_1 can thus be successfully answered, as by adhering to the modeling patterns of Sect. 3.3, `SMAPEA` QNs behave as expected.

A further result is that fulfilling the formulated hypotheses allows to point out some hints that might support decisions about system configuration(s) to adopt, e.g.:

- At design-time, a trade-off between saturation and response times might be assessed. For example, `collaborative.local` provides sub-optimality but saturates with the most intense workload, whilst `hybrid` does not provide sub-optimality but never saturates.
- At run-time, a dynamic reconfiguration strategy of the CSP might be devised, by conveniently changing the CSP based on the current workload intensity. For instance, `collaborative.local` could be adopted as sub-optimal configuration for workload intensities that are below det(1); instead, `hybrid` shall be exploited for det(1), det(0.75 and det(0.5), in order to maintain a sub-optimal configuration while avoiding saturation.

As previously mentioned, human-conceived system configurations are trivial and thus unsuitable in realistic situation. For this reason, assessing if the support that `SMAPEA` QNs may provide to performance optimization of SaSs (RQ_2) is whether valid, cannot be done by limiting the scope to such configurations. Hence, Phase 2 is executed, whose goal is to investigate non-trivial alternative configurations towards optimal performance.

Phase 2. Table 5 reports the mean response times for all the `hybrid` configurations, under the considered workload intensities. Cells of Table 5 are colored conforming to the coloring scheme used in Fig. 11, i.e.: green for ameliorative, yellow

---

[8] A pattern *dominates* another pattern when the former shows both *NormalActuate* and *CriticalActuate* mean response times lower than the latter.

for non-pejorative, pink for non-ameliorative and red for pejorative configurations. Of course, the column corresponding to `hybrid.equality` is not colored, as it represent the comparison term – namely c. Moreover, results are also plotted in Fig. 13 to allow visual comparison of the different `hybrid` configurations.

Table 5. Performance results for `hybrid` configurations.

mode → CSP → Workload	Response time (s)							
	Normal Actuate				Critical Actuate			
	equality	activities	modes	diversity	equality	activities	modes	diversity
det(0.5)	8.1585	6.6505	5.5248	5.8843	11.4902	9.8432	11.4058	9.0083
det(0.75)	4.0206	3.0131	1.5746	2.9537	7.2027	6.2644	7.1805	5.6398
det(1)	2.9869	2.0347	0.8958	2.2114	6.2358	5.3421	6.2487	4.9565
det(1.25)	2.5666	1.7077	0.6777	1.8799	5.6665	5.0166	5.7408	4.5036
det(1.5)	2.2624	1.5422	0.5596	1.6581	5.5407	4.7154	5.6659	4.3073
det(1.75)	2.1336	1.3591	0.5084	1.6158	5.3789	4.6467	5.3632	4.1812
det(2)	2.1024	1.2546	0.4324	1.5178	5.2000	4.5266	5.1574	4.1580
det(2.25)	1.9391	1.1958	0.4109	1.4952	5.2550	4.4207	5.1817	4.0750
det(2.5)	1.9206	1.1362	0.3928	1.4864	5.1792	4.3566	5.1113	4.0103

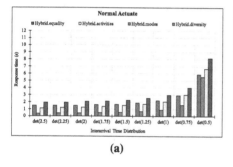
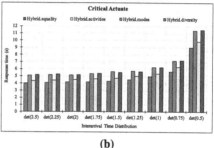

Fig. 13. Alternative system configurations mean response times for (a) normal and (b) critical mode.

As it can be noticed from Table 5, each of the three alternative configurations are ameliorative with respect to normal mode and any considered workload intensity. Instead, concerning critical mode:

- `Hybrid.diversity` and `hybrid.activities` are, respectively, ameliorative and non-pejorative, with respect to any considered workload intensity.
- `Hybrid.modes` is non-pejorative with respect to most of the considered workloads, including both the least and most intense ones, while resulting non-ameliorative with respect to three mid-intense workloads.

Based on the above observations, decisions about system configuration(s) to adopt may be taken, e.g.:

- At design-time: (a) `Hybrid.modes` might be adopted in case optimal performance was needed for normal mode; (b) `Hybrid.diversity` might be preferred in case optimal performance was needed for both system modes, especially for the critical one.
- At run-time, the system might switch between `hybrid.activities` and `Hybrid.diversity` in order to manage normal and critical mode, respectively, resulting into an optimal run-time CSP.

> RQ$_2$ can thus be successfully answered, as solutions to the CSP problem of different types, showing better performance than human-conceived ones, can be identified.

As a final remark, the fact that `hybrid.diversity` is ameliorative in any circumstance is significant, as it demonstrates that sub-optimal configurations can be "located anywhere in the search-space", paving the way to the adoption of meta-heuristics for search-space exploration.

4.6 Threats to Validity

Possible biases to experimentation can be classified in three categories: construct, internal, and external validity. As from Mansoor et al. [29], "Construct validity concerns the relation between the theory and the observation. Internal validity concerns possible bias with the results obtained by our proposal. Finally, external validity is related to the generalization of observed results outside the sample instances used in the experiment".

Construct Validity. Each `SMAPEA` QN involved in the experimentation is simulated once, because each simulation may run to infinite, especially for most intense workloads. Practically, the maximum observed durations were in the order of 3 hours, that would be infeasible in real context. In case of massive generation of `SMAPEA` QN models due to automated search-space exploration, infinite simulation shall be avoided in order to generate the models in reasonable time.

In order to mitigate unique simulations while investigating alternative system configurations with enhanced performance, we have classified the latter in terms of *ameliorative, non-pejorative, non-ameliorative* and *-pejorative*, with respect to `hybrid.equality`, by considering a simulation confidence interval of 10%.

The last threat to construct validity comes from the fact that only one SaS has been modeled, spanning over one area only. With this regard, further systems with different topologies shall be considered to mitigate this threat and assess how performance modeling and analysis of `SMAPEA` QNs actually scale.

Internal Validity. QN parameterization has been performed with the aim to "maintain control" over the `SMAPEA` QNs and their analyses, by means of the assumptions introduced in Sect. 4.2. Such assumptions allowed to point out a number of hypotheses that have been verified by experimental results, thus mitigating threats to internal validity.

External Validity. SMAPEA QNs involve specific modeling constructs that are currently available within JMT only, i.e. class-switches and fork/join. This hardens the porting of SMAPEA QNs into different performance modeling and analysis tools, as well as their adoption within other approaches for performance optimization of SaSs. However, such threat is mitigated by the fact that JMT represents a standard de-facto. Further mitigation may be achieved by providing a user-friendly SMAPEA QNs modeling and analysis framework and APIs to exploit features such as model transformation from/to other performance notations.

5 Related Work

SMAPEA QN family is related to approaches grounding on the QN paradigm for performance modeling, assessment and enhancement of SaS. Very recently, we have published a survey of those approaches at the 11th International Conference on Ambient Systems, Networks and Technologies [2].

Table 6 reports the classification of the surveyed approaches [2], namely: SimuLizar [8], QoSMOS [13,18], SAFCA [28,37], ICAC [22], Adaptive Queuing Networks (AQNs) [5,6] and EMPC [21].

Most of the knowledge base came from three literature studies, i.e. Weyns et al. [35], Becker et al. [9] and Shevtsov et al. [34]: the former two focused on approaches addressing non-functional concerns by means of formal notations and Model-Driven Engineering (MDE), respectively, until 2012, whilst the latter's scope involved approaches exploiting Control Theory to provide non-functional formal guarantees, until 2017. However, at the time our survey was written, we took into account possible evolutions/extensions of the approaches. Moreover, we investigated the existence of more recent approaches not covered by the three literature studies above; this allowed us to identify EMPC [21].

Table 6. Classification of related approaches [2].

	SimuLizar	QoSMOS	SAFCA	ICAC	AQNs	EMPC
References	[8]	[18], [13]	[37], [28]	[22]	[5], [6]	[21]
Systematic studies	[9]	[9], [35]	[9]	[35]	[34]	-
Foundations						
Foundational Paradigms	QNs, MDE	QNs, MDE	QNs, MDE	QNs, Machine Learning	QNs, Control Theory	QNs, Control Theory
Application						
Design-/Run-time	design-time	run-time	run-time	design-time	design-time	run-time
Adaptation						
Pro-/Reactive	reactive	proactive	reactive	reactive	reactive	proactive
Type	architecture reconfiguration	architecture reconfiguration	architecture reconfiguration	architecture reconfiguration	mode change	comp./par. adaptation
Architecture						
Paradigm	components	SOA	concurrent	multi-tier	components	components
Model	PCM	BPEL	(unspecified)	-	-	-
Perf. analysis						
Method	simulative	analytical	analytical	analytical	simulative	analytical
Analysis model	QN	QN	LQN	LQN	QN	QN
Transformation	yes	-	-	-	-	yes
Additional models	-	-	-	-	-	yes
Applicability						
Analysis Tools	yes	yes	yes	yes	yes	yes
MDE Tools	-	yes	-	-	-	-
Proof-of-Concept	yes	yes	yes	-	yes	-
Case Study	prototypal	-	-	yes	-	yes

By referring to the classification scheme of Table 6, we here compare SMAPEA QNs to the knowledge base in the light of the further developments performed in this paper, pointing out pros and cons, analogies and differences.

All the related approaches are founded on the QN paradigm, meaning that performance analysis models conform to either typical QNs [27] or Layered QNs [19] (i.e. a well-known extension of the former). Besides, those approaches ground on additional paradigms such as MDE (SimuLizar, QoSMOS, SAFCA), Machine Learning (ICAC) and Control Theory (AQNs, EMPC), by means of which they aim at introducing efficient adaptation mechanisms within the autonomous system of the SaS. As those approaches focus on the autonomous system and its adaptation performance, they can be applied either at design- or run-time (i.e. offline/online). Instead, SMAPEA QNs have been conceived to support both, as suggested in Sect. 4.5 by pointing out decision-making about system configuration(s) to be adopted. Moreover, the specificity of the adaptation mechanisms makes related approaches addressing either reactive or proactive SaSs, whilst SMAPEA QNs can be applied in both cases, as acting before (i.e. proactive) or after (i.e. reactive) an event happens is implicitly codified into mode-switching probabilities in our context.

The former version of SMAPEA QNs [3] was aimed at providing an instrument to model the whole SaS (i.e. not only the autonomous system) and assess its performance, without explicitly facing the problem of performance enhancement. Such problem clearly emerged in this paper, corresponding to the so-called CSP problem (Sect. 3.3), whose resolution is hard for humans, thus opening to the adoption of additional paradigms beside QNs, e.g. meta-heuristics for search-space exploration.

Defining the CSP problem allowed to introduce, beside mode-switching, a further adaptation type in terms of architecture reconfiguration. This brings SMAPEA QNs closer to SimuLizar, QoSMOS, SAFCA and ICAC, while continuing to rely on mode-based adaptation as well, similarly to AQNs (mode-switching Vs. mode-change), although such dimension of self-adaptation has not been experimented yet, as it represents part of the system's operational profile – namely mode profile [32].

Adaptation type depends on the architectural paradigm, e.g. component-based, Service-Oriented (SOA), concurrent or multi-tier. Based on the architectural paradigm, different modeling notations for architecting SaSs have been exploited by the surveyed approaches. For instance, QoSMOS relies on BPEL [24], as it addresses SOA. Instead, SimuLizar exploits the Palladio Component Model (PCM) [10] to address component-based SaSs. This latter architectural paradigm is addressed by AQNs, EMPC and SMAPEA QNs as well, by using QNs as a performance-oriented architectural notation without distinguishing between architecture and performance model. On the one hand, working on a performance-oriented architecture model allows to avoid transfor-mation from/to a performance analysis model as, e.g., in SimuLizar. On the other hand, architectural notations may enable more adaptation knobs.[9]

---

[9] A comparison between working at architecture or performance model side has been provided in previous work [4].

Furthermore, additional analysis models and transformation might be needed also while working on the performance-oriented architecture model, as for EMPC.

Performance analysis methods of related approaches equally distribute between analytical and simulative. As mentioned in Sect. 3.4, SMAPEA QNs can only be simulated, as they contain class-switches and fork/join inhibiting analytical resolution and, consequently, a rigorous definition in formal terms. However, this does not jeopardize their applicability, as demonstrated in Sect. 4, where a substantial experimentation has been conducted onto a realistic case study, differently from most of related approaches, which rely on proof-of-concepts.

6   Conclusion

This paper is an extension of our previous work introducing a generalized QN model that allows performance modeling and assessment of Self-adaptive Systems (SaSs).

Differently from existing approaches, the generalized QN model spans over the whole SaS, including its Sensing and Actuating components and not only the autonomic manager that controls them by implementing MAPE feedback loop(s). In this paper, we have defined modeling patterns to conform to during the instantiation of such a generalized QN model, aimed at representing the different parts of the system and the dynamics occurring over and among them. Furthermore, we have defined the concept of (probability-based) Controller Selection Policy (CSP) and the corresponding optimization problem, which consists in devising an optimal strategy – in terms of performance – to select which controller of the autonomous system has to process a MAPE activity.

The above contribution resulted into a novel family of QN models, namely SMAPEA QNs.

A controlled experiment has been conducted in this paper, with respect to a realistic case study in the context of emergency handling, which have been exploited in previous work to preliminarily evaluate SMAPEA QNs. The experiment was aimed at showing that (RQ_1) SMAPEA QNs can be successfully applied to performance modeling and assessment of SaSs and that (RQ_2) they may provide valid support to performance optimization of such systems. To this aim, we have firstly matched the SMAPEA QN for the case study to the defined modeling patterns, demonstrating that, by adhering to those patterns, the QN model behaves as expected. Then, have studied some solutions to the CSP problem exploiting CSPs which are very hard for a human to conceive and showing better performance than human-conceived ones, demonstrating that SMAPEA QNs may introduce significant added-value to performance optimization of SaSs.

Several future research directions have been pointed out in the paper. In particular, we plan to investigate: (i) CSPs of different nature, especially the ones that adapt during simulation based on controllers' metrics; (ii) decentralized MAPE loops [36] involving different interacting ILs; (iii) additional patterns for the S-part, introducing ad-hoc sampling rates for the different areas where sensing components are deployed.

While investigating such research directions, proper experiments shall be conducted, aimed at enforcing SMAPEA QNs validity. Experiments shall possibly span over different SaSs and include multiple simulations of QN models.

With respect to the big picture, the final goal is to develop a framework that allows to: (i) design SMAPEA QNs conforming to predefined patterns and analyze; (ii) generate huge sets of SMAPEA QNs, aimed at suggesting alternative system configurations with enhanced performance; (iii) port SMAPEA QN models from/to other architectural and–or performance notations through model transformation; (iv) fill the gap between the real system and its abstractions, by deriving SMAPEA QNs models from existing SaSs and parameterizing the former based on metrics extracted from the latter.

Enabling those activities would allow to provide an effective support to performance engineering of SaSs through SMAPEA QNs.

References

1. Arbib, C., Arcelli, D., Dugdale, J., Moghaddam, M.T., Muccini, H.: Real-time emergency response through performant IoT architectures. In: International Conference on Information Systems for Crisis Response and Management (ISCRAM) (2019). https://hal.archives-ouvertes.fr/hal-02091586

2. Arcelli, D.: Exploiting queuing networks to model and assess the performance of self-adaptive software systems: a survey. In: Shakshuki, E.M., Yasar, A. (eds.) The 11th International Conference on Ambient Systems, Networks and Technologies (ANT 2020), Procedia Computer Science, vol. 170, pp. 498–505. Elsevier (2020). https://doi.org/10.1016/j.procs.2020.03.108

3. Arcelli, D.: Towards a generalized queuing network model for self-adaptive software systems. In: Hammoudi, S., Pires, L.F., Selic, B. (eds.) Proceedings of The 8th International Conference on Model-Driven Engineering and Software Development, MODELSWARD, pp. 457–464. SCITEPRESS (2020). https://doi.org/10.5220/0009180304570464

4. Arcelli, D., Cortellessa, V.: Software model refactoring based on performance analysis: better working on software or performance side? In: Buhnova, B., Happe, L., Kofron, J. (eds.) FESCA. EPTCS, vol. 108, pp. 33–47 (2013). https://doi.org/10.4204/EPTCS.108.3

5. Arcelli, D., Cortellessa, V., Filieri, A., Leva, A.: Control theory for model-based performance-driven software adaptation. In: QoSA, pp. 11–20. ACM (2015). https://doi.org/10.1145/2737182.2737187

6. Arcelli, D., Cortellessa, V., Leva, A.: A library of modeling components for adaptive queuing networks. In: Fiems, D., Paolieri, M., Platis, A.N. (eds.) EPEW 2016. LNCS, vol. 9951, pp. 204–219. Springer, Cham (2016). https://doi.org/10.1007/978-3-319-46433-6_14

7. Barati, S., et al.: Proteus: language and runtime support for self-adaptive software development. IEEE Softw. 36, 73–82 (2019). https://doi.org/10.1109/MS.2018.2884864

8. Becker, M., Becker, S., Meyer, J.: Simulizar: design-time modeling and performance analysis of self-adaptive systems. In: Kowalewski, S., Rumpe, B. (eds.) Software Engineering. LNI, vol. 213, pp. 71–84. GI (2013). https://dl.gi.de/20.500.12116/17731

9. Becker, M., Luckey, M., Becker, S.: Model-driven performance engineering of self-adaptive systems: a survey. In: QoSA, pp. 117–122. ACM (2012). https://doi.org/10.1145/2304696.2304716
10. Becker, S., Koziolek, H., Reussner, R.: The palladio component model for model-driven performance prediction. J. Syst. Softw. **82**(1), 3–22 (2009). https://doi.org/10.1016/j.jss.2008.03.066
11. Bertoli, M., Casale, G., Serazzi, G.: JMT: performance engineering tools for system modeling. SIGMETRICS Perform Eval. Rev. **36**(4), 10–15 (2009). https://doi.org/10.1145/1530873.1530877
12. Bertoli, M., Casale, G., Serazzi, G.: Java Modelling Tools - user manual. http://jmt.sourceforge.net/Papers/JMT_users_Manual.pdf (2018). Accessed 01 Feb 2021
13. Calinescu, R., Grunske, L., Kwiatkowska, M., Mirandola, R., Tamburrelli, G.: Dynamic GoS management and optimization in service-based systems. IEEE Trans. Softw. Eng. **37**(3), 387–409 (2011). https://doi.org/10.1109/TSE.2010.92
14. Cámara, J., Garlan, D., Kang, W.G., Peng, W., Schmerl, B.R.: Uncertainty in self-adaptive systems categories, management, and perspectives. Institute for Software Research, Carnegie Mellon University, Technical report (2017). http://reports-archive.adm.cs.cmu.edu/anon/isr2017/CMU-ISR-17-110.pdf
15. Casale, G., Serazzi, G.: Quantitative system evaluation with java modeling tools. In: Proceedings of the 2nd. ACM. https://doi.org/10.1145/1958746.1958813
16. Deb, K., Pratap, A., Agarwal, S., Meyarivan, T.: A fast and elitist multiobjective genetic algorithm: NSGA-II. IEEE Trans. Evol. Comput. **6**(2), 182–197 (2002). https://doi.org/10.1109/4235.996017
17. Elkhodary, A., Esfahani, N., Malek, S.: Fusion: a framework for engineering self-tuning self-adaptive software systems. In: FSE, pp. 7–16. ACM (2010). https://doi.org/10.1145/1882291.1882296
18. Epifani, I., Ghezzi, C., Mirandola, R., Tamburrelli, G.: Model evolution by run-time parameter adaptation. In: ICSE, pp. 111–121. IEEE Computer Society, May 2009. https://doi.org/10.1109/ICSE.2009.5070513
19. Franks, G., Majumdar, S., Neilson, J., Petriu, D., Rolia, J., Woodside, M.: Performance analysis of distributed server systems. In: ICSQ, pp. 15–26 (1996)
20. Grassi, V., Mirandola, R., Randazzo, E.: Model-driven assessment of GoS-aware self-adaptation. In: Cheng, B.H.C., de Lemos, R., Giese, H., Inverardi, P., Magee, J. (eds.) Software Engineering for Self-Adaptive Systems, pp. 201–222. Springer, Heidelberg (2009). https://doi.org/10.1007/978-3-642-02161-9_11
21. Incerto, E., Tribastone, M., Trubiani, C.: Software performance self-adaptation through efficient model predictive control. In: ASE, pp. 485–496, October 2017. https://doi.org/10.1109/ASE.2017.8115660
22. Jung, G., Joshi, K.R., Hiltunen, M.A., Schlichting, R.D., Pu, C.: Generating adaptation policies for multi-tier applications in consolidated server environments. In: ICAC, pp. 23–32, June 2008. https://doi.org/10.1109/ICAC.2008.21
23. Kephart, J.O., Chess, D.M.: The vision of autonomic computing. Computer **36**(1), 41–50 (2003). https://doi.org/10.1109/MC.2003.1160055
24. Khalaf, R., Mukhi, N., Curbera, F., Weerawarana, S.: The business process execution language for web services. In: Dumas, M., van der Aalst, W.M.P., ter Hofstede, A.H.M. (eds.) Process-Aware Information Systems: Bridging People and Software Through Process Technology, pp. 317–342. Wiley (2005). https://doi.org/10.1002/0471741442.ch13
25. Kleppe, A.G., Warmer, J., Bast, W.: MDA Explained: The Model Driven Architecture: Practice and Promise. Addison-Wesley Longman Publishing Co. Inc, USA (2003)

26. Kounev, S., Brosig, F., Huber, N., Reussner, R.: Towards self-aware performance and resource management in modern service-oriented systems. In: ICSC, pp. 621–624, July 2010. https://doi.org/10.1109/SCC.2010.94

27. Lazowska, E.D., Zahorjan, J., Graham, G.S., Sevcik, K.C.: Quantitative System Performance - Computer System Analysis Using Queueing Network Models. Prentice Hall (1984). http://dl.acm.org/citation.cfm?id=2971

28. Lung, C., Zhang, X., Rajeswaran, P.: Improving software performance and reliability in a distributed and concurrent environment with an architecture-based self-adaptive framework. JSS **121**, 311–328 (2016). https://doi.org/10.1016/j.jss.2016.06.102

29. Mansoor, U., Kessentini, M., Wimmer, M., Deb, K.: Multi-view refactoring of class and activity diagrams using a multi-objective evolutionary algorithm. Softw. Qual. J. **25**(2), 473–501 (2017). https://doi.org/10.1007/s11219-015-9284-4

30. Morin, B., Barais, O., Nain, G., Jezequel, J.M.: Taming dynamically adaptive systems using models and aspects. In: ICSE, pp. 122–132. IEEE Computer Society (2009). https://doi.org/10.1109/ICSE.2009.5070514

31. Muccini, H., Sharaf, M.: Caps: architecture description of situational aware cyber physical systems. In: 2017 IEEE International Conference on Software Architecture (ICSA), pp. 211–220. IEEE (2017). https://doi.org/10.1109/ICSA.2017.21

32. Musa, J.D.: Operational profiles in software-reliability engineering. IEEE Softw. **10**(2), 14–32 (1993). https://doi.org/10.1109/52.199724

33. Perez-Palacin, D., Mirandola, R.: Uncertainties in the modeling of self-adaptive systems: a taxonomy and an example of availability evaluation. In: ICPE, pp. 3–14. ACM (2014). https://doi.org/10.1145/2568088.2568095

34. Shevtsov, S., Berekmeri, M., Weyns, D., Maggio, M.: Control-theoretical software adaptation: a systematic literature review. IEEE Trans. Softw. Eng. **44**(8), 784–810 (2018). https://doi.org/10.1109/TSE.2017.2704579

35. Weyns, D., Iftikhar, M.U., de la Iglesia, D.G., Ahmad, T.: A survey of formal methods in self-adaptive systems. In: C3S2E, pp. 67–79. ACM (2012). https://doi.org/10.1145/2347583.2347592

36. Weyns, D., et al.: On patterns for decentralized control in self-adaptive systems. In: de Lemos, R., Giese, H., Müller, H.A., Shaw, M. (eds.) Software Engineering for Self-Adaptive Systems II. LNCS, vol. 7475, pp. 76–107. Springer, Heidelberg (2013). https://doi.org/10.1007/978-3-642-35813-5_4

37. Zhang, X., Lung, C., Franks, G.: Towards architecture-based autonomic software performance engineering. In: Drira, K. (ed.) CAL. Revue des Nouvelles Technologies de l'Information, vol. L-5, pp. 144–156, Cépaduès-Éditions (2010). http://editions-rnti.fr/?inprocid=1000909

Author Index

Printed in the United States
By Bookmasters